second edition

Reading Instruction for Today's Children

NILA BANTON SMITH / H. ALAN ROBINSON

Hofstra University

second edition

Reading Instruction for Today's Children

Prentice-Hall Inc. Englewood Cliffs, N.J. 07632

Library of Congress Cataloging in Publication Data

Smith, Nila Banton.
    Reading instruction for today's children.

    Includes bibliographies and indexes.
    1. Reading (Elementary) I. Robinson, H. Alan,
        joint author. II. Title.
LB1573.S772 1980   372.4'1   79–15314
ISBN 0–13–755157–6

Reading Instruction for Today's Children, 2nd ed.
Nila Banton Smith/H. Alan Robinson

© 1980, 1963 Prentice-Hall, Inc., Englewood Cliffs, N.J. 07632

Printed in the United States of America
10 9 8 7 6 5 4 3 2 1

Photographs by Sybil Shelton
Editorial/production supervision by Joyce Turner
Interior design/Cover design by Jayne Conte
Manufacturing buyer: John Hall
Cover photo by Marion Bernstein

Prentice-Hall International, Inc., *London*
Prentice-Hall of Australia Pty. Limited, *Sydney*
Prentice-Hall of Canada, Ltd., *Toronto*
Prentice-Hall of India Private Limited, *New Delhi*
Prentice-Hall of Japan, Inc., *Tokyo*
Prentice-Hall of Southeast Asia Pte. Ltd., *Singapore*
Whitehall Books Limited, *Wellington, New Zealand*

Contents

preface xv

SECTION A
BASIC CONSIDERATIONS

chapter 1
thought, language, and reading 5

THOUGHT AND ORAL LANGUAGE:
FOUNDATIONS FOR READING 7
Stages of development 7   Relationship to reading 9

INTERRELATIONSHIPS AMONG LANGUAGE SKILLS 10
Listening 11   Viewing and listening 12   Speaking 12
Writing 14   Reading 15   Interrelating all the language skills 15

THE READING PROGRAM 18
Linguistics 18   Concept of reading 19

DISCUSSION QUESTIONS AND ACTIVITIES 20

ADDITIONAL READINGS 20

v

chapter 2

psychological-sociological guidelines 25

PSYCHOLOGICAL-SOCIOLOGICAL GUIDELINES 26

DISCUSSION QUESTIONS AND ACTIVITIES 32

ADDITIONAL READINGS 33

SECTION B
ESSENTIAL COMPONENTS

chapter 3

assessment of reading abilities 39

SELECTING AND USING STANDARDIZED READING TESTS 41
The teacher's role 43

NATIONAL ASSESSMENT OF
EDUCATIONAL PROGRESS (NAEP) 45

THE POSITIVE EXPECTANCY CONCEPT 46

APPRAISAL PROCEDURES 46
Observations 47   Checklists 48   Direct inquiry 51
Attitude surveys 51   Interviews 52   Informal tests 53
Informal reading inventories 56   Closure procedures 58
Reading miscue inventory   60   Qualitative uses of
quantitative tests and inventories 63   Self-evaluation 63

DISCUSSION QUESTIONS AND ACTIVITIES 64

ADDITIONAL READINGS 64

chapter 4
readiness for reading at all grade levels 67

PREREADING READINESS 69

Factors to be considered 69   Early readers 71   Activities 72
Foundations for vocabulary development 73   Foundations
for study skills 75   Foundations for fluent reading 76
Foundations for interest in and appreciation of literature 77

READINESS BEYOND THE PREREADING STAGE 78

Readiness principles 80   Examples of readiness procedures 83

HEALTH WORKERS 83

Medical doctors 83   Nurses 83   Dentists 84

DISCUSSION QUESTIONS AND ACTIVITIES 87

ADDITIONAL READINGS 91

chapter 5
approaches, procedures, and materials 95

BASAL READER APPROACHES 96

Uses of basal reader programs 98

LANGUAGE-EXPERIENCE APPROACHES 100

Procedures 101   Composing an experience chart 102
Types of experience charts 103
Advantages and disadvantages of the approaches 105

INDIVIDUALIZED READING INSTRUCTION 105

Six steps to individualized reading 107   More specifics
about organization for individualization 108   Evaluation of
individualized reading plans 110   Commercial programs
and systems 110

CONTRIBUTIONS FROM TECHNOLOGY 111

Television 111   The computer 112

GUIDELINES FOR CHOOSING INSTRUCTIONAL MATERIALS 112

Guide for selecting materials 113   Guide for evaluating
sex stereotyping in reading materials 114

EVALUATING READABILITY 115

DISCUSSION QUESTIONS AND ACTIVITIES 117

ADDITIONAL READINGS 119

SECTION C
GROWTH AREAS IN READING

chapter 6
developing word approximation and
identification strategies 133

STRATEGY DEVELOPMENT 135

A four-step approach 136

PICTURE CLUES 138

Picture clues in books 139   Picture dictionaries 139

CONTEXT CLUES 140

Types of context clues 140   Dangers in the context-clue
approach 142   Context-clue activities 142

SIGHT WORDS 144

Configuration 144   Letter details 144
Sight-word games 145   Self-help references 147

PHONICS 150

When should phonics be taught? 151   What phonics
should be taught? 151   Instruction in phonics 153
Practice and maintenance activities 158
Phonic generalizations 161

WORD STRUCTURE 162
Instruction in structural analysis 164

DICTIONARY USAGE 173

DISCUSSION QUESTIONS AND ACTIVITIES 175

ADDITIONAL READINGS 176

chapter 7
extending knowledge of word meanings 179

CONCEPTS AND WORD MEANINGS 180
What is a concept? 180   Building concepts 180
Confusions due to faulty or inadequate concepts 181
Improving reading through concept building 182

WORDS ARE LIKE CHAMELEONS 186

FIGURATIVE LANGUAGE 187

CHANGES IN WORD STRUCTURE 188
Compound words 190   Prefixes, suffixes, and roots 190

SYNONYMS AND ANTONYMS 190
Synonyms 190   Antonyms 192

WORD ORIGINS 192
New words 194

CRITICAL THINKING AND VOCABULARY 194
The power of words 195   Sexist terminology 195

PERSONALIZED WORD COLLECTIONS 196

GUIDING PRINCIPLES 197

DISCUSSION QUESTIONS AND ACTIVITIES 199

ADDITIONAL READINGS 201

chapter 8
nurturing reading comprehension 203

COMPREHENSION STRATEGIES 205
A model 206 General principles 207
Activities for developing basic strategies 208

COMPREHENSION GROWTH AREAS 216
Literal comprehension 216 Interpretation 218
Critical reading 220 Application 225

PURPOSES AND QUESTIONS 227
Purposes 227 Questions 228

**QUESTIONS AT VARIOUS COGNITIVE LEVELS
RELATED TO READING INSTRUCTION** 230
Knowledge questions 230 Comprehension questions 231
Application questions 231 Analysis questions 232
Synthesis questions 232 Evaluation questions 233

DISCUSSION QUESTIONS AND ACTIVITIES 234

ADDITIONAL READINGS 235

chapter 9
developing fluency and flexibility 239

FLUENCY FOUNDATIONS IN THE PRIMARY GRADES 242
Establishing phrasing 242 Breaking habits of
bodily movements 243 Setting purposes 244
Wide reading 244 Scanning 245

INCREASING RATES IN GRADES FOUR THROUGH EIGHT 245
Develop an awareness of personal rates 245
Develop the concept of reading in thought units 246
Develop habits of reading for a purpose 247
Develop the preview technique 248

SYSTEMATIC PRACTICE 251
Timed reading practice 251 Emphasis on flexibility 254

**SKIMMING AND SCANNING IN GRADES
FOUR THROUGH EIGHT** 258
Skimming 258 Scanning 258

DISCUSSION QUESTIONS AND ACTIVITIES 259

ADDITIONAL READINGS 261

chapter 10
developing study strategies in the content areas 263

STUDY STRATEGIES 264
Selection and evaluation 265   Organization 268
Recall 271   Location of information 273
Following directions 291   Survival strategies 292

PATTERNS OF WRITING 293
Specific patterns 295

VOCABULARY 297
Technical vocabulary 297   Overlap words 297
Multi-meaning words 298   Function words 299

DISCUSSION QUESTIONS AND ACTIVITIES 300

ADDITIONAL READINGS 302

chapter 11
developing interest and taste in literature 305

PERSONALITY DEVELOPMENT 306

THE STIMULATION OF INTERESTS 308
Providing functional information 309
Curricular enrichment 310

INDIRECT CONTRIBUTION TO SKILLS 312

READING INTERESTS OF TODAY'S CHILDREN 312
Primary grades 312   Grades four through six 313
Grades seven and eight 313

INTEREST-INDUCING ACTIVITIES 313
Setting the stage 313   Recommending books 316
Counseling parents 316   Making materials available 317
Classroom activities to stimulate interest 318

SELECTING, RECORDING, AND REPORTING 322
Selecting 322   Keeping records 323   Reporting 324

LIBRARY ACTIVITIES 326

The classroom library 326 The school library 327
Public library activities 330

DISCUSSION QUESTIONS AND ACTIVITIES 332

ADDITIONAL READINGS 334

SECTION D
CLASSROOM INSTRUCTION

chapter 12
reading in grades one through three 341

**DIFFERENTIATED GROUPING AND
INDIVIDUALIZATION 343**

The class as a reading group 343   Temporary
instructional groups 344   Interest groups 344
Social grouping 344   The individual 345   Overall plans 345

ORGANIZING INSTRUCTION 347

Independent activities 347   Learning centers in reading 349

TEACHING AND LEARNING 350

Planning 350   Reading to children 353   Reading by
children 353   Directed reading lessons 354
Directed reading-thinking activity 356

ADVISING PARENTS 357

Preschool reading 357   After school reading begins 357
What parents can do 358

CONCLUDING STATEMENT 360

DISCUSSION QUESTIONS AND ACTIVITIES 361

ADDITIONAL READINGS 362

xii

chapter 13
reading in grades four through eight 365

ORGANIZATIONAL PLANS 366
The Joplin plan 366 Departmentalization 367
In-class organization 367

NATURE OF THE MATERIALS 368
Basal readers 368 Other reading development
materials 368 Curriculum materials 369

INSTRUCTIONAL PLANS 370
Steps in DRTA 371 Junior great books
reflective activities 371 Alternative plans 372

INDEPENDENT READING 373
Study-reading 373 Study guides 374
Individual reading 378

ORAL READING 378

COMPLEXITIES IN LANGUAGE PROCESSING 379
Anaphora 379 Idea combining 380 Vocabulary 382

DISCUSSION QUESTIONS AND ACTIVITIES 382

ADDITIONAL READINGS 383

chapter 14
a focus on special needs 385

DIVERGENT LANGUAGE AND CULTURE 387
Building positive concepts 387
"Intelligence" and environment 389

DIALECTS AND READING 390
The roots of dialects 390 Information about
Black English 390 Dialect interference 392
Transition activities 393

BILINGUALISM AND READING 394

Learning patterns and culture 395   Learning to read 398

DISCUSSION QUESTIONS AND ACTIVITIES 402

ADDITIONAL READINGS 403

author index 407

subject index 411

Preface

This book is intended for use as a textbook in courses offered by colleges and universities and as a handbook for teachers. The chief concern of the authors in preparing the book was to help teachers obtain information and acquire techniques that can help their pupils learn to read and/or improve their ability to read.

The book is divided into four sections. In section A, the authors have formulated a structure on which the rest of the book is largely based. In chapter 1, the importance of oral language is stressed and the interrelationships among thought, language, and reading are discussed. Chapter 2 focuses on psychological and sociological principles, which form the underpinnings for a reading program.

In section B, Essential Components, important aspects of all reading programs are presented. Chapter 3 is concerned with various types of reading assessments with emphasis on evaluation within the classroom setting. In chapter 4, readiness is considered both in terms of the school beginner and in relationship to the background needed at all grade levels for reading specific kinds of materials for particular purposes. Approaches, procedures, and materials are dealt with in chapter 5 as basic ingredients of reading programs throughout the elementary and middle school.

Section C is the "heart" of the book. This is the skill and strategy part, dealing in six chapters with the major growth areas of development in reading: word approximation and identification strategies; knowledge of word meanings; reading comprehension; fluency and flexibility; study strategies in the content areas; and interest and taste in literature. Regardless of method, material, type of children, or level of development, the teacher must focus on these growth areas. Hence, over one half the book is devoted to these basic growth areas.

In section D, attention is given in turn to the learners at given grade levels and two groups of pupils: those who speak dialects of English divergent from what is considered to be the regional standard English; and those whose "dominant" language has not been, or is not, English. Organizational plans, overall teaching procedures, and specific suggestions are described for children in grades one through three, grades four through eight, and for some learners with special needs.

Before Nila Banton Smith was able to complete the manuscript for this second edition of her book, she passed away—in December, 1976. H. Alan Robinson, who had been a student of hers as well as a longtime friend, was given the honor of completing the volume. Hence, in this book, the reader will find what the authors hope is as much of an integration of ideas as two people with similar but somewhat divergent conceptual frameworks could marshall and organize. The focus is always on helping the teacher help the learner.

Although specific reading skills and strategies are discussed and demonstrated, the intent has been to build and enhance the thinking capabilities of learners during the processing of printed material. The emphasis of a reading program must be on the total development of the learner and not on the "ticking off" of skill after skill. The wise and sensitive teacher will use many of the particular ideas in this book to help the learner become a reader who not only knows *how* to read but turns to reading as a potent, necessary force and joy in life.

H.A.R.

SECTION A
BASIC
CONSIDERATIONS

CHAPTER 1 THOUGHT, LANGUAGE, AND READING

Thought and Oral Language: Foundations for Reading

STAGES OF DEVELOPMENT
Stage 1—Sensorimotor
Stage 2—Preoperational Thought
Stage 3—Concrete Operations
Stage 4—Formal Operations

RELATIONSHIP TO READING

Interrelationships Among Language Skills

LISTENING

VIEWING AND LISTENING

SPEAKING
Nursery School
Kindergarten
Primary Grades
Intermediate Grades and Above

WRITING
Classroom Opportunities for Writing

READING
Experience Stories
Reading an Organized Paragraph

INTERRELATING ALL THE LANGUAGE SKILLS

The Reading Program

LINGUISTICS

CONCEPT OF READING

Discussion Questions and Activities

Additional Readings

CHAPTER 2 PSYCHOLOGICAL-SOCIOLOGICAL FOUNDATIONS

Psychological-Sociological Guidelines

Discussion Questions and Activities

Additional Readings

3

chapter 1

thought, language, and reading

What to Expect in this Chapter:

 In this chapter, we emphasize the interrelationship between thought and language and the interrelationships among listening, speaking, reading, and writing. *Reading* is defined as an active attempt to understand a writer's message. A broad view of a language and reading program is presented.

Reading is an active attempt, on the part of a reader, to understand a writer's message. The reader interacts with, and tries to reconstruct, what a writer wishes to communicate. If the reader's anticipations and predictions are pretty much in line with what a writer says, and how it is presented, comprehension is likely to be easy and rapid. If there is great distance between the backgrounds of the reader and a writer, comprehension is likely to be slow and poor. For example:

 True or False? *Gas can grow transistors used in pacemakers.*
 To answer true, you must know that crystals are grown by adding molecules to the definite shape of a "seed" crystal. Gas is sometimes used to grow crystals. Crystals are used to make transistors. Transistors are useful for pacemakers.
 The valid italicized sentence above would be immediately understandable to anyone who could make the necessary logical connections. It is elementary for someone with appropriate background.[1]

 In order to process written language, the reader must have enough background to make contact with the writer. The interaction or contact will not always be an exact match, but if there is no match, understanding cannot take place. The same relationship exists between listener and speaker.

 A listener is actively attempting to ascertain a speaker's message. If the speaker is using language and ideas familiar to the listener, comprehension is easy and rapid. The listener anticipates and predicts much of the material. If the speaker uses words, language patterns, and ideas largely unfamiliar to the listener, comprehension is hampered. Attention is often placed on individual unfamiliar words and constructions at the expense of understanding.

---

[1] Adapted from John T. Guthrie, "Research Views: Concept Construction," *Reading Teacher* 31, no. 1 (October 1977): 111.

THOUGHT
AND ORAL
LANGUAGE:
FOUNDA-
TIONS FOR
READING

In order to bridge the gap between speaker and listener and, eventually, reader and writer, classroom emphasis should be placed on using oral language as an instrument of thought. Teachers should be aware of the stages of development of thought and language as they plan learning activities and structure the learning environment for their pupils.

Stages of Development

Practically from birth, thought and language develop side by side, sometimes touching, sometimes integrating, until for the older child and adult they become almost one in most situations. By the time a learner starts to process written language (to read), she or he must be able to integrate thought and language, or comprehending will not take place.

Cognition (knowing and thinking) and language appear to develop in chronological stages, although the chronology is not precise or fixed. It does appear, however, that the stages are hierarchical in the sense that one stage is a prerequisite for the next. The brief description of developmental stages that follows is a blend of Piaget's concepts of cognition and Menyuk's summary of language development.[2] Parts of the description of Piaget's cognitive stages were provided by Patrick McCabe, who completed his Ph.D. in reading at Hofstra University.

Stage One—Sensorimotor. This first stage in the life of human beings continues through about two years of age. The infant learns about the immediate environment through sensorimotor activities. This is a "here and now" period in which no symbolic representation occurs; the infant is bound by the moment and cannot integrate individual activities across time.

> In other words, sensorimotor intelligence acts like a slow motion film in which all the pictures are seen in succession but without fusion and so without the continuous vision necessary for understanding the whole.[3]

During the early part of this stage, babies try out their vocal apparatuses and gradually use language to express needs and react to voices. According to Menyuk, a great deal of development takes place between eight and twelve months. Infants attend to words and integrate the

---

[2] Readers interested in further information should turn to: Jean Piaget, *The Psychology of Intelligence*, trans. Malcolm Piercy and D. E. Berlyne (London: Routledge & Kegan Paul, 1950); Paula Menyuk, *Language and Maturation* (Cambridge: M.I.T. Press, 1977).

[3] Piaget, *Psychology of Intelligence*, p. 122.

phonological and semantic features. They produce words and use them (as single word units) to make statements, emphasize points, make requests. They test words and parts of words a great deal, and begin to test hypotheses about language—a vital step in categorizing and generalizing.[4] For example, "milk" may be a statement (Milk.), a point to stress (Milk!), or a question (Milk?). Language starts to become mapped onto cognition.

Between about twelve and eighteen months, there is a transition period in which children move toward two-word utterances. By eighteen months, most children produce two-word sentences, usually by combining nouns and adjectives. Right from the beginning, children use the correct rules of our language—our grammar. A child might say "milk hot" but will never say "big hot." Great progress is made during this first period of comprehensible speech. The children do a volume of meaningful talking and find that language serves them in many useful ways.

Stage Two—Preoperational Thought. From approximately ages two through seven children attempt to organize the world about them, although these attempts are not consistent. Judgments are based on intuition.

From about two or two-and-a-half years of age to four or five, there is a period of rapid and extensive development. Children are able to express themselves in patterns that are increasingly complex. Expanded use of subjects, verbs, and objects takes place along with ability to use and understand varied sentence types.

So, by the time most children are of school age they have learned their language well. They have large vocabularies, control most basic language structures and inflections, use language to communicate, to think, to learn. They have learned to comprehend the speech of others as well.[5]

Stage Three—Concrete Operations. Between the ages of about seven and eleven, a coherent "cognitive system" for organizing the world develops. Thought processes are no longer static or momentary. Language is used as a conscious and enhancing tool of thought, although children at this stage function best when objects are in their sight and they can manipulate them.

Stage Four—Formal Operations. This stage develops from the ages of about eleven to fifteen and permits individuals to deal with a world of pure conjecture. Children are able to formulate hypotheses about the world surrounding them, making use of logical thought processes, and

---

[4] Menyuk, *Language and Maturation*, p. 51.

[5] Kenneth S. Goodman, "The Interrelationships Between Language Development and Learning to Read," in *Current Emphases in Reading*, ed. David L. Shepherd, vol. 3, Proceedings of Hofstra University Reading Conferences (New York: Hofstra University, 1970), p. 130.

are now capable of thinking beyond the present. Problems can be coped with in many ways and from different perspectives. Language is used expertly, both as a facilitator and an extension of thought.

If one accepts Piaget's stages in the growth of thought, the young child and even the older learner attempting to cope with something new and complex should be involved in actual, nonlinguistic, manipulative experiences prior to using language as a medium for the new task. For example, a learner concerned with *subtraction*—what do I have left if I eat two of the five apples—should perform the task and view the result prior to attempting verbal generalizations about subtraction based on spoken or written problems. Piaget warned: "Teaching means creating situations where structures can be discovered; it does not mean transmitting structures which may be assimilated at nothing other than a verbal level." [6]

Relationship to Reading

Communication—both through listening and speaking—should be highlighted prior to, and during, the introduction of reading and writing tasks. The meaningful use of oral language serves as a readiness for processing written language. Pupils learn: (1) language as a communication tool; (2) the basic "rules" of language in regard to word order in sentences (syntax), meanings of words and word parts (semantic aspects), and sounds (phonemes); and (3) the varied purposes for listening and speaking.

In the classroom where a multitude of ideas are explored and talked about, and where children feel free to express themselves, the roots for good readers are planted. Children learn more and more about language and how to use it. They begin to look at printed materials as another source of ideas related to the world around them.

Although the wise teacher takes advantage of every opportunity to point out the similarities between oral and written language, he or she also highlights the differences. For even though oral language is a type of preorganizer, readiness, and reinforcement for written language, there are specific differences pupils must recognize. Oral and written language are most similar when children write experience stories and friendly letters, for familiar ideas and language structures are shared with peers and friendly adults within a given environment. Differences become more apparent as learners turn to books written by unknown adults. Frank Smith

[6] Jean Piaget as cited in Eleanor Duckworth, "Piaget Rediscovered," *ESS Newsletter,* Watertown, Mass.: Educational Services, Inc., June 1964, p. 3.

has said that "children who expect to read in the way they make sense of spoken language are likely to have difficulty in comprehending print and thus in learning to read."[7]

Teachers will want to help children note the similarities and differences by comparing taped dialogues with dialogues printed in books, and by comparing experience stories with passages in basal readers and trade books. (*Basal readers* are materials planned specifically for introducing reading skills at a certain pace; *trade books* are books with individual titles not planned specifically for a reading program but often used as part of one.)

Pupils need to internalize the notions that words on a page have white spaces between them, that sentence patterns frequently differ from those they use themselves, and that writing styles become increasingly more formal. They must realize that the clues to meaning are more difficult than in oral language and that they must learn certain ways of ascertaining meaning. With this kind of consciousness-raising, pupils soon become aware of significant advantages and disadvantages of both modes of communication.

INTER-RELATION-SHIPS AMONG LANGUAGE SKILLS

Researchers and writers over the years have indicated that speaking, reading, listening, and writing are interrelated, but the meaning of this interrelationship to instructional practice has been vague. Perhaps now Fillion, Smith, and Swain provide us with the key to classroom practice:

> *The four general language skills*—listening, speaking, reading, and writing—*are largely independent.* Lack of skill in one does not necessarily reflect lack of skill in another. Each skill appears to be developed through practice of that skill, although development of one skill will increase the potential of the individual for development in other skills.[8]

Potential and *practice in each* appear to be the key words. Potential for reading ability can be developed through emphasis on other language areas; a reading program should include all these important communication areas. Practice in each will strengthen each and lead to potential success with the next language area.

Guidelines for the teacher and instructional practices are highlighted in the following discussions of each communication area. Some suggestions are made for specific ways of interrelating particular listening skills, speaking skills, and writing skills with reading.

[7] Frank Smith, "Making Sense of Reading—And of Reading Instruction," *Harvard Educational Review* 47, no. 3 (August 1977): 392.

[8] Bryant Fillion, Frank Smith, and Merrill Swain, "Language 'Basics' for Language Teachers: Towards A Set of Universal Considerations," *Language Arts* 53, no. 7 (October 1976): 742.

Listening

It seems obvious that learning to listen with the object of understanding is fundamental to communication and learning. Pupils are required to listen to language a large part of each day, both in and out of school. It would seem that, in school, attention placed on specific listening activities would carry over to reading instruction because both require interaction with a message-giver.

Cunningham [9] suggested listening-reading transfer lessons to help children use a thinking strategy prevalent in listening in the reading situation. The promising technique capitalizes on the potential developed in one language area and concentrates very specifically on an identical strategy or skill in the next (listening to reading). The following example is an illustration of the technique:

> Many children have difficulty ordering the events in a story they have read. A listening-reading transfer lesson will help them. There are six steps in this lesson:
>
> 1. Set the purpose for listening: "Listen so that when I have finished reading, you can put the events of the story in the order in which they actually happened."
> 2. Read a selection to the students.
> 3. Write the major events of the story on sentence strips and tape them to the board. The children physically rearrange these strips until they agree that the order is correct.
> 4. Give the children passages to read. Tell them that they will do the exact same thing in reading that they have just done in listening. They should read to be able to put the events of the story in order.
> 5. As the children finish reading, give them a mimeographed sheet on which are written the main events of the story. They cut the sheet into strips and physically order the events.
> 6. The children share their orderings and the explanation for their orderings as a whole class or in small groups.

> This sequence-of-events lesson could be varied to suit the needs and levels of sophistication of the class. It could be made easier by displaying the events before the children listen to the story. The teacher would read the events and ask the children to "listen so as to put these events in order." When the children began the reading part of the listening-reading transfer lesson, they would have the mimeographed sheet with the events cut into strips and ready before reading their stories.
>
> A more difficult lesson would involve having the children listen

[9] Patricia M. Cunningham, "Transferring Comprehension from Listening to Reading," *Reading Teacher* 29, No. 2 (November 1975): 169–72. Reprinted with permission of the author and the International Reading Association.

so they could list the events and then put them in order. Of course, during the reading portion they would also be asked to read, list, cut the list, and put it in order. To achieve the transfer the children should be regularly reminded, "See what you just did after listening; I want you to do the same thing after reading." [10]

Viewing and Listening

There is a need for the careful analysis of the synthesis of listening and viewing skills for instructional purposes. As we capitalize more and more on the audio-visual media about us, teachers ought to be helping pupils improve their understanding and assessment of what they see when they are listening and what they hear when they are seeing. Viewing is a communication ability unto itself and in partnership with listening and reading. Lessons focused on mass media should be carefully planned and structured (see pages 79–80 in chapter 4).

Speaking

Right from nursery school on, children should be encouraged to speak and communicate freely—in their own idiolects (individual speech patterns) or in their own dialects, of course. They *must not* be told to "speak correctly." Emphasis must be on communication. How else can a child communicate except with the language patterns the child has at that point in time? There is plenty of time for learning alternative ways of saying things as children become adept at sharing ideas and comfortable in their surroundings, with their peers, and with their teachers.

Nursery School. With young children, all children really, teachers should realize the tremendous language power children have and not pick out those inadequacies that will eventually be corrected. Many two-year-olds in nursery school settings will repeat certain words and sounds over and over again as they explore language. Increasingly, as teachers structure situations in which they can mingle and interact with others, they begin to increase meaningful conversation.

Three- and four-year-olds talk with increasing fluency. They enjoy role playing familiar scenes, and such activities afford many opportunities for speaking. In addition, most nursery schools have a language period in which the children share an object brought from home or discuss a news item. Occasionally, they may dictate an announcement or two or three sentences about some event for the teacher to print on the chalkboard. They often relate personal experiences and occasionally a child tries to retell a favorite story. Thus, nursery school children engage in conversation, dramatization, discussion, dictating, announcing, and story telling.

[10] Ibid., p. 170.

Kindergarten. Many kindergarten children talk continuously and to anyone nearby. They have sizable vocabularies, and they use practically all of the sentence patterns that adults use. This inclination to talk, and these language accomplishments, enable them to expand their ability in many different types of spoken language activities if given opportunities.

They can engage in fluent conversations, dramatic play, group discussions, the making of announcements, sharing their experiences with others, and story telling. They are now able to enjoy reciting and learning poetry together with other children, and to engage in choral verse using favorite poems, rhymes, and jingles. Some of them may dictate for the teacher to write a variety of language forms: announcements, records, letters, greetings, stories based on their experiences, and simple poems.

Primary Grades. There should not be a sudden break between the atmosphere in the kindergarten and that in first grade. In fact, the atmosphere in all the primary grades should be free and happy and of such a nature as to encourage the child to talk with the teacher and with the other children. Given this kind of classroom, and opportunities to use oral language of several different types, pupils should grow rapidly in their speaking skills.

Oral reading predominates at the beginning stages of this level. This would seem to be a desirable way to make the transition from speaking words to reading words without speaking. Children have been speaking words for five years. Let them continue for a time to speak words as they struggle to learn names and meanings of symbols representing words. The wise teacher, however, even from the beginning will say something like "Read it with 'your eyes,' then read it 'aloud' because we want thinking to come before talking."

Some children may read orally to the class to explain some process or to give them directions for doing or making something.

Primary children enjoy dramatizing some stories they read, and using some of them in make-believe radio programs or television broadcasts.

Intermediate Grades and Above. Children in the intermediate grades are arriving at more advanced thought levels and have even more need for speaking than children in the lower grades. They reach out for oral expression of many types in activities that require reading in preparation and as an accompaniment. In reading instruction, silent reading predominates, and children are able now to spend considerable time in silent reading study. Their independent silent reading, however, should not crowd out opportunities to develop use of language. The speaking skills are still important and should undergo continued development in accordance with a carefully planned program.

Opportunities should be given to participate in many different types of oral language activities: conversing, planning, discussing, reporting, explaining, evaluating, solving problems, expressing creative thinking. They now enjoy preparing a mock or real radio or television presentation based on some story they have read. Most of these activities are founded on or accompanied by reading activities.

In all speaking-reading situations children at this level increasingly use and are encouraged to use richer vocabularies and more complete sentence structures, and make more frequent use of the higher thinking processes. Those who came to school speaking a dialect divergent from the regional standard English are becoming adept at using alternate speech forms and will often speak using a mixture of dialect and regional standard English.

Writing

The initial step in learning to write is taken when children manipulate a stick, crayon or pencil on some surface and notice that marks appear as a result. They enjoy repeating the experience of producing these marks. Eventually, they may try to make marks that represent pictures of objects or that imitate writing.

At the age of three or four, most children are not only drawing pictures but they are also going through a scribbling stage. Sensitive parents and teachers will treat the "writing" seriously, and children will often share their communication with adults. Cathy, for example, a four-year-old, did a lot of scribbling on a piece of paper. When asked what it said, she "read" her writing without the slightest hesitation. It was a letter to her aunt.

> Dear Auntie,
> Helen has been biting us, but not much.
> I made a house of a card table with a sheet over it.
> You can come anytime you want to because we'll be right in the house.
> I may be out in the field on my bike.

When young children's writing is treated with dignity, even though the teacher cannot really understand the scribble at all, children continue to want to communicate certain ideas in print. As they mature in language expression and production, they gradually incorporate their language generalizations in written language. First beginning consonants appear, and gradually some of the other letters in words are printed. With encouragement and acceptance of their written messages, most children will progress to writing clearly with few spelling errors. Spelling corrections should be made on demand and when teachers can help pupils perceive a need for absolute accuracy in written communication—business letters, announcements to be posted, writing to be bound in a "book" for others to read, and so forth.

Classroom Opportunities for Writing. The best way of developing writing ability is to involve children in writing activities meaningful and relevant to them. At the prereading stage, children may have contacts with writing as the teacher writes captions, plans, directions, and even some experience stories on the chalkboard. They may write their own names and names of relatives, friends, and pets. They may write labels for pictures and for items in the classroom that they have constructed in connection with class projects.

In primary grades, they continue the writing contacts and activities mentioned for the prereading period and in addition write short greetings on holiday cards, invitations, letters, short stories, labels for picture sequences, news items, short informative articles growing out of classroom interests, riddles, and poems.

In intermediate grades, they have opportunities to engage in all of the activities mentioned for primary grades in longer and more formal styles. Additional writing activities such as these may be engaged in: preparing written reports of information in connection with class assignments and interests; writing explanations of processes and methods; writing reviews of books read; and writing biographies, creative stories, and poems.

Particularly from the intermediate grades on, writing and reading seem to interrelate. Children rarely read without writing or write without reading. Teachers should direct the students' attention to the way ideas are organized by authors as models for writing. (Note the technique used by Sinatra which follows.

Reading

Many classroom activities permit the integration of reading with the other language arts. Conscious attention should be placed upon helping one aspect of the language arts reinforce the other.

Experience Stories. Experience stories offer excellent opportunities for providing reading instruction functionally integrated with other language skills. Such short stories, composed by children, permit experiences with speaking, listening, oral composition, and reading. In this activity, the teacher writes children's compositions on the chalkboard or on paper. Children may engage in this activity individually with the teacher, but there is some advantage in developing small group-experience charts and having children interact during this integrated language experience. They see the spoken words in oral composition flow into written symbols. They discuss and interpret what has been written. As they mature in writing ability, they can have many opportunities to write and read their own experience stories.

Reading an Organized Paragraph. Dr. Richard Sinatra, St. John's University, found that some pupils had trouble following the organizational pattern of a paragraph when authors presented a sequence, cause-effect, comparison, and so on. Here is an example of an approach he used to help them understand sequence.

He photographed a detailed sequence of the events in a bullfight.

Then he organized the shots in a series of slides. The pupils became involved in a discussion of the sequence and rather painlessly learned how to "read" sequence in a series of pictures. Dr. Sinatra then asked pupils to think of an experience of their own that proceeded from one step to the next. After they talked about the experiences and reviewed the sequential steps, they wrote their own paragraphs. This successful experience then carried over to their reading of paragraphs organized sequentially. Here was a focus on all the language arts culminating in a successful reading experience. (See Richard C. Sinatra, "Teaching Writing Through Visual Compositions," September, 1975, ERIC ED 105375, for further information.)

The same type of activity, with some upper-intermediate and middle-school children, can be extended across more than one paragraph.

Interrelating all the Language Skills

The following integrated language activities arose in a third-grade classroom in New Jersey as a result of reading a story about a lighthouse. The children were very much interested in the descriptions of the storm signals and asked many questions, some of which the teacher could not answer. She told them that she knew some children who lived near a lighthouse and who probably could tell all about lighthouses. (The teacher had previously taught in Truro, Massachusetts, which is near a lighthouse, and she still knew teachers and children in the Truro school.) She further remarked that if they wished to do so, they might write to these children and ask them questions.

The children were delighted with the idea and immediately began to prepare letters containing their questions. Much practice on format was necessary, and care was taken in penmanship. There were many questions about spelling because the desire to send "good letters" was strong. Standards were even developed for evaluating the letters before they were sent. Finally, a group of pupils went to the post office and mailed the letters.

The children in Truro replied with some excellent letters about Highland Light (the lighthouse), the Coast Guard, bayberries, cranberries, beachplums, and trap fishing. They also sent a collection of shells, bayberries, fish netting, and a jar of beachplum jelly. They promised to write later about the Pilgrims who landed near their town.

The letters were used as the basic material for reading lessons for quite a few days, and they also furnished leads for research. Some of the letters were read, and the gifts were shown at a school assembly. Moreover, letters of thanks were prepared and sent to the Truro children.

At Halloween time, the class sent the Truro children some masks that they had made out of paper bags as well as some samples of their craft work and paintings.

The Truro children replied with "Thank you" letters at Thanksgiving time, accompanied by a booklet that they had prepared. This booklet contained an account of a trip the children had taken to the first landing place of the Pilgrims in Provincetown and also a description of a trip they had taken to Corn Hill, where the Pilgrims first found Indian Corn. The children had copied inscriptions from tablets and statues and had written stories about the many interesting things they had seen. This booklet was eagerly read by every pupil in the room, and enthusiastic discussion ensued. The book was finally placed in the room library for the use of future classes.

The children wanted to show their appreciation by sending something worthwhile to the class in Truro. After considerable discussion they planned to make and send a booklet about Thomas Edison, who had developed many of his inventions in his laboratory in Menlo Park, which was near their school. A rich and extensive period of reading followed.

The teacher brought in a collection of clippings from magazines and newspapers that she had gathered over the years. The children brought in books from their homes and from the public library. And, in the process, they learned to use the card catalog in the school library.

All reading was done individually, except for the reading of *History Primer, New Jersey Supplement*, by Q. E. Thomson. Because this was considered to be the most authentic of the references, it was read and discussed by the group as a whole and used as a basis for comparison with the other books they had read.

The children increased their vocabulary and made and used a picture dictionary containing pictures of several words and phrases whose meanings needed clarification. Such entries as the following were included: *transmitter, incandescent light, laboratory, phonograph, telegrapher, dictating machine, Kinetoscope, filaments, electric light bulb, motion picture projector.*

Reading skills received a vast amount of practice through functional usage. Location skills needed in research included using tables of contents, indexes, dictionaries, picture encyclopedias, and card catalogs. Interpretation and critical reading were emphasized throughout the study as facts in reading materials were gathered and discussed. Word recognition skills were practiced when children needed help in pronouncing new words.

Oral reading as well as silent reading received practice as each child read to the class an incident he or she had found in a book and thought should be included in the booklet. The class decided whether or not the incident was appropriate for inclusion. In order that the class might make a fair judgment, the child reading orally was motivated to use a pleasant voice, good enunciation, and fluency of speech.

Finally, the stories were written for the booklet. After the first writing, each story was evaluated by the class and usually rewritten with improvement. The teacher typed the individual stories, and each child read her or his story back to the class for final approval.

Organization for the book was then decided upon: the stories were taped on the pages of a large blank book, and illustrations were made to accompany the stories. Finally, the book was proudly sent to the children in Truro.

However, interest was still high, and additional use was made of reading and other language art skills in two more class activities. The children wanted to share their information about their local "hero" with another class. Personal letters of invitation were written, pictures were arranged on the bulletin board, and preparation was made for telling stories about Edison and for explaining the pictures. Much purposeful practice in oral reading took place.

Finally, the principal invited the class to entertain the entire school with a program at the next assembly. Dramatizations of events in the life of Edison were prepared and enacted for this event.

The assembly program climaxed the period of rich learnings in the language arts of listening, reading, speaking, writing, and dramatization, with accompanying improvements in vocabulary, handwriting, and spelling.

THE READING PROGRAM

The school or classroom reading program draws from our knowledge of the child's stages of development, what we have learned about language acquisition and development, and the strengths inherent in the other communication areas. In beginning reading—because we do know that greater reading success will take place if the child's language, thought processes, and experiences are close to the writer's—the child should be presented with reading materials in familiar language and with content that is interesting and pertinent to the child.

As children start to reach out for other learning through reading, the reading program moves from its natural language base to the host of other materials available. Children will need to be helped to develop expanded reading strategies to cope with stories and expository passages in basal readers and in trade books. They will need special help as they turn to magazines, newspapers, and simple reference sources. Such help is imperative as the language and reported experiences of the writers become more and more distant from the language and experiences of the readers. Even when children are dictating or writing down their own experiences, their language tends to differ from that of oral communication. When they begin to read the more formal modes of written language, they usually need much guidance toward comprehension.

Linguistics

As you recognize, certainly by now, language is central to reading. The more knowledge teachers have about language, the more assistance they can give young readers as they initiate and improve their reading strategies. *Linguistics* is the name of the discipline focusing on the science and study of language. Particularly in the last decade, reading instruction has benefited from the input of linguists, psycholinguists, and sociolinguists. *Psycholinguistics* (an amalgamation of psychology and linguistics) centers on the learner (the language user) and how that learner puts language to use in a search for meaning. *Sociolinguistics* (an amalgamation of sociology and linguistics) focuses on the patterns and problems of groups of learners—speakers of a dialect divergent from a regional standard English and those who are learning English as a second language—as they attempt to use language in a search for meaning.

In this volume, we do not speak of *linguistic readers*—a term used to refer to some instructional materials devised to emphasize certain aspects of language—because all materials are linguistic. Language should not, and really cannot be, compartmentalized or departmentalized. Good materials will take all aspects of language into account and help readers develop strategies for attacking all those aspects right from the beginning stages of reading instruction. (See chapter 6.)

Written language consists of graphemes, morphemes, syntax, and semantics.

Graphemes = the written symbols that make up the words and represent the spoken sounds (phonemes) As: *ch-ai-n* in *chain.*

Morphemes = the smallest units of language that carry meaning (sometimes a single word; sometimes part of a word). *Bell* is a morpheme; *bells* consists of two morphemes, as the *s* means plural; *rewind* is two, prefix and root; *upsidedown* is three.

Syntax = the grammar of the language, not considering meaning; the way words are put together to make sensible language; sentence patterns.

Semantics = the meanings in language, not just the individual words but the interrelationships among the words.

Pupils need guidance in bringing what they know about language to the increasing complexity of the materials they must read. All the aspects of language above combine into strategies for unlocking meaning in print.

Concept of Reading

Each teacher's concept of reading will influence the classroom reading program. The rest of this book should provide enough information for a teacher to develop a concept of reading that will permit implementation of a sound program. Each concept and each program will differ from one another, but we assume all will be based on sound judgment grounded in knowledge of child development, psychological and sociological principles, and current linguistic contributions.

DISCUSSION QUESTIONS AND ACTIVITIES

1. What is your concept of reading? How do you define it? Try your hand at writing a definition of *reading* as you now see it. Write down also what you think about reading, its importance, and its uses in the classroom. As you read this book and perhaps some additional readings, look at what you have written from time to time. You may want to alter your definition and/or the ways you think you might apply it in the classroom. In all probability, you will never arrive at a definition with which you are satisfied so long as you keep thinking and learning. Both the authors of this volume have changed their concepts and definitions over the years.

2. Ask children to define *reading*. It is interesting to find out how children at various stages of their lives and from various backgrounds conceive of reading and its importance. If you are teaching, you may want to ask children about their concepts of reading during the course of the school year. They, too, will demonstrate change.

3. If you want to learn more about specific communication skills or you seek further information about psycholinguistics, Piagetian concepts, or linguistics and reading instruction, turn to the **Additional Readings** section of this chapter.

ADDITIONAL READINGS

Books and Pamphlets

ALLEN, ROACH VAN. *Learning Experiences in Communication.* Boston: Houghton Mifflin, 1976.

BURROWS, ALVINA T.; MONSON, DIANNE L.; and STAUFFER, RUSSELL G. *New Horizons in Language Arts.* New York: Harper & Row, 1972.

CARROLL, JOHN B. "The Nature of the Reading Process." In *Theoretical Models and Processes of Reading,* 2nd ed., edited by Harry Singer and Robert B. Ruddell. Newark, Del.: International Reading Assn., 1976.

CARTON, AARON S. *Orientation to Reading.* Rowley, Mass.: Newbury House Publishers, 1976.

CAZDEN, COURTNEY B. *Child Language and Education.* New York: Holt, Rinehart and Winston, 1972.

CHOMSKY, CAROL. *On Language Learning From 5 to 10: The Acquisition of Syntax in Children.* Cambridge, Mass.: M.I.T. Press, 1970.

DUKER, SAM. *Listening: Readings.* Metuchen, N.J.: Scarecrow Press, 1971.

———, comp. *Teaching Listening in the Elementary School.* Metuchen, N.J.: Scarecrow Press, 1971.

GIBSON, ELEANOR J., and LEVIN, HARRY. *The Psychology of Reading,* Cambridge, Mass.: M.I.T. Press, 1975.

GOODMAN, KENNETH S., and NILES, OLIVE S. *Reading Process and Program.* Urbana, Ill.: National Council of Teachers of English, 1970.

HENNINGS, DOROTHY D., and GRANT, BARBARA M. *Content and Craft: Written Expression in the Elementary School.* Englewood Cliffs, N.J.: Prentice-Hall, 1973.

HITTLEMAN, DANIEL R. *Developmental Reading: A Psycholinguistic Perspective.* Chicago: Rand McNally, 1978.

LUNDSTEEN, SARA W. *Children Learn to Communicate.* Englewood Cliffs, N.J.: Prentice-Hall, 1976.

———. *Listening: Its Impact at All Levels on Reading and Other Language Arts.* Urbana, Ill.: National Council of Teachers of English, revised edition, 1979.

MENYUK, PAULA. *Language and Maturation.* Cambridge, Mass.: M.I.T. Press, 1977.

MOERK, ERNST L. *Pragmatic and Semantic Aspects of Early Language Development.* Baltimore: University Park Press, 1977.

RUDDELL, ROBERT B. *Reading Language Instruction: Innovative Practices.* Englewood Cliffs, N.J.: Prentice-Hall, 1974.

RUDORF, HUGH, and HODGES, RICHARD E., eds. *Language and Learning to Read.* Boston: Houghton Mifflin, 1972.

SHEPHERD, DAVID L., ed. *Current Emphases in Reading.* Proceedings of Conferences Six, Seven and Eight, vol. 3, pt. 2. Hempstead, N.Y.: Hofstra University, 1970.

SMITH, E. BROOKS; GOODMAN, KENNETH S.; and MEREDITH, ROBERT. *Language and Thinking in School.* 2nd ed. New York: Holt, Rinehart and Winston, 1976.

SMITH, FRANK. *Comprehension and Learning.* New York: Holt, Rinehart and Winston, 1975.

———, ed. *Psycholinguistics and Reading.* New York: Holt, Rinehart and Winston, 1973.

———. *Understanding Reading.* New York: Holt, Rinehart and Winston, 1971, and second edition, 1978.

SMITH, JAMES A. *Creative Teaching of the Language Arts in the Elementary School.* Boston: Allyn and Bacon, 1973.

WALLER, T. GARY. *Think First, Read Later! Piagetian Prerequisites for Reading.* Newark, Del.: International Reading Assn., 1977.

Periodicals

CHOMSKY, CAROL. "Write First, Read Later." *Childhood Education* 47, no. 6 (March 1971), pp. 296–99.

COWE, EILEEN. "The Beginnings of Writing as an Extension of Thinking and Talking." *Elementary English* 49, no. 1 (January 1972), pp. 68–69.

SECTION A:
BASIC CON-
SIDERATIONS

DAVIS, JOEL J. "Linguistics and Reading." *Language Arts* 54, no. 2 (February 1977), pp. 130–34.

DENNISON, PAUL E. "Reading Programs are Means—Not Ends!" *Reading Teacher* 28, no. 1 (October 1974), pp. 10–12.

DEVINE, THOMAS G. "Listening: What Do We Know after Fifty Years of Research and Theorizing?" *Journal of Reading* 21, no. 4 (January 1978), pp. 296–304.

DOWNING, JOHN. "The Reading Instruction Register." *Language Arts* 53, no. 7 (October 1976), p. 762.

ELIN, RHODERICK J. "Listening: Neglected and Forgotten in the Classroom." *Elementary English* 49, no. 2 (February 1972), pp. 230–32.

FILLION, BRYANT; SMITH, FRANK; and SWAIN, MERRILL. "Language 'Basics' for Language Teachers: Towards a Set of Universal Considerations." *Language Arts* 53, no. 7 (October 1976), p. 740.

GOODMAN, KENNETH S. "Orthography in a Theory of Reading Instruction." *Elementary English* 49, no. 8 (December 1972), pp. 1254–61.

HIGGINBOTHAM, DOROTHY C. "Psycholinguistic Research and Language Learning." *Elementary English* 49, no. 6 (October 1972), pp. 811–17.

HUTTENLOCHER, JANELLEN. "Children's Intellectual Development: Acquisition of Language." *Review of Educational Research* 35, no. 2 (April 1965), pp. 114–21.

KIRKLAND, ELEANOR R. "A Piagetian Interpretation of Beginning Reading Instruction." *Reading Teacher* 31, no. 5 (February 1978), pp. 497–503.

LAWSON, ANTON E. "Teaching for Thinking: A Piagetian Perspective." *Today's Education* 65, no. 3 (September/October 1976), pp. 38–41.

McDONELL, GLORIA. "Relating Language to Early Reading Experiences." *Reading Teacher* 28, no. 5 (February 1975), pp. 438–44.

NATIONAL COUNCIL OF TEACHERS OF ENGLISH COMMITTEE. "Forum: Guidelines to Evaluate the English Component in the Elementary School Program." *Language Arts* 53, no. 7 (October 1976), pp. 828–38.

OLSON, DAVID R. "From Utterance to Text: The Bias of Language in Speech and Writing." *Harvard Educational Review* 47, no. 3 (August 1977), pp. 257–81.

RUDMAN, MASHA. "Informal Spelling in the Classroom: A More Effective Approach." *Reading Teacher* 26, no. 6 (March 1973), pp. 602–4.

RUPLEY, WILLIAM H. "Language Development and Beginning Reading Instruction." *Elementary English* 52, no. 3 (March 1975), pp. 403–8.

SMITH, FRANK. "Phonology and Orthography: Reading and Writing," *Elementary English* 49, no. 7 (November 1972), pp. 1075–88.

———. "The Role of Prediction in Reading." *Elementary English* 52, no. 3 (March 1975), pp. 305–11.

———, and GOODMAN, KENNETH S. "On the Psycholinguistic Method of Teaching Reading." *Elementary School Journal* 71, no. 4 (January 1971), pp. 177–81.

SMITH, NILA B. "Early Language Development: Foundation of Reading," *Elementary English* 52, no. 3 (March 1975), p. 399.

THOMPSON, RICHARD A. "Developing Listening Skills to Improve Reading." *Education* 91, no. 3 (February/March 1971), pp. 261–65.

TOVEY, DUANE R. "Language Acquisition: A Key to Effective Language Instruction." *Language Arts* 53, no. 8 (November/December 1976), pp. 868–73.

chapter 2

psychological-sociological guidelines

What to Expect in this Chapter:

This chapter consists mainly of guidelines that focus on the interactions of psychological and sociological principles upon the learner, the teacher, and the learning environment. When we look at the processing of language from a psycholinguistic and socio-linguistic viewpoint, we become very much aware of the complexities involved in having two people—the reader and the writer —carry on a meaningful dialogue. But, obviously, psycholinguistic and sociolinguistic insights exist that can be useful in guiding learners to strengthen strategies as they unlock ideas in a variety of materials for multiple purposes.

Psychology attempts to explain how and why individuals feel, think, and act as they do. Sociology is the study of group patterns, of the nature and development of society and community life, including its institutions, such as schools. Over the years, most educators have focused attention on the psychology of learning and, to a limited extent and as a separate area, the sociology of learning. As is true of the interrelated aspects of communication described in chapter 1, sociological and psychological factors cannot be separated when viewing learning and teaching. Each area is dependent upon the other. Pupils must be viewed from both the perspective of who they are as thinking, feeling individuals and how they function within their environments and with others.

This chapter is organized as a group of ten guidelines, for want of a better generic term, harvested from numerous sources. They are not listed and discussed in any priority order. They are unequal in scope and in the degree of immediate application to reading instruction. All, however, appear to be, in our judgment, essential psychological-sociological foundations for successful instructional practice. Teachers should consider them seriously as they plan and carry out reading experiences in their classrooms. They represent the heart of the instructional program in reading.

**PSYCHO-
LOGICAL-
SOCIO-
LOGICAL
GUIDELINES**

1. *The cultural patterns of a group or groups within the classroom should be studied, understood, and respected by the teacher.* Time spent in trying to learn about and understand group behavior patterns will pay off in establishing the kind of group empathy instrumental as a base for enlarging oral communication and beginning or enhancing pupils' interactions with written communication. Once a group believes the teacher is honestly attempting to understand and respect aspects of its traditions, goals, and interests, communication lines are opened.[1]

[1] Points, 1–5 and 10 have been adapted from H. Alan Robinson, "Psycholinguistics, Sociolinguistics, Reading, and the Classroom Teacher," in *Views on Elementary Reading Instruction*, ed. Thomas C. Barrett and Dale D. Johnson (Newark, Del.: International Reading Assn., 1973), pp. 4–7, 9–11.

Encourage pupils to speak and write about their special holidays and customs. Let children represent their particular ethnic groups by dramatizing their special events, share group experiences, bring interesting foods to class. Develop with all pupils the concept of respect for others by giving each of them opportunities to share as well as to listen.

2. *The behavior of individuals within the classroom should be studied and understood by the teacher.* Teachers should get to know as much about each child as possible: verbal ability; reactions to different situations and people; interests; ways of learning; feelings about school, parents, peers, and so forth; past learning history; strengths and needs in reading. Granted, doing case studies of the individuals in a classroom is time consuming and often complicated, but the result can be significant. Teachers may want (at first) to conduct "minicase studies" of those few pupils who seem to present particular problems. However, case studies applied to one individual often help teachers' insights and procedures as they look at other individuals. Gates said that conducting comprehensive case studies with learners has transformed many teachers ". . . from routine operators to insightful artists." [2] The result of a case study is bound to help the learner and the teacher undertand and respect each other—the basic ingredient of instruction.

A minicase study focuses on a problem that has surfaced. You will want to talk with the pupil and those others who might be able to cast some light on the particular problem. Having the pupil execute an assignment while you are observing is a useful means of gaining insight into how the pupil tackles a specific skill.

3. *The learner's language should be understood and respected.* Language is used (normally) to communicate meaning. The pupil comes to school with a remarkable knowledge of how to gain meaning from oral language. Specifically, pupils are adept at obtaining meaning from their dialect or language—that which has been heard and used in the learner's environment prior to school entrance and during school attendance.

If the pupil comes to school and finds that communication is

[2] Arthur I. Gates, "Characteristics of Successful Teaching of Reading," in *Reading: Seventy-Five Years of Progress*, ed. H. Alan Robinson, Supplementary Educational Monograph No. 26 (Chicago: University of Chicago Press, 1966), p. 15.

impossible because the teacher does not speak and/or understand Spanish, or Chinese, or Greek, and so on, the learner has serious problems. The best solution is, of course, for the teacher to speak and understand the language and be receptive to communicating in it. If this is impossible, the next best solution is for the English-speaking teacher to get help from peers or community volunteers; at the same time, the teacher should try to learn as much about the language as possible and have a good bilingual dictionary at hand. If the learner recognizes the intent and desire to communicate, much interaction is possible. (See chapter 14 for further discussion.)

If the learner comes to school speaking a dialect of English divergent from the regional or local standard English, and the teacher tries to understand and respect it, rather than deprecate it, the individual will be able to express his or her thoughts. If the teacher studies the dialect and learns what is part of the dialect system and what is not, the teacher will know when corrections are called for.

If the dialect or language is denigrated and not understood, the learner will stop using language almost completely in the classroom or will cease to use it for positive communication and may look for ways of using it in negative behavior. In any case, learners will most likely make little conscious effort to learn the new and "dominant" language or dialect.

If pupils are given many opportunities to use language to express meaning and to search for meaning in the language of others, they will gradually learn to cope with "standard English," which, at this time, they need to learn in order to succeed in society. Without doubt, in our opinion, transitions to "standard English usage" must be made, or the school is failing in its task. *Transitions* imply over time and at a pace that is slow enough for pupils to learn alternative structures in a positive way without being asked to give up their own language or dialect. *Standard English usage* refers to that English usage spoken by "educated" people in a region of the country—the language used in educational circles, in business, by announcers on radio and television, and so on. (See chapter 14 for further discussion.)

4. *Initial reading experiences should capitalize on the learner's language or dialect*. The learner should recognize a need to transfer from oral to written language in order to receive a message of importance. Such an abstract, high-flung goal as "you need to learn to read because it will help you all the way through school and life" is a feeble reason to read in the minds of most pupils—particularly in today's multimedia world. Initial messages to be read should parallel the learner's native language or the learner's dialect semantically (the words should represent concepts the learner already possesses) and syntactically (language patterns or structures should be familiar to the learner).

For native speakers of a very definite regional English or a dialect, it is unnecessary to write the message to match the sounds of their speech; that is, it is not essential for there to be a phoneme- (sounds spoken)

Be careful that the messages you write and the materials you select for pupils to read initially, coincide with oral language experiences. Such a message as, "For several reasons, you should occupy only your own seat," introduces a syntax or word order difficult for young learners to process, as well as words whose meanings may be very hazy in their minds. "Sit in your own seat because. . . ." makes use of the simple imperative sentence (which they are used to hearing and saying) followed by reasons (which is the pattern they will usually use themselves).

grapheme (spoken sounds represented in print) match. If children are permitted to use their own way of speaking when reading orally—for there is surely no problem when they are reading silently—there is little need to have the orthography (the way the words are spelled) printed or written in a dialect or regionalism.

5. *Instructional materials and recreational materials, particularly in the early stages of learning, should be selected on the bases of significance and relevance to the learner.* Reading, especially in beginning stages, should (as implied earlier) satisfy immediate goals. The messages should have significance and relevance in terms of solving problems, supplying enjoyment, and enhancing ability—as seen by the pupils. Too often, our reading programs have been largely literature programs emphasizing the literary and the narrative. Certainly, part of the reading diet should be narrative in nature, but the diet should be well-balanced. In all probability, a large number of boys and girls would gain more from initial reading experiences if the materials placed more stress on expository (explanatory) and utilitarian reading.

6. *Expectations about individual learner's ability, progress, and achievement should be flexible and positive.* From the time of Rosenthal and Jacobson's *Pygmalion in the Classroom,*[3] a number of studies and examples have been cited in the professional literature to demonstrate that learners usually live up to teachers' expectations of them. Browne[4] and Angelo[5] have demonstrated that teachers usually have low expectations of pupils in low reading groups, and the pupils reward teachers with low performance. On the plus side, Dworkin[6] has shown that negative expectations can be changed to positive under appropriate conditions.

[3] Robert Rosenthal and Lenore Jacobson, *Pygmalion in the Classroom: Teacher Expectation and Pupils' Intellectual Development* (New York: Holt, Rinehart and Winston, 1968).

[4] Margaret P. J. Browne, "An Exploratory Study of Teacher-Pupil Verbal Interaction in Primary Reading Groups" (Doctoral dissertation, University of Alberta, 1971).

[5] Evangeline B. Angelo, "Teacher Cue Patterns Related to Pupil Mastery of Contextual Aids," (Doctoral dissertation, Hofstra University, 1975).

[6] Nancy Dworkin, "Changing Teachers' Negative Expectation Towards Educationally Vulnerable Children Through the Use of a Brief Interactive Process," (Doctoral dissertation, Hofstra University, 1974).

Teachers can frequently help pupils learn cognitive tasks through affective means; that is, if a teacher will anticipate that a learner can do something and the learner is provided with the setting and structure in which to do it, the learner will frequently succeed without interference or specific direction from the teacher. Just the trust and faith of the teacher, in a number of instances, permits the child to work through the task. It would seem, of course, that learners could function best in environments where they are expected to succeed and are also given the necessary guidance to do so.

7. *Each learner should be helped to develop a positive self-concept and a strong feeling of self-esteem.* Athey [7] reported that the research literature suggested that good readers tended to have more positive self-concepts than poor readers—feelings of adequacy and personal worth, self-confidence, and self-reliance. These research reports raise the question of the chicken and the egg, of course—Which came first? On the other hand, it seems evident that if teachers would work to help individual learners develop positive psychological concepts related to themselves, the effect would be felt in language achievement and in the relationships essential to the sociological settings in which the learners find themselves.

The following practices work against the establishment of positive self-concepts:

a. Maintaining static reading groups in the classroom and labeling them—the blackbirds, the sweet peas, or the bears. Whatever is chosen as a name will become a negative term for the "low" reading group. (See chapter 12 for further discussion.)

b. Conducting round-robin oral reading sessions in order to have children "practice" their reading. Purposeless oral reading—one paragraph or section by one child and then on to the next—cements attitudes of dislike and uselessness for the poorer reader particularly, and often serves as a direct instrument of lowering self-concept. (See chapter 12 for further discussion.)

c. Having children call out how many wrong they received on a given classroom test of reading comprehension, vocabulary knowledge, or spelling. This practice serves no purpose except to embarrass the low achiever.

d. Introducing group competition for number of books read, best scores on language-related tests, speed of reading, and so forth. It is the low achiever who always feels the burden and shame of being last. The most visible offender, we guess, is the traditional spelling bee. It takes a strong, positive self-image and relative success in language-related tasks to compete with the knowledge that you might lose, but you will do "pretty well." It would take a massive, potent, positive self-image to know that you will be at the bottom of the heap; most of us

---

[7] Irene Athey, "Reading Research in the Affective Domain," in *Theoretical Models and Processes of Readng*, 2nd ed., ed. Harry Singer and Robert B. Ruddell (Newark, Del.: International Reading Assn., 1976), p. 357.

cannot cope with this. Competition situations need to be viewed cautiously! Helping a learner set up a self-competition situation is a very different story but even self-competition needs to be looked at carefully in relation to the tasks, the learner, and the learning situation.

8. *As suggested by Bloom* [8] *and others, learning tasks should be carefully programmed for success. The old adage that "success breeds success" remains a valid concept.* Lessons should begin with examples and experiences that pupils understand. Instruction should then proceed in easy steps. If the instruction is being carried on with a group, individuals within the group should have opportunities to respond at each step. Too many times, it is assumed that all individuals understand when the "group" response only represents a small percentage of the learners. Pupils should experience immediate feedback so they may know how they are doing. If a pupil appears to be misunderstanding, the correction should be encouraging and nonjudgmental. Pupils who are not "turned off" when they make errors will continue to try—and they will succeed if instruction is programmed adequately.

If a pupil responds to the question, "How many days does each month have?" with the response of 31, the teacher might say, "Good answer for most of the months; let's look at each one." The teacher might then help the pupil develop a list of the seven months with 31 days, and encourage the pupil to make decisions about the others.

---

9. *For children in the primary grades, especially, instructional periods should be planned in developmental increments from kindergarten through third grade; that is, the time allotted to a specific lesson should be adjusted as learners are able to contend with longer periods of concentration on sedentary tasks.* Large blocks of time should be set aside for instruction in processing oral and written language (speaking, listening, reading). This time should be used flexibly with groups and/or individuals so that it does not overrun their attention spans or tolerance for physical inactivity.

10. *Reading tasks are dictated by the nature of the language user, the nature of the environment in which the reading is accomplished, the nature of the material, and the purposes for reading.* There is no specific sequence of skills to be taught in reading instruction. Sequences of skills to be learned in various published reading programs have most frequently been devised on the bases of speech development, developmental needs of

[8] Benjamin S. Bloom, *Human Characteristics and School Learning* (New York: McGraw-Hill, 1976).

children, and/or the logical thinking of program designers. In reality, though, sequence is only relevant when related to the language knowledge and inadequacies of particular learners, the learning situation, the nature of the materials to be read, and the purposes for reading. Reading skills are actually a clustering of tools that form a strategy the learner can utilize to unlock the writer's meaning. Additional strategies are then employed to interpret, evaluate, and make use of what has been read. If the strategies are appropriate for the purpose of the reading and the nature of the material on hand, a given reading task will be successful.

The execution of reading tasks will differ when learners work on their own, must interact with others, or must make presentations to others. Most learners react best to informal learning environments and need direction and assistance in moving toward more formal situations. Except for the overall superior reader, pupils need much assisted practice and encouragement prior to reading a selection to others. This is especially true if reading presentations are to be made outside of the home classroom. (See chapter 4.)

The nature of the material to be used must also be carefully explored, for there is no reason for the learner to attempt to acquire a strategy at a given point if it will not be functional. A complete reading program cannot be presented in any meaningful way within the framework of a given set of materials. Strategies for unlocking ideas should be acquired as a reader utilizes printed materials throughout a school curriculum. The wide variety of writing patterns requires a variety of strategies for interpretation.

Purpose constantly interacts with the reader, the writer, and the material to be read. Any piece of material can be read utilizing different strategies for different purposes, and the task is hardly ever clear-cut. For example, if the reader is searching for the solution to a problem, she or he does not care much what the writer's purpose was—so long as the information is available. The reader probably has specific questions in mind that can be used to ferret out the desired answers. A very different set of strategies has to be employed, however, when the reader is trying to discover the writer's purpose—particularly if the writing is somewhat subtle. In such cases, most readers need guidance from teachers before their eyes even hit the page.

DISCUSSION QUESTIONS AND ACTIVITIES

1. Do you work with children from cultural backgrounds differing from your own? Have you learned about important holidays, customs, traditions, beliefs? Ask the children. Incorporate them into classroom activity.

2. What topics are relevant and exciting to pupils as they compose group stories or experience charts—or their own stories? Help pupils write and/or dictate potent experiences as the basis for reading. Explore the chil-

dren's interests, fears, superstitions, hopes. Consult Sylvia Ashton-Warner's *Teacher* (New York: Simon and Schuster, 1963) for some ideas.

3. Tape yourself interacting with a group of pupils and then play the tape back. Were you clear and supportive? Think of how you can improve your interactions with pupils.

If your ego is strong, play the tape (or another) for a group of your peers. Discuss strengths, weaknesses, and ways of improving the performance. Children can sometimes profit by listening to the playback of interactions, too. Discussions of interrelationships with peers may be profitable if evaluative sessions are carefully prepared.

If you are really brave, study an interaction analysis technique, like Flanders, and apply it in a class session, recording it on audio or, if possible, video equipment. (See Edmund J. Amidon and John B. Hough, *Interaction Analysis: Theory, Research, and Application.* Reading, Mass.: Addison-Wesley Publishing Co., 1967.) Interaction analysis techniques are organized ways of looking at the way you interrelate with your pupils during a teaching situation.

4. Ask pupils which class practices bother them and why. Be sure not to generalize in one direction or the other on the basis of individual feelings, but bear those feelings in mind as you work with those individuals. For example, use the four practices that work against positive self-concept (see pages 30–31) and see how children react. Add practices of your own for discussion as well as other practices you question.

ADDITIONAL READINGS

Books, Pamphlets, and Microfiche

ALEXANDER, J. ESTILL, and FILLER, RONALD C. *Attitudes and Reading.* Newark, Del.: International Reading Assn., 1976.

AUSUBEL, DONALD P. *The Psychology of Meaningful Verbal Learning: An Introduction to School Learning.* New York: Grune and Stratton, 1963.

BLOOM, BENJAMIN S. *Human Characteristics and School Learning.* New York: McGraw-Hill, 1976.

BLUMER, HERBERT. *Symbolic Interaction: Perspective and Method.* Englewood Cliffs, N.J.: Prentice-Hall, 1969.

BRAUN, CARL; NEILSEN, ALLAN R.; and DYKSTRA, ROBERT. "Teacher Expectation: Prime Mover or Inhibitor?" In *Reading Interaction: The Teacher, The Pupil, The Materials,* edited by Brother Leonard Courtney. Newark, Del.: International Reading Assn., 1976.

CAZDEN, COURTNEY B.; JOHN, VERA P. and HYNES, DELL, eds. *Functions of Language in the Classroom.* New York: Teachers College Press, Columbia University, 1972.

ELASHOFF, JANET D., and SNOW, RICHARD E. *Pygmalion Reconsidered.* Worthington, Ohio: Charles A. Jones Publishing Co., 1971.

JENSEN, GALE E. "The Sociopsychological Structure of the Instructional

Group." In *The Dynamics of Instructional Groups*, Fifty-ninth Year-book, pt. 2, edited by Nelson B. Henry. Chicago: National Society for the Study of Education Press, 1960.

MacDonald, James B., ed. *Social Perspectives on Reading*. Newark, Del.: International Reading Assn., 1973.

Manis, Jerome G., and Meltzer, Bernard M. *Symbolic Interaction, a Reader in Social Psychology*. Boston: Allyn and Bacon, 1967.

Quandt, Ivan. *Self-Concept and Reading*. Newark, Del.: International Reading Assn., 1972.

Rose, Arnold, ed. *Human Behavior and Social Processes: The Interactionist Approach*. Boston: Houghton Mifflin, 1962.

Rosenthal, Robert, and Jacobson, Lenore. *Pygmalion in the Classroom: Teacher Expectation and Pupils' Intellectual Development*. New York: Holt, Rinehart and Winston, 1968.

Shuy, Roger W., ed. *Linguistic Theory: What Can It Say About Reading?* Newark, Del.: International Reading Assn., 1977.

Singer, Harry, and Ruddell, Robert B., eds. *Theoretical Models and Processes of Reading*. 2nd ed. Newark, Del.: International Reading Assn., 1976.

Smith, E. Brooks; Goodman, Kenneth S.; and Meredith, Robert. *Language and Thinking in School*. 2nd ed. New York: Holt, Rinehart and Winston, 1976.

Smith, Frank. "Twelve Easy Ways to Make Learning to Read Difficult." In *Psycholinguistics and Reading*, edited by Frank Smith. New York: Holt, Rinehart and Winston, 1973.

Soar, Robert S. *An Integrative Approach to Classroom Learning*. Public Health Service, Final Report, no. 7–R11–MH02045. Philadelphia: Temple University, 1966. ERIC ED 033 749.

Spaulding, Robert L. *Achievement, Creativity, and Self-Concept Correlates of Teacher-Pupil Transactions in Elementary Schools*. U.S. Office of Education, Cooperative Research Project No. 1352. Hempstead, N.Y.: Hofstra University, 1965. ERIC ED 024 463.

Periodicals

Estes, Thomas H., and Johnstone, Julie P. "Twelve Easy Ways to Make Readers Hate Reading (and One Difficult Way to Make Them Love It)." *Language Arts* 54, no. 8 (November/December 1977), pp. 891–97.

Kaufman, Bel. " 'Here's to Children Everywhere!' " *Today's Education* 67, no. 1 (February/March 1978), p. 22.

Muller, Hans. "Two Major Approaches to the Social Psychology of Reading." *Library Quarterly* 12, no. 1 (January 1942), pp. 1–28.

Rubovits, Pamela C., and Maehr, Martin I. "Pygmalion Analyzed: Towards an Explanation of the Rosenthal-Jacobson Findings." *Journal of Personality and Social Psychology* 19, no. 2 (August 1971), pp. 197–203.

Sanacore, Joseph. "Reading Self-Concept: Assessment and Enhancement." *Reading Teacher* 29, no. 2 (November 1975), pp. 164–68.

SECTION B
ESSENTIAL COMPONENTS

CHAPTER 3 ASSESSMENT OF READING ABILITIES

Selecting and Using Standardized Reading Tests
THE TEACHER'S ROLE

National Assessment of Educational Progress (NAEP)

The Positive Expectancy Concept

Appraisal Procedures
OBSERVATIONS
CHECKLISTS
DIRECT INQUIRY
ATTITUDE SURVEYS
INTERVIEWS
Interests
Reading Experiences
Background Experiences
INFORMAL TESTS
Criterion-Referenced Tests
Skill Tests
Writing Questions for Informal Tests
INFORMAL READING INVENTORIES
CLOSURE PROCEDURES
READING MISCUE INVENTORY
QUALITATIVE USES OF QUANTITATIVE TESTS AND INVENTORIES
SELF-EVALUATION

Discussion Questions and Activities

Additional Readings

CHAPTER 4 READINESS FOR READING AT ALL GRADE LEVELS

Prereading Readiness
FACTORS TO BE CONSIDERED
Attention Span
Visual and Auditory Development
Psycho-sociological Development
Cognitive Development

EARLY READERS

ACTIVITIES
Informal, Functional Contacts
FOUNDATIONS FOR VOCABULARY DEVELOPMENT
Visual Discrimination
Auditory Discrimination
Emphasis on Meaning

FOUNDATIONS FOR STUDY SKILLS
Locating Information
Following Directions
FOUNDATIONS FOR FLUENT READING
FOUNDATIONS FOR INTEREST IN AND APPRECIATION OF LITERATURE

Realistic Stories
Fanciful Tales
Poems

Readiness Beyond the Prereading Stage

READINESS PRINCIPLES

EXAMPLES OF READINESS PROCEDURES
Primary Grades and Above

Health Workers

MEDICAL DOCTORS

NURSES

DENTISTS
Teacher A
Teacher B
Teacher C
Intermediate Grades and Above

Discussion Questions and Activities

Additional Readings

CHAPTER 5 APPROACHES, PROCEDURES, AND MATERIALS

Basal Reader Approaches

USES OF BASAL READER PROGRAMS
Misuses
Desirable Uses

Language-Experience Approaches

PROCEDURES

COMPOSING AN EXPERIENCE CHART

TYPES OF EXPERIENCE CHARTS
Narrative Charts
Question Charts
Suggestion Charts
Rule Charts
Planning Charts
Diary Charts

ADVANTAGES AND DISADVANTAGES OF THE APPROACHES

Individualized Reading Instruction

SIX STEPS TO INDIVIDUALIZED READING

MORE SPECIFICS ABOUT ORGANIZATION FOR INDIVIDUALIZATION

EVALUATION OF INDIVIDUALIZED READING PLANS

COMMERCIAL PROGRAMS AND SYSTEMS

Contributions from Technology

TELEVISION

THE COMPUTER

Guidelines for Choosing instructional Materials

GUIDE FOR SELECTING MATERIALS

GUIDE FOR EVALUATING SEX STEREOTYPING IN READING MATERIALS

Evaluating Readability

Discussion Questions and Activities

Additional Readings

chapter 3

assessment
of reading
abilities

What to Expect in this Chapter:

Chapter 3 focuses on several aspects of the assessment of reading abilities. Standardized tests and some of the problems related to them are discussed, and specific suggestions are made for test selection and evaluation. A variety of appraisal procedures, including the use of checklists, attitude surveys and interviews, informal tests and inventories, closure procedures, and the Reading Miscue Inventory, are discussed. Suggestions are also made for looking at product as well as process, qualitative uses of tests, assessment of the functions of reading, and pupil self-appraisal.

In a sincere effort to understand the strengths and needs of pupils, educators over the years have developed evaluation tools. In the United States and elsewhere, prior to the onset of the twentieth century, most assessments of pupils' abilities were made through direct observation. With the start of the "scientific movement" in education in the early 1900s, the United States in particular began the development of survey and diagnostic tests and inventories to measure individual and group achievement and/or needs. The effort continues today, although many educators question a number of our contemporary assessment instruments.

In general, standardized tests (tests administered to groups of learners whose scores are set up as norms for other learners) have been designed to measure "subskills" of reading. Measuring the subskills is a peculiar happenstance. Most reading educators believe that reading is either a process or group of processes employed by an individual to discover what an author has to say. They would agree that many thinking processes intertwine in order to get the message. Some educators believe that the processes of reading need to be broken down into subskills in the instructional situation; others believe in a more holistic approach to instruction. The authors of this book believe that the holistic approach must be used in helping learners develop strategies for dealing with written language *and* that there are certain skills that must be used as tools for specific reading tasks. But whatever the belief about instruction, what does this have to do with the isolated nature of reading subskills in most of our standardized tests?

One can understand how it came about. We needed group assessment devices. Tests had to be given to groups during school time in limited sessions. We wanted to know how pupils compared with other groups and even other school systems. We wanted to cover a variety of subskills in as short a period of time as possible. And—an evil misuse— we sometimes wanted to use our crude assessment devices to evaluate teacher performance.

Survey tests were designed to provide grade norms for ability to recognize and/or understand the meanings of isolated words; to comprehend details, main ideas, and sometimes inferences; and sometimes to read fast. Norms in grade equivalents, percentiles, stanines, and the like told us where groups of pupils and individual pupils scored in relation to the norms on total score (an averaging of vocabulary, comprehension, and sometimes rate) and on each part. Diagnostic tests, although usually containing unreliable subtests, attempted to help us look at strengths and weaknesses in such specific subskills as word analysis, auditory discrimination, aspects of vocabulary or comprehension, or rate.

Today, we appear to be evaluating these tests in light of information we have received in the past decade, particularly in regard to language and its sociological and psychological ramifications. Tests or inventories are beginning to emphasize process as well as product. In the past, we tended to judge a learner's reading ability through what he or she did— the test result. Today, we tend to look also—and perhaps more intently— at what he or she is doing during the processes of reading. In all probability, tests directed toward learning more about the reading strategies will "pay off" better for instruction.[1]

SELECTING AND USING STANDARDIZED READING TESTS [2]

Typical standardized survey tests of reading used to look at rough standards for a school or school system are of limited help to the teacher because they report the products of very specific types of reading behaviors usually not closely related to the types of reading pupils are called upon to perform in the classroom. Results on standardized reading tests should not be used to make decisions about the overall reading ability of pupils or their ability to read in a given area. Other evaluative techniques are needed to give substance to the picture.

Not only do standardized reading tests contribute little knowledge about performance in the classroom, but they also contribute to the lowering of "ego-strength" for many pupils. Placement in a stanine or percentile, or even percentile range, only serves to suggest that a given pupil always reads at or within some given statistical level. Grade-equivalent scores are even worse—the labeling of a pupil as a 3.6 or 5.9 or even 8 + reader just does not make sense and is certainly not functional.

The concept of reading at any certain level is at best an average of peaks and valleys on a given test or over a variety of classroom reading tasks. "Level" will change, depending upon the test, the task, the environment, the reader's interest, and so on. Some writers in the field of reading feel that the level a pupil achieves on a standardized reading test is usually indicative of a frustration level in reading. This may be so. It might be more accurate to say that we really do not know what the level indicates for a given pupil other than some average of performance at that time

---

[1] H. Alan Robinson, "Testing Reading: Product Versus Product," *Reading Teacher* 26, no. 3 (December 1972): 303–4.

[2] Adapted from H. Alan Robinson, *Teaching Reading and Study Strategies: The Content Areas,* 2nd ed. (Boston: Allyn and Bacon, 1978), pp. 32–37.

on certain reading tasks. In the main, these tasks are far removed from the type of reading expected in the usual classroom setting.

The statistical basis of such scores is straightforward enough, but those reported to be "below grade level" are left with a false sense of failure and low achievement. The eternal struggle to bring everyone "up to grade level," laudable though it sounds, is doomed from the start because it is inherent in a norm-referenced, standardized reading test that 50 percent of the children taking it will be below grade level. Schools so fortunate that all of their pupils are at or above grade level simply mean that elsewhere, where the health and social welfare of the children may not be so favorable, there will be schools almost all of whose children will "fail." While we believe that teachers and schools have important and lasting effects upon children's reading abilities, we also know that socioeconomic factors have a strong influence.[3]

Several professional educational organizations have recently suggested a moratorium on norm-referenced standardized testing. Other organizations such as the National Council of Teachers of English, although not calling for a moratorium, stress the need for

. . . new processes of assessment that are more fair and effective than those currently in use and that more adequately consider the diverse talents, abilities, and cultural backgrounds of children.[4]

Buros, in the preface to *The Sixth Mental Measurements Yearbook* (1965), stated:

Unfortunately, the rank and file of test users do not appear to be particularly alarmed that so many tests are either severely criticized or described as having no validity. Although most test users would probably agree that many tests are either worthless or misused, they continue to have the utmost faith in their own particular choice and use of tests regardless of the absence of supporting research or even of the presence of negating research.[5]

In the introduction to volume 1 of *The Seventh Mental Measurements Yearbook*, Buros said: "At least half of the tests currently on the market should never have been published. Exaggerated, false, or unsubstantiated claims are the rule rather than the exception."[6]

[3] Slate Steering Committee of the National Council of Teachers of English, *Slate* 1, no. 8 (October 1976): 1–2.

[4] North Dakota Study Group on Evaluation of the National Council of Teachers of English, reprinted in *Slate* 2, no. 1 (November 1976): 3.

[5] Oscar K. Buros, reprinted in *Slate* 2, no. 1 (November 1976): 4.

[6] Oscar K. Buros, *Seventh Mental Measurements Yearbook*, vol. 1 (Highland Park, N.J.: Gryphon Press, 1972).

The Teacher's Role

Under these circumstances, how should a classroom teacher view standardized tests? Should assessment or evaluation through standardized techniques be abandoned? Houts responded by saying:

> No one should interpret the current controversy over standardized tests as an effort to abandon assessment. Rather, it is an effort to develop assessment procedures that are more in keeping with a new set of educational and social assumptions that we as a society are working on: that the purpose of education is not to sort people but to educate them; that in a knowledge society we need to expose as many people to education as possible, not to exclude them from it; that human beings are marvelously variegated in their talents and abilities, and it is the function of education to nurture them wisely and carefully; and, not least, that education has an overriding responsibility to respect and draw on cultural and racial diversity. Assessment of students must begin to reflect that philosophy, and that is the true reason for the current call for test reform and an end to IQ testing.[7]

If standardized tests are to be used in a school system or in a given classroom, the following steps should be taken as part of the selection process.

1. Consult these sources:

The Mental Measurements Yearbooks, compiled and edited by Oscar K. Buros. At the time of this writing, the eighth *Mental Measurements Yearbook* was not yet published. Teachers should consult *The Seventh* and earlier yearbooks when necessary. Yearbooks contain reviews of tests by experts who have examined tests quite carefully. Published by the Gryphon Press, Highland Park, New Jersey.

Reviews of Selected Published Tests in English, edited by Alfred H. Grommon, 1976. Suggests questions to be asked in test selection and evaluates over fifty widely used English tests. Published by the National Council of Teachers of English.

Common Sense and Testing in English by the Task Force on Measurement and Evaluation in the Study of English, 1975. Discusses tests and lists criteria for selection and interpretation. Published by the National Council of Teachers of English.

Testing in Reading: Assessment and Instructional Decision Making by Richard Venezky, 1974. Discusses assessment procedures and use of results. Published by the National Council of Teachers of English.

Measuring Reading Performance, edited by William Blanton, Roger Farr, and J. Jaap Tuinman, 1974. Offers partial solutions to some problems in measuring reading behavior within the contexts of performance contracting, criterion-referenced tests, and testing the "disadvantaged child." Published by the International Reading Association.

[7] Paul L. Houts, "Behind the Call for Test Reform and Abolition of the IQ," *Phi Delta Kappan* 57, no. 10 (June 1976): 673.

Reading Tests and Reviews II, edited by Oscar K. Buros, 1975. Descriptions and reviews of reading tests. Published by the Gryphon Press.

2. If there is a vocabulary or word-knowledge subtest, choose the standardized reading test only if the words in this particular subtest are presented in context. The practice of having students read an isolated word and then having them try to find another isolated word to match is a far cry from measuring vocabulary power. Emphasis should be placed, as much as possible, on examining strengths in using strategies to unlock ideas across a language context.

3. Although the measurement of comprehension is a difficult task, be sure that the emphasis in the comprehension section of the standardized test is on examining strengths in using strategies to unlock ideas also. If multiple choice is used, be certain that a wide range of thinking processes are tapped and that the forced choices are all sensible and plausible. The use of the cloze procedure (using blanks to fill in within the running context) is a promising technique for measuring the ability of readers to use many language skills in their search for meaning. In all probability, however, it should not be the only method of measuring comprehension. The cloze procedure may not be tapping the reader's abilities to synthesize and integrate what they read. Several ways of measuring comprehension, used within the same test, might be an interesting way of learning more about the readers' search for meaning as well as the product of that search.

4. Examine several tests that seem suitable. Look carefully to be sure that the type of reading material is representative of what your pupils are asked to read within your curriculum. Be sure the content is not too distant from the background of the youngsters to be tested; if it is, you may be testing lack of background experience rather than ability to read. Consider the way the material is presented. The written discourse should at least represent some match between both the readers and the material they have been accustomed to read.

5. As much as feasible, choose tests that describe norms or populations somewhat equivalent to yours. If this is impossible, or even if the norms seem somewhat satisfactory, consider the possibility of developing local norms.

6. Although validity (and there are many kinds) of a reading test is often complex to ascertain, be sure that the test publisher offers evidence about validity. Do not jump into the administration of a new test with the promise from the publisher of information to come. The information may not be available for a long while, *and* it could be unsuitable.

7. Do not choose a test when reliability is questionable. An unreliable test means that you cannot trust it, or its alternate forms, to give consistent results over administrations.

Should standardized reading tests be used? Undoubtedly with all the criticism levied at them in recent years, they will be improving. They can be used with a great deal of caution and with the realization that they measure particular kinds of reading performances in particular ways. They largely measure some type of product of the reading act rather than process. They do not permit adequate evaluation of any individual's reading ability. And certainly a score of 4.5 or thirty-seventh percentile or sixth stanine has little relationship to overall performance in reading because students are asked to read materials at many "levels."

To a limited extent, standardized reading tests can provide rough, initial information, particularly for the instructor who is meeting a new class. Even though there is no such thing as *a* reading level for pupils, an individual score shows where a given pupil stands on that test in relation to other pupils. Although the score itself might be different on another test, the pupil would probably stand in approximately the same place in relation to peers. Hence, although there will not be a one-to-one correspondence between the kind of reading ability measured on the test and the reading in a classroom, the teacher learns that a variety of levels of reading materials ought to be provided for instruction and reference. The teacher might also be able to plan in advance some study and reading techniques that would help poorer readers attack some of the essential but complex material. Even so, such planning and instruction would need to be followed up with observations and appraisals of performance, described later in this chapter.

NATIONAL ASSESSMENT OF EDUCATIONAL PROGRESS (NAEP)

Since 1970–71, reading has been assessed on a national level twice, and planning for a third cycle is under way at the time of this writing. Although these assessments are largely product oriented, they have been built on a somewhat holistic conceptual framework endeavoring ". . . to reveal how well students (1) comprehended what they read, (2) analyzed what they read, (3) utilized what they read, (4) reasoned logically from what they read, and (5) made judgments from what they read." [8] These, too, are crude, broad measures that cannot be used as criteria for what pupils ought to be doing, but they do show some encouraging trends when the first and second cycles are compared.

The most encouraging finding is that nine-year-olds during the second assessment read significantly better than did nine-year-olds four years earlier. The improvement was noted in all reading skills but was greatest for reference skills. Black nine-year-olds showed the most dramatic improvement, a finding which a panel of reading specialists convened by NAEP attributed to intervention programs that have been implemented at the primary level since the first assessment.

For the other two age groups tested (thirteen- and seventeen-year-olds), results were less consistent. Both groups showed a slight improvement in literal comprehension and a slight decrease in inferential comprehension. Students at all ages had little difficulty comprehending straight-

[8] Slate Steering Committee of the National Council of Teachers of English, *Slate* 2, no. 6 (October 1977): 1.

forward, literal material, but their comprehension dropped off quickly as the reading tasks became more difficult.[9]

In our opinion, another reason for the increased improvement in the reading of the black nine-year-olds is the growing awareness of, and sensitivity among teachers to, psycholinguistic and sociolinguistic insights that must be considered in any reading program. The results with older students also points up the importance of helping students develop the types of study strategies discussed in chapter 10 of this book.

THE POSITIVE EXPECTANCY CONCEPT

In this chapter the terms *appraisal, evaluation,* and *assessment* are used rather than *diagnosis.* Dictionary definitions indicate that *diagnosis* is the process of determining by examination the nature of a diseased condition. And this is what we are saying to the pupil when we diagnose. Some people might say, "Oh, that's just semantics!" We feel that it is a serious problem and one that affects children's concepts of themselves. We suggest that education stop operating from a medical model—diagnosis, treatment, prescription—and develop its own positive expectancy model.

In a positive expectancy model or concept, all children are expected to succeed, although they will proceed in different ways at different paces. Assessment, as part of the instructional cycle, is ongoing and hardly thought of as a separate entity. Some learners may be given special help in succeeding with special tasks, but there are no remedial, corrective, or retarded readers. All learners progress in stages along a continuum.

Evaluation should feature a search for the strengths of learners. Needs should be determined on the basis of the insufficiencies of some of the strengths to succeed with certain reading tasks. Appraisals should be centered around meaningful tasks that include purposes. Instead of "checking one's phonics," an assessment of a pupil's ability to understand the complex directions in completing a science experiment can include an appraisal of strengths—as well as weaknesses—in using certain phoneme-grapheme (sound to print) relationships as an aid in unlocking meaning. (For further discussion of word-recognition techniques, see chapter 6.)

APPRAISAL PROCEDURES

The evaluation procedures described and discussed in the remainder of the chapter range from the informal use of standardized procedures through specific task analysis.

The teacher appraises each pupil continuously, although some special emphasis to assessment may take place at the beginning of the year, at the beginning of a new unit of work, or at the conclusion of a unit. Information gained from these evaluations can be used to differentiate instruction and plan for future instruction. The greatest value of informal appraisal procedures is that small pieces of work can be evaluated at once, and pupils can be helped to strengthen specific strategies or skills im-

[9] Ibid., p. 2.

mediately. Another, perhaps obvious, value is that reading behaviors are analyzed in fusion with the materials used in the classroom rather than in the isolated context of a formal reading test.

A number of the informal procedures are process-product oriented. They are used to look at both what the reader is doing during the reading act and what the reader *appears* to have learned from the reading. *Product* is difficult to appraise because teachers are not always sure of what the reader had in her or his head prior to the reading. *Product,* or the number of answers right on any evaluation instrument, is probably a combination of information and ideas gained and what the readers had in their heads prior to the reading.

In addition to relatively narrow, cognitive (pertaining to knowledge) assessments of the reading processes, teachers are more and more concerned with broad affective (pertaining to feelings and emotions) and cognitive questions directed toward their pupils' widening utilization and concerns about their reading. Such questions are:

> Was this reading experience sufficiently satisfying to aid in developing in this child a sense of personal dignity, worth, and achievement?
>
> Have new interests arisen that will lead on to further reading?
>
> Has worthwhile information been acquired from the reading content?
>
> Has the child done some real thinking in connection with the reading content?
>
> Have deeper insights into human living and deeper understandings of human relationships been developed from the import of the content read or from the discussions concerning it?
>
> Are individual children extending and refining the reading strategies and skills that they will need in realizing personal and social goals in school, in work, in community life, and in recreational pursuits?

The teacher who continuously evaluates the deeper growths of human beings as well as growth in reading achievement will probably be successful in applying any of the new ideas that are in our midst at the present time or that are likely to develop in the future. He or she will dare to try new ideas, will know how to judge their worth, and will be able to adjust them in ways most conducive to growth in the particular children under consideration.

Observations

General, unrecorded observations of reading behaviors in the classroom are of some value in the identification of pupils who appear to have few or no problems as well as those who have many. But, as with the standardized test, such observation can only help to identify gross strengths and weaknesses and possibly succeed in assisting the instructor to place pupils on some sort of performance continuum, at least in relation to the task being performed at the time of observation.

To be most meaningful, observations should be made in relation to the objective(s) of a given instructional situation. Pupils should be observed as they work independently, as they respond to questions formulated by the teacher, and as they interact with their peers. The teacher should concentrate on one or at most a few pupils at one time and record dated impressions. In this way, the instructor is able to compare observations for given pupils over time while coping with specific reading tasks. The instructor then has a product—dated written comments—to view in conjunction with other evaluative evidence.[10]

Because appraisal is a continuing and continuous part of the instructional cycle, the reading lesson directed by the teacher also serves as an excellent vehicle for looking at the behaviors of particular children. The directed reading activity (DRA), Stauffer's directed reading-thinking activity (DRTA), or other teacher-directed lessons introduced and discussed in chapters 12 and 13 permit the teacher to observe specific activities with a group or an individual. Stauffer suggested the following questions, among others, as useful for evaluative purposes while teaching a lesson.[11]

> How readily does a pupil set purposes when reading fiction? Nonfiction?
> Can the pupil deal with hypotheses that may or may not be true?
> To what degree does he or she reread and reflect?
> How readily does the pupil locate lines needed to support or refute a point?
> How effectively does she or he use a glossary or a dictionary?

As the teacher learns about pupils through observations during teaching sessions, during independent activities, and during the time they interact with each other, records are being accumulated that will be useful for future teaching lessons, for future independent work, for future interactions with pupils. Sometimes the records and/or anecdotal notations of other teachers may be useful—*after* teachers have observed pupils on their own. Additional points that other teachers noted may fit into the total picture, but they should not be allowed to guide the picture. Children change.

Checklists

Inexperienced teachers and also some experienced teachers looking for a way of organizing the data to be gathered from observations may want to use individual checklists similar to the example shown, created by Braun [12] for primary-level readers.

Depending upon the teachers' concepts of reading, the checklist may

[10] Robinson, *Teaching Reading*, p. 37.

[11] Russell G. Stauffer, *Directing the Reading-Thinking Process* (New York: Harper & Row, 1975), pp. 321–22.

[12] Carl Braun, "Diagnostic Teaching in a Language Experience Context," in *An Experience-Based Approach to Language and Reading*, ed. Carl Braun and Victor Froese (Baltimore: University Park Press, 1977), pp. 103–4.

be suitable or not. Adjustments can, of course, be made. Such individual checklists, as suggested by Braun, can be summarized in group charts to facilitate small-group instruction and obtain a view of group strengths and needs.

Checklists can also be derived from observations of each child, and analysis of such checklists can give direction to instruction. For example, Zintz cited another checklist that, when looked at in its entirety,

Name: _____ Date: _____

Skill area	Seldom or never	Usually	Always
A. Word recognition			
I. Sight vocabulary			
1. Recognition			
a. Recalls most words	_____	_____	_____
b. Recalls interesting words	_____	_____	_____
B. Word analysis			
I. Phonic			
1. Integrates auditory and visual skills in identifying:			
a. Beginning consonants	_____	_____	_____
b. Consonants in final position	_____	_____	_____
II. Structural			
1. Uses word parts to aid recognition of:			
a. Compounds	_____	_____	_____
b. Inflectional endings	_____	_____	_____
III. Semantic-associational context clues			
1. Predicts unknown words from association of surrounding meaning clues			
a. Semantic clues	_____	_____	_____
b. Syntactic clues	_____	_____	_____
IV. Syntactic-graphic content clues			
1. Predicts unknown words from syntactic-graphic clues	_____	_____	_____
V. Integration of phonic, structural, and context skills			
1. Uses semantic, syntactic and phonic-structural clues in combination to unlock words	_____	_____	_____
C. Comprehension [a]			
I. Literal			
1. Recognizes			
a. Details	_____	_____	_____
b. Main ideas	_____	_____	_____

Skill area	Seldom or never	Usually	Always
2. Recalls			
a. Details	_____	_____	_____
b. Main ideas	_____	_____	_____
II. Inferential—uses implied information to			
1. Draw simple inferences	_____	_____	_____
III. Evaluative—uses information to			
1. Make simple judgments	_____	_____	_____
2. Respond emotionally to ideas in print	_____	_____	_____

[a] If the teacher finds that reading comprehension breaks down at any given level, she [he] should determine the reason. The problem may be that the readability of the material used is too high or that the child has difficulty with the particular type of comprehension at a listening level. Immediate adjustments should be made.

highlights strengths (1–11), plays down needs (12–15), and yet paints enough of an individual picture so that further instruction may be planned.

1. Reads with understanding
2. Applies phonic skills
3. Reads independently
4. Finishes assignments
5. Reads well orally
6. Uses independent study time efficiently
7. Follows directions
8. Understands reading assignments
9. Pronounces new words efficiently
10. Works well in small groups
11. Brings in new information from outside of school
12. Is embarrassed in front of class
13. Reads in too soft a voice to be heard
14. Misses little words (basic sight words)
15. Reads in a monotone [13]

Again, the teacher's concept of reading might call for a different checklist. For example, a teacher could indicate that he or she is not interested in items 2, 9, and 14 above if the pupil reads with understanding. Teachers will also differ on how they would help this particular pupil. Nevertheless, this type of checklist serves an important function in helping teachers characterize observations in an organized manner.

[13] Miles V. Zintz, *The Reading Process: The Teacher and the Learner,* 2nd ed. (Dubuque, Iowa: Wm. C. Brown Co., 1975), p. 532.

Direct Inquiry

Teachers may also learn about their pupils through informal conversations with individuals and groups, checklists and questionnaires filled out by pupils, planned interviews with children and sometimes with parents. Such direct inquiries are useful for obtaining information about attitudes, interests, and background experiences in particular. Such information, of course, is valuable in planning a reading program for an individual because fostering positive attitudes toward reading can only result in improved reading. In addition, children will read about something that interests them with much more gusto than they would topics of little or no interest to them. Reading that capitalizes on interests and needs nourishes positive attitudes.

Attitude Surveys

Attitude-toward-reading inventories or surveys are usually Likert-type scales (responses on a scale from one extreme to another). Smith and Johnson suggested some typical attitudinal questions:

> *Directions to pupil:* Read each statement and circle the answer that describes how you feel:
>
> 1. I like to check books out of the library.
>   Strongly agree   Agree   Sometimes   Disagree
>   Strongly disagree
> 2. I'd rather watch TV quiz shows than read a book.
>   Strongly agree   Agree   Sometimes   Disagree
>   Strongly disagree
> 3. I like to read at night before bedtime.
>   Strongly agree   Agree   Sometimes   Disagree
>   Strongly disagree

Teachers of very young children or nonreaders can use the same technique by reading the questions to the children and having them circle an appropriate "face."

Teacher: "I like to check books out of the library." [14]

[14] Richard J. Smith and Dale D. Johnson, *Teaching Children to Read* (Reading, Mass.: Addison-Wesley Publishing Co., © 1976), p. 203.

For older pupils, sentence-completion techniques often work well. For instance, pupils can be asked to complete such statements as:

Reading is _____
To me, books are _____
I'd read more if I _____

Answers to attitude surveys may not always be honest, but if the stage is properly set they can be. Also, information gathered from such surveys must be combined with information from other sources.

Smith and Johnson also wisely pointed out that ". . . it seems more sensible to access pupils' attitudes toward reading *specific* things than to determine their *general* attitude about reading."[15] They suggested the use of Smith and Barrett's short inventory, which asks pupils to react to whether or not a given selection was enjoyed, was boring, held the pupil's attention, or was disliked.[16]

Interviews

Interests. Although pupils can be asked to respond to survey instruments such as those described above to assess interests, planned questions asked in interview situations appear to get the best results. Patience and fortitude are necessary when first questioning pupils who indicate no interests. Such is not the case, but they are timid or cannot find the words to talk with the teacher about their interests. Some children need help in understanding what is meant by "interests," simply because they have never thought of them so consciously before. Such questions as these can be useful:

If you were allowed to do whatever you wanted to do, what would you do?
If you could have your choice, what would you like to have someone read to you about? Or what would you want to read about more than anything else?
What are your favorite TV shows?
Do you have hobbies or special things you like to do? What are they?
Do you have a pet? What is it? Would you like a pet? What kind?

Reading Experiences. Such questions as these that follow are useful in ascertaining the extent of reading experiences individuals have at home.

[15] Ibid.

[16] Richard J. Smith and Thomas C. Barrett, *Teaching Reading in the Middle Grades* (Reading, Mass.: Addison-Wesley Publishing Co., 1974), pp. 180–81.

Do you have books of your own at home?

Do you look at your books by yourself?

Can you (or do you) read any of the stories in the books?

Do you have some books with old, old stories in them? What are they?

Do you have books with stories in them about children like you? What are they?

Does anyone read to you? What does he or she read to you? Do you ever look at the lines of print as she or he reads?

Do you know your name when you see it in writing?

Can you write your name?

Can you tell when the Stop-Go signal says "Stop"? When it says "Go"?

Do you know any words on the grocery packages in the kitchen cupboard? What words?

Background Experiences. Interview questions directed toward gathering information about background experiences serve three purposes: (1) to have reading experiences capitalize on background experiences, particularly in generating language-experience stories; (2) to learn more about each individual and to make each child realize the importance of bringing his or her experiences to the classroom; (3) to reveal what experiences ought to be designed to acquaint individuals with concepts that will emerge in reading but, at this point, are not a part of their background experiences. The questions that follow are aimed at a variety of levels.

What games do you have at home?

What pets do you have?

Do you play with other children? What do you play?

Do you help at home? What do you do?

Do you ever go to a store? What kind of store? What do you see there?

Have you ever seen a train? Have you ever ridden on a train? Have you ever ridden on an airplane?

Do you have a garden? Is it a vegetable garden or a flower garden? What are the different plants that grow in it?

Do you ever go on trips with your father and mother? How do you travel? Where do you go?

Have you ever visited a farm? What did you see there? (In case of a farm child ask: Have you ever visited a city? What did you see there?)

Informal Tests

In this chapter, the informal instruments that follow are classified as tests or inventories. The tests discussed and exemplified below focus on discrete skills or a group of specified skills. They are not standardized, although some informal tests are produced commercially.

Criterion-Referenced Tests. Popham and Husek explained criterion-referenced tests in this way:

> Criterion-referenced measures are those which are used to ascertain an individual's status with respect to some criterion, i.e., performance standard. It is because the individual is compared with some established criterion, rather than other individuals, that these measures are described as criterion-referenced. The meaningfulness of an individual score is not dependent on comparison with other testees. We want to know what the individual can do, not how he stands in comparison to others. For example, the dog owner who wants to keep his dog in the back yard may give his dog a fence-jumping test. The owner wants to find out how high the dog can jump so that the owner can build a fence high enough to keep the dog in the yard. How the dog compares with other dogs is irrelevant.[17]

Some commercial companies have prepared criterion tests. Others are developing them. A number are prepared by teachers or reading specialists for use in the particular classes with which the testers are concerned.

In our opinion, criterion-referenced tests make sense—theoretically. Children compete with themselves, not others. They are assessed on their ability to master a given skill or strategy. These seem like sound criteria. However, one must be certain that the performance or behavioral objectives focus on meaningful, purposeful activities. Fragmenting the curriculum into a multitude of behavioral objectives such as *being able to pronounce* CH *correctly eight out of ten times* endangers the reader's overall search for meaning. How can we assume that eight out of ten or two out of three indicates mastery in other reading situations and with other materials?

Important reading-thinking skills, such as ability to locate specific information to solve a problem or understanding the steps in a process, can be considered criterion-referenced tasks. When accomplished successfully in one situation with specific materials, the criterion has been met. One hopes and assumes that consecutive successful experiences with the major objectives of a reading curriculum will eventually be transferable to a multitude of similar tasks.

Skill Tests. Reading specialists and/or teachers sometimes devise individual tests of an aspect of reading without spelling out the behavioral or performance objectives. This is usually done with the type of material to be used for instruction so it is closer to the needs of the pupils than standardized tests. Sometimes, a test is created to focus on one skill area. The example below concentrates on pupils' ability to recognize simple antecedents (word or words to which a pronoun refers) and referents (the pronoun).

[17] W. James Popham and T. R. Husek, "Implications of Criterion-Referenced Measurement," *Journal of Educational Measurement* 6, no. 1 (Spring 1969): 2.

EXAMPLE:

The antelope is a hoofed mammal that lives in Asia or Africa. It is related to the cow and the deer, but it is more like the deer. Both the antelope and the deer are graceful and speedy. They also have horns, and each is timid of human beings.

Pupils are to tell or write the antecedent for each underlined pronoun. This short paragraph and one-time test cannot provide all the information a teacher must know about pupils' ability to process the *anaphora* (antecedent and referent), but it begins to provide some insights into the pupils' strategies at this point.

Tests that attempt to assess pupils' abilities to handle several discrete skills can be devised. These are most meaningful to learners and for teachers if they cluster around a particular strategy for unlocking meaning. For instance, if pupils are having problems locating information (or if a teacher wants to find out their ability to do so), an informal test might center on knowledge of alphabetical order, looking up entry words in dictionaries and telephone books, and a series of questions based on a section of a simple index. A similar type of test could be designed to ascertain flexibility in reading two different types of material, such as expository and narrative.

Writing Questions for Informal Tests. Reading comprehension is an elusive concept and difficult to define. Hence, comprehension of something that has been read needs to be defined as that understanding shown by a given testing procedure—comprehension as measured by multiple choice, by completion, by essay, and so forth. Each type of measurement has its own characteristics and its own problems. The teacher devising an informal test must take this into consideration. True and false leaves no options; multiple choice gives cues and foils (choices other than the correct answer), which are difficult to write; deletion in closure material is often dependent upon the nature of the material; essay involves organizational skill, and so forth.

Haupt [18] suggested that when writing open-ended questions of a literal nature, teachers locate the meaningful parts of sentences (subject, predicate, and adverbials) and base their questions on specific parts. He indicated, in line with such case grammarians (linguists focusing on specific semantic relationships) as Chafe,[19] ". . . that predicate questions will

---

[18] Edward L. Haupt, "Writing and Using Literal Comprehension Questions," *Reading Teacher* 31, no. 2 (November 1977): 193–99.

[19] Wallace L. Chafe, *Meaning and the Structure of Language* (Chicago: University of Chicago Press, 1970).

often be the most important ones for assuring comprehension of all the information in a passage." [20] (See chapter 8 for further discussion about questioning procedures.)

Informal Reading Inventories

Sensitive teachers have always tried out books and selections with pupils to determine the match. The procedure is sensible because it allows teachers to view process as well as product and to determine strengths and needs with materials to be used for instructional purposes. Trial procedures usually involve both silent and oral reading. Although not standardized, some of these informal procedures have been organized into semiformal inventories. Inventories have been published by Betts and Welch,[21] Botel,[22] McCracken,[23] Nila B. Smith,[24] and others. A problem with these published informal reading inventories (IRIs) is that they are based on one set of materials, and often the results do not carry over to other sets of materials.

For the teacher who wants to set up such an inventory, the following steps should be taken:

1. Procure a series of readers or content-area textbooks ranging from at least two years below and two years above the grade level of a child.

2. Select about six passages (100 words or more each, depending upon the level), two from the beginning, middle, and end of each book. Start a year below grade level.

3. Have the child read the first pair of passages, one orally and one silently, and do the same for the other two pairs.

4. During the oral reading, note and write down the deviations from the printed page and the reading behaviors engaged in. What words were omitted? What words were substituted for others? Did the youngster self-correct? When and probably why did the child go back or regress?

5. After the oral reading, ask pupils to tell you about what they read through a series of questions, a closure procedure (see pages 59–60), or retelling (see pages 61 and 62). Keep a record of the result.

6. During the silent reading, time the youngster and note reading behavior. Record the time in seconds and write down any unusual behaviors during the reading.

[20] Haupt, "Writing and Using Literal Comprehension Questions," p. 196.

[21] Emmett A. Betts and Carolyn Welch, *Informal Reading Inventory* (New York: American Book Co., 1964).

[22] Morton Botel, *Botel Reading Inventory* (Chicago: Follett Publishing Co., 1961).

[23] Robert A. McCracken, *Standard Reading Inventory* (Klamath Falls, Oreg.: Flamath Printing Co., 1966).

[24] Nila B. Smith, *Graded Selections for Informal Reading: Diagnosis for Grades 1 Through 3* (1959); *Diagnosis for Grade 4 Through 6* (1963) (New York: New York University Press).

7. After the silent reading, ask pupils to do the same as in number 5 above.

8. Compare the results across passages for a given book and then across all the passages for all books used. Look at types of deviations from the print, reading behaviors, comprehension, and time for silent reading.

9. Make a decision about which levels of those specific materials the child can read independently and which levels can be used for instructional purposes (without frustration).

10. If you are able to use multilevel materials, assign a given child to suitable material for independent work and then for instruction. If multilevel materials are not available for instructional purposes, study the IRI results carefully to design structured assistance as a child uses difficult material. You should also look for high-interest, easy materials dealing with similar content to which the child may turn on his or her own. Be prepared, also, to develop your own materials at suitable levels.

Some teachers use somewhat rigid criteria for establishing the independent level (99 percent word recognition; 90 percent comprehension), the instructional level (95 percent word recognition; 75 percent comprehension), and the frustration level (90 percent or less in word recognition; 50 percent or less in comprehension). In our opinion, the comprehension percentages are more or less adequate if the teacher allows leeway for the individual reader's nature and the nature of the material. We do not, however, give much credence to the word-recognition score as an isolated percentage; the accuracy of word recognition only becomes important when it interferes with comprehension. We advise *informal* use of informal reading inventories! Level is not as important as knowledge about the child's strategies. Level changes from one type of material to the next in relation to a child's interests, background experiences, linguistic competence, and purpose.

Aside from the IRI described above, different types of inventories can be organized, particularly in relation to content-area materials. An inventory differs from a test in that it endeavors to look for strategies and outcomes that are more holistic in nature, as contrasted to viewing specific skills or clusters of skills. Edwin H. Smith, Guice, and Cheek, in their article on informal reading inventories in science and math, presented many examples at increasingly difficult reading levels. Here are two: The first is about third grade science; the second is about fifth grade mathematics.

I. A scientist may work in a *laboratory*. That is a place where experiments take place. Some of these are controlled experiments or ones that are done in different ways. Both ways are almost the same, but there is one thing that is different. Suppose you want to know how light changes the growth of a certain kind of plant? Then you need two of the same kind of plants. They would have to be of the same age and size. The dirt they grow in would have to be the same. Both would have to have the same amount of water. The temperature of the room in which they grow should be the same for both. Then you would change one thing. One plant would get more light than the other plant. You would watch them carefully and keep notes to see what differences happen between the plants. You would find out how light changes the growth of that kind of plant.

Draw a line under the best answer.

1. How many things are different in a controlled experiment?
   one   two   three
2. The two plants in the experiment would not have the same amount of
   water   light   dirt
3. The experiment would work without
   notes   water   temperature control
4. The experiment would be best done with how many plants?
   two   four   eight

II. Bill and his father were planning a trip. Their cottage, near the river, was 240 miles away. They estimated that if they left home at 1:00 p.m. they could be at the house by 5:00 p.m. They could have the car unloaded by a quarter of 6:00 and walk the eighth of a mile to the river in 5 minutes. There they would fish until 8:30 and then go back to the house for, hopefully, a fish dinner.
   The cottage lacked a water supply They would take water with them. They estimated that they would need 30 gallons for 3 days. Since a pint of water weighs a pound, the water alone would weigh 240 pounds plus the weight of the containers. Bill and his father were careful planners.

Draw a line under the best answer to each question.

1. How many miles an hour did they plan to average for the trip?
   45   60   70
2. How much does a gallon of water weigh?
   10 lbs.   8 lbs.   5 lbs.
3. About how many feet was the house from the river?
   50   700   1000 [25]

Closure Procedures

Various forms of closure procedures are useful in determining a type of comprehension. They may be used in connection with other evaluative procedures or as tools unto themselves. The most common type of closure procedure is word deletion.

[25] Edwin H. Smith, Billy M. Guice, and Martha C. Cheek, "Informal Reading Inventories for the Content Areas: Science and Mathematics," *Elementary English* 49, no. 5 (May 1972): 660–61, 664–65. Copyright 1972 by the National Council of Teachers of English. Reprinted by permission.

> *EXAMPLE:*
>
> *The new driver crashed the* _____ *into the fence.*

The learner is to supply the missing word in writing (spelling doesn't count, but precise synonyms do) or orally for beginning readers. This procedure forces the learner to use his or her background experiences and the context surrounding the blank. Deletions may be every so many words at random, or specific types of words may be deleted. Teachers can gather a great deal of information about the pupils' abilities to process written language in general and in particular. For instance, in the example about the antelope and the deer on page 55, ability to cope with *anaphora* in another way would have been to delete the pronouns and ask pupils to fill them in. See pages 208–214 in chapter 8 for instructional uses of closure that can be used to appraise.

The most frequently used closure procedure is the *cloze* technique created by Wilson.[26] Wilson suggested that every *n*th word be deleted from a passage a pupil is asked to read. (In practice, every fifth word is deleted most of the time.) Usually, the first sentence of the passage is left intact and sometimes the final sentence is, too. Pupils are then asked to fill in the deleted words; they may retrace their steps and erase when desired. The objective is to find out how capable pupils are of making connections among ideas as they utilize the syntactic and semantic clues in the material. There is no right or wrong. The teacher is searching for strengths that pupils put to work in processing particular types of material. As indicated earlier, synonyms are acceptable. This procedure is particularly useful in viewing how the pupil searches for meaning, what cues she or he uses, and in determining how to help some pupils make connections among ideas in and across sentences.[27]

Notice that all blanks are the same size to avoid space cluing. Some of the blanks can be filled in because pupils are aware of logical word sequence. Some may be filled in because of normal redundancy, and pupils are able to pick up semantic clues within the material. Other blanks can only be filled in when the learner has prior knowledge to bring to the material. Depending on the situation, information can be gained in the following ways:

1. Have the pupil attempt to fill in all answers and discuss the results. Both you and the pupil draw conclusions about why some of the responses would not be accurate for that particular blank.

[26] Wilson L. Taylor, "Cloze Procedure: A New Tool for Measuring Readability," *Journalism Quarterly* 30, no. 4 (Fall 1953), 415–33.

[27] Discussion of cloze adapted from Robinson, *Teaching Reading*, pp. 40–41.

EXAMPLE:

> *Your body is built around a frame of bones. There are 206 bones _____ your body. They are _____ shapes and sizes. Their _____ and sizes depend on _____ jobs. Some bones, like _____ tiny bones of the _____, are small. Others are _____ and heavy like the _____ of the legs. Some are flat, others _____. Some are curved, others _____ straight. If you have _____ picturing this frame, look _____ a Halloween skelton. That _____ give you some idea _____ all these different bones.*[28]

2. Have a pupil fill in only those answers she or he feels are possible—in light of the pupil's background. Discuss the responses.
3. Provide the missing words in scrambled fashion and have the pupil insert them. Discuss the responses. The exact words in correct order are: *in, different, shapes, their, the, ear, big, bones, round, are, trouble, at, will, of.*

Reading Miscue Inventory

Pupils should rarely be asked to read out loud without specific purpose and preparation. A valid exception is to have pupils, on a one-to-one basis, read orally in order to find out more about the strategies they might employ when reading silently. Kenneth Goodman, reading specialist and psycholinguist, views the exploration of oral reading in this fashion as a means of learning about the strengths readers put to use as they interact with writers.

Yetta Goodman and Burke[29] developed a useful procedure called the *Reading Miscue Inventory.* This inventory, although packaged as a training kit for teachers with its own materials, can be applied to all materials and all pupils. The *Inventory* is based on Kenneth Goodman's concept[30] that pupils miscue or deviate from the expected responses during reading for a variety of reasons. In the traditional sense, these *miscues* might appear to be synonymous with *errors*, but there is a distinct conceptual difference. In such standardized oral reading tests as the *Gray Oral Reading Test* or the *Gilmore Oral Reading Test,* for example, mispronunciations and other types of word recognition errors are added up; results are

---

[28] Passage from BE A BETTER READER, Level B. Basic Skills Edition, by Nila Banton Smith, © 1977, 1968, by Prentice-Hall, Inc. Reprinted by permission.

[29] Yetta M. Goodman and Carolyn L. Burke, *Reading Miscue Inventory* (New York: Macmillan Co., 1972).

[30] Kenneth S. Goodman, "Analysis of Oral Reading Miscues: Applied Psycholinguistics," *Reading Research Quarterly* 5, no. 1 (Fall 1969): 9–30.

based on the *number* of errors—a quantitative assessment. In the Reading Miscue Inventory, the miscues, or deviations from the expected responses, are classified in relation to specific questions about the reader's strategies in handling language and ideas. The evaluation is largely *qualitative.*

The full miscue analysis inventory takes a long time to administer. Hittleman's modification [31] based on suggestions from Burke appears to save some time and yet honors the intent of the analysis. In our opinion, teachers who use this analysis will learn a great deal about the reading strengths and needs of their pupils. Essential steps as we see them are presented below; for deeper analysis, further discussion, or clarification, turn directly to the original inventory and/or Hittleman's presentation.

1. Record on tape a pupil reading orally from a selection that is difficult but not frustrating. Do not have the pupil stop reading until he or she has made at least twenty-five miscues. If the pupil does not make twenty-five miscues during the first hundred words or so, the material may be too easy for the analysis. Find a more difficult selection. (Miscues consist of word substitutions, insertions, omissions, word reversals, repetitions, incorrect intonation in terms of the author's presentation.)

2. When the oral reading is done, keep the recorder on and ask the pupil to retell the story. Use an outline of the story you have prepared in advance to follow the story as it is told. Have the pupil retell without assistance first but use prodding, general questions if all the information is not given: What else happened? Tell me more. Once the retelling is done, turn off the recorder and dismiss the pupil.

3. Mark the miscues on a copy of the selection you have prepared for this purpose. (This marking of miscues may be done while the child is reading and then confirmed when the tape or cassette is replayed.)

   a. Substitutions: "The moon is a heavenly body that revolves around the earth."

   b. Insertions: "The candy fell on the dirty floor."

   c. Omissions: "She said, 'Please (don't) leave now.'" (Circled word was omitted.)

   d. Word reversals: "Once upon a time there were three pigs." (Draw a light line through the part that was reversed.)

   e. Repetitions:
      (1) Correction of miscue: "The moon is a heavenly body."
      (2) Repetition of uncorrected miscue: "It revolves around the earth."

[31] Daniel R. Hittleman, *Developmental Reading: A Psycholinguistic Perspective* (Chicago: Rand McNally College Publishing Co., 1978), pp. 113–32.

(3) Repetition that changes correct response: "It was a
trembling (ch)
tremendous earthquake."

4. Analyze substitutions first through the use of three questions. As
Hittleman suggested, "Answers to these questions indicate the extent of the pupil's use of grapho-phonological cues and knowledge
of grammatical functions." [32]
Question 1: Does the miscue look like the word in the text?
Question 2: Does the miscue sound like the word in the text?
Question 3: Does the miscue retain the same grammatical function
as the word in the text? [33] (Noun for a noun, verb for a verb, and
so forth.)

5. Use the two questions that follow to analyze knowledge of language.
They are asked of all sentences containing one or more miscues of
any kind. Language is acceptable if the child is producing sensible
language, irrespective of dialect.
Question 4: Is the sentence as finally produced an acceptable and
grammatical sentence? (Irrespective of other sentences.)
Question 5: Does the sentence as finally produced have an acceptable meaning? [34] (Irrespective of other sentences.)

6. Ask the following question of each sentence containing a miscue.
Question 6: Does the sentence as finally produced change the
meaning of the story in relation to its plot and theme? [35] (If the
material is expository, does the sentence change the meaning of the
larger selection in relation to major ideas and their supporting
ideas?)

7. Tally the number of *yes* or *almost yes* responses to the first five
questions for each miscue for each pupil and convert them to percentages. Example: If Teresa substituted fifteen times, and twelve
of the miscues looked like the word in the text, in response to question one her graphic similarity score is 80 percent. Or if, of Jonathan's twenty-five miscues only fourteen were grammatically acceptable, in response to question four his grammatical acceptability
score is 56 percent.

8. Tally the number of *no meaning change* miscues and convert to a
percentage.

9. Score the retelling record you made. Goodman and Burke assign
fifteen points for recall of characters and an additional fifteen
for descriptive information about them. They suggest twenty points
for theme, twenty points for plot, and thirty points for recollection
of specific events. You will need to reorder the scoring of the retelling, particularly if expository material is used.

10. Hittleman suggested a convenient evaluation form for each individual on pages 127–28 of his book. The form is keyed to the six
basic questions. The manual for the *Reading Miscue Inventory*
contains a coding sheet on pages 40–41 for the full inventory.

[32] Ibid., p. 124.
[33] Ibid., pp. 124–25.
[34] Ibid., pp. 125–26.
[35] Ibid., p. 126.

Qualitative Uses of Quantitative Tests and Inventories

Standardized tests and informal inventories may be used to ascertain the reading strategies of children. They must first be given as directed if the standard or structured results are needed for purposes of comparison or as rough measures of achievement. Qualitative uses should be made only once the tests or inventories have been scored as directed.

For example, the *Gray Oral Reading Test* and the *Gilmore Oral Reading Test,* as already indicated, direct the examiner to tally the types of errors, but the scores and grade equivalents are based on number of errors. Here is an opportunity for the teacher to look at the errors, or miscues, and determine what specific strengths and needs particular pupils have. Some of the same kinds of questions asked in the *Miscue Inventory* can be applied.

Informal reading inventories (IRIs) may also be put to double use. As pupils read the oral selections, teachers can record miscues and analyze them as suggested by Hittleman or even less formally.

If teachers can retrieve standardized silent reading tests once they have been scored—sometimes an impossibility—they, too, can be analyzed in terms of the kinds of questions pupils cope with well or poorly. As the standardized measures begin to use closure procedures more frequently, these responses can be analyzed much as one would analyze the results on an informal closure passage. These tests can then serve double duty.

Although pupils may not always give honest answers or wish to express their feelings and thoughts, retrospection can sometimes be a useful tool with both scored standardized instruments and informal inventories or tests. Retrospection is the process of thinking back over what you did and why you did it. The teacher can obtain useful insights from some pupils by discussing closure and miscue responses with them.

Self-Evaluation

Pupils should be helped to appraise themselves and their reading performances. Individual conferences planned periodically at which teacher and pupil focus on strengths and successes will help pupils also look at needs. Such conferences should include examination of dated work samples, results of tests and inventories, types of books read, recordings of oral reading situations, and so forth. Pupils need to react to and think about specific abilities and needs related to purposeful tasks. "You're a good reader" or "You're not a good reader" has little meaning.

Some pupils like to graph their achievements on their own personal profiles, which the teacher can help them develop if they wish. Such profiles should be private and only shown to peers when and if the individual child wishes to do so.

Positive self-evaluation guided carefully by the teacher can result in heightened self concept—the cornerstone of reading success.

1. What standardized reading tests are used in the school in which you teach? If you are not teaching, what tests are used as part of the course work in the program in which you are enrolled? Select one or more of them and read reviews in one of the Buros' publications. Inspect the tests(s) yourself and compare them with the evaluative criteria listed in the chapter. Look at them in relation to the pupils who must take them. Read about some other tests. Are there others that you would like to try out?

2. If possible, observe one pupil carefully for a week as the pupil engages in reading and writing activities. Jot down major observations. At the end of the week, cluster together all the pupil's strengths. Then cluster together some needs. Think of how you might use the strengths to help the pupil improve in one specific need area.

3. Try out some attitude and interest questions on a group or an individual. Devise some questions not exemplified in the chapter and see if they help you develop increased insights about the pupil(s).

4. Devise and administer a skill test or some type of informal reading inventory to a pupil.

5. Try out the cloze procedure on pages 59–60 if you have access to pupils who are usually able to contend with materials labeled grade five or higher. If you do not have access to these older children, write your own with easier material.

6. You ought to learn how to administer the modification of the *Reading Miscue Inventory* because it will help you develop insights into the reading of all children, not just the one or two with whom you might practice initially. Try your hand at it.

ADDITIONAL READINGS

Books and Pamphlets

BEERY, ALTHEA; BARRETT, THOMAS C.; and POWELL, WILLIAM R., eds. *Elementary Reading Instruction: Selected Materials.* 2nd ed., pp. 590–630. Boston: Allyn and Bacon, 1974.

BRAUN, CARL. "Diagnostic Teaching of Reading in a Language Experience Context." In *An Experience-Based Approach to Language and Reading,* edited by Carl Braun and Victor Froese. Baltimore: University Park Press, 1977.

COOPER, CHARLES R. *Measuring Growth in Appreciation of Literature.* Newark, Del.: International Reading Assn., 1972.

DAUZAT, SAM V. "Informal Diagnosis: The Nucleus." In *Classroom Practice in Reading,* edited by Richard A. Earle. Newark, Del.: International Reading Assn., 1977.

FARR, ROGER, and ANASTASIOW, NICHOLAS. *Tests of Reading Readiness and Achievement: A Review and Evaluation*. Reading Aids Series, edited by Vernon L. Simula. Newark, Del.: International Reading Assn., 1969.

HARRIS, ALBERT J. "The Reading Teacher as Diagnostician." In *Classroom Practice in Reading*, edited by Richard A. Earle. Newark, Del.: International Reading Assn., 1977.

JOHNS, JERRY L.; GARTON, SHARON; SCHOENFELDER, PAULA, and SKRIBA, PATRICIA, comps. *Assessing Reading Behavior: Informal Reading Inventories*. Newark, Del.: International Reading Assn., 1977.

JOHNSON, MARJORIE S., and KRESS, ROY A. *Informal Reading Inventories*. Reading Aids Series, edited by Ira E. Aaron. Newark, Del.: International Reading Assn., 1965.

MACGINITIE, WALTER. *Assessment Problems in Reading*. Newark, Del.: International Reading Assn., 1973.

RANKIN, EARL F. *The Measurement of Reading Flexibility: Problems and Perspectives*. Newark, Del.: International Reading Assn., 1974.

SMITH, RICHARD J., and JOHNSON, DALE D. *Teaching Children to Read*. pp. 193–221. Reading, Mass.: Addison-Wesley Publishing Co., 1976.

Periodicals

BOYD, RACHEL M. "Differences Underlying Multiple-Choice Items in a Reading Comprehension Test." *Journal of Reading* 14, no. 3 (December 1970), pp. 173–78.

CUNNINGHAM, PATRICIA M., "Match Informal Evaluation to Your Teaching Practices." *Reading Teacher* 31, no. 1 (October 1977), pp. 51–56.

GOODMAN, KENNETH S. "Analysis of Oral Reading Miscues: Applied Psycholinguistics." *Reading Research Quarterly* 5, no. 1 (Fall 1969), pp. 9–30.

HILLERICH, ROBERT L. "A Diagnostic Approach to Early Identification of Language Skills." *Reading Teacher* 31, no. 4 (January 1978), pp. 357–64.

MONTEITH, MARY K. "ERIC/RCS Report: Screening and Assessment Programs for Young Children: Reading Readiness and Learning Problems." *Language Arts* 53, no. 8 (November/December 1976), pp. 921–24.

PIPHO, CHRIS. "Minimal Competency Standards." *Today's Education* 67, no. 1 (February/March 1978), pp. 34–37 .

POPHAM, W. JAMES. "The Standardized Test Flap Flop." *Phi Delta Kappan* 59, no. 7 (March 1978), pp. 470–71.

Reading Teacher 26, no. 3 (December 1972), 260–310.

RUDMAN, HERBERT C. "The Standardized Test Flap." *Phi Delta Kappan* 59, no. 3 (November 1977), pp. 179–85.

RUPLEY, WILLIAM H. "ERIC/RCS: Miscue Analysis Research: Implications for Teacher and Researcher." *Reading Teacher* 30, no. 5 (February 1977), pp. 580–83.

SMITH, EDWIN H.; GUICE, BILLY M.; and CHEEK, MARTHA C. "Informal Reading Inventories for the Content Areas: Science and Mathematics." *Elementary English* 49, no. 5 (May 1972), pp. 659–66.

chapter 4

readiness
for reading
at all grade levels

What to Expect in this Chapter:

Readiness was not a common educational term until about the 1920s. At that time, and for many years afterward, it was used to refer to that stage of learning prior to reading instruction—prereading activities. Today, it is used to refer to several different but similar concepts. In this chapter, we first discuss readiness as applied to the young child and the prereading stage. We then focus on the child who is reading and the kind of readiness essential for success in reading as the elementary-school curriculum unfolds. Finally, we suggest some readiness procedures related to specific reading situations.

Readiness is a desire and/or a willingness, plus the ability to accomplish a task. *Ability* refers to the possession of adequate background experience to understand the task. For example, the authors of this text might be able to generate a desire and willingness to read about nuclear physics for some purpose, but their ability to do so is very limited. Unless the text were simplified in some way and helped them relate whatever background they have to the reading, the going would be very difficult.

Background experience, in the example cited above, refers to understanding both the concrete and abstract aspects of the discipline, the terminology, and the interrelationships between mathematical and verbal language. Perhaps our "general" intelligence might help us, but we suspect that intelligence is highly related to the specific task at hand.

No real learning takes place without readiness because readiness is highly related to the nature of instruction. Gates and Bond [1] (referring to readiness for reading) and Bruner [2] and Bloom [3] (referring to readiness for general learning) suggested that the instructional process is highly interrelated with readiness. Hence, the notion of readiness is a significant one for the school to focus on, not only as the child enters the school but throughout a child's school career. Although we are concerned with the child's readiness for general learning, our actual concern at each level of instruction is readiness for the task at hand and the way the task will be learned.

Reading readiness, of course, involves this same desire, and/or willingness, and ability to read. But reading readiness is task-oriented, as is any other type of readiness for learning. The learner wants to read something, not everything. Granted, at first some learners are so thrilled with reading

[1] Arthur I. Gates, and Guy L. Bond, "Reading Readiness: A Study of Factors Determining Success and Failure in Beginning Reading," *Teachers College Record* 37, no. 8 (May 1936): 679–85.

[2] Jerome Bruner, *The Process of Education* (Cambridge, Mass.: Harvard University Press, 1960).

[3] Benjamin S. Bloom, *Human Characteristics and School Learning* (New York: McGraw-Hill, Inc., 1976).

that they are ready to read anything, but this is not the case for most learners.

In the early decades of American education, ready or not, children were sent to school at two or three years of age. At this time, they were immediately *taught* the alphabet and inducted into the intricacies of spelling out and sounding out words.

We have come a long way in American education. Readiness is now respected. Although we may have children enter at young ages (prenursery school), we usually engage in informal activities and help children develop their own readiness for more formal learning activities. Few teachers of today would "give such a hard time" to a child as the experiences encountered by Scout, portrayed by the author of the Pulitzer Prize winning novel *To Kill a Mockingbird*.

You will remember that Jem said of his four-and-a-half-year-old sister:

"Scout yonder's been readin' ever since she was born, and she ain't even started to school yet." [4]

Then upon entrance in first grade, Scout, whose real name was Jean Louise, was asked to read something that [the teacher] Miss Caroline wrote on the chalkboard. She read it so well that Miss Caroline was visibly bothered. Miss Caroline then had her read most of the first reader and finally the stock market quotations in the *Mobile Register*. All of this time Miss Caroline's irritation was building up and she finally told Scout to tell her father to stop teaching her, as it would interfere with her learning to read in school. Scout said that her father did not teach her and reading just seemed easy. Her troubles continued, however, as her school days went by. Miss Caroline became increasingly annoyed and frequently implied that Scout wasn't supposed to know certain things until next year.

PREREADING READINESS

Factors to be Considered

Attention Span. As suggested in chapter 2, teachers must be conscious of the ability of children to attend to learning tasks. The younger the child, normally, the shorter the attention span. The nursery school or kindergarten child not only has a short span psychologically but also physically. Concentrated language-learning activities should be limited to short periods of time with breaks for physical activities.

Visual and Auditory Development. Young children particularly should not be asked to concentrate visually on close work—such as reading readiness and reading tasks—for long periods of time. Although there is no definitive evidence that proves when or if a young child is too visually immature to read, common sense suggests slow, carefully programmed

[4] Harper Lee, *To Kill a Mockingbird* (New York: Popular Library, Inc., 1962), p. 13.

sequences of instruction. The teacher should also look for specific indications of possible vision problems in young children, or learners of any age, such as avoidance of close-work activities; tenseness during such close work; frequent headaches; tilting the head to the side; rubbing the eyes; and exhibiting such facial distortions during close work activities as frowning, excessive blinking, scowling, or squinting.[5] Other symptoms that might indicate the need for a visual examination can be complaints of blurred vision; an eye or eyes that turn inward, outward, or upward involuntarily; and complaints of or visible fatigue following near-point activities.[6]

Visual perception is undoubtedly related to the act of reading, but there is no conclusive evidence to suggest that visual perceptual training on commercial or teacher-made programs is a helpful readiness procedure.[7] Visual discrimination training, in our opinion, should focus on meaningful readiness activities directly related to the symbols of print—letter forms, words, phrases, and clauses.

Auditory discrimination is, of course, also related to readiness and reading. Some emphasis should be placed on this area in the readiness stages of reading by providing many opportunities for children to use and hear language in numerous meaningful situations. Asking and answering questions and following specific oral directions help to develop the discrimination abilities. Conscious attention directed toward the sounds of language, in rhyming situations, alliteration, and so forth, are helpful activities. "Playing with language has not usually been included in the beginning reading program, but it is suggested here that such activities may foster continued linguistic growth, including that of auditory discrimination."[8]

Although visual anomalies are more frequently related to problems with reading than are poor auditory acuity for certain sounds, the latter may also be related. Teachers should be on the lookout for such symptoms as frequent headaches, turning the head or body to one side in the direction of the speaker, lack of ability to follow spoken directions, a great deal of inattentiveness, frequent requests for repetition of directions, or constant use of a loud voice. Obviously such symptoms may not always point toward auditory problems, but discernible patterns might call for referral.

Psycho-sociological Development. As suggested in chapter 2, children will function best when they have developed positive concepts about

[5] *Do You Know These Facts About Vision and School Achievement?* (St. Louis, Mo.: American Optometric Assn., 1969).

[6] Violet B. Robinson, Dorothy S. Strickland, and Bernice Cullinan, "The Child: Ready or Not?" in *The Kindergarten Child and Reading*, ed. Lloyd O. Ollila (Newark, Del.: International Reading Assn., 1977), p. 14.

[7] Donald Hammill, Libby Goodman, and J. Lee Wiederhold, "Visual-Motor Processes: Can We Train Them?" *Reading Teacher* 27, no. 5 (February 1974): 469–78.

[8] Violet Robinson, et al., "The Child: Ready nor Not?" p. 16.

themselves and can function well within the framework of the learning environment. In the readiness and beginning-to-read stages, special attention must be given to provide opportunities for children to develop positive concepts about themselves and others. Attention placed on sharing ideas and materials and on learning how to resolve conflicts that are bound to occur in social situations become important aspects of a readiness program.[9]

Cognitive Development. Piaget has helped us realize that children proceed through stages of cognitive growth. Nursery school and kindergarten children need to develop readiness for language activities by physically manipulating objects in their environment. Their thinking is usually semilogical. As indicated by the title of Waller's pamphlet, *Think First, Read Later!* [10] young children probably develop readiness for reading activities by dealing with parallel and concrete situations prior to reading about them. The Piagetian stages of development, described briefly on pages 7–9, are particularly relevant for readiness activities throughout the elementary grades.

Early Readers

Like Scout, in *To Kill a Mockingbird,* some children develop readiness for reading extremely early and read well before school entrance. In a longitudinal study, Durkin [11] followed two groups of preschool readers into the third and sixth grades. Among these children, age four appeared to be a common time for interest in reading to begin. These children tended to come from "reading" homes and had parents who were involved with them and involved their children in a variety of experiences. Only the children who were *tutored* by parents did not appear to maintain their early lead in reading. Durkin's study and the events of the late fifties and early sixties (when her study was in progress) combined to spur the movement for reading in kindergarten. Commercial programs were introduced and carefully structured readiness programs were developed. We were off again on a typical pattern in American education—jump on the bandwagon.

Recently, Durkin cautioned that, although there is no evidence to indicate that help in reading before first grade is harmful,

> . . . future benefits will be reaped only if schools alter their instructional programs to accommodate the pre-first grade learnings.
> If reading instruction *is* initiated earlier than has been traditional,

[9] Ibid., p. 18.

[10] T. Gary Waller, *Think First, Read Later!* (Newark, Del.: International Reading Assn., 1977).

[11] Dolores Durkin, *Children Who Read Early* (New York: Teachers College Press, Columbia University, 1966).

it also ought to be of a kind that will add enjoyment and greater self-esteem to the fifth year of a child's life.[12]

Activities

This section of the chapter concentrates on activities for some children in the nursery school, some children in the kindergarten, and some children in the introductory period in first grade. As stated earlier, all children will not be ready for them and should not be "pushed" to become involved. Further on in the chapter, more specific types of readiness activities are discussed both for older children and for particular kinds of reading lessons.

Informal, Functional Contacts. Informal, functional reading contacts will arise as the need presents itself. Teachers who are watching for such opportunities will find many as daily activities proceed. In these informal contacts, children should simply be *exposed* to the symbols. If some of them start reading the content, whatever it may be, it is all right. Such children should not be denied this privilege. It should be encouraged. For those with whom the exposures do not "take," be content with the exposures only; eventually they will "take."

1. Print name cards and let the children, if they so desire, wear their cards pinned to their clothing for a time. Invite children to hold up their name cards when their names are called to check attendance; or they may place their names in a pocket chart when they are called during attendance taking. Later, some children might like to group together all names that begin with the same letter.

2. After discussion with the children, when a need arises place labels on objects in the room when they may serve some functional purpose; for example, if difficulty arises in finding the scissors, label the cupboard where the scissors are kept; place *in* and *out* signs on swinging doors to prevent an accident; label hooks in the hall with the children's names; and so on. The children themselves may prepare simple labels for their construction work on large paintings and drawings, as *City Airport, Tom's Home.*

3. Frequently, print memoranda on the chalkboard; for example, orders for school lunches, as "milk 6, cocoa 8, crackers 10, apples 3"; names of committees and their members, as "Plant Committee—Jay, Sal, and Sue"; simple rules, such as "Work quietly"; simple directions for some activity, such as making applesauce—"Pare. Wash. Cook. Sweeten."

4. Place "surprise" sentences on the bulletin board each morning, such as "Susan will bring her pet rabbit this afternoon." Let the children gather around the bulletin board and try to guess what the surprise is; then read it to them.

[12] Durkin, "Facts about Pre-First Grade Reading," in *The Kindergarten Child and Reading,* p. 10.

5. When taking a walk or going on an excursion, call attention to the names on packages in a grocery store window; signs on store buildings; names of streets; names on trucks, street cars, and buses; danger signs; and so on.

6. The children may make class or individual scrapbooks, each page of which contains a picture or a collection of pictures that they have cut from magazines. The teacher may pass out labels (consisting of individual words, phrases, or even short sentences) typed on a typewriter with a primer-sized type, and place them under the pictures. The children may then paste these labels under the pictures on the pages of their scrapbooks.

During the entire prereading period and during any necessary preparatory period in first grade, teachers should frequently let children see their own words flow into printed symbols as teachers print them on the chalkboard or on tagboard. Advantage should be taken of every opportunity to print, as the children watch, notices, plans, suggestions, or directions that they, themselves, have composed. Although the children should not be required to *read* the words, phrases, or sentences, they will have had the valuable experience of seeing meanings put into reading symbols, meanings that grow out of their own experiences; and some of them will begin to read words or sentences of their own accord.

Foundations for Vocabulary Development

After children have had many opportunities to see words as labels for familiar things, and after they have seen a number of messages on the chalkboard and elsewhere, some become interested in (and ready for) learning to recognize—on sight—recurring words.

Visual Discrimination. Matching is a good way of promoting visual discrimination ability. At first, children should match words and pictures. One way of doing this is to paste a picture on each of several large cards about 4″ × 9″ in size. Print the name of the picture at the bottom of the card. On another card about 4″ × 2½,″ write the name of the picture only. Place several of the picture cards on the chalk ledge. Give one of the matching word cards to each of the children. Ask children to place the card that each holds under the word of one of the picture cards that looks just like the word held. Continue until all the children have had a chance to match their words.

As children learn more words and sentence patterns, matching can be undertaken with both isolated words and simple sentences. For example: Functional words used as labels in the school and classroom may be grouped and children should be asked to match them by circling or underlining.

crayons / books   pencils   <u>crayons</u>

boys / girls   coat room   (boys)   paper

Or, in the case of simple sentences that are used, children can be asked to look for the similarities. This is also a good way of developing metalinguistic awareness of written language (such features as spaces between words, lower case and upper case, punctuation). For example: Pupils can be asked to circle or underline the words that are not the same or that are the same within sentences.

(Theresa) is a <u>girl</u>.

(John) is a <u>boy</u>.

<u>This</u> <u>is</u> <u>a</u> (toy.)

<u>This</u> <u>is</u> <u>a</u> (car.)

Auditory Discrimination. Words in isolation or in sentences may also be presented orally so that children must listen for similarities and differences. An enjoyable and useful experience for prereading pupils is that of listening for words that sound alike in rhymes and jingles. The teacher starts by reciting some to children but eventually children will compose some themselves.

Little Bo <u>Peep</u>   A rat and a <u>mouse</u>
She lost her <u>sheep</u>.   Both lived in one <u>house</u>.

          I like this <u>school</u>
          And I'm no <u>fool</u>.

Emphasis on Meaning. Foundations for reading to understand the author's message, interpretation, and evaluation can be laid informally during the prereading period. In discussing a picture, a teacher may ask: "What does this girl have in her hands? On what is she sitting? What pet is lying beside her?" In discussing a story that has been read to the children, the teacher may ask: "What was the name of the girl in the story? Where was she going? Whom did she meet on the way?" Such literal questions call for simply naming objects or reproduction of statements within the story. They have importance in terms of understanding the basic information and are necessary. They should not be overemphasized, however, at the expense of interpretation, which has a much wider service to render.

Considerable experience may be given in interpreting pictured situations. The teacher may make a collection of thought-provoking pictures; for example, one picture may show a little boy peeling onions, and he is crying; another may show three puzzled, brown kittens gathered around a large, black, china cat used as an ornament on a table; another may show a little girl eating spinach with her eyes turned toward her dessert.

Teachers of young children should frequently guide them in interpreting deeper meanings in stories. For example, while reading the story of Bambi, a teacher read that *Bambi* was in an open space in the forest that was really screened in on all sides. She paused to ask, "How could this space be screened in on all sides?" In reading *The Lively Little Rabbit*, another teacher read about the owl, who, like practically all owls, did not like to travel in the daytime. To stimulate thinking about what was said in the text, this teacher asked, "Why don't owls like to travel in the daytime?"

Still closer to the reading situation are the opportunities in which children are guided by the teacher to evaluate some incident or statement in a story. "Do you think it was fair for Peter Rabbit's mother to put Peter to bed with only a dose of camomile tea while his brothers and sisters had bread and milk and blackberries?" asked the teacher during a discussion after she had read *Peter Rabbit* to the children. Some children did think it was fair and gave their reasons; others did not think it was fair and gave their reasons. All had an opportunity to express personal reactions to something read from a book.

Words are often used in stories that do not occur in the ordinary conversation of children. These should be noted and explained—not lightly passed over. In reading the "fox lived in a shady glade in the woods," the vocabulary-conscious teacher paused for discussion and explanation of "glade." After reading about a poor mother and child who "drank from the cool spring," the teacher remarked, "This season is called the *spring* of the year. We talked about spring flowers this morning. Yet it says here that the mother and child drank out of a *spring*. Could this same word mean two different things?" The children, through discussion, arrived at the two different meanings for *spring*.

Foundations for Study Skills

This possibility may seem the most remote of all reading-development possibilities with the prereader. How can you do anything about study strategies or skills with children who cannot even read—let alone study?

In chapter 10, several different study strategies and skills are discussed. It is entirely possible to lay foundations for these before formal reading experiences. Possibilities for developing bases for two major study-skill areas are discussed briefly below.

Locating Information. The very useful cluster of skills needed in finding information in books should not be overlooked by the teacher of prereading groups. Consider the following opportunities:

1. Finding a new page in a book by matching it with a picture or number in an identical book held by the teacher.
2. Finding pictures of specific objects in books.
3. Identifying the content of a book by the picture on the cover.
4. Having attention called to the titles of books and stories.

5. Having attention called to the numbers on the pages of books as the teacher names them.

6. Turning pages in a picture book to find continuous developments in a pictured story.

7. Making booklets in which definite sections are devoted to different topics (pictures of dogs, pictures of cats, pictures of pet birds). The teacher should give children experience in finding the different sections.

8. Having attention called to books as a source of information and pleasure: the teacher finds information and reads from a book or encyclopedia to answer children's questions; or perhaps she or he looks through a book, reading titles of stories to the children until they find one they think they would like to hear.

9. Turning to a "library corner" in the classroom for pleasure and information to be gleaned by looking at the pictures in self-chosen books.

Following Directions. Children often come across directions that must be read and followed accurately as they study in the later grades. In prereading periods, children have many experiences in following oral directions. They should be exposed also to situations in which they follow printed directions exactly, even though the teacher reads these directions to them. For the most part, however, they should participate in composing the directions that are to be used in making something, going somewhere, conducting room activities, and so on, such as:

MAKING A VALENTINE
Draw a picture.
Color it.
Cut it out.
Paste it on the heart.

ROOM DUTIES
_____: Water the plant.
_____: Feed the fish.
_____: Get the crayons out.
_____: Put the crayons away.
(A different child's name is written in the blank space each day.)

Foundations for Fluent Reading

It seems desirable to give some attention during the prereading period to developing a sense of direction, with experience in following objects or pictures in lines from left to right and back again. Here are some suggestions.

1. After an art period, children often display their pictures. These pictures might be grouped in the following ways:
   a. The characters who are walking or moving toward the right.
   b. The characters who are going toward the left.

    c. The characters who are looking toward the right.

    d. The characters who are looking toward the left.

2. During discussion periods, the teacher and the children might note the border designs on books, tablets and pictures, and observe whether the objects are going in a certain direction. The figures in fancy wrapping paper, such as used for gift packages, may be used for this purpose also.

3. Place pictures in the pockets of a wall pocket chart. Ask a child to name these pictures, picking up each picture as he or she does so. Watch carefully that the child proceeds in an orderly manner from left to right across the first line of pictures; then guide him or her in returning accurately back to the line and down to the beginning of the next line, and so on. Then give other children opportunities to engage in this same type of activity.

    A variation of this activity is to arrange pictures that accompany a story in sequence in the pocket chart and then let a child or different children hold up the pictures in order as the teacher or one of the children tells the story.

    At another time, have different children arrange pictures in the chart into two groups according to the direction in which objects are facing, one group facing to the right, the other to the left.

4. Children may find pictures of objects going in different directions. The teacher prepares a set of pictures of objects in which direction is clearly indicated. Several of these pictures are placed before the children, and a child is asked to find the picture that shows something:

	going to the left	going down
	going to the right	going away
	going up	
or	looking up	looking away
	looking down	looking back
or	climbing up	and so on
	climbing down	

Be sure to encourage each child to tell about the picture that she or he selects, using such responses as: "This car is going to the left," "The boy is climbing up," and so on. This activity has an added value in that it acquaints children with meanings of adverbs and prepositions—frequently the root of difficulties in beginning reading.

Foundations for Interest in and Appreciation of Literature

An abiding interest and a full and satisfying appreciation and enjoyment of different types of literature is a lifetime contribution that reading instruction can make to the individual. Early childhood is not too soon to begin laying the foundation for the full measure of satisfaction that reading can bring to girls and boys of school age, as well as to adults.

Realistic Stories. Young children should have ample opportunities to hear stories about boys and girls of their own age living in their own world. Their vision of life would become quite distorted if they were told only fanciful tales. They need to have realistic stories, not only as a means of developing their taste for this kind of literature, but also as a means of helping them grasp relationships and clarify concepts concerning present-day living.

Appreciation for realistic stories can be developed easily in young children. Great care, however, should be taken in the choice of a realistic story for listening purposes. It *must* be related directly to the interest and experiences of the children at their particular level of development. Teachers should study the environment and out-of-school activities of the group of children with whom they are working in order to choose realistic stories that will be most satisfying to the pupils.

If teachers can tell realistic stories and guide discussion concerning them in a way that will throw back upon actual life a glow of art, then teachers will have taken a long step forward in developing appreciation in young children for this particular type of literature.

Fanciful Tales. Folk tales and fairy tales are the heritage of every child, and all young children should have an opportunity to listen to such stories, to retell them, to dramatize them if they like.

Showing pictures that accompany a fanciful tale contributes much to children's appreciation of it. Calling their attention to an attractive book in which an old tale is found will help to awaken within them a desire to read such stories for themselves.

Poems. Rhymes, jingles, and short poems are greatly enjoyed by children of this age. The rhythm, the cadence, the pat collocations of syllables are all pleasing to small children.

The teacher should keep choice collections of rhymes, jingles, and poems always at hand. He or she should memorize many of them to use spontaneously, because enjoyment of poetry often reaches its greatest depth when the teacher recites a stanza or two of some appropriate poem just at the time that the children are having an interesting experience related to the subject of the poem.

READINESS BEYOND THE PREREADING STAGE

Paul was reading a story that had its setting in an old Greek school. In the course of his reading, he came to the word *stylus*. "Do you know what a *stylus* is?" asked the teacher. "Sure," said Paul. "A man that cuts women's hair."

Paul knew the meaning of *stylist*. As a younger child, he had gone to the beauty parlor with his mother, and the stylist had trimmed her hair. The symbol *stylus* to him sounded the same as *stylist*, so he brought a meaning gathered from his experience to the new symbol, which was embedded in an entirely different situation and had an entirely different denotation.

Particularly when pupils engage in reading experiences that are unlike their own experiences, as in Paul's case, it becomes the responsibility of the teacher to help develop readiness. Teachers must be sensitive to the fact that even in grade one, for some children the reading matter may not mesh with their backgrounds. Whenever and wherever teachers find a distance between author and reader, readiness must be built. Obviously, as reading tasks become more complex through the grades, and ideas become more abstract, the job of readiness-building becomes even more significant.

Dale's Cone of Learning Experience [13] is a useful way of looking at a progression of experiences from most concrete—*direct purposeful*—to most abstract—*verbal symbols*. When possible, it would seem best to help the learner become involved in a direct experience in order to best understand the printed concepts. For example, readers are going to read about the 747 airplane, but none have been on one and only a single pupil has seen the plane up close. The experience that would help the pupils really become familiar with the plane would be a tour of the 747 and, of course, a flight on one. The tour *might* be arranged, but a flight for the group is probably not feasible. A flight would be a direct and potent experience; the tour would be next best as a direct experience. Pupils would certainly be able to bring rich experience to the reading.

On the other hand, direct experiences are not always possible, desirable, or economical. Some vicarious experiences may serve well as readi-

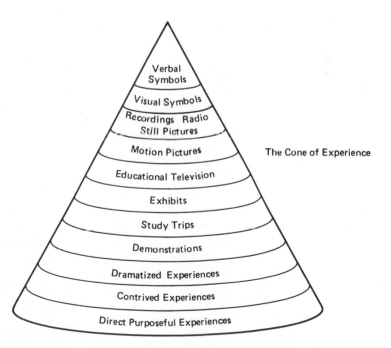

The Cone of Experience

Verbal Symbols

Visual Symbols

Recordings Radio Still Pictures

Motion Pictures

Educational Television

Exhibits

Study Trips

Demonstrations

Dramatized Experiences

Contrived Experiences

Direct Purposeful Experiences

[13] Edgar Dale, *Audiovisual Methods in Teaching*, 3rd ed. (New York: Holt, Rinehart and Winston, 1969), p. 107. Copyright 1946, 1954, 1969. Reprinted by permission.

ness for certain concepts. A dramatic presentation on film or television of the flight of a 747 including selected scenes showing what it is like to be a passenger on the plane might serve as well or even better as a readiness experience for some learners.

One way or another, learners need help in getting ready to read material distant from their experiences. The readiness must be specific to the task. Readiness experiences focused on the flight of a 727 will relate to reading about the 747 but cannot help young readers realize the enormity or the service functions of the 747. Or, back to Paul, if his teacher had taken him and his classmates to a museum to see dioramas of Greek life, he would not have placed a hair stylist in the Greek school.

Readiness Principles

The principles that follow are useful for readers who are about to embark on reading tasks that diverge from their experiential backgrounds. Teachers need to direct and guide pupils in developing readiness for specific kinds of reading, although some of these principles, when brought to the consciousness level, can be put to use directly by pupils without teacher direction. In the final analysis, because it is anticipated that pupils will become independent readers, the pupils need to learn how to make themselves ready for reading by cutting down the distance between themselves and the authors whose works they intend to read.

1. Analyze the material to be read to be sure that pupils have some actual or vicarious experiential background to bring to the concepts presented by the writer. Decide on the major ideas or concepts that they ought to know before engaging in the reading situation.
2. If you realize that the pupils have reasonable background experiences to bring to the material, help them retrieve such experiences from their minds through discussion, through brief visual and/or audio presentations related to major concepts, or through a preview of the material. (See number 5 below for more information about previewing.)
3. If you realize that the pupils have little background to bring to the material, spend as much time as necessary in prereading experiences to help pupils close the distance between themselves and the author. As indicated earlier, and exemplified later in this chapter, use trips, television, films, filmstrips, tapes, models, simulated experiences, illustrations, and so forth, to develop readiness.
4. If the style of writing and the use of language patterns differs from the styles and patterns pupils have become used to reading, spend time giving examples and discussing the language until pupils feel somewhat comfortable with it. If the language is rather archaic (as in some of the primary source material in social studies), they should know that you are available to help them with the concepts even after the readiness period. They should be helped to realize that some of the words can be skipped without hindering comprehen-

sion; however, they should call on the teacher or a peer assistant when understanding is inhibited.

5. The readiness technique of previewing should be used under any condition prior to engaging in study-type material. Previewing serves as an organizer and reminder for those with considerable background, and as a vital means of helping to develop background for those without it. Previewing is the process of examining the material to be studied in an organized fashion: (1) Study the title and think about its meaning; mentally review what you already might know about the topic. (2) Inspect the illustrations and their captions; relate them to your experience when you can. (3) Read the introductory paragraph or section, which usually sets the stage for your reading. (4) Study the headings and think about their meanings. If there are no headings, read the first sentence of each paragraph (or every few paragraphs in a long selection) to get some idea of the major ideas. (5) Read the concluding section or paragraph if it acts as a summary of the material.

The five steps above can be utilized in any order. They are directed toward pupils, although teachers will want to guide application until pupils begin to use the technique automatically. They will learn flexibility as they come in contact with a variety of organizational styles.

6. In addition to bringing the pupils' life and language experiences to bear on what they are about to read, try to interest them in the reading as well. At least focus some curious attention on the task. Some of the media mentioned in number 3 above are useful for this purpose. A teacher cannot "motivate" each pupil for each reading task, but pupils should be able to recognize some pertinence to themselves and/or to the learning activities in which they are engaged.

7. Some teachers deal with what Thomas and Robinson call "stopper words" [14] during the readiness period. They intertwine within the framework of a discussion or presentation several words or phrases that they feel will be particularly important for comprehension. If this is done, the words should be few in number, not defined in the material to be read, and of major importance. They should be placed on the chalkboard in a sentence context so pupils may utilize the context to help them remember the words as used in the selection. One of the authors of this volume remembers with horror a session in which he observed one of his student teachers. The student did a marvelous job in getting the group interested in what they were about to read; in fact, the children could hardly wait to find out. *But* then, before turning to the material, the student teacher rolled up a map that had been covering a section of the chalkboard and exposed thirty-two isolated words from the selection. The teacher and the group began to discuss the words—pronunciation and meaning. Dictionaries were used when needed. By the time the thirty-two

[14] Ellen L. Thomas and H. Alan Robinson, *Improving Reading in Every Class: A Sourcebook for Teachers,* 2nd ed. (Boston: Allyn and Bacon, 1977), pp. 22–24.

words were reviewed and hardly remembered by many, the pupils could not even remember what the selection they were to read was about. Their enthusiasm dwindled below the level of a small spark!

8. An idea gaining in popularity is the concept of advance organizers based on the work of Ausubel.[15] Research related to whether or not advance organizers facilitate learning is by no means definitive (a statement that could be made of many techniques in use today), but from a logical point of view the concept seems worthwhile for some pupils and some materials.[16] Advance organizers may take the form of questions about major concepts asked in advance of the reading, reactions to statements about major concepts, or organized frameworks that represent the relationships of one concept to another—a structured overview.

Herber indicated that the purpose of a structured overview

. . . is to present familiar words and to teach new words for the unit (or lesson) in such a way as to: (1) demonstrate the relationships among the words which form the overall concept; (2) provide a framework into which new ideas and information can be fitted; (3) develop a context from familiar words which will help clarify definitions and meanings of new words; (4) provide an opportunity to teach or reinforce specific vocabulary-acquisition skills implicit in the words themselves as appropriate to the students' needs.[17]

A structured overview should be developed with the pupils so they have an involvement in the organization and content of the material to be read well in advance. (See pages 83–85 for an example.)

9. Whatever techniques are being used to help readers get ready for the reading, purpose or purposes should always be an important aspect of the readiness period. Perhaps more important than any other single readiness ingredient, clarity of purpose aids comprehension. Purposes should be developed with pupils during the course of the readiness discussions and/or presentations. As pupils become used to conducting their own previews, they will be able to establish their own purposes for reading. At first, of course, and with complex material, the teacher is needed as a guide. Purposes should be listed on the chalkboard or on paper if the reading is to be done at home.

In content area textbooks, the pattern of terminal aids (structured sections at the ends of chapters) should be pointed out by the teacher and noted by pupils when on their own. Such aids frequently consist of vocabulary review (sometimes placed at the start of a chapter); comprehension, interpretation, and/or reaction questions; activities. Pupils should learn to examine such material in advance of study (as part of preview) in order to help them set purposes for the reading.

[15] David P. Ausubel, *The Psychology of Meaningful Verbal Learning* (New York: Grune & Stratton, 1963).

[16] David P. Ausubel, "In Defense of Advance Organizers: A Reply to the Critics," *Review of Educational Research* 48, no. 2 (Spring 1978): 251–57.

[17] Harold Herber, *Teaching Reading in the Content Areas,* 2nd ed. (Englewood Cliffs, N.J.: Prentice-Hall, 1978), p. 152.

10. For important reading assignments that are advertised in advance, some pupils can help themselves develop readiness through the wide reading of simple books. Part of this kind of readiness is the existence of a classroom library collection that imports and exports reading materials on curriculum-related topics every few weeks from the school library and other sources. For example, if the science text or texts are difficult for some readers and a unit on *magnetism* is coming up, many pupils can turn to easier books about magnetism prior to reading the chapter in the text.

The ten principles above should be applied to any kind of expository materials that are to be read and studied by pupils. All but numbers 5 and 8 may be used with narrative materials as well. Undoubtedly, the depth and extent of readiness activities will be moderated by the significance of the reading to pupils and teacher, the nature of the pupils, the nature of the material, and the purposes for the reading activity. Too much structured readiness can "turn off" the reader; too little can leave some readers in a hopeless mire. The ultimate goal is to help pupils develop their own readiness for specific kinds of reading. A bonus resulting from readiness activities is the building of ego strength and self-concept. If pupils delve into the reading with success because they were prepared for it, they understand and remember what they read. The feeling of success carries into further reading activities.

Examples of Readiness Procedures

Primary Grades and Above. The following selection is a short piece of expository writing that some third graders are going to read.

HEALTH WORKERS

There are many kinds of health workers. Three kinds of health workers are of great importance to you.

Medical Doctors

When you are sick you sometimes need help from a medical doctor. A medical doctor is someone who knows many things about your body. If you have a broken bone, a doctor knows how to set it for you. Such a doctor knows what medicine you need to make you well.

Nurses

Nurses can take care of you after the doctor has been to see you. They also help keep you healthy. They even look after children in school.

Dentists

If you have ever had a toothache, you have probably been to see a dentist. Dentists help keep teeth healthy. They clean teeth, straighten them, and fix them when something needs to be done.[18]

Teachers have many choices available for developing readiness to read the short selection above. Teachers A, B, and C exemplify different approaches that could be intermixed, and, of course, there are many other techniques that might be used.

Teacher A. "Do you know any health workers? Do you know what I mean when I say health workers?" (Pupils volunteer answers and teacher A develops a simple definition with them.) Pupils, in their free discussion, also mention several health workers, which teacher A lists on the chalkboard—in structured overview form.

"We're only going to read about three of these health workers this time—doctors, nurses, and dentists. Do you know any doctors who are not health workers?" (Pupils—with guidance—realize they must modify the word *doctors*. One pupil volunteers *medical doctor*.) The teacher asks a pupil to alter the structured overview to conform with the result of the discussion.

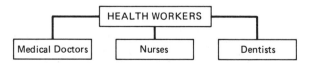

Teacher A now suggests that pupils read to find as many ways as they can that these health workers help us. Pupils are given a dittoed sheet with the structured overview at the top of it plus some large empty but lined boxes. They are asked to fill in three ways that each health worker helps us.

[18] H. Alan Robinson and Charlotte Reynolds, *EDL Study Skills Library*, 2nd ed., C-Science-2, More Practice (New York: McGraw-Hill, Inc., 1978).

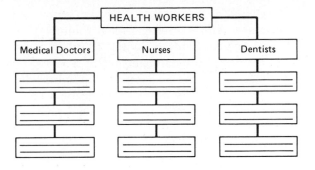

After the pupils have written their responses on the lines within the boxes, the teacher may open up the discussion for purposes of verification and discussion. Some pupils may have felt that they could not find three ways for each health worker; other pupils may have felt there were more ways in some cases. Although the discussion is not part of the readiness development, it is included here for purposes of closure.

Teacher B. "You all know Ms. Calderone, our school nurse. She'd like to talk with you about the important topic of *Keeping Yourself Healthy.*" (Ms. Caledrone speaks about health and health workers for about ten minutes and then asks for questions. As the questions and answers interplay, teacher B writes the following sentences on the chalkboard; they grew from the discussion.)

Medical doctors help you when you are sick or hurt.

Nurses help to keep you healthy.

Dentists help you when you have a toothache.

Dentists sometimes straighten your teeth.

When Ms. Calderone leaves, teacher B tells the pupils that they are going to read about three health workers and try to get even more information about them than Ms. Calderone furnished. Teacher B directs the pupils' attention to the chalkboard to be sure they are certain about the four underlined words. Pupils read through them silently and volunteers read them out loud. Then pupils are directed to read the selection and write the ways each health worker helps us on a piece of paper.

Teacher C. Pupils are asked if they have watched any TV stories about nurses. They discuss their experiences and succeed in drawing a rather accurate picture of how nurses help people. Teacher C has them view a brief filmstrip about nurses to confirm their information and see if they can add any information. The words *medical* and *healthy* are used in the filmstrip. Teacher C, after a discussion of the filmstrip, asks pupils what *health workers* means. After discussion, one of the pupils frames a helpful sentence about *health workers*, which teacher C writes on the chalkboard. The same discussion ensues with the same result for *medical* and *healthy*. Teacher C then volunteers the information that this word—*straighten* (written on the board in isolation)—is used in a story they are going to read about *health workers*. One pupil pronounces the word adequately and suggests that it means *the doctor straightens the bone*. Teacher C asks if any other health worker, other than a medical doctor, might *straighten something*. One pupil said orthodontist, and after discussion, was willing to have this sentence placed on the board: "The orthodontist, a kind of dentist, straightens your teeth."

Teacher C tells the group that they already have a great deal of information about health workers—particularly nurses. Teacher C asks pupils to quickly survey the selection by just reading the title and headings to learn who they are going to read about. The three headings are put on the chalkboard. The children volunteer the information they already have, which is written under each heading. Then teacher C asks them to read through the material to see if they obtain any additional or different information. They do so and make appropriate adjustments to the categories on the chalkboard.

Intermediate Grades and Above. Although Thomas and Robinson's book, *Improving Reading in Every Class*, was directed toward the secondary-school teacher, the following example of a readiness technique they presented is suitable and interesting for independent library research.[19] The readiness activity was created and used initially by Edgar Bernstein, University of Chicago Laboratory School social studies teacher.

Never a Dull Moment in Zinch Valley

Each pupil is handed a dittoed sheet. On the sheet they find only the following:
A group of ten people enters and settles in Zinch Valley. Write an essay answering the following questions:

1. What are the immediate and long-range problems these people face?
2. What are the solutions these people bring to bear on both the immediate and the long-range problems?

That's all! No other information is provided.

But in class there will be an opportunity for questions. For 30 minutes and 30 minutes only, the students may ask questions. They may have *all* the information they can pull out of their teacher in those 30 minutes.

Questions come pell-mell: "How did they arrive—by jet plane?" "Did they bring guns?" [The students soon begin to realize that they are dealing with very ancient times.] "Where did this happen?" [In the Middle East—Egypt through Mesopotamia.] "When?" [The late upper

[19] Thomas and Robinson, *Improving Reading*, pp. 105–6.

Paleolithic Age.] "What's the climate of the valley?" "Are there mountains?" "What are the resources?" "What can these people do?" "What do they bring with them in the way of equipment?" [The students are led to understand that clues to these answers have already been given—that the dating clue is the one to research further to discover what prehistoric man of that time and place could do.] "Are they male or female?" "Any children?" "How old?" [Answer: Five males, five females, nine between ages 10 and 45, a mother, a father, one small child.]

The session is lively and the time is up too soon. No more questions are permitted. The students are provoked and frustrated, yet challenged. Of course it is "permitted" to learn more about Zinch Valley through reading! Some of the students react, "I don't *need* all the answers from you—I can find out for myself." A list of readings spanning the reading levels within the class is provided which include everything from easy adventure stories of a Stone Age family menaced by cold, hunger, and wild beasts, to advanced scholarly discourses. What happened in Zinch Valley, the wellspring of some of man's first painting, sculpture, music, and complex social patterns, becomes a thrilling chapter in the upward march of human progress.

DISCUSSION QUESTIONS AND ACTIVITIES

1. If you are not a nursery school, kindergarten, or first-grade teacher, try to get an opportunity to observe these young children in a school-type situation. Note the differing degrees of readiness children have—particularly for reading and writing.

2. Try out some of the activities described in the chapter with children. Devise some of your own patterned on the examples or create new activities.

3. The approach used by teacher A on pages 83–85 seems to be promising for helping intermediate pupils and above grasp both the concepts and the organization of a piece of writing. Try the technique with other kinds of material. Be sure, at least at the beginning, to use materials that have a very visible structure.

4. Ask pupils to suggest readiness activities for given selections. Sometimes children involved in readiness activities for reading selections come up with potent ideas that spark and capture the interest of others.

5. An interesting way of helping pupils realize the importance of the previewing technique is to have them preview and then ask questions about what pupils learned prior to their studying the material. The selection and activities below are taken from pages 17–19 of the *Be a Better Reader* series, Level C (1977). Pupils can use this selection or one you choose, to preview and amass a good deal of information prior to study-reading.

Here is what you would do with this selection. Ask pupils to: (1) study the title and think about its meaning; (2) read the first heading;

(3) read the first paragraph; (4) read each of the other headings; (5) study the diagram. When they finish, ask them to do activity one and activity two. Discuss the results. Then have the pupils study-read the material to answer another set of more detailed questions, activity three. They will be convinced of (1) the value of preview as a readiness tool; and (2) their improved comprehension of what they studied.

THE SOLAR SYSTEM [20]

The Solar System Contains the Sun and Nine Planets

The earth is a part of the solar system. *Solar* is from the Latin word meaning *sun*. The solar system is made up mainly of the sun and the nine planets that travel around the sun. The earth is only a tiny part of this system. Also, the whole solar system is only a very tiny part of the enormous universe. Our sun is just one of the many billions of stars in the universe.

The Sun Makes Life on Earth Possible

The sun is very hot. It gives off both light and heat produced within itself. The energy which the earth gets from the sun makes it possible for us to live. All the fuels which run automobiles and heat houses contain energy from the sun. All of our food contains energy from the sun. If the sun were to burn out, the earth would soon become cold, dark, and without life of any kind.

The diagram shows the path of each of the nine planets as they travel around the sun. Such a path is called an *orbit*. Planets are held in their orbits by the balancing of two forces. One is the force of gravity, which prevents them from sailing out into space. The other is *centrifugal* force, which pulls away from the center, thus keeping the planets away from the sun.

Mercury is the Smallest Planet

On the diagram shown, if we look outward from the sun, we see first the planet Mercury. This is the smallest of all the planets. It is also the fastest in its movement around the sun. It travels around the sun once in 88 of our days. The length of time it takes a planet to circle the sun is known as its *year*. Mercury's year is, therefore, 88 of our days.

[20] From BE A BETTER READER, Level C, Basic Skills Edition, by Nila Banton Smith, © 1977, 1968, by Prentice-Hall, Inc. Reprinted by permission.

Venus is the Brightest

The next planet we come to is Venus. It is often called the *sister* of the earth. It is only slightly smaller. Venus was named for the ancient goddess of beauty because it is the brightest planet in our sky. It can be seen in the morning and early evening.

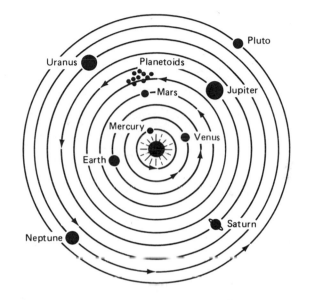

The Earth Has a Satellite

The next member of the planet family is our own earth. The earth is the fifth largest planet. It is the third planet from the sun. It takes a little more than 365 days for the earth to revolve around the sun. The earth has a little follower, the moon, which revolves around the earth.

A body that revolves around a larger body in the sky is called a *satellite*. The moon is a satellite of the earth. Many manufactured satellites, shot up by great rockets, are now circling the earth, hundreds of miles out in space.

Mars Goes Through Seasons

Mars is smaller than the earth. It takes Mars almost twice as long as the earth to circle around the sun. Mars is reddish in color. Because of this fiery color the ancient Romans named it after the god of war. Mars is better known by scientists than any of the other planets which can be observed with telescopes from the earth. Through telescopes they have discovered that Mars goes through seasons like the earth. At this time, however, there is no real proof of life on Mars. You will hear more about this in your lifetime.

Jupiter is the Largest Planet

The largest of all the "children" of the sun is the giant planet Jupiter. Its diameter is more than ten times that of the earth. Heavy clouds encircle Jupiter near its equator. Scientists think that the surface temperature of Jupiter is about 200° below zero. Jupiter has 12 moons.

Saturn Has Three Rings and Nine Moons

Saturn is an unusual planet. It has three rings which encircle it at its equator. The three rings are made up of small satellites whose orbits are very close together. They may be the result of the explosions of moons which encircled the planet at one time. Since these bodies are very close together the rings appear to be a solid mass. In addition to the three rings, Saturn also has nine moons.

Uranus, Neptune, and Pluto Are Farthest Away

Uranus, Neptune, and Pluto are the planets farthest away from the sun and earth. They can be seen only with a telescope and were discovered only within the last two centuries.

Uranus was discovered in 1781 by an English astronomer. At first he thought it was a comet. Neptune was discovered in 1846 by two astronomers who believed that another planet was pulling on Uranus. With mathematics, they were able to tell just where this new planet was located.

Pluto was observed first in 1930. These outermost planets take a long time to circle once around the sun. One "year" on Pluto is equal to 248 of our years on earth. Scientists know less about Pluto than about the other planets. Its yellow color, however, suggests that this planet probably has very little atmosphere.

Activity 1

Answer these questions to see how much you got from previewing the diagram.

1. Tell in three words what the diagram shows.
2. Which planet is nearest to the sun?
3. Which is farthest away from the sun?

4. How many planets revolve around the sun?

5. Name these planets.

Activity 2

Find out how much information you got from reading the headings. The first few words of each heading are given below.

1. The solar system contains. . . .
2. The sun makes life. . . .
3. Mercury is. . . .
4. Venus is. . . .
5. The earth has a. . . .
6. Mars goes. . . .
7. Jupiter is. . . .
8. Saturn has. . . .
9. Uranus, Neptune, and Pluto. . . .

Activity 3

Try to answer these questions without looking back at the article. If you have to look back, the headings will help you.

1. What is the solar system?
2. Why would the earth be without life if the sun were to burn out?
3. Which planet is better known by scientists than any of the other planets which can be observed by telescope from the earth?
4. What is a satellite?
5. What is the earth's satellite?
6. What are manufactured satellites?
7. Upon what is the length of year for any planet based?
8. What is an *orbit*?
9. What may have caused the three rings around Saturn?
10. What were the last planets to be discovered?

ADDITIONAL READINGS

Books and Pamphlets

AUKERMAN, ROBERT C., ed. *Some Persistent Questions on Beginning Reading.* Newark, Del.: International Reading Assn., 1972.

BEERY, ALTHEA; BARRETT, THOMAS C.; and POWELL, WILLIAM R., eds. *Elementary Reading Instruction: Selected Materials.* 2nd ed., pp. 335–80. Boston: Allyn and Bacon, 1974.

DOWNING, JOHN, and THACKRAY, D. V. *Reading Readiness*. Newark Del.: International Reading Assn., 1971.

DURKIN, DOLORES. *Teaching Them to Read*. 3rd ed., pp. 147–75. Boston: Allyn and Bacon, 1978.

HEILMAN, ARTHUR W. *Principles and Practices of Teaching Reading*. 4th ed., pp. 25–95. Columbus, Ohio: Charles E. Merrill Publishing Co., 1977.

HITTLEMAN, DANIEL R. *Developmental Reading: A Psycholinguistic Perspective*. Pp. 143–80. Chicago: Rand McNally College Publishing Co., 1978.

JOHANSSON, BROR A. *Criteria of School Readiness*. Uppsala, Sweden: Almqvist & Wiksell, 1965.

OLLILA, LLOYD O., ed. *The Kindergarten Child and Reading*. Newark, Del.: International Reading Assn., 1977.

SPACHE, GEORGE D., and SPACHE, EVELYN B. *Reading in the Elementary School*. 4th ed. pp. 143–225. Boston: Allyn and Bacon, 1977.

THOMAS, ELLEN L., and ROBINSON, H. ALAN. *Improving Reading in Every Class: A Sourcebook for Teachers*. 2nd ed., pp. 102–36. Boston: Allyn and Bacon, 1977.

Periodicals

BLATT, GLORIA T. "Playing With Language." *Reading Teacher* 31, no. 5 (February 1978), pp. 487–93.

BORDEN, JULIET P.; HANDLEY, HERBERT H.; and WOLLENBERG, JOHN P. "Head-Start Can Contribute to Reading." *Elementary English* 51, no. 6 (September 1974), pp. 874–76.

BUTLER, ANNIE L. "Early Childhood Education: A Perspective on Basics." *Childhood Education* 50, no. 1 (October 1973), pp. 21–25.

DURKIN, DOLORES. "A Six Year Study of Children Who Learned to Read in School at the Age of Four." *Reading Research Quarterly* 10, no. 1 (1974–1975), pp. 9–61.

FOULKE, PATRICIA N. "How Early Should Language Development and Pre-Reading Experiences be Started?" *Elementary English* 51, no 2 (February 1974), pp. 310–15.

HALL, MARYANNE. "Prereading Instruction: Teach For the Task." *Reading Teacher* 30, no. 1 (October 1976), pp. 7–9.

HANSELL, T. STEVENSON. "Increasing Understanding of Content Reading." *Journal of Reading* 19, no. 4 (January 1976), pp. 307–10.

HOSKISSON, KENNETH. "Reading Readiness: Three Viewpoints." *Elementary School Journal* 78, no. 1 (September 1977), pp. 44–52.

KING, ETHEL M. "Prereading Programs: Direct Versus Incidental Teaching." *Reading Teacher* 31, no. 5 (February 1978), pp. 504–10.

———, and FRIESEN, DORIS T. "Children Who Read in Kindergarten." *Alberta Journal of Educational Research* 18, no. 3 (September 1972), pp. 147–61.

KIRKLAND, ELEANOR R.. "A Piagetian Interpretation of Beginning Reading Instruction." *Reading Teacher* 31, no. 5 (February 1978), pp. 497–503.

MacGINITIE, WALTER H. "When Should We Begin to Teach Reading?" *Language Arts* 53, no. 8 (November/December 1976), pp. 878–82.

Readiness for Reading at all Grade Levels

O'DONNELL, C. MICHAEL, and RAYMOND, DOROTHY. "Developing Reading Readiness in Kindergarten." *Elementary English* 49, no. 5 (May 1972), pp. 768–71.

VACCA, RICHARD T. "Readiness to Read Content Area Assignments." *Journal of Reading* 20, no. 5 (February 1977), pp. 387–92.

chapter 5

approaches, procedures, and materials

What to Expect in This Chapter:

The term *approaches,* as used in this chapter, refers to the broad ways reading programs are packaged and delivered as instructional programs: basal reader approaches; language-experience approaches; individualized approaches. The term *procedures* is used to indicate some of the more specific teaching activities found within an approach or across approaches.

Materials are discussed in connection with approaches and procedures. In addition, attention is paid to the two very important concepts of (1) criteria for selecting and evaluating materials; and (2) judging the readability of materials.

Abraham Fuller, an English scholar of the seventeenth century, wrote: "Marshall thy notions into a handsome method. One's work will carry twice more weight packed up in bundles, than when it lies flapping and hanging about his shoulders."

Fortunately, in America there is opportunity to develop many "handsome methods." In our educational system, we have a chance to express different philosophies, to evolve different approaches, to experiment with different methods and procedures. At the present time, we most certainly are taking advantage of these privileges. Consequently, our teachers are using and experimenting with many different procedures and approaches in a never-ending quest to find better ways to help children master the many skills involved in reading. Unless involved in some closely controlled experiment, few teachers use only one approach to reading instruction.

BASAL READER APPROACHES

These approaches are based on the stories, skills, and suggestions of a group of qualified authors who have put together a sequential reading program or system designed for specific instruction across the grades. For many years, it was *the* approach used in our schools, and it still enjoys a very prominent place today, although there is the promising trend of teachers using many other kinds of materials in their instructional programs. Because reading instruction must be a part of the total curriculum and permeate every content area, basal reading instruction can only be one component of a total program.

Basal programs of the past had many criticisms leveled against them because they frequently concentrated on the middle-class culture alone, controlled vocabulary very tightly, presented an overdose of narrative material, and did not allow for too many individual differences. Today's basals have not managed to solve all their problems, but much progress is evident. There is a trend toward more stimulating and relevant con-

Teachers have different techniques for evaluating student's work.[1]

[1] From The Phoenix Reading Series—Level B Teacher's Guide by Marion Gartler and Marcella Benditt, © 1974 by Prentice-Hall, Inc., Englewood Cliffs, N.J. Reprinted by permission.

tent spanning the interests and needs of many pupils. There is a tendency for the basals to be making more contact with the reality of many cultures. There is an effort to avoid the sexist stereotyping of earlier times. In addition, the basal programs are trying to reach out to the rest of the curriculum by recommending much supplementary reading and also often provide some of that reading within the scope of the basal program.

Many of the modern basal programs are providing larger and richer vocabularies than in the past. This movement is a positive and needed effort because there is little evidence to show the need for any given vocabulary—other than the several hundred function words that recur in all writing. The vocabularies of basal series do not overlap greatly. In addition, we know that children appear to learn words best in context, making use of the redundancies of our language. In this mass media world, children are likely to be familiar with a vast number of the "new" words to be introduced at certain points in the basal readers. One of the fathers of modern basal reader series, Arthur Gates,[2] questioned tight vocabulary control when he found that elementary school youngsters knew in advance many of the words to be introduced in the subsequent books they were to read.

Today's basal programs come in many shapes, sizes, and packages. Some of them are called reading systems, which consist of graduated levels, and an organization of skills, which features consistent reinforcement and evaluation. They are, in most cases, quite different from their predecessors and often include a host of supplementary activities. Most include some well-written literature and specific selections from content areas. A teacher, even with help, must become a good classroom manager in order to cope with the varied components of the program.

The majority of the large educational publishing companies produce basal programs or systems. Books and other materials proceed from the prereading stage through grades six or eight. Each publisher perceives the system as moving from one instructional level to the next in anywhere from thirteen to twenty steps. All have teachers' editions or guides and workbooks. Most offer a multitude of supplementary materials.

Uses of Basal Reader Programs

Much of the criticism of present-day basal programs is unwarranted. The criticism should be directed more at how the programs are being misused.

Misuses. The discussion below focuses on some of the misuses and then proceeds to suggest desirable uses.

1. Considering the basal reader, itself, as the whole program for reading instruction.
2. Using one grade level of a basic reader with an entire class regardless of the different instructional levels of the children.
3. Setting up the goal of having children cover all pages in a certain reader as the objective of a semester's work.
4. Insisting that no children should work with a reader higher than the grade represented in the classroom so that the book for the next grade level may be fresh when all children begin to work in that grade.
5. Using the teachers' guide as a detailed prescription to be followed exactly in all its aspects, or on the other hand disregarding it entirely.
6. Confining reading instruction largely to reading selections from the reader without a sufficient number of interspersed periods of skill development.

[2] Arthur I. Gates, "The Word Recognition Ability and the Reading Vocabulary of Second- and Third-Grade Children," *Reading Teacher* 15, no. 8 (May 1962): 443–48; "Vocabulary Control in Basal Reading Material," *Reading Teacher* 15, no. 2 (November 1961): 81–85.

7. Failing to keep records of specific skills on which certain children need help and providing extra practice on these skills over and above that provided for in the basic materials.

8. Using the basal reader for busy work by instructing the children to read from this book at their seats when they have nothing else to do.

9. Using workbooks indiscriminately with all children; failing to check workbook activities; failing to develop workbook pages with children who are not able to work independently with them without preceding explanations.

10. Simply directing children to read a story as a routine matter, without first building background and stimulating purpose.

11. Requiring purposeless rereading.

12. Failure to develop interest in reading many supplemental books.

Desirable Uses. Until the beginning teacher becomes better acquainted with reading skills and techniques, it may be advisable to follow the sequence of the stories in the reader and to make careful use of the aids and instructions in the teachers' guide. As teachers become more proficient in the teaching of reading, they will refer to the teachers' guide only as a source for helpful suggestions as needed rather than slavishly following this manual page by page. They may upon occasion have children read certain stories out of order (if the stories are not too advanced in difficulty) as these stories carry with them possibilities for skill development needed by the children at the time. They will use numerous and varied materials and activities for skill development, many of which they personally create and prepare. They will stimulate extensive reading from other books.

There are several ways in which the use of basal readers may be strengthened by some teachers, both experienced and inexperienced.

1. Request sets of readers of different levels appropriate for the reading levels of different groups in your classroom.

2. Use sets of books from different series for variety and to prevent constant repetition of the selections by pupils who move upward so they do not read what they have heard over and over again in class.

3. Keep a record of the names of the basal readers and other books each child reads during the year to pass on to the next teacher; also prepare a record of the instructional level of each child to pass on to the next teacher at the end of the year.

4. At the beginning of the school year, refer to the records mentioned above when procuring your basal readers from the school's stockroom and when organizing reading groups. If there are some children in your class who are new to the school or whose instructional level you question, give these children an informal inventory (see pages 56–60), to ascertain their respective reading levels.

5. If a child or certain groups of children finish the reader at their grade level before a semester is over, have them use a somewhat more difficult reader at the same level from another series; or, if they are ready

to read from a book at the next higher grade level in the same series, by all means let them do this. The teacher in the next grade should take pupils where they are and have them read from readers appropriate to their reading competency regardless of the label of the grade in which he or she is teaching.

6. Make a study of teachers' guides to ascertain the different skills to be developed, prepare a table or chart of these skills and have it duplicated, check the ones on which each pupil needs the most help, and leave space on the chart to indicate progress as it is made in each skill area.

7. If a skill is seriously needed by several children, introduce it at the time that it is needed rather than waiting until they reach the point in the reader program at which it is introduced.

8. Although the children read a story from the reader for enjoyment, the chief function of having them read a story from your standpoint should be diagnosis—finding out on what skills they need practice.

9. Prepare for the reading of a new story by building informative background and pointing up a motive for reading the story as a whole. Clear the way for easy reading by clarifying new concepts that promise to interfere with clarity of comprehension.

10. Usually when working with children in first and second grades and often when working with some children in more advanced grades, it is advisable to stop after they have read two or three pages or one episode and give practice on skill needs revealed while they were reading these few pages.

11. Use workbooks as they are needed as a whole or in parts, the latter being more desirable. Develop new workbook activities before leaving the children to work by themselves. By all means *check* the workbook results carefully after each use. Study these results to ascertain skill needs. Follow up with additional help for children whose workbook activities reveal special needs.

LANGUAGE-EXPERIENCE APPROACHES

Books, and in some cases commercially prepared charts, were the reading fare for beginning readers for many years in the United States and elsewhere. The experience chart was introduced before 1900 as a rather separate learning tool and certainly not as part of the broader language-experience approaches of today. Having pupils use stories of their own composition based on their own experiences as a base for a thorough reading program was a radical departure not well accepted for many years. We first read about using children's experiences as a basis for reading instruction in Roma Gans' publication *Children's Experiences Through Reading* (Columbia University, 1941) and *Learning to Read Through Experience* by Lamoreaux and Lee (Appleton-Century-Crofts, 1943). The approach suggested in these early books has been broadened and expanded through applications of current psychological, linguistic, and educational concepts. At present, it is used in the majority of schools and in connection with many other approaches, including a considerable number of basal series of reading textbooks.

Today, there is no one language-experience approach. Teachers use a variety of techniques, and several commercial programs exist that present somewhat structured language-experience approaches. As the name implies, language-experience approaches are language arts or communication skills programs based heavily on children's experiences. No distinction is made among the communication strands of speaking, listening, writing, and reading. Equal emphasis is placed upon all these skills as each feeds into, facilitates, and reinforces the others.

Procedures

The philosophy of language-experience approaches as phrased in the child's language by Van Allen is:

What I can think about, I can talk about.
What I can say, I can write (or someone can write for me).
What I can write, I can read.
I can read what others write for me to read.[3]

Reading and writing as well as speaking and listening may take place even during the first days of school. As a child paints, the teacher may ask. "What are you painting?" If the child answers, "My house," the teacher may write the caption "My house" under the picture. If the pupil has several objects in the picture, the teacher may ask what each one is and write the name that the child gives for each object above its picture.

As the children go about their creative work, they talk. Tom, who is modeling with clay, may say, "See the dog I made!" The teacher may then suggest, "Let's write what you just said," and writes on the chalkboard or paper, "See the dog I made." Tom "reads" what the teacher has written.

At the beginning, as indicated, the teacher writes what the children dictate. Eventually, and one by one, the children say they want to write. The teacher then helps each child to write what he or she personally wishes to say or what others say in making a group chart or perhaps a booklet of group-composed charts.

In addition to art and construction activities, many other types of experiences are provided for the purpose of stimulating talk, for talk is the stuff out of which skills in listening, reading, and writing emerge. The children go on excursions, view films and television, listen to recordings, sing songs, bring objects from home for discussion, relate their personal experiences, play games, listen to poems and stories, make individual and class books, dictate stories to each other, learn the use of the alphabet in meeting their spelling and reading needs. Thus, they use language as a

[3] Roach Van Allen, "More Ways Than One," *Childhood Education* 38, no. 3 (November 1961): 108–11.

tool to meet their own needs and interests and at the same time become acquainted with language as others use it.

Insofar as specific reading skills are concerned, word recognition of written or printed words comes easily in beginning years as the words are already in the child's vocabulary or arise from new school experiences. In addition, as teachers write on the chalkboard or a chart they call attention to word forms and help pupils cement their pronunciations and meanings through wise use of context. Comprehension is stressed as pupils interpret their stories and the stories of others.

Composing an Experience Chart

Although many of the children's language-experience stories will be written or printed on sheets of paper to be brought home, put on the bulletin board, or bound into a personal booklet, a number of them—especially when done by a group—should be put on chart paper. The first essential of chart construction is that the children must have had some vivid, interesting experience, real or vicarious (preferably real), which fills their minds with ideas and stirs them to active discussion concerning it. In other words, the subject must be something that is vital to them and something that they wish to talk about.

Once this prerequisite has been fulfilled, the teacher should proceed to give the children an opportunity to engage in free discussion concerning this event of mutual interest and to let them talk it over spontaneously and happily.

The second essential of chart construction is that the children have some motive for recording their expressions. It may be interesting to talk over experiences, but why should they be written down and read?

There are several ways in which chart work may be made purposeful to children. Perhaps they will wish to record an experience so that the principal or other visitors coming to the room may know what they have been doing. Perhaps they will wish to record an experience to be read as part of a program that they are preparing on some general topic. Perhaps they will wish to record plans and rules and directions as guides to themselves in future work.

After the children have expressed themselves freely and pleasurably on a topic of mutual interest and have decided to write it down for some purpose, the teacher proceeds to ask a series of organizing questions to guide them in making a composition that will have unity and interest, that will be simple enough to read, and that will sometimes include essential vocabulary words. All this does not mean that the teacher will lead the children to author some predetermined chart story that he or she has already formulated. Nothing of the sort! Every question asked should stimulate a variety of answers, and the children should have the privilege of selecting the sentence that they think is best in each case. Thus it is that teacher and children work together suggesting, weighing, considering, evaluating, and revising until a creditable but childlike composition is prepared.

The first draft of the chart may be printed on the chalkboard. If the teacher is expert in printing, the first draft may be made directly on lined chart paper as the children compose it.

Types of Experience Charts

Experience materials lend themselves to a variety of forms. A few of these different types of materials are described and illustrated with examples taken from typical classrooms. The teacher is urged to make use of several of these different forms rather than confining practically all charts to narrative accounts shown in the first example.

Narrative Charts. This frequently used type of chart contains a running account of some group or individual experience.

EXAMPLE:

Our Trip to a Farm
We went to a farm.
We played in the barn.
We found some eggs.
We ate lunch under the big apple tree.

Question Charts. The question chart is useful as a means of recording and capitalizing on interests demonstrated by questions the pupils raise. The teacher jots down questions the children ask about a topic, and prints them on a chart. These questions are then used as a nucleus of research and are checked off as the children find the answers.

A first-grade class became interested in learning more about mail delivery and the job of the mail carrier. They raised questions in advance, which were put on a chart. Then, the mail carrier came to class. They checked off their questions and added some new ones.

Suggestion Charts. Recording suggestions children make when discussing a new activity can become a profitable reading activity. In the example that follows, a group of second graders had insisted that they wanted to build a stage in the classroom. The teacher asked, "Why?" Suggestions came thick and fast. The teacher recorded them on the board, and they were carried out later. Here is the list.

1. Tell stories.
2. Read from the stage.
3. Invite our parents and have a play.
4. Do stunts.
5. Play instruments.
6. Make moving pictures and show them.
7. Sing songs.

Rule Charts. Rules made up by a group or the class to be observed by them form the basis for this type of chart. A group who had decided they were not working profitably during their workshop period discussed the problem. They came up with the following rules, which they printed on a very visible chart.

Plan our work.
Help each other.
Share our tools.
Finish our work.
Stop on time.
Clean up.

Planning Charts. Plans form the content of this type of chart. It can be hung up in the room and reviewed from time to time so that pupils can keep track of how plans for an activity are progressing. Some primary youngsters who were planning to build a library corner formulated this chart.

Bring in boxes.
Bring in spare lumber.
Pull out all old nails.

Another class planned its activities for the year as follows:

Learn to read.
Draw pictures.
Work with clay.
Make things out of wood.
Tell stories.
Paint pictures.
Play on slide.
Make a train.
Make a farm.

The class added and deleted activities as the year progressed.

Diary Charts. These charts are used as a means of recording the progress of a prolonged activity. One third grade class planted a garden and kept this chart:

April 18. We wrote for our seeds.
April 25. We planted our garden.
May 14. The cucumbers came up.
May 21. All the seeds are up.
May 26. Our garden is growing fine.
June 10. We picked some lettuce today.
        We made sandwiches with the lettuce.

The examples above illustrate only a few possible varieties of chart content. Almost any topic of relevance to a pupil or a group of pupils can become an experience chart and, therefore, a pertinent reading experience. In addition, language-experience charts and individual stories are not limited to the primary grades; they are valuable as part of the program in any classroom.

Advantages and Disadvantages of the Approaches

A language-experience approach has the distinctive advantage of working with the experiences and language of the child. Motivation to read is usually good because children are able to read what they have dictated or written. There are many opportunities for problem-solving activities.

A major disadvantage, if the approach is used through the grades, is that some teachers cannot cope with the lack of an organized, structured program. Some publishers have produced language-experience programs that help the teacher in this regard. Also, there are several professional books on the market that are helpful. (See **Additional Readings** at the end of this chapter.) Nevertheless, the program demands knowledge of reading skills, flexibility, and careful attention to record-keeping and classroom organization.

In our judgment, language experience approaches have validity and many uses throughout a reading program. Certainly children should first learn reading through their own language-experience stories and charts before turning to basals or other materials. As the reading program develops through the grades, the approach should be used along with other approaches so that children have an opportunity to read many kinds of materials. Both the basal reading approach and an individualized approach permit and welcome language-experience approaches.

INDIVID-UALIZED READING INSTRUCTION

It is interesting to note that three different cycles of individualized instruction in reading have taken place in America in its over two hundred years of existence.

In the earliest times, reading instruction was conducted exclusively on an individual basis. Children were first taught individually by a parent, minister, or priest. In our early "Dame Schools," each child was taught individually and progressed at her or his own rate. Two or three children would gather in the Dame's kitchen, and each one would "recite" to her from a primer or Bible as she busied herself with her household duties.

These individualized arrangements were of course discontinued when our population increased and public schools, organized in classes, were established.

The second cycle began with the advent of the scientific movement in education between 1910 and 1920; intelligence and reading tests were developed and put into use. As a result, school personnel became keenly aware of individual differences in the reading achievement of children in the same grade and class. This discovery stimulated interest in making several group adjustments in classroom organization, but the pulsating new idea was that of breaking up class organization entirely to permit individual progression. This plan of organization received almost as much attention at this time as it is receiving at the present moment. Speeches, articles, and yearbooks dealt with the subject, and many school systems reported the results they had obtained from using the individual instruction plan.

The third cycle is the one that we are now experiencing—an interest in providing children with opportunities for learning to read through the use of individualized plans and materials. It seems that the seeds of the second cycle lay dormant for many years, then began to spring up in the late 1950s in vigorous growth. Olson [4] made several studies of growth, behavior, and development of children, and synthesized his results and conclusions into three terse terms: *seeking, self-selection,* and *pacing.* It is this crystallization of Olson's psychology that has provided the basis for most individualized teaching in recent years. Lazar,[5] and particularly Veatch,[6] were mainly responsible for carrying Olson's thinking to reading instruction.

In this third cycle, interest and uses of individualized approaches are higher and more widespread than any previous time in our history. The present concepts about individualized reading instruction extends far beyond the earlier plans permitting children to progress at their own rates. It is primarily concerned with reading as it meshes into and promotes child development in many different aspects—physical, mental, social, emotional, linguistic, and experiential. It focuses on not only children's reading achievement but also on their interests in reading, their attitudes toward reading, and their personal self-esteem and satisfaction in being able to read.

[4] Willard C. Olson, *Child Development* (Boston: D. C. Heath, 1949); "Seeking, Self-Selection, and Pacing in the Use of Books by Children," *The Packet* (Boston: D. C. Heath, 1952), pp. 3–10.

[5] May Lazar, "Individualized Reading: A Dynamic Approach," *Reading Teacher* 11, no. 2 (December 1957): 75–83.

[6] Jeannette Veatch: *Individualizing Your Reading Program* (New York: G. P. Putnam's Sons, 1959); *Reading in the Elementary School* (New York: John Wiley & Sons, Inc. 1978). With the assistance of Philip J. Acinapuro.

Six Steps to Individualized Reading [7]

1. Build a climate or atmosphere for productive reading. This step takes careful planning, nurturing, and time. The goal is to have pupils learn how to read productively on their own. The steps that follow are parts of that climate.

2. Develop a variety of silent reading activities that move toward having pupils direct themselves during the reading period. "The perfect situation requires that everyone be so engaged in silent reading (or working on responses thereto) that the teacher is free to interact with pupils in a variety of ways, individually or in groups." [8] Visible charts that list activities provide a structure for the reading period. Here is a sample chart suggested by Hunt:

Quiet Reading Time
1. Select book or other printed material.
2. Read quietly (see how much you can get done).
3. Have a book talk or conference (be prepared—know what to say).
4. Record your results—write about reading, chart your progress.
5. Study vocabulary.
6. Work with a partner. [9]

Hunt also cautioned that teachers not move too quickly to conferences or book talks prior to establishing the framework for, and habit of, uninterrupted sustained silent reading (USSR).

3. During the reading period, no one may interfere with the productive reading of someone else. Pupils must be trained to obey this rule of noninterference unless they are engaged in some planned activity productive to both. This kind of instructional guidance is vital if the program is to work.

4. Plan book talks or conferences with individuals or with groups to discuss parts of books, articles, and the like. This time is not set aside for book reports on everything read by a child. It is a sampling of each pupil's accumulated reading. The teacher uses perceptive and penetrating questions to get at the major ideas with which the pupil has been dealing. Comprehension, interpretation, and evaluation are the goals. It is *not* a time for checking oral reading errors.

5. Help pupils learn to sustain themselves with print over longer and longer periods of time. The greatest reading skill to be developed is the ability to read silently with *understanding*. *Understanding* refers to the large ideas and not every detail in the material. Teachers may encourage

[7] This section is based on Lyman C. Hunt, Jr., "Updating the Individual Approach to Reading: IPI or IRP?" *Meeting Individual Needs in Reading*, ed. Helen K. Smith (Newark, Del.: International Reading Assn., 1971), pp. 45–51.

[8] Ibid., p. 46.

[9] Ibid.

USSR with individual time-keeping charts or through other means. Oral reading is confined to the verification of ideas, and teacher interference is limited to those times the pupils want assistance with words, sentences, or interpretations of some ideas.

6. Record-keeping and evaluation is keyed to the individual. Teachers may keep a card or notebook page for each child to record notes during conferences. Some teachers organize more formal checklists and record observations periodically. Evaluation is directed toward helping pupils perform effectively and toward helping them become self-evaluators.

More Specifics about Organization for Individualization

Materials used may consist of individual trade books, basal readers, magazines, and newspapers. Self-selection is the keyword, of course, although the collection to choose from is usually provided by the teacher. Sometimes teachers may limit or guide selections for some of the pupils. Some teachers use the conference period to work with other reading skills or strategies.

During a general conference period, teachers may plan with the children how they will occupy themselves while the teacher is working with individuals. Individual plan charts may be set up in addition to the class planning chart visible to everyone. Individual conferences usually vary from two to ten minutes. Each child does not have to have a conference each day.

As indicated above, individual record keeping is essential. A number of teachers suggest that the following should be recorded at each conference: name of book; number of pages last read; special progress; special needs; specific help given if any; notes on interests and attitudes. An example of a simple format for recording such data is given below.

JOHN MORRIS

Date	Book and Page	Progress	Special Needs	Interest and Attitude	Other Remarks
Feb. 17	*Charlie and the Chocolate Factory,* pp. 68–69.	Reads more smoothly.	Doesn't use context to get at words with meanings different from those he knows. Gave help with strategy.	Keenly interested in this story. Delighted that he had read so many pages.	Behavior problems subsiding.

Group sessions are held as needed. Some people make the mistake of thinking that the teacher in an individualized plan always works with a pupil individually, that there is never any instruction given to groups. This is not true. It is possible and desirable upon occasion to make use of several different types of grouping.

Total class grouping may occur at times. Charts evolving from a mutual experience or based on plans for activities, questions to which answers are sought, directions for going somewhere or doing something— all such mutually prepared charts call for whole-group participation and provide opportunities for whole-group reading. Notices placed on the chalkboard or bulletin board are read by the entire group.

The whole class may also be involved in planning activities, such as planning procedures for book selection or for individual conferences, planning what to do for independent work, and planning sharing experiences in which one child or a group will share their reading with the class as a whole. Sometimes a new reading skill is introduced to the group as a whole. Whenever there is a need or a reason for the entire class to work together, whole-class grouping may ensue. It is up to the teacher. There is nothing in the philosophy of the individualized plan itself that precludes functional whole-group participation in a reading activity.

Small-group arrangements also take place often. Sometimes children who are reading or have read the same book gather in a group to "talk it over." Such discussion may lead to plans for some sharing activity, such as a dramatization, puppet show, or mock radio or television program. At other times, children reading the same book may work with the teacher as a group during the usual individual conference period.

Now and then, two or three children who like to be together socially gather in one spot when reading from their individual books. Usually, there is considerable oral reading to each other in such a group, and often the children help each other with unrecognized words.

Interest groups emerge at times. Four or five children may become interested in elephants, for example. Regardless of their different levels of ability, they may work together, each sharing information and interesting incidents from his or her book or story geared to individual ability levels.

Skill groups are frequently formed to meet individual needs. If two or three or several children need help on the same skill, these children meet as a group with the teacher for development of and practice on that skill. This group is disbanded one by one as children master the skill, and new groups, possibly composed of some of these children and others, assemble to meet other skill needs.

Thus, group work proceeds on many different bases: common purpose, common social preference, common interest, common skill needs. Proponents of the individualized plan stoutly proclaim that no teacher who fully understands the broader concepts of the individualized plan would deny children the opportunity for group work motivated by some of the common purposes mentioned above. (Grouping and classroom organization are discussed in more detail in chapters 12 and 13.)

Evaluation of Individualized Reading Plans

Opinion in regard to the use of an individualized plan varies. Most teachers who are using a plan are highly enthusiastic about its values. They recognize problems attendant upon implementing the plan, but they feel that the values justify the effort expended in coping with these problems. Another group believes that children should be taught through the use of a carefully organized, sequential skill development program making use of basic readers and their accompanying materials designed for this purpose, with provision also for supplemental reading. Still a third group believes that the answer is to be found in some combination of the two plans. One example of a combination is a plan that permits those children who are making excellent progress to proceed exclusively under the individualized method, but that provides for having slower pupils, who seem to require more carefully systematized skill practice and more developmental work and supervision, to work with the teacher in a group using organized materials. In this case, however, the basic reader instruction is supplemented by individual selection and the conference plan in a program of supplemental reading.

Commercial Programs and Systems

There are a number of management systems and individualized programs available today for a given classroom or for an entire school. For example, in IPI (Individually Prescribed Instruction) pupils are placed in a unit on a skills continuum by a placement test. They take a pretest to determine what skills must be worked on; on the basis of the pretest, the teacher writes a prescription to fit the pupil's needs. After the skill has been worked on, mastery is evaluated. A post-test is given at the end of each unit.

Another example: In IGE (Individually Guided Education) pupils may be placed for varying time spans, depending on the needs and the work at hand, into one of four basic learning modes: (1) independent (working alone at own rate); (2) one-to-one study (tutoring by teacher, teacher aide, or another pupil); (3) small group (four to eleven pupils working on a common objective; (4) large group (thirty-five pupils or more involved in a suitable group activity—speaker, film, and so forth.

Another example: In PLAN (Program for Learning in Accordance with Needs), learning is individualized through the grades in language arts, mathematics, science, and social studies. The PLAN project involves six thousand behavioral objectives and in addition to its own materials uses available commercial materials, adjusting them to individual needs.

Although such systems have the salubrious effect of increasing individualization and turning the teacher's attention to the individual, there appear to be two major hazards operating. First, they do not seem to succeed in reducing the managerial jobs of the classroom teacher. Second, the large number of behavioral objectives in some systems and programs fragment the reading process into so many little parts that the pupils may never be able to put it back together again.

Television

We live in a television world. We need to capitalize on it as a significant medium for communication, not just as a source of infrequent entertainment in the classroom. Actually, television serves the function that reading served alone once upon a time for many people. We need to help pupils become more discriminating users of television.

Television can also be and is used as a direct source of instruction in reading. In the 1970s, television made a dramatic entrance as a medium for teaching reading with the nationwide readiness program, *Sesame Street*. It has been followed by a number of other programs, both national and local. Although these initial programs have been useful for many children, we look forward to the further development of such programs as they begin to place more emphasis on reasoning and less on isolated decoding.

Closed-circuit television becomes increasingly important in helping teachers evaluate themselves, in teacher training programs, and in conferences. The "playback" has the advantage of allowing one to view the behaviors that accompany speech in contrast to the limitation of audiotapes alone. Some schools have purchased playback units and are able to have pupils and/or teachers view a variety of programs on video cassettes.

Probably by the early 1980s, a number of us will have units in our homes which can play *videodiscs* in our homes. Three hundred 250-page books can be stored on one side of such disc and played back on our television screens. Films can be intermixed with print and music. The units will probably be selling for under $1,000 and discs may be about $10 each. Perhaps by the time this innovation has been out a few years, we will benefit from it in our schools.[10]

As cable television expands, it will be possible for us to call on certain programs when we want them and have them piped into the classroom. Because cable television can be programmed as two-way communication, dialogs can be set up between groups of children and teachers.

Television (coordinated with radio, computer, and written materials) was the main means of instruction in a massive satellite experiment called "The Rocky Mountain Region Experiment." [11] Although a very small part of the program dealt with reading, it gave many insights into

[10] R. Kent Wood and Kent G. Stephens, "An Educator's Guide to Videodisc Technology," *Phi Delta Kappan* 58, no. 6 (February 1977): 466–67.

[11] Kenneth A. Polcyn, "Future United States Educational Broadcast Satellite Experiments: The Rocky Mountain Region Experiment," *Educational Technology* 13, no. 8 (August 1973): 46–52.

the practical uses of satellites in distributing educational assistance over wide areas of the United States.

The Computer

In 1966, exciting news came from the Brentwood Elementary School in Palo Alto, California. First-grade children there were being taught to read with the use of a computer. Thus, the computer made its entrance into reading instruction.

It was in the 1970s that we began to hear for the first time about large-scale computer experiments. Today, there are a number of computer-assisted instruction (CAI) projects, although the costs have prevented the wide use anticipated. Minicomputers and microcomputers offer some possibilities in reduced cost.

Some critics of CAI say that computers and other technological devices dehumanize education, mechanize instruction, make automatons out of children, and replace teachers. The authors of this book disagree. Just as with basal readers, for example, more abuses come from misuses than from the educational tool itself. We feel that the role of the teacher in the technologically oriented school of the future is both promising and challenging. In such a school, teachers have the opportunity of becoming true professionals—directors of learning rather than largely dispensers of knowledge and exercises. The media can perform most of these two services and free the teacher to attend to those aspects of learning that only a human being is competent to execute.

There always will be moral, social, and educational values that cannot be developed solely through the use of machines, but that from now until eternity must be achieved through association of human beings with other human beings. Most definitely, teachers of reading will still be needed in the future.

**GUIDELINES
FOR
CHOOSING
INSTRUC-
TIONAL
MATERIALS**

The guides below are particularly pertinent to basal and supplemental materials used in a reading program, although aspects of them can certainly be used with content-area texts and trade books. The *Guide for Selecting Materials* was organized by combining our ideas with some of the suggestions made by Colvin,[12] Dallman and others,[13] Durkin,[14] Goodman and others,[15] and Smith and Johnson.[16] The *Guide for Evalu-*

[12] Cynthia M. Colvin, "Psychological Principles in Materials Selection," in *Elementary Reading Instruction: Selected Materials*, 2nd ed., ed. Althea Beery, Thomas C. Barrett, and William R. Powell (Boston: Allyn and Bacon, 1974), pp. 147–52.

[13] Martha Dallman and others, *The Teaching of Reading*, 4th ed. (Holt, Rinehart and Winston, 1974), pp. 576–77.

[14] Dolores Durkin, *Teaching Them to Read*, 3rd ed. (Boston: Allyn and Bacon, 1978), pp. 63–65.

[15] Kenneth S. Goodman and others, *Choosing Materials to Teach Reading* (Detroit: Wayne State University Press, 1966).

[16] Richard J. Smith and Dale D. Johnson, *Teaching Children to Read* (Reading, Mass.: Addison-Wesley Publishing Co., 1976), pp. 91–93.

ating Sex Stereotyping in Reading Materials was originally published in the December 1977 issues of *The Reading Teacher* and the *Journal of Reading.*[17]

Guide for Selecting Materials

1. Be aware of your goals for a reading program *before* selecting materials. Think through what you would like to accomplish with your youngsters by the end of the year. Do the materials help you get there?

2. Select materials that match your philosophy of teaching-learning as much as possible. Examine the materials and be sure that you can live with them—in terms of how you would like the children in your class to learn and how you would like to teach.

3. Also consider what is known today about the related disciplines of child growth and development, psychology, sociology, and linguistics. Be sure the construction and suggested uses of the material are consistent with sound principles in those disciplines.

4. Examine the material carefully to be sure that it does what it promises to do. Too often, scope and sequence charts, for example, list exposures rather than learnings.

5. In the first two grades, it is probably necessary to expect some consistent vocabulary and sentence pattern control. Be sure that control does not result in meaningless, tedious discourse. Beyond the first two grades of school, look for wide expansion of vocabulary and writing styles with attention paid to their introduction.

6. Anthologies and basals should include selections from interesting literature as well as representations from the various content areas. Selections in the content areas should be as up-to-date and accurate as possible.

7. Strategies and skills for dealing with different kinds of materials for different purposes should be clearly differentiated.

8. Particular attention should be paid to sensitive areas such as cultural background, sex differences, and race. As Smith and Johnson said, "Check carefully for discrimination shown by commission and *also by omission.*" [18]

9. Although the material should be varied, look for material that will match the interests and needs of your pupils as much as possible. As Colvin pointed out, "The kinds of materials used to introduce children to the reading process influence the way they perceive reading, learning, and school. Many children fail to see reading as useful, pleasant, or relevant to their life styles." [19]

[17] Committee on Sexism and Reading, "Guide for Evaluating Sex Stereotyping in Reading Materials," *Reading Teacher* 31, no. 3 (December 1977): 288; *Journal of Reading* 21, no. 3 (December 1977): 240.

[18] Smith and Johnson, *Teaching Children to Read,* p. 92.

[19] Colvin, "Psychological Principles," p. 148.

10. Attempt to ascertain the readability ·of the material for your pupils to the best of your ability. Do not accept the publisher's rating. Try the material out with your pupils.

11. Determine whether or not there is enough practice material included for your pupils to be able to handle on their own. Check clarity of directions, clearness of formats, interest of exercises, and amount of practice available for learning a skill or strategy.

12. Be sure there are provisions for individual needs—the individual needs represented in your groups.

13. The material should be organized and clear so that you can manage them without too much bookkeeping. Too many components often cause problems with classroom management and defeat the objectives. Be sure all components are functional and necessary.

14. Although this criterion is not necessarily valid always, it is wise to examine the credentials of the authors and the publisher. Authors who are recognized leaders in their field will undoubtedly try to produce materials based on sound principles. Large educational publishers have a large stake in their products and want to be sure they answer the needs of consumers. Be sure, though, to also inspect the wares of new, innovative authors and publishers who may be making some fine contributions.

15. Attempt to gain evidence about the material prior to purchase. Examine reports on use or observe use and question users in other situations. Order samples and try them out for a while with some pupils.

16. Evaluate the expenditure. Consider the costs of consumable materials over the years. Compare cost with cost of comparable materials. Don't turn down excellent materials because they are more expensive than others. Compare values.

Guide for Evaluating Sex Stereotyping in Reading Materials

The Committee on Sexism and Reading of the International Reading Association has developed the following checklist to assist teachers in analyzing educational materials for sex stereotypes and related language usage. All persons responsible for selecting books for classroom, school, or district-wide use or functioning in any capacity as educators should be aware of the implications of sex-role stereotyping and exclusionary language.

Directions: Place a check in the appropriate space. Most items should be evaluated separately for each sex.

	Almost always	Occasionally	Rarely
1. Are girls and boys, men and women consistently represented in equal balance?	____	____	____
2. Do boys and girls participate equally in both physical and intellectual activities?	____	____	____

		Almost always	Occasionally	Rarely
3. Do girls and boys each receive positive recognition for their endeavors?	Females	___	___	___
	Males	___	___	___
4. Do boys and girls, fathers and mothers participate in a wide variety of domestic chores, not only the ones traditional for their sex?	Females	___	___	___
	Males	___	___	___
5. Do both girls and boys have a variety of choices and are they encouraged to aspire to various goals, including nontraditional ones if they show such inclination?	Females	___	___	___
	Males	___	___	___
6. Are both boys and girls shown developing independent lives, independently meeting challenges and finding their own solutions?	Females	___	___	___
	Males	___	___	___
7. Are women and men shown in a variety of occupations, including nontraditional ones? When women are portrayed as fulltime homemakers, are they depicted as competent and decisive?	Females	___	___	___
	Males	___	___	___
8. Do characters deprecate themselves because of their sex? (Example: "I'm only a girl.") Do others use denigrating language in this regard? (Example: "That's just like a woman.")	Females	___	___	___
	Males	___	___	___
9. Do the illustrations stereotype the characters, either in accordance to the dictates of the text or in contradiction to it?	Females	___	___	___
	Males	___	___	___
10. Is inclusionary language used? (For example, "police officer" instead of "policeman," "staffed by" instead of "manned by," "all students will submit the assignment" instead of "each student will submit his assignment," and so on.		___	___	___

EVALUATING READABILITY

The best way of judging the readability of any given piece of material is to try it on for size with the pupils who will be using it. Let them do some silent reading and oral reading and question them about the author's message. If they understand somewhere about 70 to 80 percent of the ideas conveyed by the author, across a number of samples, that material is probably suitable for instructional use. Comprehension at the level of about 85 percent or better probably means pupils can manage the material on their own. (See chapter 3 for a more precise way of matching pupils and materials.)

Another technique is to use Bormuth's cloze readability procedure. With this procedure, the teacher prepares one or more cloze passages (see page 118 for details of preparation) taken from the material slated for use. Pupils then fill in the deleted words.

> Bormuth found that student scores falling between 44 and 57 percent on a cloze test indicated their ability to handle the material with supervised instruction. Scores above 57 percent indicated that students could read the material on their own with adequate comprehension. For specifics in conducting readability tests using the cloze procedure, consult Bormuth's clear explanation in *Elementary English*.[20] Bormuth counts only exact word responses in his readability procedure.[21]

For teachers who must estimate the readability of a large number of books and cannot try them all out with pupils, a readability formula may be used. As Fry said, "These are mechanical procedures, sometimes involving use of average sentence length, vocabulary lists, or counts of syllable length, which give you an *estimate of readability* or reading difficulty level."[22] They cannot include interest, purpose, language complexity for given children, or concepts given children have for particular words. The Spache Readability Formula[23] is widely used for primary grade materials; the Dale-Chall Readability Formula[24] spans grades four through sixteen. The Fry Readability Graph,[25] grades one through college, is also used particularly because of its simplicity.

In addition to trying the book on for size, using a cloze procedure, or computing a readability formula, teachers will want to inspect books carefully and apply their own readability criteria. The criteria that follow are particularly useful for content-area texts. Numbers 1 through 11 were contributed by Krause;[26] the remaining four were added by H. Alan Robinson.[27]

---

[20] John R. Bormuth, "The Cloze Readability Procedure," *Elementary English* 45, no. 4 (April 1968): 429–36.

[21] H. Alan Robinson, *Teaching Reading and Study Strategies: the Content Areas*, 2nd ed. (Boston: Allyn and Bacon, 1978), p. 131.

[22] Edward Fry, *Elementary Reading Instruction* (New York: McGraw-Hill, 1977), p. 216.

[23] George D. Spache, *Good Reading for Poor Readers*, 9th rev. ed. (Champaign, Ill.: Garrard Publishing, 1974).

[24] Edgar Dale and Jeanne S. Chall, "A Formula for Predicting Readability," *Educational Research Bulletin* 27 (January 21 and February 17, 1948): 11–20, 37–54. Also available in a separate booklet from Ohio State University, Bureau of Educational Research.

[25] Fry, *Elementary Reading Instruction*, p. 217.

[26] Kenneth C. Krause, "Do's and Don'ts in Evaluating Textbooks," *Journal of Reading* 20, no. 3 (December 1976): 213.

[27] Robinson, *Teaching Reading and Study Strategies*, p. 132.

1. The density of concepts *isn't* intended to frustrate the student. In other words, each sentence isn't packed with several ideas.
2. The sentence complexity *isn't* usually high. That is, the authors don't tend to always use long compound and complex sentences.
3. The authors *don't* continually choose to use long, difficult words when simpler synonyms would suffice.
4. Captions under graphs, tables and diagrams are clearly written.
5. The text contains both a table of contents and an index.
6. The table of contents shows a logical development of the subject matter.
7. When a text refers to a graph, table, or diagram, that aid is on the same page as the textual reference.
8. Pictures are in color and are contemporary, not dated by dress unless the author's intention is to portray a certain period.
9. Difficult new vocabulary words are highlighted, italicized, or underlined.
10. The main idea or purpose for reading a chapter is stated at the beginning.
11. The authors include a summary at the end of each chapter.
12. Passive tense is used only when essential, since frequent use seems to trouble poor readers.
13. The variety of connectives (consequently, in spite of, thus, however, etc.) is somewhat controlled so they are used sparingly as important signals to the reader.
14. Antecedents and referents are clear, particularly across sentences
15. Relative clauses are limited in number in a given sentence, clearly written, and clearly attached to a referent.

Specific materials were not cited in this chapter for fear of omission or bias. In addition, new materials will be on the market between the time this book went to press and was published. For annual, objective, and brief descriptions of new materials on the market, consult the January or February issues of *The Reading Teacher* as well as the *Journal of Reading*. For more extensive analyses and user reports, write to the EPIE Institute, 475 Riverside Drive, New York, New York 10027, for their latest publications.

**DISCUSSION
QUESTIONS
AND
ACTIVITIES**

1. Compare books from two or more basal reading series that are supposed to be at the same reading level. Try them out with pupils. Ask pupils why one seems more difficult than another. Ask pupils why they like one better than another.

2. Stauffer suggested the technique of developing a word bank with each youngster. He indicated that children are extremely interested in the activity because they gather words from their very own individually dictated stories. Words are stored in some type of box, nonalphabetically at first. As the children see a need for some organization, alphabetical order is introduced and children are able to review and use their words readily. Such activity also serves as excellent readiness for dictionary work.[28] The vocabulary file is a good technique to try out with individual language-experience stories because the children begin with a feeling of "word ownership," and they appear to retain most of the words—usually—for future reading and writing. Try it with children of all ages.

3. Subject the materials you use most to the *Guide for Evaluating Sex Stereotyping in Reading Materials.* Compare their ratings.

4. If you have not already done so, try your hand at preparing a cloze passage. Select a passage from material you would like to try out. For primary youngsters, be sure the number of deletions do not exceed twenty-five; for intermediate grades and above, use fifty deletions. This means your passages will range from about 140 to 270 words. The first and last sentences are left intact, but every fifth word is left out for the sentences in between. Administer the passage or passages to a whole group and have them write the answers in the blank spaces. Spelling does not count, and they may erase any time they want to. When you review the papers, only count exact word responses as correct. Assign four points to each primary sample and two points to each of the upper-level samples. Scores between 44 and 57 percent suggest that comprehension is adequate. As you've learned, above 57 percent indicates that pupils can read the material on their own. (Some teachers want to count synonyms as correct. Such a procedure is fine when closure procedures are used for instructional purposes. But for the evaluation of readability, stick to exact words. A body of research indicates that the counting of synonyms—and all the problems involved in deciding on what is a synonym—does not improve the readability scoring significantly.)

5. A comprehension aid and a technique to use in language-experience, individualized programs is to have children read each other's experience stories on composition paper or charts and ask them to think about the "main idea" of the story. Then prepare simple sentences, using only the words of the story writer, that represent the main idea of each story. Separate the beginnings and endings of the sentences and place them in a mixed arrangement. Children are to draw a line from the beginning of each sentence to its appropriate ending. Such sentences may be used for chalkboard development or duplicated and passed out for independent seat work.

---

[28] Russell G. Stauffer, *Directing the Reading-Thinking Process* (New York: Harper & Row, 1975), pp. 190–95.

An example of content to use for this activity is:

Julia likes to help	for his dog.
Lin likes to fly	for the party.
Dorothy made a dress	his toy airplane.
Paul made a house	her father.

ADDITIONAL READINGS

Books and Pamphlets

ALLEN, ROACH VAN. "How a Language-Experience Program Works." In *A Decade of Innovations: Approaches to Beginning Reading*, edited by Elaine C. Vilscek. Proceedings of the Twelfth Annual Conference, vol. 12, part 3. Newark, Del.: International Reading Assn., 1968.

———, and ALLEN, CLARYCE. *Language Experience Activities*. Boston: Houghton Mifflin, 1976.

AUKERMAN, ROBERT C. *Approaches to Beginning Reading*. New York: John Wiley & Sons, 1971.

BARRETT, THOMAS C., and JOHNSON, DALE P., eds. *Views on Elementary Reading Instruction*. Pp. 43–55, 65–76. Newark, Del.: International Reading Assn., 1973.

BECKER, GEORGE J. *Television and the Classroom Reading Program*. Newark, Del.: International Reading Assn., 1973.

BEERY, ALTHEA; BARRETT, THOMAS C.; and POWELL, WILLIAM R., eds. *Elementary Reading Instruction: Selected Materials*. 2nd ed., pp. 146–66. Boston: Allyn and Bacon, 1974.

BRAUN, CARL, and FROESE, VICTOR, eds. *An Experience-Based Approach to Language and Reading*. Baltimore: University Park Press, 1977.

DALLMAN, MARTHA; ROUCH, ROGER L.; CHANG, LYRIETTE Y., and DeBOER, JOHN J. *The Teaching of Reading*. 4th ed., pp. 481–509. New York: Holt, Rinehart and Winston, 1974.

DURKIN, DOLORES. *Teaching Them to Read*. 2nd ed., pp. 11–50. Boston: Allyn and Bacon, 1974.

FRY, EDWARD. *Elementary Reading Instruction*. Pp. 134–53, 167–89, 208–21. New York: McGraw-Hill, 1977.

HALL, MARYANNE. *The Language Experience Approach for Teaching Reading: A Research Perspective*. 2nd ed., Newark, Del.: International Reading Assn., 1978.

HEILMAN, ARTHUR W. *Principles and Practices of Teaching Reading*. 4th ed., pp. 97–129. Columbus, Ohio: Charles E. Merrill Publishing Co., 1977.

HUNT, LYMAN C., JR. "Philosophy of Individualized Reading." In *Reading and Inquiry*, edited by J. Allen Figurel. Conference Proceedings, vol. 10. Newark, Del.: International Reading Assn., 1965.

MUSGRAVE, G. RAY. *Individualized Instruction: Teaching Strategies Focusing on the Learner*. Boston: Allyn and Bacon, 1975.

SMITH, RICHARD J., and JOHNSON, DALE D. *Teaching Children to Read.* Pp. 46–56, 91–135. Reading, Mass.: Addison-Wesley Publishing Co., 1976.

SPACHE, GEORGE D., and SPACHE, EVELYN B. *Reading in the Elementary School.* 4th ed., pp. 39–140, 314–58. Boston: Allyn and Bacon, 1977.

STAUFFER, RUSSELL G. *Directing the Reading-Thinking Process.* Pp. 170–260. New York: Harper & Row, 1975.

————. *The Language Experience Approach to the Teaching of Reading.* New York: Harper & Row, 1970.

VEATCH, JEANNETTE. *Reading in the Elementary School.* 2nd ed., New York: John Wiley & Sons, 1978. With the assistance of Philip J. Acinapuro.

Periodicals

ADAMS, ANNE H., and HARRISON, CATHY B. "Using Television to Teach Specific Reading Skills." *Reading Teacher* 29, no. 1 (October 1975), pp. 45–51.

ATKINSON, R. C., FLETCHER, J. D., LINDSAY, E. J., CAMPBELL, J. D., and BARR, A. "Computer Assisted Instruction in Initial Reading: Individualized Instruction Based on Optimization Procedures." *Educational Technology* 13, no. 9 (September 1973), pp. 27–32.

BARTH, RODNEY J., and SWISS, THOM. "ERIC/RCS: The Impact of Television on Reading." *Reading Teacher* 30, no. 2 (November 1976), pp. 236–39.

BUSCH, JACKIE S. "Television's Effects on Reading: A Case Study." *Phi Delta Kappan* 59, no. 10 (June 1978), pp. 668–71.

DIETERICH, DANIEL, and LADEVICH, LAUREL. "ERIC/RCS Report: The Medium and the Message: Effects of Television on Children." *Language Arts* 54, no. 2 (February 1977), pp. 196–204.

JOHNSON, DALE D., and PEARSON, P. DAVID. "The Weaknesses of Skills Management Systems." *Reading Teacher* 28, no. 8 (May 1975), pp. 757–64.

KIDDER, CAROLE L. "Choosing a Basal Reading Program." *Reading Teacher* 29, no. 1 (October 1975), pp. 39–41.

PIENAAR, PETER T. "Breakthrough in Beginning Reading: Language Experience Approach." *Reading Teacher* 30, no. 5 (Febraury 1977), pp. 489–96.

ROGERS, JOHN R. "Should Experience Charts Be Edited?" *Reading Teacher* 30, no. 2 (November 1976), pp. 134–36.

ROSECKY, MARION. "Are Teachers Selective When Using Basal Guidebooks?" *Reading Teacher* 31, no. 4 (January 1978), pp. 381–84.

STAUFFER, RUSSELL G., and HARRELL, MAX M. "Individualizing Reading-Thinking Activities." *Reading Teacher* 28, no. 8 (May 1975), pp. 765–69.

WHEELER, ALAN. "A Systematic Design for Individualizing Reading." *Elementary English* 50, no. 3 (March 1973), pp. 445–49.

WHEELER, KIRK, and WHEELER, MARY. "Research Report: The Other Classroom." *Instructor* 83, no. 10 (June/July 1974), p. 15.

Approaches,
Procedures,
and Materials

Wood, R. Kent, and Stephens, Kent G. "An Educator's Guide to Videodisc Technology." *Phi Delta Kappan* 58, no. 6 (February 1977), pp. 466–67.

SECTION C
GROWTH AREAS
IN READING

CHAPTER 6 DEVELOPING WORD APPROXIMATION AND IDENTIFICATION STRATEGIES

Strategy Development

A FOUR-STEP APPROACH

Picture Clues

PICTURE CLUES IN BOOKS

PICTURE DICTIONARIES

Context Clues

TYPES OF CONTEXT CLUES

DANGERS IN THE CONTEXT-CLUE APPROACH

CONTEXT-CLUE ACTIVITIES
Supplying Words in Chalkboard Sentences
Supplying Words in Completion Sentences
Guessing Riddles
Exchanging Sentences Written by Pupils
Sentences from Outside Reading

Sight Words

CONFIGURATION

LETTER DETAILS

SIGHT-WORD GAMES
Avoid Contrived Games
Avoid Presenting Words in Isolation
Use a Variety of Games
The Guessing Game

SELF-HELP REFERENCES
A Chalkboard Dictionary
A Class Dictionary Booklet
Pictures with Captions
Key Sentences
Individual Word Booklets

Phonics

WHEN SHOULD PHONICS BE TAUGHT?

WHAT PHONICS SHOULD BE TAUGHT?

INSTRUCTION IN PHONICS
Proceed from the Known to the Unknown
Avoid Misrepresentation of Natural Sounds
Children's Phonic Needs Differ
Incidental Development "On the Spot"
Planned Development

PRACTICE AND MAINTENANCE ACTIVITIES
  Practice with Beginning Consonants
  Practice on Vowel Sounds
  Practice in Recognizing Unpronounced Letters

PHONIC GENERALIZATIONS

Word Structure

INSTRUCTION IN STRUCTURAL ANALYSIS
  Compound Words
  Little Words in Big Words
  Root Words, Inflectional Endings, and Affixes
    Root Words
    Inflectional Endings
    Affixes
  Syllabication

Dictionary Usage

Discussion Questions and Activities

Additional Readings

CHAPTER 7 EXTENDING KNOWLEDGE OF WORD MEANINGS

Concepts and Word Meanings

WHAT IS A CONCEPT?

BUILDING CONCEPTS

CONFUSIONS DUE TO FAULTY OR INADEQUATE CONCEPTS

IMPROVING READING THROUGH CONCEPT BUILDING
  First-Hand Experience
  Relating to Personal Experience
  Models and Construction Projects
  Dramatization
  Exhibits
  Chalkboard Sketches
  Pictures
  Audio-Visual Aids
  Context
  Abstract Meanings

Words Are Like Chameleons

Figurative Language

Changes in Word Structure

COMPOUND WORDS

PREFIXES, SUFFIXES, AND ROOTS

Synonyms and Antonyms

SYNONYMS

ANTONYMS

Word Origins

NEW WORDS

Critical Thinking and Vocabulary

THE POWER OF WORDS

SEXIST TERMINOLOGY

Personalized Word Collections

Guiding Principles

Discussion Questions and Activities

Additional Readings

CHAPTER 8 NURTURING READING COMPREHENSION

Comprehension Strategies

A MODEL

GENERAL PRINCIPLES

ACTIVITIES FOR DEVELOPING BASIC STRATEGIES
Closure Procedures
Introductory closure activities, especially for primary pupils
Closure activities, especially for pupils beyond the primary grades
Closure activities, especially for pupils with demonstrated needs
Retrospection Procedures

Comprehension Growth Areas

LITERAL COMPREHENSION

INTERPRETATION

CRITICAL READING
A Caution

Propaganda
Planned Activities for Critical Reading

APPLICATION
Teaching Creative Reading

Purposes and Questions

PURPOSES

QUESTIONS
Types of Questions

Questions at Various Cognitive Levels
Related to Reading Instruction

KNOWLEDGE QUESTIONS

COMPREHENSION QUESTIONS

APPLICATION QUESTIONS

ANALYSIS QUESTIONS

SYNTHESIS QUESTIONS

EVALUATION QUESTIONS

Discussion Questions and Activities

Additional Readings

CHAPTER 9   *DEVELOPING FLUENCY AND FLEXIBILITY*

Fluency Foundations in the Primary Grades

ESTABLISHING PHRASING

BREAKING HABITS OF BODILY MOVEMENTS

SETTING PURPOSES

WIDE READING

SCANNING

Increasing Rates in Grades Four Through Eight

DEVELOP AN AWARENESS OF PERSONAL RATES

DEVELOP THE CONCEPT OF READING IN THOUGHT UNITS

DEVELOP HABITS OF READING FOR A PURPOSE

DEVELOP THE PREVIEW TECHNIQUE
Introducing Previewing
Practicing Previewing

Systematic Practice

TIMED READING PRACTICE
Materials
Instructions for Giving Timed Practice
Ascertaining Rates and Grasp of Content
Keeping Personal Records
Controlled Reading

EMPHASIS ON FLEXIBILITY

Skimming and Scanning in Grades Four Through Eight

SKIMMING

SCANNING

Discussion Questions and Activities

Addtional Readings

CHAPTER 10 DEVELOPING STUDY STRATEGIES IN THE CONTENT AREAS

Study Strategies

SELECTION AND EVALUATION
Examples from Textbooks
Social Studies
Mathematics
Development of Selection and Evaluation Strategies
First Grade
Second and Third Grades
Upper Grades

ORGANIZATION
Examples from Textbooks
Science
Social Studies
Mathematics
Development of Organization Strategies
First Grade
Second and Third Grades
Intermediate Grades and Above

RECALL
Examples from Textbooks
Science
Social Studies
Mathematics
Development of Recall Strategies
First Grade
Second and Third Grades
Intermediate Grades and Above

LOCATION OF INFORMATION

Primary Grades
    Finding Page Numbers
    Finding Specific Phrases or Sentences in Context
    Using Titles
    Recognizing Chapters
    Using Tables of Contents
    Reading Illustrations
    Alphabetizing
    Contacts with Reference Materials
Grades Four and Above
    Using Parts of Books
    Using Dictionary and Glossary Skills
        Alphabetizing
        Using guide words
        Using pronunciation aids
        Finding definitions
        Finding synonyms
Using an Index
    Finding key words
Dictionaries for Grades Four through Eight
Encyclopedias for Grades Four through Eight
Reading Illustrations
Library Skills
    Organization of books
    Card Catalog
    Cards in the card catalog

FOLLOWING DIRECTIONS

SURVIVAL STRATEGIES

Patterns of Writing

SPECIFIC PATTERNS
    Literature
    Science
    Social Studies
    Mathematics

Vocabulary

TECHNICAL VOCABULARY

OVERLAP WORDS

MULTI-MEANING WORDS

FUNCTION WORDS

Discussion Questions and Activities

Additional Readings

CHAPTER 11   DEVELOPING INTEREST AND TASTE IN LITERATURE

Personality Development

The Stimulation of Interests

PROVIDING FUNCTIONAL INFORMATION

CURRICULAR ENRICHMENT

Indirect Contribution to Skills

Reading Interests of Today's Children

PRIMARY GRADES

GRADES FOUR THROUGH SIX

GRADES SEVEN AND EIGHT

Interest-Inducing Activities

SETTING THE STAGE

RECOMMENDING BOOKS

COUNSELING PARENTS

MAKING MATERIALS AVAILABLE
CLASSROOM ACTIVITIES TO STIMULATE INTEREST
Reading Orally and Telling Stories
Planning for Specific Periods of Sharing
Using Table or Shelf Arrangements
Using Bulletin Board Displays
Preparing for Assembly, Television, or Community Programs

Selecting, Recording, and Reporting

SELECTING

KEEPING RECORDS

REPORTING

Library Activities

THE CLASSROOM LIBRARY
Reading Materials
Use of the Classroom Library

THE SCHOOL LIBRARY
Value of the School Library
Use of the School Library
Cooperation between Teachers and Librarians

PUBLIC LIBRARY ACTIVITIES
Taking Excursions to the Library
Story Hours
Reading Clubs

School-Representative Clubs
Supplying Teachers with Book Lists

Discussion Questions and Activities

Additional Readings

The explorer found a hidden cave.

Maps are made by cartographers.

chapter 6

developing word approximation and identification strategies

What to Expect in This Chapter:

Emphasis is placed on the development of functional strategies for unlocking the meanings and pronunciations of unfamiliar words. Each special aid is discussed and illustrated: picture clues, context clues, sight words, phonics, word structure, dictionary usage. The focus is on the development of comprehensive strategies suited to the needs of the individual child and the specific reading task at hand.

"Normal" native-born speakers of English enter school reasonably proficient in coping with the language of their communities. They are able to extract meaning from what they hear and are able to communicate meaning to others. In a wholesome classroom and school environment, they also gradually learn to add to their repertoire of oral communication abilities. They learn to communicate (listen and speak to others) in the regional standard English of their expanding spheres of activity.

As they are introduced to the processes of reading, they must be helped to realize that the same *listening* goals are involved: What is the writer *saying?* Do I understand the message? In contrast to oral language acquisition, which appears to develop quite naturally over time, many learners must now consciously learn to unlock the code of written language. In order to unlock the code, learners use much of what they already know about oral language plus new strategies appropriate to written language.

Written language consists of three parts—all of which must be mastered in order to become an effective reader: phonographological, syntactic, and semantic. All parts work together for learners as they attempt to unlock the code in their search for meaning.

Phonographological refers to the application of the *sound* system of oral language to written language (often referred to as phonics or phonic analysis). Without this knowledge, one cannot read. With *only* this knowledge, one becomes word-bound and usually a retarded reader.

EXAMPLE:

Jackson: a word-bound reader, comes across this sentence: "I used the new **encyclopedia** *to look up the information I needed." Jackson uses his one aid, phonographological or phonic skill, successfully until he reaches the word* encyclopedia. *He realizes it is difficult and starts to work on it—eh-uhn-seye-klowe-pee-deye-uh. By the time he gets done, he is uncertain of the*

*sounds at the beginning and either loses his struggle or succeeds
after tremendous effort.*

*If Jackson had learned to combine other language clues
with his phonographological attack, his mission would have been
accomplished quickly and efficiently. He would have understood
the author's message with little need to struggle. If he had been
trained to be aware of* **syntactic clues**—*the order of the words in
phrases, clauses, sentences, and paragraphs*—*he would have
reduced some of his uncertainty by saying to himself, "That
word's a thing; it's the name of something." Jackson, if aware of
syntax, would realize this because of the noun marker* **the** *and the
intervening adjective. He would know it is the object because of
its position in the sentence. Granted, syntax alone will not, probably cannot, unlock the word for Jackson, but it is an aid not to
be overlooked.*

Semantic *refers to meaning the learner is able to attach to
individual words and the interrelationships of words. Had Jackson, armed with knowledge of sounds and syntax, skipped the unknown word and processed the rest of the material in search of
meaning, he would probably have determined that the unknown
word was some sort of book.*

*"I used the new _____ to look up the information
I needed."*

*With little doubt, once Jackson then looked at the beginning
of* encyclopedia *(through his reduction of uncertainties), he would
have recognized the word and the total message.*

STRATEGY DEVELOP-MENT

Pupils need to learn many ways of attacking unknown words when
they come across them in print. One approach may be effective in one
situation, and a different approach in another. In the main, the most
efficient and economical approach is a combination or integration of
several. Teachers must take the time to help pupils who demonstrate a
need to develop specific techniques; the goal, though, must be integration
of approaches into ever-developing strategies that will help learners become independent readers.

Some strategies will enable the reader to arrive at the exact word
(word identification); other strategies will enable the reader to understand the message, but not the exact word (word approximation).

On the other hand, if the reader's purpose was to be sure to learn
that word—not only to gain the author's message—then phonic and
dictionary skills might be put into play. Or suppose the reader were faced
with: "A *reapplication* of paint did not help." In this case, an elementary
level reader might get little help from context and be forced to resort
to phonic analysis, word structure analysis, and the dictionary.

Generally speaking, however, context (syntactic and semantic) is a
potent tool for helping pupils unlock ideas in print. In our opinion, the

EXAMPLE:

"Patricia has just had two front teeth removed. Will she be able to masticate her food?"

A given reader will probably be able to receive the author's message just through the use of context; the word **chew** *will probably be substituted without any need to "sound out" the word* masticate. *In fact, many elementary level readers might even "sound out" the word without knowing what it means.*

development of strategies for unlocking unknown words in print should start with an examination of context and then proceed to other strategies if context alone is not enough.

A Four-Step Approach

1. Examine the Context. Is it language? Does it make sense even if you are not sure of the word? Is the word a person or a thing? Is the word an action? Does the word describe something? What does it seem to mean in relation to the rest of the sentence(s)? Think of the word it might be. Try it in the sentence. Does it make sense?

If the purpose is satisfied and the author's message is understood, the strategy of examining context and arriving at the word or a word approximation is sufficient in that instance. If, however, the reader is uncertain or a reading purpose calls for exact word recognition, the reader should move on to the next strategy.

2. Examine the Beginning of the Word. Do you know how to pronounce the first letter or letters? Perhaps you recognize the first part of the word or syllable. Does the word you selected when you just looked at the context alone start the same way? Is it the same word? If it is, now you are sure of the word. If it seems different, try it in context again. Is there another word that begins the same? See if it is correct.

Most of the time, if the word is in the reader's meaning vocabulary, the word will now be recognized. If not, the reader has the option of trying strategy three below. Sometimes, the reader might want to go directly to strategy four, however.

---

3. *Examine Other Parts of the Word.* (If the reader just cannot figure out the word—approximate or actual—with the help of strategies one and two, the reader may want to try dividing the word into parts. This strategy is successful for some words with some readers.) Take the word apart if you can. Do you recognize a syllable? a root? a common prefix? an ending? Words that at first look difficult can often be broken down into well-known building blocks. Considering the context again, do you now recognize the word? [1]

4. Use a Dictionary. If you just cannot get the word and do not understand its meaning in the sentence after using the earlier strategies, you can consult a classmate or your teacher. On the other hand, getting used to using a dictionary will provide you with a life-long friend. Use the phonetic respelling of the word to help you pronounce it. Use the pronunciation key if you need sample words to help you understand what a certain symbol means. If there is more than one pronunciation, check the context again to be sure of how the word is used. Bring the sentence to the dictionary when you look for its meaning. Select the definition that suits the context.

In order to make use of the four-step approach explained above, learners have to gain increasing knowledge about written language, and they need the guidance of their teacher. The major portion of this chapter is focused on discussion and application of specific word identification and word approximation strategies. Although particular strategies are empha-

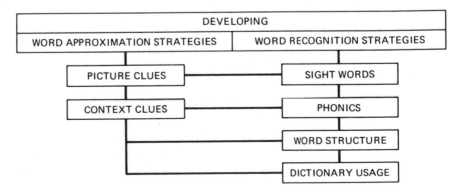

---

[1] Adapted from Ellen L. Thomas and H. Alan Robinson, *Improving Reading in Every Class: A Sourcebook for Teachers,* 2nd ed. (Boston: Allyn and Bacon, 1977), p. 95.

sized at times, they should be integrated into an overall approach that will be of use to the reader—as described above.

PICTURE CLUES

Pictures most frequently serve to help readers approximate words in normal reading situations. However, during the beginning stages of reading, particularly as an approach to introduce words, picture clues are useful in actual word identification.

Beginning dictionaries, workbook exercises, charts, and other materials often use pictures of objects, people, and animals to be sure that the learner identifies a word. Often, there is actual instruction in word discrimination starting from a pictorial stimulus. Children are asked to look at a picture and are helped to read a simple sentence related to it. Emphasis is placed on the pictured object. Then pupils are asked to pick out that word in a similar sentence pattern when the picture is not there.

This technique often helps when pupils have limited experiences and when they are just beginning to develop a stock of words. They will usually pick out the anticipated answer, "This is a dog." As experience increases and sight-word knowledge builds, the technique becomes one of approximation more than actual word identification. For example, if in the situation above, the sentence had read, "This is a poodle," and the reader had responded, "This is a puppy," the reader would not have been wrong—just using the picture as a clue.

This is a cat.   This is a dog.
This is a boy.   This is a game.

"Taffy" by Irene Springer.

Picture Clues in Books

The first books that children use for reading are often picture books with a few words and/or sentences appearing beneath the pictures here and there. The skillful teacher helps children deduce the names of the important words from the pictures. Sometimes there is a one-to-one match between the picture and a word—it could hardly be anything else. At other times, the pictures are used to help cement the names of certain important characters; this is really just a temporary use of picture clues that is only useful in the beginning stages of reading. For example, before reading a book, teachers might give the names of the chief characters as they show their pictures in the book. They might say, "The girl's name is Nancy, and this word under the picture is Nancy." Later, the children refer to the picture to refresh their memories.

Although the picture-clue technique is more valuable at beginning stages than later, it is of use throughout the elementary school. Books today are beautifully illustrated, and great strides have been made in recent years in providing pictures that supplement information given in the context and that help children to visualize the concepts presented.

Picture Dictionaries

Picture dictionaries also identify words through the use of picture clues. Learning new words through meaningful association, developing the ability to help one's self, and establishing dictionary habits are all products of using picture dictionaries. There are numerous picture dictionaries put out by publishers of elementary materials; also, some pre-primers and other materials for beginning readers have miniature picture dictionaries at the backs of their books. The dictionaries prepared in the classroom, however, are probably the most useful in terms of developing word identification abilities through pictures. Three ways of preparing such dictionaries are presented below.

1. Teacher and pupils may make a wall dictionary for use in recognizing new words met in their reading material. Each entry word is printed first, followed by a picture. The words are kept in alphabetical order. (The sophistication of alphabetical order should be determined by the knowledge of the group.)

2. Pupils may make a class dictionary book. The teacher binds together large sheets of paper and attaches alphabet tabs to the edges of the sheets. As the children meet new words they can put into pictures, the teacher has them find the place in the class dictionary where the word should appear and the teacher prints it on the page. The children then draw or find a picture to illustrate the word, and this is pasted or drawn, in the dictionary at the appropriate place. The book is left in a readily available place, and the pupils refer to it for help in word recognition and spelling. This plan may be used also in connection with the spe-

cial vocabulary of a unit or textbook topic, such as "Farm Animals" or "The Sky Above Us."

3. Pupils may make individual dictionaries. Each child may provide a looseleaf notebook with alphabetical tabs pasted on the page edges. They keep a record in their books of words that they do not recall reading or do not know how to spell. The nouns and verbs are illustrated with drawings or pictures cut from magazines. A pictured label is used for unpicturable words; for example, if *are* is the troublesome word, a picture showing children skipping rope may be accompanied with the label, "These children *are* skipping rope." When they look for *are* in the *a* section of their dictionaries, they find the labeled picture, read through the label, and find *are*, which is identified from the label.

**CONTEXT
CLUES**

"What word would it have to be to make sense?" Teachers up and down and around the countryside have been asking this question of their pupils for years. In so doing, they have been encouraging the use of *context clues* in finding out an unidentified word. This method is fine, but teachers need to do much more in developing ability to use context clues. This is an important tool for the pupil, and one that should be developed through planned, thoughtful, and intelligent guidance. It should take precedence over other word identification and/or word approximation strategies because it is the one that comes to the aid of the mature reader most often. In addition to putting more planned time and effort in helping pupils use context clues, it—along with picture clues—should receive initial emphasis.

Types of Context Clues

A number of investigators have identified types of context clues, but for purposes of utilization in the elementary and middle grades, a combination of the ideas of Artley [2] and McCullough [3] appear to still provide the most viable means of making use of context revelation. Although teachers should help children learn how to cope with the various types in relation to their maturity and background (both experiential and linguistic), the types should not be "taught" point by point. They should be added to readers' strategies through conscious practice with materials that are being read for their ideas—not for their context-clue types. The names of the context-clue types are usually unimportant to the pupil.

1. *Experience Clue.* Children who are reading material not too distant from their life and language experiences can figure out words or word approximations by tapping their own experiences, both actual and vicari-

[2] A. Sterl Artley, "Teaching Word-Meaning Through Context, *Elementary English Review* 20, no. 2 (February 1943): 68–74.

[3] Constance McCullough, "The Recognition of Context Clues in Reading," *Elementary English Review* 22, no. 1 (January 1945): 1–5.

ous. "Do I see a *present* for me under the Christmas tree?" "The police officer put the prisoner's arms behind the prisoner's back and then put handcuffs around his *wrists.*"

2. *Definition Clue.* This type of clue is used frequently in exposition and, hence, it becomes a valuable tool for reading in the content areas. Authors use a variety of ways of defining and usually signal the reader in some way. In elementary and middle-grade textbooks, the most frequent means are through *direct explanation* and *statements in apposition.*

Examples of direct explanation: "An antipollution device is an instrument that helps to reduce the amount of pollution given off by cars and many factories." "*Horizontal* means level or lying in the same direction as the horizon." (The verbs *is* and *means* in these sentences signal that an explanation is to be given. In the second sentence, the italicized word signals the fact that the writers will define the word.)

Sometimes, the definition precedes the word: "The common end point A where the rays AB and AC meet in an angle is called the vertex."

Sometimes, the word is in one sentence and the explanation in another. "The *cerebellum* is an important part of the brain. It controls our posture and balance as well as how the muscles of our body work together." (In this instance, a small part of the definition was given in the first sentence, but the major part of the explanation was given in the second sentence. Pupils need to suspend conclusions until they are sure all the information is given.)

Examples of statements in apposition: "As *commerce,* or business, grew in the eastern United States, many ships traveled between Europe and the United States to bring goods for trade." [4] "The *machete*—a large, heavy knife—was used to cut through the dense growth in the jungle." These sentences are representative of the ways statements in apposition appear in instructional materials at elementary and middle-school levels. Occasionally, parentheses are used and, once in a while, the words *that is* are used to signal a definition. "The term he used was *struggle for existence, that is,* the competition in nature among organisms to maintain themselves, survive, and produce others in a given environment." [5]

3. *Synonym Clue.* Learners should be guided to search for synonyms within the sentence context and/or within the context of subsequent or even preceding sentences. Knowledge and utilization of this frequently used clue is a giant step toward independence for the reader who is focused on a search for meaning. "The children's clothes were soaked through and through. The storm had *drenched* them."

4. *Comparison or Contrast Clue.* The reader's knowledge of a word or idea already known is compared or contrasted with the meaning of an unknown word(s). "Peggy excels in basketball, photography, and music,

---

[4] From *Be a Better Reader,* Level B, Basic Skills Edition by Nila Banton Smith, 1977, by Prentice-Hall Inc., p. 53. Reprinted by permission.

[5] H. Alan Robinson, *Teaching Reading and Study Strategies: the Content Areas* (Boston: Allyn and Bacon, 1975), p. 63.

and her older brother is even more *versatile*." [6] "When the light brightens, the pupils of the eyes contract; when it grows darker, they *dilate*." [7]

5. *Mood or Tone Clue.* Although this clue appears to be rather elusive at the cognitive level, it is easy for the reader—at the affective level. Once the mood or tone is understood, the reader usually recognizes or approximates the unknown word(s). "I've never seen such a *sentimental* person. He cries at sad movies. He is touched by poetry and stories that tell a tender story."

Dangers in the Context-Clue Approach

The first danger in developing the context-clue strategy arises from indiscreetly instructing the child to "guess the word." Finding out an unidentified word through the use of context is different. In this case, children carefully consider the meaning implied in a sentence or paragraph as a whole, and in the light of this meaning and their growing knowledge about types of clues, deduce the word as a result of their reasoning. The meanings conveyed by a combination of other words in a passage constitute the evidence on which learners base their conclusions in supplying the unidentified word.

The second danger is that an overemphasis on the use of context clues may cause some children to look upon this procedure as *the* only way to get words, and may result in retarding or diminishing their attempts to use other strategies. To avoid this state of affairs, the teacher should continuously emphasize to children the need of having "several different tools to unlock new words," so that if one does not work they will have another one to use or to serve as a check.

Context-Clue Activities

Teachers will think of numerous activities to help learners build context-clue power. Here are a few suggestions.

Supplying Words in Chalkboard Sentences. The teacher may write sentences on the chalkboard, including in each one a word that the children probably do not know and that can be supplied readily through the context in the rest of the sentence. The words *home* and *bed* are examples of such words in the sentences below.

When school is out we will go home.
At night we go to bed.

[6] Thomas and Robinson, *Improving Reading*, p. 24.
[7] Ibid., p. 25.

The children are asked to read the sentences to themselves. One child is then asked to read the first sentence orally but not to say the last word. The teacher asks, "How many know what the last word is? Raise your hand. Don't say it." If there are some children who cannot supply the word, the teacher guides these children with comments and questions until they are able to deduce it from the context in the rest of the sentence. Work with the next sentence proceeds in the same way, and so on.

Supplying Words in Completion Sentences. The same plan as discussed above may be used, except that blanks appear where the children are to fill in words. At first, separate words may be provided for them to use in making a selection of an appropriate word for each blank. There should always be a joker in the list of words provided. Later, they may try filling in blanks without the accompaniment of word choices.

Examples of completion sentences to use in working with context clues are:

Squirrels like to climb _____.
Ducks like to _____ in water.
Jan washed her face and _____.
The huge plane _____ high in the sky.
Pete _____ fast in order to get to school on time.
hands   ran   swim   trees   climbed

The teacher may work with a group at the chalkboard while choosing and supplying words in such sentences; or if the children needing practice can write, the sentences may be duplicated and given to them for independent work at their seats.

Guessing Riddles. Simple riddles provide excellent content in developing ability to get a word from context because children have to supply a word in terms of the total meaning of three or perhaps several related sentences. The riddles may be written on the chalkboard and used for group or individual work with the teacher, or they may be duplicated and passed out to each child who needs such practice. The word that is the answer to each riddle may be written or illustrated with a drawing.

Here are some examples of riddles:

Mother gave me something for my birthday. I can read in it. What is it?

It has long ears and a short tail. It can hop. It likes to eat carrots. It has soft brown fur. What is it?

Children may make up their own sentences for context work. After they become acquainted with materials of the types suggested above, invite them to make up sentences leaving out one word for the other children to supply. The sentences may be given orally, and the children needing practice may supply the missing words orally. Riddles that the children make up may be used in a similar manner.

Exchanging Sentences Written by Pupils. In the more advanced grades, children may make up and write a set of sentences (whatever number the teacher thinks is advisable), leaving out one word in each. Then they may exchange papers and try to fill in the appropriate words in each other's sentences. A score of one should be given for each sentence in which the correct word was supplied. After the papers are returned, the answers should be discussed and the children guided in deciding why the use of context clues worked in some cases and not in others.

Sentences from Outside Reading. Invite pupils to bring in one sentence encountered in outside reading in which they found an unidentified word they were able to figure out from context. Have each pupil read this sentence to the group, and discuss what was in the sentence that helped the pupil figure out the word.

**SIGHT
WORDS**

One goal of reading instruction is to assist pupils to read fast enough so they may integrate ideas. Slow, laborious reading—stopping to figure out almost every word—hampers comprehension. Learners must develop an ever-increasing stock of sight words that they identify instantaneously as they are processing ideas in print. There are several ways of helping them to do this.

Configuration

Word configuration—general contour or shape—is used by some teachers as a sight-word technique. If used at all, it can only be a temporary aid for beginning readers. Once readers possess a large stock of sight words, the use of configuration as a sight-word tool is confusing—too many words look alike. At the beginning stages, however, long words and words with unusual configurations may be learned easily. Children may have less difficulty in learning to recognize *grasshopper* or *grandfather* because of their shapes and lengths than they do *is* with its nondistinctive shape.

Letter Details

When one focuses on the whole word, without using context clues, letter details have an influence on recognition. The specific details that are of particular aid to one reader may be different for another reader, depending on their language knowledge and competence. According to Frank Smith,

> . . . there are two sources of information available for the identification of words: one is featural, the visual information available to the eye, and the other is sequential, our knowledge of the way words are constructed.[8]

Letters at the beginnings of words (and sometimes at the ends of words) are frequently more helpful to young learners than are letters in the middle—unless the middle letters have something distinctive about them for the given pupil. Children will usually, however, discover some cue on their own to help them identify the word when they meet it again. Frank Smith (using the word *John* as an example) pointed out the following:

> That is the problem for the child: to discover cues that will distinguish *John* from other configurations. The child may decide that a good cue lies in the length of the word, or the two upright strokes, or the shape of the "fish-hook" at the beginning. In selecting a cue that will be the basis for recognition of the word, a child will establish the first tentative "distinctive features" to be looked for in the future when testing whether to allocate a configuration to the category "John." [9]

Sight-Word Games

Focusing pleasurable attention on word forms through the use of games in which the words are repeated orally is a method widely used by primary teachers in fixing sight words. Of course, such games are used more extensively in beginning reading classes than elsewhere because children at this stage have not yet developed ability to attack words independently and are largely dependent upon memory. The value of such games depends upon the type of game, its content, and the way in which it is played. A teacher should choose these games with care.

Avoid Contrived Games. Many devices widely used in the past for sight-word practice are artificial and farfetched. For example: An apple tree is drawn on the chalkboard, a word is printed on each apple, and children pretend they are picking apples; that is, each time a child names a word he or she has "picked an apple." Or a brook is drawn on the chalkboard, with stones placed at intervals across it. The words to be given practice are written on the stones. Children try to walk across the brook by stepping on the stones; that is, each time they pronounce a word correctly, they are supposed to have taken another step across the brook. There are several reasons why it is not desirable to rely heavily on

---

[8] Frank Smith, *Understanding Reading* (New York: Holt, Rinehart and Winston, 1971), p. 134.

[9] Frank Smith, *Understanding Reading*, 2nd ed. (New York: Holt, Rinehart and Winston, 1978), p. 128.

such devices as these. Although they are taken from real-life situations, their application is so far removed from the original activity that it seems almost an insult to the intelligence of any child to resort to such pretense in order to give practice on words. Probably the more serious objections, however, have their roots in modern psychology. The use of such devices builds up wrong associations. Suppose one of the words is *fly;* is there any reason why connections should be built up between *fly* and picking apples or walking across a brook? It is better not to associate a word with anything at all than to build up a wrong association. Another objection is that attention is divided between concentrating on the words and enjoying a vivid play experience. For this reason, practice probably is not as effective as it would be if the attention were sharply focused on the words to be fixed, rather than being diluted and overshadowed by a play activity.

Avoid Presenting Words in Isolation. Flash-card games, games played with lists of words on the chalkboard, or spinning disk games in which the child is to pronounce the word pointed to when ·the hand stops spinning are examples of the isolated-word type of game. Practice in word identification should be directed not only toward ability to pronounce a word but also toward recognizing its meaning. Words have many different shades of meaning, and the particular shade of a certain word meaning is apparent only when the word is surrounded with other words. The word *can,* a very common word in beginning reading, may mean one thing in the sentence, "I can help Mother," and another thing in the sentence, "Tom has a can of dog food." The words that surround any particular word give that word its meaning.

Use a Variety of Games. Interest is a strong factor in acquiring new words in a reading vocabulary, and variety in game playing keeps interest high. Teach the children how to play several worthwhile games. Play one for a few minutes one day, another for a few minutes the next day, and so on, all as a part of (and we hope tied in with) current reading experience and the needs of participating pupils.

Try the game below. It avoids some of the disadvantages pointed out above and incorporates some of the desirable features. It also gives practice on words in content close to the life experiences of the children, and it provides for maximum participation. The creative teacher, and perhaps the pupils themselves, may design other games that include these features.

The guessing game. The teacher prepares sentences containing sight words that have been troublesome for some children. For example, the words causing the most difficulty with children in a certain second grade were *said, here, is, my, you,* and *can.* The teacher made up these sentences:

Susan said, "Here is my cake, Bill.
You and I can eat my cake."

If possible the sentences should be tied in with some experience the children are having or have had recently or with something they are reading. In this particular case, Susan, one of the pupils in the group needing help, had told about a little cake she had baked the day before; she had shown it to her brother Bill and had invited him to eat with her. The sentences above were meaningful because they related to Susan's personal experience.

If it appears that sentences containing the sight words on which practice is desired cannot be an outgrowth of current experience or reading, then the teacher may make the sentences more meaningful by preparing a short background story leading up to the sentences and telling it to the children when they are about to work with those sentences. In some cases, the children are able to make up sentences containing words on which they need practice.

Just one short sentence may be used in beginning reading stages. In later stages, several sentences may be used in one composition, and several different groups of sentences may be used if it seems advisable.

After the sentences are composed, the teacher prints them on tagboard, cuts the sentences and words apart, and places them in the pocket chart. (If a pocket chart is not available, the sentences may be written on the chalkboard.)

In playing the game, one child goes out in the hall. Another child in the group selects a word for the child in the hall to "guess." He or she pulls out the card for this word, shows it to the other children, and they read the word orally. This ensures that everyone in the group knows what the word is that the child in the hall is to "guess," and it also offers everyone a chance to have some initial practice in recognizing that particular word.

The child who is in the hall is then called back to the classroom. He or she pulls each card up in turn, but does not take it out of its context. As the child pulls a card up, he or she asks, "Is it *Susan?*" "Is it *is?*" "Is it *my?*" and so on until the word that was chosen is mentioned. Each time the child asks a question, all the children in the group reply, "No, it is not *Susan*," "No, it is not *is*," and so on. Thus, not only the child who is trying to find which word was chosen has practice in associating the spoken word with the sight word symbol, but all the children in the group actively participate in the practice.

After the child who is trying to "guess" which word was chosen finds the word, another child goes out in the hall, and the game continues. When first playing the game, it is desirable for the child who is guessing to pull up the cards in order. Later, it adds to the interest if children are permitted to skip about, selecting words out of order.

Self-help References

Supplying self-help references for children's use in finding out sight words for themselves is one of the most commendable provisions a teacher can make. Both the attitude toward and the habit of finding out unrecognized words by oneself are important assets in learning to read. Furthermore, when children use their own initiative in finding out a word, the activity is reinforced by success, and they are able to continue reading unimpeded by word identification difficulty, the word is more apt to "stick." Here are some self-help references to try out.

A Chalkboard Dictionary. Some teachers prepare a dictionary for use during the early stages of reading instruction on one section of the chalkboard or on a large tagboard chart. To make the foundation for the dictionary, the teacher draws horizontal lines about four inches apart, one for each letter of the alphabet, except that only one line is allowed for XYZ. The appropriate letter, both in capitalized and lower case forms, is placed at the left of each line. Whenever a new, depictable word comes up in reading, the teacher draws or pastes the appropriate picture for the word on the line containing its beginning letter and prints the name beside the word in both lower case and capitalized form. Stick figures are especially appropriate for action words such as *run, hop,* and *jump.* Sometimes, the children find pictures to illustrate the words.

The section of the chalkboard dictionary for *a, b,* and *c* might look something like this:

The teacher and children read the words together as new ones are added to the dictionary. If children fail to identify one of these words while reading in a book, they refer to the picture dictionary on the chalkboard or chart and find it for themselves.

A Class Dictionary Booklet. A dictionary booklet may be built up for use by all children in the class in any of the primary grades. To prepare a class dictionary, the teacher may procure a large notebook and a set of alphabet tabs to be attached to the edges of the leaves. As a new word comes up that the children wish to record for future reference, they find the place for it in the class dictionary, and the teacher (or a child in second or third grade) prints the word in the appropriate spot. Children and teacher then search for a picture to illustrate the word.

They may look in old catalogs, magazines, newspapers, and discarded books for an appropriate illustration. When a good picture is found, it is pasted above the word in the class dictionary. Sometimes, children draw or paint pictures of a word, and the best one is chosen for the dictionary.

As the dictionary develops, children are free to go to this reference and look up a word at any time while reading. (See additional picture-dictionary suggestions, pages 139–40.)

Pictures with Captions. Not all words that children need can be pictured. In fact, the most difficult sight words are those that do not lend themselves to picturization, such as *was, here, their, of,* and so on. Captions beneath pictures can be used as self-help references for such words.

In preparing material to use in connection with this activity, teachers should make a collection of attractive colored pictures. They should also jot down the undepictable words that are causing the most trouble, then select a picture that lends itself to a caption that will include some of these difficult sight words. The class discusses the picture and composes an appropriate caption to be pasted beneath the picture or attached to it. With skillful guidance, the caption may be one that contains several of the difficult words.

For example, several children in one second grade group were having difficulty with the words *these, their, were, was,* and *while.* It was during the maple sugar season, and the children were interested in the process of making maple sugar and were engaged in some language activities in connection with this topic. The teacher brought out a picture showing some children in the woods tending a pan of maple syrup as their father was disappearing far down the road. After some discussion, the pupils in the classroom made up this label for the picture: "These children were making maple syrup while their father was away." The teacher printed the sentence on a strip of tagboard, attached it to the picture, and hung it up in the classroom. The children found the hard words (*these, their, were, was, while*) in the sentence, and the teacher drew a "box" around each of these words to make it stand out. The children referred to the label whenever they had trouble with one of these words.

A few labeled pictures of this sort can take care of nearly all the undepictable sight words that cause trouble.

Key Sentences. Some teachers have found it valuable to prepare a group of key sentences containing each of the sight words giving difficulty, printing each group of key sentences on a separate chart, and assembling all the key-sentence charts in one place for permanent reference.

The key sentences should be given by the children themselves. For example, the teacher tells the children that he or she is going to print several sentences on a chart with the word *where* in each of them, and places the chart beneath the chalkledge in the front of the room. If they forget the word *where* they can look at the chart, read the sentence, and thus find out the word. The teacher then asks them to give several sentences with *where* in each one. The teacher prints the sentences on the chalkboard and transfers them to tagboard later. The suggested sentences might be the following:

where
Where is your hat?
Where is your book?
Tell me where your mother is.
Where is your pencil?

Individual Word Booklets. Each child may have a little notebook in which the words causing difficulty are recorded by the teacher. Each word may be followed by an appropriate sentence suggested by the child, such as: "*How*—How old are you?" The child studies these sentences and during certain times set aside for the purpose reads them to the teacher or another pupil. The goal of the child will be to beat his or her own record each time by identifying more and more of the words.

PHONICS

Phonics, phonics instruction, or phonic analysis focuses on the relationships between the sounds used in speech and their representations in written language. Because numerous terms must be clarified in order to discuss phonics, the following definitions will be useful to the reader as a prelude to the discussion.

Phonemes and graphemes. Phonemes are speech sounds; there are forty or so such distinctive sounds in the English language. **Graphemes** are the twenty-six **letters** of the alphabet **that represent** those **sounds.**

Phoneme-grapheme relationships. Phonics is concerned with the nature of the relationships between speech sounds (phonemes) and their written or printed representations (graphemes). Over time—with personal experience, teacher guidance, and the help of a dictionary—pupils learn to handle graphemes that both correspond and deviate from phonemes. Examples: The sound /p/ is always represented as **p**; the sound /k/ can be represented as **c**oal, **k**ind, **ch**orus. The sound /i/ as in **i**ce can also be represented as **tie, try, righ**t, **ai**sle, **buy** (to name a few).

Morphemes. *Morphemes* are the *smallest units of meaning* in language. Morphemes may consist of several phonemes or a single phoneme. The word **cat** is a morpheme consisting of three phonemes. The word **cats** consists of two morphemes because the -s ending signifies plural and hence contributes meaning.

When Should Phonics Be Taught?

It seems important to take into account a child's level of linguistic development. He need not be taught that which he already knows nor should he be frustrated by that for which he is not ready. A supposedly sacred hierarchy of phonics skills, all considered essential for maximum reading growth at times in the past took precedence over our knowledge and understanding of children and how they learn and acquire language. It is suggested that different children learn phonics, like everything else, differently, and that one sequence, unless it is broad and general in nature, is unlikely to be appropriate for all pupils. Many individuals learn to read with some degree of efficiency without exposure to a single schwa, circumflex or diphthong-digraph distinction.[10]

The following criteria should be observed in regard to the time at which children should begin to utilize phonics as a strategy for unlocking words:

1. Children should develop an interest in reading and a desire to read before working with such technical aspects of reading as sounding letters.

2. Children should acquire the attitude of reading for meaning before having their attention directed to the analysis of words into sound elements—an activity that could distract from meaning.

3. Children should have practice in using context and picture clues in a search for meaning.

4. Children should first acquire a reading vocabulary of word wholes sufficient in size to represent the phoneme-grapheme correspondence to be learned; in this way, they may generalize from known words the relationship of phoneme and grapheme they need to unlock new words. For example, if the phoneme /f/ and its graphic representation as **f** is to be learned in the initial position in a word, the children should have had previous experience in identifying a few words beginning with **f**, such as *fox, fat, for.*

What Phonics Should Be Taught?

Artley pointed out that ". . . there is no question about the fact that phonic cues are important in the identification of unfamiliar words, not as the primary means of identification, but as a support to the other cue systems." [11] He indicated that when a reader has to choose from among several possible words that would make sense in a given context, knowledge of phonics is invaluable. He used this example: "The postman put a _____ in a mailbox." Artley pointed out that the unknown word could have been *package, letter,* or *message.* When the reader

[10] Pose Lamb, "How Important is Instruction in Phonics?" *Reading Teacher* 29, no. 1 (October 1975): 18.

[11] A. Sterl Artley, "Phonics Revisited," *Language Arts* 54, no. 2 (February 1977): 124.

notes that the unknown word begins with a *p*, the combination of context clues and initial consonant sound provides the accurate answer.[12]

This being true, what should be included in the phonics program to make it a useful aid in word identification? Certainly consonant symbol-sound relationships are important, since words usually begin and/or end with consonants. Instruction would include, of course, the single consonants, consonant digraphs (*ch*, *th*, etc.) and consonant blends or clusters (*st*, *bl*, etc.). If one knows that the word begins with /*b*/, /*wh*/, or /*sw*/, this knowledge alone gives the reader a powerful leverage over unfamiliar words.[13]

Pupils should be helped to ascertain the differences between vowels and consonants, but a great deal of stress should not be placed on instruction with vowel sounds. Most words can be figured out with knowledge of consonant sounds and context clues. If vowel sounds are taught, emphasis should be placed on working out a vowel strategy related, essentially, to *long, short*, and *schwa* sounds. Pupils should try each of the possible sounds as they examine the unknown word in its context setting. Other vowel sounds can be dealt with when and if the need arises.

The charts below present the basic phonic elements with which the teacher ought to be familiar. Obviously, in light of what has been discussed earlier, they are reference tools for the teacher and not charts to be mastered by the pupil.

CONSONANTS*

Single Consonants			Consonant Blends		Consonant Digraphs		
One Sound		Two or More Sounds			One Sound		Two Sounds
b	m	c (came	bl	sc	ch		th (those
c	n	face)	cl	sk	gh	ng	thin)
d	p	g (go	dl	sm	ph	nk	wh (what
f	r	gem)	fl	sn	sh		who)
h	t	s (hiss	gl	sp	shr		
j	v	rose	pl	st	thr		
k	w	sugar)	sl	sw	sch		
l	x	x (box	br	tw	(schwa)		
	y	exit	cr	spl			
	z	xylophone)	dr	scr			
			fr	spr			
			gr	str			
			pr	sch			
			tr	(school)			

* A *consonant blend* is a cluster of two or three consonants that are blended together to make one sound but that do not lose their separate identities. A *consonant digraph* is formed when a cluster of consonants produce one sound and the sound is a new sound—the separate letters appear to lose their individual identities.

[12] Ibid., pp. 124–25.
[13] Ibid., p. 125.

VOWELS*

Long	Short	Schwa (ə)	Other Sounds	OU Sounds
ā (ate)	a (at)	a in above	ä (father	bough
ē (be)	e (end)	e in parcel	far)	cow
ī (ice)	i (it)	i in pencil	ér (term	journey
ō (open)	o (hot)	o in lemon	bird)	though
(show)	u (up)	u in circus	ô (order	through
ū (mule)	y (bicycle)		often	touch
(few)			all	
y (by			awe)	
candy)			oi (oil	
			boy)	
			ú (put	
			wood)	
			ü (rule	
			move	
			blue	
			loose)	

* The most common sounds are represented on this chart. For exceptions to the patterns represented and for rarely used sounds, pupils will need to refer to the pronunciation guide of a dictionary and carefully interpret the diacritical marks. A most important concept is that there is not always a one-to-one phoneme-grapheme relationship—note that the ô sound may be applied to *all* and the ü sound may be applied to *move*, for example. The vowel patterns that result in only one vowel being pronounced are not represented in the chart, although they may be long, short, or schwa. Examples: rāin, cōat, bāy, certaín, bread, frēe, liēn, breāk.

The phonic charts are not precise tools; they are useful in grouping sound approximations together. Regional and dialectic differences must be honored; there will be many deviations from the sounds, as listed, by individuals and groups—especially in pronouncing the vowels. The goal is not absolute "standard English" accuracy of pronunciation but enough differentiation among the sound productions to enable individuals to sound out words or syllables or letters when necessary. There are no such entities as long and short vowels; they are just handy terms for us to use as we differentiate between two major categories of sounds that occur frequently. Even the consonant sounds, which seem so stable in isolated words, change at times when we are reading the words in context.

Instruction in Phonics

Proceed from the Known to the Unknown. In phonics, as in all learning, teachers should start with something within a child's experience and build upon that in proceeding to a new and/or unknown learning element; that is, proceed from the known to the unknown. Also, it is better to start with a meaningful unit as a whole and then break it down into its parts than to start with small, meaningless parts and put them together to make a meaningful whole.

The synthetic method of teaching phonics used in the past proceeded in direct opposition to the principles above. Children were first taught the sounds of the letters of the alphabet. These sounds and letters were not in the experience background of most of the children, nor did they have any meaning for them. Once these smallest of language units were learned, they were put together to make a word, and the words in turn were put together to make a sentence.

Today most successful instruction in phonics makes use of the analytic method. Children begin reading through the use of an entire composition—language experience story—and then break it down into sentences, phrases, and words when and if necessary. This activity is usually accompanied by other experiences with whole words as labels on familiar objects, words with pictures, and then as words in simple, meaningful sentences as captions and in books. Children in need of help with specific phonic elements then get such help on letters or letter patterns, drawn from the word wholes they already know.

Avoid Misrepresentation of Natural Sounds. Sounds are frequently exaggerated in classroom instruction, especially when the children try to verbalize the isolated sound of a consonant or consonant combination. In such cases, the children give the sound of /c/ as "*cuh,*" /b/ as "*buh,*" /k/ as "*kuh,*" /l/ as "*e-e-ell,*" /r/ as "*errr*" and so on. One cannot articulate the sound of a separate consonant unless a vowel is added, and when a vowel is added the result is usually a syllable, not a consonant sound. When children try to blend this syllable or cluster of sounds with other elements in a word, they meet with difficulty. Thus, the practice of having children verbalize separate consonant sounds may do more harm than good.

Children's Phonic Needs Differ. Some children do not need phonics. Among those who do, needs may differ. Some children may be particularly weak in auditory discrimination and especially need practice in listening to sounds; others may be especially weak in visual discrimination and need practice particularly in developing keenness in *seeing* word elements, and so on. Occasionally, there is a child who simply does not grasp phonics instruction at all, and emphasis must be placed on other means of unlocking words.

Incidental Development "On the Spot." Perhaps one of the most effective ways of developing new phonic elements or generalizations is to capitalize upon opportunities as they arise. For example, children read about a boy "who had a bowl of soup. He sat down to eat it." John pronounced *bowl* with the same sound of /ow/ as in *down.* The teacher wrote *bowl* and *down* on the chalkboard and asked John to underline the *ow* in each. Then she explained, "/ow/ has two sounds, one as in *cow,* another one as in *own.*" She wrote the two words on the chalkboard, and added other words as the children mentioned them and told her under which heading to write each one. The words so classified were: *now, brow, owl, fowl, clown, show, blow, crow, snow, slow.* The teacher then explained that they could be more sure of an /ow/ sound in a word if they would try it both ways and see which sound makes sense, and then continued, "Which sound did John use for both of the *ow* words? Did it make sense? John, do you want to try the other sound in this word (pointing to *bowl*)? Read the sentence pronouncing the word that way. Does it make sense?" Thus, John worked out the pronunciation of *bowl* and checked it with context, and everyone learned about the two sounds of /ow/.

Warning: The teacher must use judgment in regard to the amount of time that it is expedient to use in working with "on the spot" phonics. The child should be told the word so that he or she can proceed with the reading, and then the phonic development or practice should follow directly afterwards while the child's need for help with the particular word is still fresh in mind.

Planned Development. The procedure described below, is planned to help the child who meets difficulty in recognizing a word in a sentence. This word is one he or she is about to encounter in reading a story in a book. An element needed in recognizing this new word is pulled out for development through the use of known sight words from which the new sound is deduced. As a result of this practice, children return to the original sentence and read the previously unrecognized word. They then apply the results of all this practice when encountering the word in reading story context in their books.

The best way to explain this procedure is to give an example. Developing the initial consonant *h* is used for this example, but the same general procedure is equally effective when used in developing a final or medial consonant, a blend, or a digraph.

Providing a contextual setting. The teacher selects from the larger context a sentence containing a new or difficult word that begins with *h* and that lends itself to phonic treatment. An example of such a sentence is "Nancy took the kitten in her *hand.*" *Hand* is a new word to be read by the group and is appropriate for use in developing the consonant *h.* The teacher then prints the sentence on the chalkboard.

This part of the procedure enables the teacher to introduce the new consonant in a contextual setting rather than as an isolated letter, and it provides for immediate application in reading context following the introductory practice.

Meeting a need in context. The children are asked to read the sentence. They have difficulty with the word *hand.* (Supplying the word through context alone does not help completely because the word could be *basket, doll-buggy,* and so on). At this juncture, the teacher explains that they will now be shown how to find out this word all by themselves, whenever and wherever they see it.

Visual discrimination. Children need to become sensitive to the appearance of *h* at the beginning of words, to *see* that many words begin with *h*. Practice designed to develop the sensitivity might be as follows: The teacher lists known sight words beginning with *h*. The list might look something like this before and after the children work with it:

Before	After			
hen	h̲ en	(h) en	hen
home	h̲ ome	(h) ome	home
help	h̲ elp	(h) elp	help
him	h̲ im	(h) im	him

The teacher explains that there is something that is alike in all these words, and then asks a child to draw a long box around the letter that is the same in all of them. Others may have a turn, some drawing a circle around each copy of *h*, others underlining each copy of *h*, and so on.

Auditory discrimination. Not only must children be able to *see h* in a word, they must be able to *hear* its sound.

The teacher explains: "This letter *h* has a sound all its own. If you know what this sound is, it will help you many times in figuring out the pronunciation of a new word. Listen to see if you can hear this sound as I pronounce the words on the chalkboard."

The teacher then reads the words, slightly emphasizing but not isolating the sound of the initial consonant /h/. Different pupils are asked to read the words, emphasizing the sound of /h/ in each, so that the others can hear this sound.

An auditory perception game is then played. The teacher may say several words that begin with different letters, including some that begin with /h/. The pupils clap *once* whenever a word is said beginning with the sound of /h/, or individuals may take turns and name the word(s) in a given list. An example of lists of words that might be used for this purpose is:

girl	have	table	chair
hat	told	flower	tick
home	head	hands	fall
boy	house	horns	hall

In addition to serving the practice function in auditory discrimination, this game is diagnostic. Children who clap at the wrong time or who say the wrong words are in need of further practice.

Blending. After children have had practice in recognizing the initial consonant *h* both visually and aurally, they are ready for blending this sound with other vowels and letter patterns. One of the most satisfactory ways of doing this is again to proceed from the known to the unknown.

The teacher writes a known sight word such as *top* on the chalkboard, and asks the children to read the word. Then he or she explains, "I am going to take the first letter off *top* and write the letter *h* in its place to make a new word." The teacher then proceeds to erase the *t* from *top* and add *h*, making the new word *hop*. The children are asked to read this word.

In a similar fashion *h* is substituted for the initial consonant in other known sight words such as: told (hold), fall (hall), catch (hatch), mouse (house), corn (horn), good (hood), say (hay).

Finally, the teacher presents a known word that can be changed into *hand*, the new word needed in the original sentence written on the chalkboard. As an example, suppose that the children know *sand* as a sight word. Then the teacher would explain, "Now, you will be able to read the new word in the sentence that I wrote on the chalkboard. What is this old word that you already know (writing *sand* on the chalkboard)? Now I am going to take the *s* off this word and replace it with the new sound of *h* (erasing *s* and replacing it with *h*, making the word *hand*). What is this new word?"

Contextual application. At this point, the children may be asked to read sentences containing the new words that they have made by substituting *h* for the other initial consonants; that is, they are given a chance actually to apply the results of their practice while reading words in contextual situations.

Some sentences that might be used for this purpose are as follows:

Mary saw the robin { top. / hop.   Chickens { hatch / catch out of eggs.

The bowl was not large enough to { told / hold the milk.   David can blow his new { corn. / horn.

Ralph walked down the { fall. / hall.   Mildred has a new red { hood. / good.

Sylvia lives in a big white { house. / mouse.   Horses like to eat { say. / hay.

In later stages, the multiple-choice word may be omitted, and the new word may be written directly into the context of the sentence.

Applying practice to an immediate reading need. The teacher refers to the sentence written on the chalkboard at the beginning of the devel-

opmental activity: Nancy took the kitten in her *hand*. "Now you can read this sentence and get the new word without any trouble, I'm sure." The children read the sentence. "We shall see if you can read the new word that well when you find it in the story that we soon will read."

The result of all this practice is applied in reading the story in which *hand* is a new word. It also is applied in working out any other unrecognized words beginning with *h* in the immediate story and in successive stories.

Practice and Maintenance Activities

The development of a given phoneme-grapheme relationship is sufficient for a few children, but most require continued practice throughout the primary grades and frequent review and maintenance in the upper elementary grades. Needs will vary, and practice should be given in accordance with needs. The practice and maintenance activities that follow are illustrations of the many possible. If games are played that remove words from context, teachers should make every effort to have pupils meet those words in meaningful contextual situations in the immediate future.

Practice with Beginning Consonants.

1. After a common experience, such as taking an excursion or building and equipping a playhouse, the teacher may say, "Let's think of all the things we saw" or "all the things we have in our playhouse that begin like *Ted*." Such lists as *turtle, turkey, toad,* or *table, telephone, tub, tack* may result. These are written on the chalkboard, and attention is called to the sameness of the appearance and sound of the beginning letter.

2. Riddles may be used to give practice in auditory discrimination, such as:

I am round.
Children play with me.
My name begins like *book* and *baby.*
What am I?

3. A description word activity is especially desirable for auditory and visual practice because the recognition of an initial consonant sound takes place in a contextual setting.

Write on the chalkboard a sentence containing a noun that begins with a consonant on which you wish to give practice, as: I have a *book*. Ask the children to add other words that start with *b* that might be used to describe the book, as:

I have a beautiful book.
I have a big book.
I have a blue book.

Use the same activity for other consonants.

4. *Blending.* Write words on the chalkboard that can be changed by substituting different initial consonants (and some that can be changed by substituting different final consonants). Let the children erase the preceding consonant, add the new one, and pronounce the resulting word as the teacher gives instruction, for example:

Change *cat* to *bat*
Change *cat* to *cap*
Change *fan* to *tan*
Change *see* to *bee*

Have the children read sentences containing the new words:

A *bat* can see at night.
Ted has a new *cap*.

5. Place sentences on the chalkboard containing words representing elements you wish to review. Have children find and read words in the sentences that begin like a word you mention. For example, if you wish to review *st*, *bl*, and *ch*, write sentences something like the ones given below. Then give such directions as "Find a word that begins with the same sound as *cheese*. Show the word. Then read the sentence."

Janice saw a bright star.
Michael has red cheeks.
Marie built a house with her blocks.

Practice on Vowel Sounds.

1. If children need practice with vowel sounds, have them substitute vowels in words similar except for the vowel sound. They should pronounce each new word they make and read it in a sentence. As an example of content for such activity, the key words *big* and *hat* are given, together with words that the children might make by substituting vowels. Sample context sentences are also given.

big: **bag, beg, bug**
The man put candy in a **bag.**
My dog will sit up and **beg** for a bone.
Julia found a **bug** on the plant.
hat: **hit, hot, hut**
Bill could not **hit** the ball.

The soup was too **hot.**
The old man lived in a little **hut.**

2. Filling words in with vowels provides extra practice on the vowel sounds. A sample of sentences to be used for this purpose is:

Sylvia has a new **h—t.**
It is **r—d.**
It has a **b—nd** of ribbon on it.
Her aunt **s—nt** it to her.

3. After pupils have generalized some principles about vowels and the sounds of vowels, they may put words to which the principle applies in sentences on the chalkboard or find words on pages in a book. Sentences appropriate for chalkboard practice in finding words to illustrate the principle of final *e* are as follows:

Our bird's **name** is Susan.
We put her in a **cage.**
The cage is made of **wire.**

A sample appropriate for finding words to illustrate the principle of two vowels coming together might be:

Susan likes to **eat** often.
We gave her some **wheat seed.**
She has never **laid** an egg.

Practice in Recognizing Unpronounced Letters. Practice in detecting unpronounced vowels and consonants may be given by writing on the chalkboard words similar to those suggested in the sample below. Ask children to cross out the letter(s) they do not pronounce in each one. If they have difficulty recognizing any of the words in isolation, write them in sentences.

Cross out the vowels you do not pronounce in:

date	throat	ridge
health	beetle	tube
brake	wise	crate
aid	soap	float
seize	reason	lie
lay	hoarse	raise

Cross out the consonants you do not pronounce in:

weight	wrapped	frighten
own	stretch	tight
wrist	thought	catch
knuckle	bomb	wreck
half	two	through

Phonic Generalizations

Studies by Bailey,[14] Burmeister,[15] Clymer,[16] and Emans [17] have demonstrated that a large number of the rules or generalizations that have been taught to children over the years do not work. Certainly, pupils can establish their own generalizations about common letter patterns, but they must be ready to try another strategy if the generalization does not work. For example, in a one-syllable word ending in *e*, they may generalize that the *e* is an unpronounced marker that tells them the vowel before the *e* is frequently pronounced *long*; they must be ready, however, to try the *short* sound, or another sound, if the generalization does not hold up—sense in context is usually the ultimate test.

Some of the principles or generalizations suggested by Spache and Spache [18] and Richard Smith and Johnson [19] that seem useful and stable follow. Many children will arrive at them inductively (meeting a number of examples and arriving at the generalization, probably unconsciously, on their own). Other children may need directed guidance in order to arrive at the generalization.

1. When the letter *g* is followed by *e, i,* or *y,* it is pronounced "soft" like /j/, as in *gentle.* Otherwise the *g* sounds "hard," as in *good.*

2. When *c* is followed by *e, i,* or *y,* it is pronounced as /s/, in *city* or *lace.* Otherwise, the *c* is pronounced as /k/, in *cable* or *attic.*

3. When two of the same consonants are side by side, only one is sounded, as in *ladder.*

4. The sound of /t/ is usually that heard in *tap* or *cat,* but in *-tion* endings it is pronounced as in *nation* or *mention.*

5. When a consonant and *y* are the last letters in a one-syllable word, the *y* is given the long sound of /ī/, as in *try.* In longer words, the *y* is given the long sound of /ē/, as in *baby.*

[14] Mildred H. Bailey, "The Utility of Phonic Generalizations in Grades One Through Six," *Reading Teacher* 20, no. 5 (February 1967): 413–18.

[15] Lou E. Burmeister, "Usefulness of Phonic Generalizations," *Reading Teacher* 21, no. 4 (January 1968): 349–56, 360.

[16] Theodore Clymer, "The Utility of Phonic Generalizations in the Primary Grades," *Reading Teacher* 16, no. 4 (January 1963): 252–58.

[17] Robert Emans, "The Usefulness of Phonic Generalizations Above the Primary Grades, *Reading Teacher* 20, no. 5 (February 1967): 419–25.

[18] George D. Spache and Evelyn B. Spache, *Reading in the Elementary School,* 4th ed. (Boston: Allyn and Bacon, 1977), pp. 382–83.

[19] Richard J. Smith and Dale D. Johnson, *Teaching Children to Read* (Reading, Mass.: Addison-Wesley Publishing Co., 1976), p. 148.

6. The first vowel is usually long, and the second is unpronounced in *oa, ay, ai,* and *ee,* as in *coat, day, rain,* and *seed.*

7. In *ea,* the first letter may be pronounced as a long /ē/ and the second unpronounced, or it may be pronounced as a short /e/ as in *bread.*

8. The combination *oo* may be pronounced in one of two ways, as in *soon* or as in *wood.*

Pupils must be conscious of the fact that most of the generalizations here and those they will arrive at on their own are subject to change. They will find exceptions and often those exceptions will increase in magnitude as their word stock grows. If they will couple their knowledge of phoneme-grapheme relationships with the four-step approach suggested on pages 136–37, they will meet with success most of the time.

WORD STRUCTURE

Structural analysis and phonic analysis are frequently confused. They are, however, quite different in content and application. Phonics is concerned with individual sound elements in words; structural analysis focuses on the units that make up the structure of a word or that change the meaning of a word.

The content of structural analysis, as phonics, is made up of several elements that lend themselves to classification. A total graphic picture of word structure elements and processes from the teaching standpoint, together with examples, is presented in the chart on page 163. Each aspect is then discussed in subsequent pages.

It is not possible, of course, to list all the root words, compound words, contractions, and possessive forms that youngsters will meet in their reading in the elementary grades. The common inflectional endings are established by the grammar of the English language as *s, es, ing, er,* and *est.*

Studies that have been made of the frequency of *prefixes* and *suffixes* offer some, but not complete, guidance in regard to the teaching content of these elements.

According to Stauffer's study [20] of Thorndike's *The Teacher's Word Book,* the following prefixes appear with the highest frequency: *ab, ad, be, com, de, dis, en, ex, in* (into), *in* (not), *pre, pro, re, sub, un.* Thomas and Robinson [21] added *ante, circum, inter, mis, non, post, trans,* and *anti.*

Thorndike [22] made a study of suffixes appearing in his word list. He found the following to be the most commonly used suffixes:

-ion	-ment	-ence	-ant
-tion	-ful	-ance	-able

[20] Russell G. Stauffer, "A Study of Prefixes in the Thorndike List to Establish a List of Prefixes that Should be Taught in the Elementary School," *Journal of Educational Research* 35, no. 6 (February 1942): 453–58.

[21] Thomas and Robinson, *Improving Reading,* pp. 49–50.

[22] Edward L. Thorndike, *The Teaching of English Suffixes* (New York: Bureau of Publications, Teachers College, Columbia University, 1941).

WORD STRUCTURE ELEMENTS

Words in a Compound Word	Stem or Root Word	Inflectional Forms	Prefixes	Suffixes	Possessive Forms	Contractions	Syllables
Example: *snowman* Children learn to identify the two separate words in a compound word as *snow, man,* when having difficulty in reading a compound word.	Example: *joy* Children learn to look for the stem word in words changed by adding affixes as *joyful, enjoyed, enjoyment* when meeting unrecognized words.	Examples: Words changed by adding *s—cats* *es—boxes* *ed—walked* *ing—walking* *er—sweeter trainer* *est—sweetest* Children learn to recognize and pronounce these endings when encountered in reading words.	Examples: *re—return* *dis—disappointed* Children learn to recognize prefixes and their meanings when encountered in reading words.	Examples: *ment—amusement* *less—helpless* Children learn to recognize suffixes and their meanings when encountered in reading words.	Examples: *John's* hat the *girl's* doll Children learn to identify possessive forms by noting apostrophe *s* in reading words.	Examples: *didn't* *aren't* *haven't* Children learn that the one word stands for two words, and that the apostrophe shows where a letter was left out.	Examples: *dan ger* *wis dom* Children learn the concept of a syllable, and learn several ways of dividing words into syllables, when reading words.

-ation	-ity	-en	-an
-er	-ty	-ly	-ian
-y	-ent	-ary	-n
-al	-ure	-ive	-ic
-ous	-ness		

The teacher will not necessarily teach the prefixes and suffixes in the order of frequency indicated above; nor will the elementary teaching program as a whole be confined to those elements listed. Although all these most common elements should be included in the total elementary program, specific ones should be taught in relation to children's needs and maturity; and if a particular prefix or suffix not in these lists appears in children's reading, it may well be given attention.

Instruction in Structural Analysis

Compound Words. One of the easiest beginnings in structural analysis is that of helping children to see the two word units in a compound word. Even in the earliest stages of reading, children meet such compound words as *playhouse, something, into, policeman, grandfather.*

In chart and chalkboard activities, the teacher may call attention to the two separate words in a compound word in some such way as this: "This word *playhouse* has two words in it (placing one hand over house). You see if I cover up *house,* I have *play;* if I cover up *play,* I have *house* (covering *play*). Show me *play* in this word, Julia. Mark it off with the sides of your two hands, placing one hand on each side of *play.* (Julia does as directed.) What word did you show me?" (Julia answers, *"play."*) Similarly, the teacher may have *house* marked off with the sides of a pupil's hands or indicated in some other way.

Here is an example of the use to which a child may put knowledge of a compound word even after its first introduction. Mr. Hill had called attention to the *in* and *to* in the new word *into* with the use of a procedure similar to the one described above. Cathy met this word *into* in her book soon afterwards and did not recognize it by sight. "Don't tell it to me. Don't tell it to me!" she cautioned the teacher. "Wait a minute till I part it." Cathy covered *to* with her index finger, and looking at the remaining word said, "This is *in*"; then she covered *in* and read *to.* Removing her finger she victoriously announced *"into!"*

It is helpful to synthesize as well as to analyze compound words. For example, a new word that the children may meet is *bird.* They have already had the color words *black* and *blue.* Ms. Blau writes *bird* on the chalkboard saying, "I can make a big word with bird in it." She then writes *black* on the chalkboard. "Now watch while I run these two words together to make one big word." Ms. Blau writes *blackbird* and the children read it. Similarly, *blue* is combined with *bird* to make *bluebird*. They thrill with achievement at being able to read "big words" like this.

Some children will "catch on" to the technique of analyzing compound words as a result only of introducing the procedure described above. Others will need practice in order to develop a keener sensitiveness to the use of this technique. Two ways of providing additional practice are suggested below.

1. Select eight or ten compound words to which the children have been introduced. Print duplicate copies of each compound word in large letters on strips of cardboard about 18 × 4 inches.

Hold up one of the copies saying for example, "This is *bedroom*. I am going to cut the word into two parts and see what we have." Cut the card, holding up the two parts of the word, which the children read separately. There are now three separate cards for the compound word:

bedroom

bed

room

Pass out to the children the smaller cards upon which are printed the single words, such as *bed, room, cow, boy, cow, girl*, and so on. Hold up a large card upon which is printed one of the compound words, such as *bedroom, cowboy*, or *cowgirl*. As the compound words are held up, each pupil who has one of the smaller words runs up, says his or her word, and holds it in the appropriate place under the large card. The class then tells what the entire word is. The activity continues in this way.

As a later step, dispense with the large cards, on which the compound words are written as a whole, and use only the smaller cards containing the component words of the compound. Distribute these cards, one to each child. Ask a child to stand and hold his or her card up before the other children. The other children look at their cards, and the one who finds that he or she has a word to go with the word held up comes and places the card by the side of the other card. (It may go before or after the word held up.) For example, the child who first holds up a card may have the word *with*; the child who has *out* comes up and places his or her card beside the other card, thus making the word *without*. Each child reads his or her word and the class tells what the "big" word is. The children should, of course, understand that the two words they put together must make a real word—it must make sense.

This activity may well serve the double purpose of aiding in the identification of words in compound words in general and of giving practice on troublesome words in particular. As an example: The teacher passes out the separate cards for *some, body, time, thing, where, my, him, her, self*. A child holds up the word *some*; four children may come up, each having one of these cards: *time, thing, body, where*. Each in turn holds his or her card beside *some*, making the words *sometime, something, somebody, somewhere*. The children looking on read the words as they are made.

2. A variety of marking techniques may be used in giving practice in the analysis of compound words. Select the words from material that is being read or that is about to be read. Write the words on the chalkboard and call upon different children to indicate the two words by some marking plan such as that described below. Different plans may be used upon different occasions, or a variety of marking plans may be used upon any one occasion.

Have the children:

Draw a box around each of the words as | sail | | boat. |

Draw a circle around each word as (pop) (corn.)

Underline each word separately as side walk.

Draw a line between the two words as bee / hive.

Connect the parts of compound words in opposite columns by drawing a line from one part to the part that goes with it, as:

Little Words in Big Words. The practice of having children look for "little words in big words" is highly questionable and should not be considered as part of a word-structure program. This is such a widely used and misused technique, however, that it warrants discussion in the interest of clarification.

One way in which teachers make use of this technique is to teach children to "look for the little word" when they have trouble in pronouncing a new word, such as *at* in *pat*. It might work in this case, but what about *at* in *what*?

Some children who had been taught always to look for a little word first in working out a new word were reading silently about *Timmy, the Toad*. In the midst of the story, Terry burst out with this inquiry: "Miss Anderson, what is a *to ad*?"

The little-word technique misleads very often in the pronunciation of one-syllable words, and even more often in the pronunciation of polysyllabic words. Imagine a pupil trying to pronounce *dynamite* by first looking for *am, Jonathan* by looking for *at, territory* by looking for *it,* or *recreation* by looking for *eat.*

One legitimate use of this technique is finding root words in words modified by inflectional endings, prefixes, or suffixes, such as finding *walk* in *walking, load* in *unload,* and *sweet* in *sweetness.* In these cases, children are perceiving whole word units, which is an excellent structural-analysis technique.

Root Words, Inflectional Endings, and Affixes. The development of sensitivity to root words is necessarily related to the development of inflectional endings and affixes and is, therefore, discussed in connection with them.

Root words. A beginning in auditory discrimination of root words can be made very early. Suppose that the children have the new word *playing.* The teacher may say, "What whole word do you hear in *playing;* if we left off the *ing* part, what word would we have left? Can you tell me the main word in these other words as I say them: *hunted, walking, shouted, sleeping . . .?*" and so on. "The teacher may continue in this way when other new modified words come up in reading situations.

Visual discrimination of root words may be developed first by pointing out the root word and separating it from its inflectional ending whenever such a word comes up in reading context, as: "The word *holding* is a new one (writing it on the chalkboard). What is the main word in this word? Yes, it is hold" (boxing or underlining *hold*).

Inflectional endings. Perhaps the first inflectional ending that children will meet in their reading is *s*, added to make plurals. Some classroom situation may be used to develop the concept. For example, the first word of this type to come up might be *boys*, with *boy* having been learned previously as a sight word. When the word *boys* is encountered, the teacher may write both *boy* and *boys* on the chalkboard, explaining that when we want to talk or read about more than one boy we add an *s* to the word. The teacher might then have one boy stand and write *one boy*, then have two boys stand and write *two boys*, then have one girl stand and write *one girl*, and so on. The children may then read the phrases (with help on the number words) and finally be given turns in circling the *s* in a word that means more than one.

Similarly, when an *ing* ending first appears in reading, the teacher may develop this element through a classroom situation; for instance, let us suppose that the new word is *walking,* and that it appears in the sentence "Tom was walking to the store with his father." The teacher may write this sentence on the chalkboard, call attention to the word *walking,* and then ask different children to dramatize such actions as *walk, laugh, jump, pull, push,* and so on. While the children are performing these actions, sentences similar to the following may be written.

John is walking.	Bob is pulling.
Dick is laughing.	Camille is pushing.
Mabel is jumping.	

The children may read the sentences, with help if necessary on any of the proper names or verbs. The teacher may ask what is alike in all the words that tell what the children were doing. The *ing* ending may be underlined in each word and the sentences read again, making sure that everyone can hear the *ing*.

The *ed* ending might be introduced in the same way, except that each sentence would be written after the action had taken place rather than while it is in progress, as was the case with the *ing* words.

After the pupils have had a few sight words containing one of the endings, an organized development may take place. All the suggestions applied to the development of phonic elements should also be applied to the development of inflectional endings. An example of one way in which these suggestions may be applied is described below.

Suppose that the children had met the word *standing* in a sentence and had experienced difficulty with it. The teacher might write the sentence on the chalkboard: *The man was standing on the walk.* Then *visual discrimination* might be sharpened by listing in a vertical column known sight words ending with *ing*, such as *looking, walking, going.* The children might find the part that was the same in each word and box or circle it.

For *auditory discrimination*, the children might listen as the teacher pronounces words and clap or stand each time one is pronounced ending in *ing*. Words of this type might be used: *quickly, helping, eating, waited, standing, shouted, falling.*

Known root words might then be written on the chalkboard and the children asked to add *ing* to each and to pronounce the word so modified: *help (helping), play (playing), sleep (sleeping), stand (standing).*

After the word-building experience, the children might read sentences containing the new words they had built and choose the right word from multiple-choice endings, as:

          help
Mike was helped his mother with the dishes.
          helping

          playing
Sus was played with a ball.
          play

          sleep
Carol found the kitten sleeping on her bed.
          slept

          stand
Billy was standing out in the rain.
          stood

Finally, the children should read the sentence in which the word *standing* originally gave trouble.

Affixes. Affixes—prefixes and suffixes—should be taught in accordance with the same general procedures suggested for inflectional endings, but with increased emphasis upon the effect of these elements in changing word meanings.

Discussion may take place whenever children first encounter a word containing a new prefix or suffix. Call attention to the prefix or suffix. Have the pupils find the root word and see if they can tell in what way the prefix or suffix changes its meaning. The two suggested procedures below may be used interchangeably for prefixes and suffixes.

1. Suppose the youngsters have had the word *retold* and *return,* and the new word *repaint* appears in their reading. Write on the chalkboard the words *return* and *retold* in a vertical column. Have children tell what is alike in both words. Erase the *re* in each word and ask what the word means. Add *re* again and ask how the meaning is changed. Write several roots, including *paint,* as *paint, write, tell.* Discuss their meaning. Have *re* added to each one and and discuss the changed meaning. Ask children to give sentences using first the root word and then the changed word. Have them read sentences containing the root words, as:

John will paint the doghouse.
Ruth will write her composition in class.
Ed, will you tell your story?

After pupils have read each sentence, erase the verb and write in its place the same verb modified by the prefix *re*. Discuss the change in meaning. Underline the prefix.

2. Write a sentence on the chalkboard: Lillian put a full spoon of sugar in the iced tea. After having the sentence read out loud, ask the pupils if they can think of another way of saying the same thing. When offered, write: Lillian put a spoonful of sugar in the iced tea. Have the children realize that the suffix *ful* means *full.* Have them circle or underline the suffix. Write additional sentences containing root words with the suffix *ful.* Have the children read the sentences, underline the words with the suffix, and tell the meanings.

It is always desirable to have children visualize the element *and* understand how it affects the meaning and/or function of a root. Continue from easy-to-understand, concrete affixes to the more difficult and abstract as pupils are able to proceed.

Many children need to refresh their knowledge of prefixes and suffixes previously developed and review the function of these elements in helping with their word-recognition ability. Two suggested activities are offered below.

1. Children may state orally or write prefixed or suffixed words to match definitions, as:

Prefixes

un—not	*pre*—beforehand or in advance
de—take away or remove	*over*—too or too much
mis—wrong or wrongly	*under*—under or not enough

set in advance _____	not able _____
not sold for enough _____	a wrong deed _____
price is too much _____	remove the frost _____

Suffixes

ful—full of	*en*—to make or to be made of
ment—result or process of	*ist*—one who does a certain thing
er—one who	*able*—that can be

one who plants _____	one who plays a harp _____
that can be enjoyed _____	made of wood _____
pail filled with water _____	process of governing _____

2. Filling in blanks in sentences with prefixed or suffixed words is a meaningful activity. Examples are given: In this challenging activity, pupils should be told that all the prefixes are to be used, but two of the root words will not be used.

un, mis, re, out, over, under

fed	wit	time	planted
formed	laid	view	ground
current	directed		

The horse was very thin. It was because he had been _____ for five days.

Many desert plants will not live when _____ in other parts of the country.

The soldiers made their way into the city through an _____ passage.

Hal went to the top of the mountain where he could get a good _____ of the country.

Tom's letter never reached the person to whom he wrote, because it was _____.

Jack's father was late getting home last night. He worked _____.

In many of the old fables, one animal tried to _____ another.

Syllabication. Formal rules of syllabication are more useful for the writing of compositions than for reading. The good and/or mature reader is more able to use syllabication as a tool than the poor or beginning reader. One needs to have generalized a great deal of information about language in order to recognize the ways words are divided into parts by syllables—and even then the inconsistencies prevent accuracy. Syllables are units of sound; hence, children must be able to pronounce a word and know that the pronunciation is correct before they can determine syllables. The more experience readers have with polysyllabic words, the more success they will have with syllabication. These remarks are not meant to imply, however, that pupils should not be helped to attack polysyllabic words in collaboration with context aids. The help must be functional; rather than emphasis on formal rules that frequently do not work, the focus should be on meaningful strategies.

Young readers often need some guidance in learning to hear separate pronounceable units in words. As soon as learners begin to meet a number of polysyllabic words—whatever the grade level—teachers may begin developing some sensitivity to syllables, incidentally and casually. For example, when the new word *wonderful* is being discussed, the teacher might say something like this: "This long word has three parts in it. Count them (pronouncing *won der ful*). Some words have two parts, as *princess*. Count them (pronouncing *prin cess*). And some only have one part, as *spot*."

When it seems advisable to develop the concept of a syllable, both auditory and visual discrimination should be given attention. As in the case of the development of other word elements, familiar words should be used as a working basis. The concept that a syllable usually contains one vowel that is pronounced should be generalized by the children. An example of one type of procedure that has been used for this purpose is given below.

The teacher first developed ability to *hear* two syllables in a word. This was introduced as follows: "Some words have two parts. Listen while I say *darkness*. One part of the word is *dark* and the other part is *ness*. Can you hear two parts in *surprise*? What are the two parts?" This procedure was continued with the words *Johnson, watchman, grinding, blanket, Sunday,* and so forth.

The children were then asked to see if they could tell the difference between words that have one part and those that have two parts. They were told to clap once every time the teacher said a word that had one part and twice when a word was said that had two parts. Such words as *rang, shallow, morning, Ray, wife, happen, button, top,* and *garden* were pronounced.

After the children were able to hear the difference between one-syllable and two-syllable words, the teacher introduced the term *syllable.* "Each part of the word that you can hear separately is called a syllable. In *darkness, dark* is a syllable and *ness* is a syllable." The word *syllable* was written on the chalkboard and the children were asked to read it.

Following this introduction, the concept of syllables was developed by vowel sounds. The teacher wrote on the chalkboard several one-syllable words, as: *big, top, rich, bell, had.* "How many vowel sounds can you hear in *big*? How many syllables are there in *big*? Let's make a note of that." The headings below were written together with *big*. The children were asked to tell the number to write under each heading.

	Vowels	Syllables
big	1	1

The teacher then added other one-syllable words, and the number of vowels and syllables in each were written.

Two additional headings were written—*Vowels, Syllables*—and the procedure repeated using two-syllable words, as *river, stupid, broken, farmer, basket*.

As a result of this experience, the children arrived at these generalizations: (1) Every syllable has one vowel sound. (2) There are as many syllables in a word as there are vowel sounds.

A similar procedure may be used in extending the development to three- and four-syllable words when it seems practical to do so.

Teachers may use these patterns in giving as much practice as is necessary. They will of course use words with which the children are working currently in reading and other subjects.

1. Have children respond to questions and lists as indicated.

	How Many Vowels Are Pronounced?	How Many Syllables?
main	_____	_____
twins	_____	_____
branch	_____	_____
Benjamin	_____	_____
complete	_____	_____
historical	_____	_____

How many syllables can you hear?

get _____	wave _____	huge _____
coastline _____	grownup _____	multiply _____
happen _____	sail _____	handful _____
paragraph _____		science _____
		crack _____

2. The riddle technique in auditory identification of syllables is enjoyed by children. Teacher and children may make up such riddles as this:

There are two syllables in my name.
I am a bird. I come early in the spring.
I have a red breast. What am I?

Children supply the answer.

After the basic concept of the existence of syllables in longer words has been established, pupils should be helped to work out strategies for themselves. Groff [23] has pointed out that readers should be guided to break a word into parts that seem logical and that coincide with the readers' developing maturity and knowledge about the letter patterns in our language. He suggested that syllabication is, in the main, intuitive. Hence, for the pupils attempting to use syllabication as they attack poly-syllabic words, the definition of a *syllable* can be, "any word part that seems to have a vowel in it which I pronounce." The vowel sound can be any one of the varied vowel sounds—including schwa. The syllable divisions made by a given pupil do not have to equal the syllable divisions shown in a dictionary. Such divisions are important only for accuracy in dividing syllables at the ends of lines in written composition.

DICTIONARY USAGE

Dictionary usage involves a composite of skills, which call for skillful introduction and practice.

One teacher, Ms. Hughes, introduced dictionary usage in this way:
"I heard a man on television last night say "al'mond." I have always thought the word was pronounced a'mond. Have you heard people say al'mond? Do you suppose they are right? How can we find out for sure?"

She followed this discussion by looking up the word in the dictionary in front of the pupils and placing the main entry and the respelling with its diacritical markings on the chalkboard. She asked the youngsters to help her to work out the pronunciation with the use of the dictionary aids, some of which she explained briefly as she followed up with later development.

It is in ways like this that the astute teacher develops attitudes toward the use of a dictionary as a source of reference for, and authority on, word pronunciation. Attitude is of great importance in developing dictionary skills, as well as other skills. Of what avail is effort expended in developing word-attack skills unless a positive attitude toward using skills is developed simultaneously?

Both attitudes and skills in dictionary usage are developed most effectually in "on the spot" situations in which a doubt about the word exists. This might happen during discussion any time in the day; it might

---

[23] Patrick Groff, *The Syllable: Its Nature and Pedagogical Usefulness* (Portland, Oreg.: Northwest Regional Educational Laboratory, 1971).

happen while reading in any subject area. A teacher should take advantage of every opportunity to encourage pupils to develop their dictionary attitudes and skills and to apply them in functional situations.

Dictionary skills, however, cannot be left entirely to chance. They are too numerous and complex. Their development needs to be carefully planned in terms of specific clusters of skills. One cluster consists of those skills necessary in locating a word in the dictionary; another is concerned with working out pronunciation of words; and a third is concerned with getting meanings from words.

Children usually develop some ability in using rudimentary location skills and rudimentary meaning skills in the primary grades. Each of these clusters needs further development and refinement in the upper grades. (See Chapter 10, pages 278–80, for a discussion of dictionary location skills and pages 281–82 for a discussion of dictionary meaning skills.) Because the pronunciation cluster is built upon all the phonic and word-structure skills discussed in this chapter, it is usually the last of the dictionary skill clusters to be developed. Fortunately, pupils usually have had acquaintance with several of the pronunciation skills through their phonic and word-structure activities preceding the use of pronunciation aids in the dictionary.

The work that follows needs to be directed and guided until pupils are somewhat adept at reading respellings, diacritical marks, and accent marks. For some children, a fair amount of attention must be placed on hearing the accented syllables—best done in meaningful sentence situations.

The pupils may be told that when they look up a word in a glossary or dictionary they will find after the word a second spelling in parentheses. This second spelling tells them how to pronounce the word by showing the syllables, the accent mark, and the sounds of the vowels. But in some cases the second spelling is different from the one used in the text of the story, for example, *English* (ing'glish), *pygmy* (pig'mē), *dense* (dens), *curds* (kérds). The teacher may explain that many of our words are not pronounced just as they are spelled; thus, in a glossary or dictionary, words are often respelled just the way they are pronounced. The children should be urged always to look for the spelling in parentheses as an aid in working out the pronunciation.

Then the diacritical markings may be taken up as applied to the word in question, which for the sake of illustration we shall say is *archive* (är'kīve). The teacher may explain the markings in some such manner as this: "As you know, vowels are pronounced in many different ways. In order to help you know how to pronounce a vowel in a certain word, a marking scheme has been developed and is used in glossaries and dictionaries. You will find it at the beginning of some glossaries, always at the beginning of dictionaries, and in large dictionaries at the bottom of the pages." At this point, it would be advisable to let the pupils turn to these sources to get an overview of the entire marking system. The children should be told that marking keys vary somewhat from one dictionary to another, and that they will need to make use of the system appearing in the particular dictionary they are using at the time.

If there are not enough dictionaries to accommodate each child in the group, the teacher may place the entire key for diacritical marks on the chalkboard. To follow up with illustrations, it is advisable to read the key through, with the children stopping, of course, to work out the pronunciation of *är* in *archive* when discussing the /ä/ so marked in the key, and the /ī/ in *kīv* when discussing the /i/ so marked in the key. (The word, of course, should be one with which the children have had trouble, not necessarily this particular one.)

After the general introduction of the key, the teacher will probably wish to concentrate on just a few of the sounds until the children have become thoroughly familiar with them. Then, the teacher concentrates on a few more of the sounds at another time, and so on, until the children can interpret diacritical marks when looking up any word in the dictionary. The introductions to abridged school editions of dictionaries usually include suitable exercises to serve as models for teacher-made exercises on the words pupils meet in their reading.

DISCUSSION
QUESTIONS
AND
ACTIVITIES

1. Observe pupils as they tackle different kinds of reading assignments. Ask them what they are doing. Ask them such specific questions as: Why are you using your finger at this time? What are you looking for? When you come to a word you don't know, what do you do? Attempt to learn as much as possible about the word identification strengths of each pupil in order to help develop the strategies that will aid each in gaining additional strengths. See Chapter 7 for additional suggestions related to evaluating word identification and word approximation strategies.

2. Develop a set of word identification strategies with the class as a group. Emphasize flexibility! The set or sets of strategies might be printed on chart paper and kept in the classroom as a point of reference—a point of reference subject to modification.

3. Use interesting exercises to help pupils learn to interpret phonetic respelling. Thorndike and Barnhart, in the 1974 edition of their intermediate dictionary, have pupils read a story interspersed with a number of words written phonetically. Pupils are to rewrite the story and spell out the phonetically spelled words.[24] It is an interesting approach that incorporates "phonics" with the use of context clues. You can prepare

[24] E. L. Thorndike and Clarence L. Barnhart, *Thorndike Barnhart Intermediate Dictionary*, 2nd ed. (Glenview, Ill.: Scott, Foresman, 1974), p. 23.

suitable material for your own pupils at any level—once they have begun to use a dictionary. For instance, try this:

Question: Do you (līk) the (tel′ ə vizh′ ən) show, (ôl) in the (fam′ ə lē)? Why or (hwī) not?

ADDITIONAL READINGS

Books and Pamphlets

BECK, ISABEL L. "Comprehension During the Acquisition of Decoding Skills." In *Cognition, Curriculum, and Comprehension*, edited by John T. Guthrie. Newark, Del.: International Reading Asso., 1977.

CARROLL, JOHN B. "Comments on Comprehension During the Acquisition of Decoding Skills." In *Cognition, Curriculum, and Comprehension*, edited by John T. Guthrie. Newark, Del.: International Reading Asso., 1977.

EHRI, LINNEA C.; BARRON, RODERICK W.; and FELDMAN, JEFFREY M. *The Recognition of Words*. Newark, Del.: International Reading Asso., 1978. *and Thinking in School*. 2nd ed., pp. 265–83. New York: Holt, Rinehart and Winston, 1976.

SMITH, E. BROOKS; GOODMAN, KENNETH S.; and MEREDITH, ROBERT. *Language and Thinking in School*. 2nd ed., pp. 265–83. New York: Holt, Rinehart and Winston, 1976.

SMITH, FRANK. *Understanding Reading*. 2nd ed., pp. 99–150. New York: Holt, Rinehart and Winston, 1978.

SPACHE, GEORGE D., and SPACHE, EVELYN B. *Reading in the Elementary School*. 4th ed., pp. 361–436. Boston: Allyn and Bacon, 1977.

STAUFFER, RUSSELL G. *Directing the Reading-Thinking Process*. Pp. 263–314. New York: Harper & Row, 1975.

TINKER, MILES A., and McCULLOUGH, CONSTANCE M. *Teaching Elementary Reading*. 4th ed., pp. 159–95. Englewood Cliffs, N.J.: Prentice-Hall, 1975.

Periodicals

ALLEN, DAVID P. "Cue Systems Available During the Reading Process: A Psycholinguistic Viewpoint." *Elementary School Journal* 72, no. 5 (February 1972), pp. 258–64.

ALLINGTON, RICHARD L., and STRANGE, MICHAEL. "The Problem with Reading Games." *Reading Teacher* 31, no. 3 (December 1977), pp. 272–74.

ARTLEY, A. STERL. "Phonics Revisited." *Language Arts* 54, no. 2 (February 1977), pp. 121–26.

DURKIN, DOLORES. "Phonics: Instruction that Needs to be Improved." *Reading Teacher* 28, no. 2 (November 1974), pp. 152–56.

EMANS, ROBERT. "When Two Vowels Go Walking and Other Such Things." *Reading Teacher* 21, no. 3 (December 1967), pp. 262–69.

Developing Word Approximation and Identification Strategies

JOHNSON, DALE D., and MERRYMAN, EDWARD. "Syllabication: The Erroneous VCCV Generalization." *Reading Teacher* 25, no. 3 (December 1971), pp. 267–70.

LAMB, POSE. "How Important is Instruction in Phonics?" *Reading Teacher* 29, no. 1 (October 1975), pp. 15–18.

PERFETTI, CHARLES A., and HOGABOAM, THOMAS. "The Relationship between Single Word Decoding and Reading Comprehension Skill." *Journal of Educational Psychology* 67, no. 4 (August 1975), pp. 461–69.

chapter 7

extending knowledge of word meanings

What to Expect in This Chapter:

This chapter builds on the previous chapter by emphasizing the meanings of words—vocabulary development. Attention is paid to the many levels of vocabulary development—varied meanings, figurative language, changes in word structure. Critical thinking and vocabulary development are stressed as important partners with special emphasis on the power of words to control and persuade. The chapter concludes with some guiding principles useful in balancing a vocabulary development program.

No matter what conceptual framework one operates out of in regard to reading comprehension, vocabulary is a major element. Every effort should be made by classroom teachers to encourage vocabulary development through wide reading and other experiences, but, in addition, direct instruction must be planned if the vocabularies of most pupils are to grow significantly.

CONCEPTS AND WORD MEANINGS

What Is a Concept?

A concept, in the sense we use it here, is the cementing of an idea in one's mind. Concepts usually grow from a series of experiences. For example, the child who consistently experiences the word *pitch* in the context of throwing or tossing, generalizes that specific concept which she or he applies when meeting the word *pitch* in varied contextual settings. As the contexts change and bring different meanings to the word, the child learns to enlarge his or her concept and *pitch* becomes both a noun and a verb with varied meanings.

Building Concepts

Because concepts play such a versatile role in reading, it is important that teachers be fully aware of the processes by which concepts are built. The first step in building a concept is that of having experiences. Experiences are the self-starters of concepts, but concepts do not necessarily result from experiences; just experiences are not enough. There must be a second step, that of drawing conclusions from the experiences and later classifying and summarizing conclusions from several experiences. These classifications or summaries derived from experiences are called concepts. These concepts may be sound or faulty, full or meager, complete or inadequate. Regardless of their state of perfection, we use them in interpreting words verbally or as they appear in text. Concepts constitute the medium that makes experiences usable in interpreting reading symbols. So, the third step in concept building, insofar as reading is concerned, is that of applying concepts to new experiences that are encountered on the printed page.

Confusions Due to Faulty or Inadequate Concepts

What happens during the process of reading interpretation if concepts have not been well built? What happens if concepts are meager, lacking or inaccurate, and are still in isolated strands instead of classified and generalized?

Perhaps a concrete example will answer this question better than a discussion. Let us consider the case of a group of first-grade children who were reading a farm story. The story had its setting in a vegetable garden, a typical large farm garden in which vegetables were grown in sufficient quantities, not only to supply the immediate needs of the family, but also to feed the hired men and to can or store for winter.

The children who were reading the story lived in Los Angeles. Few of them had ever seen a vegetable garden; none of them had ever had any contact with an acre garden plot, such as one finds on Midwestern farms, or with many of the other objects mentioned that had to do particularly with farm life in the Midwest. The "new" words in the story were: *garden, plant, earth, vegetables,* and *row.*

As the children read, they had a great deal of difficulty. They hesitated and repeated, and stumbled and stopped—not because of pronunciation difficulties but because of confusion resulting from faulty or inadequate concepts. A checkup revealed the following disparities in interpretation: A *garden* to these children meant a small round space in the backyard in which pansies and forget-me-nots were blooming. *Plant,* which was used in the story as a verb, to these children meant the philodendron that grew in a container placed on a table in the living room. *Earth* to them meant the place on which we live, rather than the soil in which the garden seed had been planted according to the story. *Vegetables* to them meant several grown edibles such as corn, peas, oranges, carrots, figs, avocadoes, and so on. They had not yet arrived at generalizations to guide them in distinguishing between vegetables and fruit.

The word *row,* which was used in the context as "a row in the cornfield," was a universal source of difficulty. It was found that all the children could pronounce this word, but as with the other words, they were confused about meaning. The school was near a small lake. Nearly all the pupils had gone for a row with their parents in a rowboat on this lake. When they read about "a row in the cornfield," they thought they must have made a mistake, and at this point the reading process really broke down.

This example illustrates a very important consideration, namely: words have different meanings in terms of the experience of the author, in terms of the experience of the reader, and in terms of the contextual setting in which they are found. Teachers have a tremendous task in attempting to bridge the gap among these important factors. They not only need to bridge the gap between author and reader, they also need to provide new experiences where concepts are lacking and to help children generalize and classify ideas gathered from both old and new experiences. In these ways, they can assist their pupils to form flexible, versatile, usable concepts, that will enable pupils to see through the crystal-clear substance of experiences to the full meaning behind reading symbols.

Improving Reading through Concept Building

Although children will build their own concepts ultimately, we agree with Vygotsky[1] that wise assistance and some guidance from adults—teachers—is valuable and often necessary. Teachers can help pupils improve in their ability to interpret what they read through concept building.

First-Hand Experience. The semanticists tell us with repeated emphasis that "the word is not the thing," that at best the word is simply an abstract symbol that stands for experience. This being the case, one of the most basic functions of teachers is to ensure experiences for pupils that will equip them to interpret symbols, which in turn stand for these experiences. The example about farm life in the Midwest is a case in point. How much clearer the concepts would have been if the children had first-hand experience!

Relating to Personal Experience. When class experiences are not feasible, the practice of having a discussion recalling and relating personal experiences has proved beneficial. One third-grade class read a poem in which the poet spoke of "the melancholy sky." Different children were asked to express their opinions as to the meaning of the word "melancholy." One or two were able to define the word acceptably. They and several of the other children were asked to recall and relate instances in which they had felt "melancholy." By guided discussion, the teacher then brought out the point that the sky, of course, could not feel "melancholy," but that it had the effect of making people who looked at it feel "melancholy"; that it was a dark, gray, somber sky that caused one to feel sad, rather than a light, bright, sunny sky that had the effect of making people feel glad and happy.

Models and Construction Projects. Reading content is so broad in scope that it is not possible, of course, to give children first-hand contacts with all the things that they will read about. However, models and construction projects serve very well in building accurate concepts. A modern child reading a story about medieval life in Europe might not

[1] Lev S. Vygotsky, *Thought and Language* (Cambridge, Mass.: M.I.T. Press, 1962).

have the slightest idea of the meaning of *moat, drawbridge, parapet,* and so on. Constructing a representation of an ancient castle and its surroundings under the skillful guidance of a teacher who is "concept conscious" would substitute for a first-hand experience in a very realistic way. The use of models and construction projects is all to the good in concept building.

Dramatization. An effective but simple medium to use in developing concepts of new words is that of dramatization. For example, the children in one classroom were reading a story that contained the sentence, "The pool was surrounded by tall grass." Questions revealed that some children were confused about the meaning of "surrounded." The teacher clarified their concept by having a group of children "surround" one of the tables in the classroom. Such an informal performance requires no preparation and very little time. This technique should be used more often.

Exhibits. Using an exhibit of objects pertaining to some new topic in a book serves a useful purpose in concept building. In one classroom, the children were about to read a series of stories with settings in jungles. Preceding the reading of the stories, they talked about jungle life, and each pupil was asked to bring in something that might have come from a jungle. A table, set aside for the purpose, was soon covered with such articles as coconuts, bananas, Brazil nuts, palm leaf fans, a reptile-skin bag, and pictures galore. Discussions of these objects as they affected or contributed to the lives of the people provided these children with many meaningful concepts to bring to their reading of jungle stories. Even the simplest exhibits are valuable in building concepts.

Chalkboard Sketches. Chalkboard sketches require no material other than chalk and chalkboard, and the teacher doesn't necessarily have to be an artist in order to draw a simple sketch or diagram that will help children to understand the meaning of a word or phrase. Some third-grade children were reading a selection on astronomy, in which the constellation commonly known as "The Big Dipper" was featured prominently. Because the utensil known as a "dipper" passed away with the pump and water bucket, very few children today know what a "dipper" is. In this case, the teacher drew a picture of a dipper on the chalkboard and explained its use and then drew a representation of the constellation, placing the stars appropriately, and called to the children's attention the similarity in the shape of the constellation to that of a "dipper."

Pictures. Undoubtedly, teachers could make much greater use of still pictures in building concepts than is usually done. One illustration is given to show the usefulness of still pictures in reading interpretation.

A fifth-grade class in California was about to read a story that had as its underlying theme the conservation of wild flowers. The "Spring

Beauty" was the particular wild flower that was dealt with throughout the story, yet at no time was it called a flower. Spring Beauty grows profusely in the Middle West and East, but it does not grow in California. The children in California, who were not acquainted with this particular flower, might have deduced an abstract meaning from the phrase "Spring Beauty," interpreting it as "the beauty of the season of spring" or "the beauty of spring water bubbling from the ground." Their wise teacher, anticipating this possible mental confusion, procured several colored pictures of Spring Beauties, which she showed preceding the reading of the story. The children then had a clear mental concept of "Spring Beauty" as it was used in this story, and their interpretation of the entire selection benefited accordingly.

More abundant use should be made of the excellent illustrations that are provided in modern textbooks. Careful study and discussion of these illustrations yield rich returns in concept building. In addition to pictures in texts, every teacher should have a collection of pictures, adding to it continuously and drawing from it whenever concept building can be served.

Audio-Visual Aids. Those who have the facilities and budget for showing moving pictures and television tapes are fortunate, indeed, in having such strong allies to assist in concept building. Consider how much more meaningful an informative selection on the bulb industry in Holland could be to children if the reading of this selection were preceded or accompanied by a moving picture showing all the steps involved, from planting the bulbs to harvesting and shipping them. For those experiences that cannot be provided first hand because of remoteness in distance or time, instructional films, television, slides, and filmstrips can be extremely useful. Guidance and discussion are still necessary, of course, and for concept-building purposes great care must be taken to choose films that convey accurate information on a suitable grade level.

Context. Giving more attention to contextual influences is a *must* in concept building in reading. Words have the chameleon-like property of changing their color according to the other words that surround them in context. Consider the word *people,* for instance. If *people* were written on the chalkboard by itself and children were asked to tell its meaning, the response might be "just a lot of folks." The word would be abstract—not colored with any particular meaning. But if the teacher should write on the chalkboard a sentence containing *people,* then this word would immediately take on meaning from its neighboring words. Suppose the sentence were, "The old people of the tribe, in rags and tatters, bent and emaciated, followed in the rear." This entire group of words, in which the one word *people* is embedded, makes the word itself immediately bristle with lively meaning and become a vivid and picturable concept.

As word relationships and their influences upon interpretation in reading are brought more sharply to the attention of teachers, they rightly will devote larger portions of their pupils' reading time to the study of context upon word meanings. Some of them will also come to realize more fully why modern methodology points a finger of disapproval at the once very prevalent practice of starting each reading lesson by having the children pronounce a list of new words that had been written on the chalkboard, or by having them say words in isolation as these words were flashed before them one by one on cards.

Abstract Meanings. When pupils first meet most words in text, the word usually represents a fairly concrete meaning and one that has probably been encountered before in oral language. As the reading material moves further away from experience, many of the techniques suggested above can be used to bring author and reader together. The more difficult phase of concept building, however, has to do with the abstract meanings of words, far removed from the very concrete meanings children probably met in their first encounters with such words in print.

As an example, consider the word *capital*. Children may have their first experience with this word while playing with ABC blocks when someone calls attention to "capital H" on one side of the block and "small h" on the other side. They soon learn the difference between "capital" and "small" letters, and in this sense *capital* has a concrete meaning. A little later in life, children may take a trip to the capital of the state. Here, the youngsters see a building with a large round dome and many steps leading up to it, and are told that it is the capitol building where the law-making bodies sit while discussing the affairs of state. After this, when children read that a certain city is the *capital* of the state, they have a fairly concrete idea of the meaning of the sentence. When passing a local bank, at another stage in life, children may read on the window, "Capital $2,900,000." Now *capital* is associated with a bank and money.

In all of the cases above, *capital* was tied to a concrete object—a letter, a city, a bank and money. Although pupils may need some additional help in getting the meaning of capital city or the capital in a bank, they are usually not puzzled or confused when these terms are encountered in print. But they do start to have problems in more advanced reading when *capital* is used in describing more generalized and abstract nouns, as "a capital error," "capital goods," "capital punishment." The most remote level of abstraction is reached when pupils meet the word as part of a term that represents an idea embracing a vast expanse of territory, that is, "capital and labor." The shift to this highly generalized use of the word *capital* is quite a long stride to take. If left alone to struggle with the interpretation of this meaning of *capital*, unaided by mental interaction and clarifying discussion, pupils may leave the reading with only a vague or partial understanding of the meanings involved; or their understanding may be definitely erroneous; or it may be highly colored by emotive language with which the word was surrounded. Yet the word used in this sense has much to do with the structure, thought, and feeling of American society, and as such deserves careful study and interpretation.

The teacher needs to cultivate a keen awareness of different levels of abstraction and be ever on the alert for shifts from one level to another as children meet such words in their reading. The class should be invited as a whole to study such a word and to tell what it means to them in terms of their individual experience. Out of all their experiences and their combined mental reactions, they should then attempt to construct a common meaning for the word in the particular situation that is acceptable to everyone in the group.

**WORDS
ARE LIKE
CHAMELEONS**

"Words are like chameleons. They change their color—their shade, too—to harmonize with their surroundings." [2] Most words are polysemantic, although some seem to take on many more meanings than others. These changes in relation to context become more numerous as pupils move beyond the first two grades and meet more materials in specific content areas. (See pages 297–300 in chapter 10.) The *denotation* of a word is supposed to be its exact or literal meaning, and the *connotation* is supposed to be something beyond the literal. Such labels for words, however, are inadequate and inaccurate for individuals and groups of individuals, particularly as they digest increasing amounts of words. The labels are inaccurate even if *denotative* is thought to mean the most common or concrete meaning. Even the word *mother* brings varied meanings to the minds of different readers—even at different times. Hence, most of the time words cannot be considered in isolation; their meanings are linked to their contextual environments.

As an example, consider the word *note:* In a selection about music, the word *note* would probably mean an elliptical character placed in a certain position on the staff. If the context referred to *note* in connection with a business transaction or mathematics, it might mean "a written promise to pay." If *note* were encountered in text having to do with English, it might mean an informal communication; or on the other hand, if it appeared in social studies, it might mean a formal communiqué between the heads of two nations. In the directions for an experiment in science, readers might be told to carry out certain directions and then to *note* results, meaning to observe; in a selection in literature, they might read about a character who was of great *note* in her community.

So many words in the English language have multiple meanings that children are sometimes confused and unable to make the transition from one meaning to another. A mother tells of such an incident that led to a very erroneous interpretation. She told her young son, Martin, a story

---

[2] The heading of this section and the first two sentences are from Ellen L. Thomas and H. Alan Robinson, *Improving Reading in Every Class: A Sourcebook for Teachers,* 2nd ed. (Boston: Allyn and Bacon, 1977), p. 37.

about the Garden of Eden, after which she explained that he might draw a picture of the story if he liked. Martin proudly showed the resulting picture with lush flowers and trees, a man and a woman, and a box-like object in one corner of the sheet of paper. "What is that?" asked the mother. "It's the car" replied Martin. "I didn't say anything about a car when I told the story," remarked the puzzled mother. "Well, you said God drove them out of the garden." The only meaning of *drove* that he knew was the one associated with manipulating an automobile while in motion. *Drove* in this sense is, of course, derived from *drive,* meaning to "impel forward," but Martin had not made that generalization yet. He would probably have been quite nonplussed upon hearing someone talk about a farmer who "drove his cattle to pasture," or a rancher who had "a drove of cattle."

The various functions that one word may perform in speech is another aspect of multiple meanings and one in need of special attention. We encounter *sound* as a noun, the subject of a sentence in the statement, "The sound of thunder was not pleasant to Esther." It has a different meaning when it is used as a verb in, "Sound the chimes, Bill." And still a different meaning when used as a modifier in "Uncle Fred was sound asleep."

One of the authors of this book was in a classroom one day when the teacher wrote on the chalkboard a sentence from a selection the children had read, telling them to draw a picture of the sentence. The sentence was, "The great golden sun rose high above the mountains." Seven of fifteen children drew a picture of high mountains, a blazing yellow sun, and a red rose. They knew the meaning of *rose* in its noun function, but they did not recognize it in its verb sense. Because of this, they misinterpreted the meaning of the sentence.

In promoting reading interpretation, teachers should help children in sensing different meanings according to the functions of the word, and assist them in becoming aware of any differences in pronunciation or spelling that may accompany these changing functions. In dealing with multiple meanings in reading, it is advisable for the teacher to check frequently upon the new use of a word and explain its meaning, guiding children to make the transition from one meaning to another. The goal should be to help each child build up a constellation of multiple meanings for words so that he or she can pull out any one meaning in bold relief whenever it is needed in interpreting a particular context.

FIGURATIVE LANGUAGE

Figurative language surrounds children. It appears in a thousand subtle forms in nearly every moment of verbal communication. Every hearing child has heard uncountable figurative expressions and understands, at least at some level, most of them. Figurative language is prominent in the dialects as well as the idioms of mainstream language. It characterizes the greater part of most slang expression.[3]

[3] Thomas N. Turner, "Figurative Language: Deceitful Mirage or Sparkling Oasis for Reading?" *Language Arts* 53, no. 7 (October 1976): 758.

Yet it seems generally recognized that children have difficulty reading (comprehending) figurative expressions. According to Turner, there seem to be three reasons for this: (1) Children are pushed to think at abstract and complex levels. (2) Children often do not have the necessary background experience to bring to the abstractions represented in the figurative language. (3) The kinds of figurative language used in the reading materials are usually not those encountered in oral communication.[4]

Here are a few samples taken from a beginning second-grade reader: "The little house sitting high up on the hill was shining like a new penny." How could a house shine like a new penny, children might wonder. "They found little Sally curled up in a ball." One of the authors of this volume asked some children what this sentence in the reader meant. They thought it meant that Sally was curled up inside of a big ball. They did not understand that she was curled up in the shape of a ball. "Tom found a brown flint arrowhead in a cup of sand." Several children thought that the arrowhead was found in a tea cup filled with sand. They did not understand that the "cup of sand" was a small depression in the soil. Many similes and many examples of metaphorical language can be found in books for elementary children even very early in the primary grades. The frequency of such comparisons increases and becomes more abstract, of course, as children read books at successively higher levels. Teachers do not know how much such comparisons mean to children unless they ask them. Children's answers usually are quite convincing for the need for giving special attention to passages of this type.

CHANGES IN WORD STRUCTURE

The increasing need for giving more attention to the analysis of word elements in interpreting meanings is important. In our frantic search for words to express new meanings in this rapidly changing world, and in our haste to say everything in the quickest possible way, we are adding suffixes and prefixes to thousands of words that heretofore have not been so modified. If we are feeling low we seek a *pepper-upper* in the way of an *enriched* food that might contain *flavoprotein*. In the laundry, we use a *wonder-working soapless* powder to *activate* the water, which in turn has a *super-wetting* effect on our *washables*. In years past, we might have said "I am going to take a tonic to pep me up," or "I am going to use some Scrub-Clean soap in washing my soiled clothes." But now verbs and adverbs become nouns, nouns become verbs and adjectives—all with the aid of prefixes and suffixes.

If you want convincing evidence of the prevalence of modified words in modern reading text, try the experiment of counting the number of variant forms in a paragraph or two of reading matter in a current newspaper, magazine, or novel.

Here is an example from a newspaper:

[4] Ibid., pp. 758–59.

American military personnel were *restricted today* to stay *within* the Saigon city *limits. Military officials also urged* the *soldiers* to travel with *companions whenever* possible.

The *action followed official confirmation* by the *military advisory* group that a *26-year-old American* army *specialist* was *missing.*

In these short paragraphs, there are twenty-four words that have been changed in some way from their root form, and nineteen that remain unchanged. More than half the words in the paragraph have been modified.

The example is typical of the large proportion of words that are being modified in modern text by adding different beginnings and endings.

Another manifestation of this same trend is seen in the rapidly increasing use of hyphenated and compounded words. If you should doubt the prevalence of such words in recent writing, just choose any selection in a current newspaper or magazine and count the number of words of this type. If you start with a page of fiction, you may read about a *streamlined* bit of femininity with an *upswept hair-do*, wearing an *eye-catching, waist-hugging* gown of *sharkskin* with a *pencil-slim* skirt and a *figure-flattering* bodice.

If news items are selected, you may find that "*Freeholders* voted this *afternoon* to guarantee $15,000,000 in *short-term* notes to establish a *wholesale* food center in the *Meadowlands*"; or that "Losses stemming from the *nationwide* steel strike *sky-rocketed into* billions as the labor dispute hit the *100-day* mark"; or that "There was an *all-out* drive to subdue the reign of terror *shake-up.*"

Turning to advertisements, you may read such highly compressed statements as "*wet-weather raincoats* that can be *home-dried* or *dry-cleaned*"; or a "jacket for young *on-the-go* life from morning till *date-time, zephyr-light, sheer-wool, high-lighted* with satin trim"; or "*anti-gray-hair* vitamins," a "*magno-low writing-ring* and *ruby-red* setting," a "*performance-engineered* radio," and a "*medically-proven* cough syrup"—all of which can be procured in a local *budget-tailored* store.

This extraordinary trend toward increased use of variant forms is not limited to reading materials in life; school texts also are moving in this direction. Geographies, history books, and science texts are all using modified forms more freely.

Because textbooks include large numbers of modified words, and because variant forms are not always included in the vocabulary lists of basic readers after they have once been introduced, it is desirable for the teacher to look ahead in any material that the children are about to read to see if there are words in modified forms that may give trouble. If so, he or she may then plan to clarify the changed meaning of these words (and pronunciation also, if necessary) through discussion or chalkboard explanation.

Compound Words

Children rarely have difficulty with compound words when each part retains its own meaning or stays close to it. But they can have problems when both parts do not add up to the literal meaning anticipated. This may sometimes be true of hyphenated words as well. For instance, in the examples above, *streamlined* could be difficult, but most children probably have the meaning stored in their heads from oral communication. *Upswept hair-do* might present some difficulties, although experience might carry the reader through; *upswept* can be explained rather literally but *hair-do* could be a problem if not in the child's experiential background. Certainly, most young readers would have difficulty with *sharkskin*, *freeholders*, and possibly *wholesale*.

Prefixes, Suffixes, and Roots

Teaching prefixes and suffixes (affixes) and roots in isolation or in some list is unwise, unprofitable, and boring. Help pupils learn to use word parts by making them conscious of their constant appearance in the material they are reading. As Dale and O'Rourke pointed out, we want pupils to generalize through their own discovery ". . . that *tele* means distant or far away, as in *television, telemeter, telephone, telegraph,* and *telepathy.*" They believe that instruction begins with familiar words that are broken up into meaningful parts, and then the meanings of the parts can be transferred to new words. They suggested, in addition to the pupils generalizing from their own words, that teachers group known words together and help pupils infer meanings from them (automobile, autobiography, automatic) to more difficult words in contextual settings (automation, autonomy, autopsy). Dale and O'Rourke indicated that "our aim is to move by easy steps from some knowledge (automobile) to increased knowledge (autonomous). It is not to move from zero knowledge to increased knowledge." [5]

Dale and O'Rourke included detailed lists of prefixes, suffixes, and roots on pages 326–60 in the appendix of their fine volume devoted to the teaching of vocabulary.

The crossword puzzle exercise below is an example of an activity that can be used with prefixes, suffixes, or roots. In this case, the focus is on prefixes. The four prefixes used were first taught separately with groups of known words taken from material being read by a fourth-grade group.

SYNONYMS AND ANTONYMS

Synonyms

Synonyms may be single words or short phrases that are substituted for a variety of related words expressing similar meanings. The word

---

[5] Edgar Dale and Joseph O'Rourke, *Techniques of Teaching Vocabulary* (Palo Alto, Calif.: Field Educational Publications, 1971), p. 116.

un: not   *re:* back, again

in: not, into   *dis:* not, apart from

Write ACROSS words in the spaces going across and DOWN words in the spaces going down. The number tells the number of the space where you should start writing.

ACROSS

1. To form again
4. Not aided
5. Not even
6. Not covered
8. Not able
9. Not used
10. Not liked
12. Lack of order
15. Not safe
16. Not hidden
17. Build again

DOWN

2. To view again
3. To read again
4. Not usual
5. Not arched
7. Not to agree
10. Not honest
11. Not jointed
13. Not to favor
14. Into the land

[6] From BE A BETTER READER, Level A, Basic Skills Edition, by Nila Banton Smith, © 1977, 1968 by Prentice-Hall, Inc. Reprinted by permission.

similar is important because few related words have identical meanings. Because writers usually choose the appropriate word for a given context, readers need to learn how to interpret the shades of meaning. For example, common usage permits us to say, "She gets *little* exercise," but we would not say, "She gets *small* exercise."

Pupils can be helped to extend word meanings as they meet interesting words in their reading materials, but they should also be involved in direct instruction. Dale and O'Rourke suggested an exercise that calls for pupils to substitute one noun for another. A portion of that exercise follows [7]:

1. Another name for *basement* is c_____.
2. Another name for *rug* is c_____.

     [7] Dale and O'Rourke, *Techniques*, p. 218.

3. You can turn on a *light* or a l_____.
4. You can turn off a *spigot* or a f_____.
5. Carpenters often use *brads* or small n_____.
6. Another word for *belly* is a_____.
7. Another word for *leg* is l_____.
8. *Adders* and *asps* are also called s_____.

A discussion should always follow such an exercise—not to correct the papers but to consider the reasoning processes and the possibilities of synonyms other than those normally anticipated: *cellar, carpet, lamp, faucet, nails, abdomen, limb, snakes.* Here is an opportunity to discuss the varied nature of synonyms: "*Lamp* is really an example of *light. Limb* is the larger category under which *leg* fits. The same synonym could be used for *arm.*"

Antonyms

As with synonyms, antonyms are rarely exact opposites. We can only classify them in terms of general meanings. On the other hand, learning opposites or antonyms helps pupils ". . . to think in terms of contrasting or contradictory concepts and statements." [8] When possible, pupils should be helped to learn antonyms as well as synonyms for new words they meet. And, as with synonyms, incidental exposure is not enough; pupils should be presented with many varied examples and exercises. The best exercises use context and give the pupils an opportunity to sort out synonyms from antonyms as they complete each item. Discussions similar to those mentioned for synonyms should follow exercises.

The portion of an exercise dealing with antonyms below was recommended by Dale and O'Rourke.[9] Pupils are to read each sentence and underline the word in parenthesis that *cannot* complete the sentence correctly.

1. A *huge* bear is a (big, tiny, large) animal.
2. *Heat* is related to (flame, blaze, frost).
3. The windows were *damp* because of the (humid, moist, dry) weather.
4. The slight surface of the rock was almost as *smooth* as (glass, burlap, silk).

WORD ORIGINS

Children can be "turned on" about studying word origins. Excitement about words can claim the attention of all kinds of children from varied backgrounds. Much depends upon the contagious enthusiasm of the teacher as well as the way the study of word history is undertaken. It

[8] Ibid., p. 56.
[9] Ibid., p. 59.

is valuable because it helps pupils become more word conscious and is an additional way of extending word knowledge.

Cook [10] spoke of how the enthusiasm he developed for studying word origins transferred to a class of fourth-grade "underachieving," "reluctant," male readers. The pupils became "active participants in their learning" through collecting and buying books, reading to one another, asking questions, and plastering the room with posters related to changes in word meanings. Other classes from fourth grade up shared the enthusiasm with the exception of a few pupils.

In a mimeographed supplement to his article, Cook demonstrated the areas touched upon by these children; examples follow.[11]

Words That Changed With Time

Word	Current Meaning	Past Meaning	Classification
nice	pleasant	ignorant	ameliorated
propaganda	to mislead	to inform	pejorated
shipped	to move by air, land, or sea	to move by sea	generalized
rumor	news without proof	a great uproar	specialized

Slang

Expression	Meaning
cooking on the front burner (1943)	doing extremely well
Jackson (1940)	all around popular boy

Names That Have Become Words

Word	Origin
shrapnel	From Henry Shrapnel, an army officer, who invented a shell that exploded into small fragments in the air.
maverick	From Samuel Maverick, a Texas rancher, who refused to brand his cattle.

Idioms

Idiom	Origin
Charley horse	A lame horse named Charley, used to drag a roller around the baseball field in Chicago. As a result, a muscle injury to athletes became known as a Charley horse.
ham	Actors used fat from the upper part of a pig's hind leg to remove heavy makeup. As a result, actors are called hams.

Acronyms

Acronym	Meaning
POGO	Polar Orbiting Geophysical Laboratory
RADAR	Radio Detecting and Ranging

Blendwords

[10] Jimmie E. Cook, "Teacher Survival Kit: The Dictionary," *Language Arts* 53, no. 7 (October 1976): 755–57.

[11] Parts of a mimeographed outline prepared by Cook and reprinted with his permission.

Word	*Origin*
smog	smoke and fog
motel	motor and hotel

Additional ways of working with word origins are suggested in the Eisiminger article and the Dale and O'Rourke book listed in the bibliography for this chapter.

New Words

One other point related to word origins should be mentioned—that is, the need that some people are feeling for new words. There are those who are urging that it would be better to coin some words for new concepts rather than trying to fit our new concepts into old words that have had a long history of established meanings.

Some new words are emerging, particularly in the scientific fields of medicine, chemistry, computers, and to some extent in the fields of industry. Examples of such words that have come into wide usage are *penicillin, barbiturates, electronics, telegenic, astronaut, launching pad*.

Many words originate because of the popularity of events, books, movies, and television shows and are used widely for a time. For example, the term *a Jaws Alert* is used at beach resorts when sharks are sighted close to land; obviously the term was derived from the popular book and movie, *Jaws*.

It seems to be in the field of social studies that new words are most needed for new concepts or vice versa. Some people are saying that the new patterns of world crisis require new forms of expression, new words, if misunderstanding is to be eliminated. For example, consider the word *Americanism*: many verbal and even legal battles have been fought over this word, yet who can define this term definitely and specifically? Webster states that *Americanism* is "loyal attachment to the United States, its traditions, interests, and its ideals." Here, we are confounded with abstract words, each of which is subject to wide variation in interpretation: loyal *attachment, traditions, ideals*. Each of us brings to bear upon such words concepts arising from our own personal experience, and while we have a hazy impression of what each of these words means to us personally, we would have difficulty in stating it concretely.

Perhaps some of the children with whom we are working in the schools today, if encouraged, will make contributions by inventing new words and new definitions that will help to clarify and unify thinking and promote international understanding.

CRITICAL THINKING AND VOCABULARY

As part of the major effort that should take place in every classroom—nurturing critical reading—attention should be paid to (1) the power of words used to persuade and/or control our emotional and intellectual reactions, and (2) sexist terminology. Through discussion, inspection of written text, and exercises, teachers should develop a consciousness of how the choice of certain words may cause us to think in certain ways. Pupils should be helped to think about vocabulary critically.

The Power of Words

In advertising and political campaigning as well as in other more subtle ways, writers of material for all communication media carefully choose words that have the chance of persuading people to buy their wares. Writers who want to sway opinion in a given direction choose words that they know have certain meanings for the particular audience they want to attract. For example, *egghead* may present a positive stereotype for some people and a negative one for others.

Pupils should be on the lookout for words used as stereotypes and words used in an effort to control thought. Debates and discussions in class will make pupils more conscious of such usage. Thomas and Robinson created an exercise called " 'Good Guys' or 'Bad Guys'?" for use in high-school classrooms. We have adapted it for upper-intermediate and middle-school use.[12]

GOOD GUYS OR BAD GUYS?

"Good guy" words are often used to persuade you to support a particular person or a cause. "Bad guy" words are often used to turn you away from a particular person or cause.

Which of the words below do you think are *good guys* and which are *bad guys*? Make two columns on your paper and head the first one GOOD GUYS and the second one BAD GUYS. Place each word in one column or the other. When you're done, we'll discuss the possible answers in class. Be ready to support your choice.

step-mother	police officer
100% American	Black
egghead	square
father	Women's Lib
patriot	capitalist
dictator	peace
terrorist	war

Sexist Terminology

Consciousness of "male" and "female" terminology in the materials children read should be developed right from the beginning of school. For those stories written years ago but handed down through the generations, children should be made aware of and give thought to why the world seemed to be seen through the eyes of men only. But new ma-

[12] Thomas and Robinson, *Improving Reading*, p. 78.

terials should be evaluated for their freedom from sexist terms and thought. Pupils should be on the lookout for sexism, and classroom discussions should focus on sexist terminology and stereotyping. We should not have to accept the rationale that "he" is used as part of our language but it really means *he and she*.

When pupils do find sexist terminology, it is fun and important to change the words to include both sexes. Children will enjoy the ludicrous notion of changing *manhole* to *peoplehole*, but at the same time will be made conscious of the male-oriented terms used so widely in our society. See chapter 5, pages 114–15, for the guidelines recommended by the Committee on Sexism and Reading of the International Reading Association.

PERSON-ALIZED WORD COL-LECTIONS

In addition to incidental learning and direct teaching of vocabulary, pupils should be encouraged to collect words on their own. Early development of a method for collecting words, with support from the teacher, often succeeds in establishing a lifelong interest in words.

Thomas and Robinson [13] recommended a way of developing personalized word collections. Words and pertinent information about them can be put on individual slips of paper or cards (uniform in size) and filed alphabetically in a small manila envelope. Each child has her or his own collection and adds to it from material read, television, classroom discussion, and so on. A line may be added to the Vocabulary Slip giving the pronunciation of the word if the teacher or pupils desire. Pupils should be cautioned to collect only those words they think they will want to use or words that seem particularly important to remember. The teacher can help develop a "feel" for which words to retain if pupils are uncertain at first.

Pupils can play solitaire at times to see if they are remembering the words. They can choose partners and help each other with the words. They can separate words into those they know well and those that need further work. As they study they should (1) read the word and the

---

VOCABULARY SLIP

Word _____ *lee* _____

Sentence where found *The wind was so terrible that we stayed on the lee side of the house.*

Specific Meaning *sheltered from the wind; part way from the wind.*

Your example sentence *The lee side of a ship is sheltered from the wind.*

---

[13] Ibid., pp. 63–67.

meaning; (2) say the word, even in a whisper; (3) write the word and even create another sentence that puts the word to good use.

GUIDING PRINCIPLES

The following principles [14] can be helpful in guiding and extending vocabulary development in every elementary and middle-school classroom.

---

1. Children learn to read and write familiar words best—those that have already found a place in their listening and speaking vocabularies. If an unfamiliar word, important to the learners, is found in a reading assignment or independent reading situation, carry it to the oral level for development.

2. Children whose dialects diverge from standard regional English need the patient assistance of the teacher in learning certain words that have different meanings in their dialects. Learning alternate meanings enriches the learners' repertoires, but retention of those meanings will not occur overnight.

3. "Consciousness-raising" is particularly important in extending knowledge of word meanings. When young learners become aware of their needs to improve their vocabularies, they will be on the lookout for interesting and necessary words.

4. Provisions should be made, through school activities and parental encouragement, to give children a multitude of direct and indirect experiences that can add new words to their word banks and give "old" words new meanings. Such experiences can be stimulated and extended by specific classroom activities: involving children in simulation situations; carefully planned trips; television programs chosen with particular goals in mind; films and filmstrips viewed for given purposes; classroom experiments in science; viewing and analyzing models, pictures, and objects pertinent to subsequent units of work. (See chapter 4 for additional readiness activities.)

5. Wide reading permits children to meet many words for the first time but also serves to reinforce learning. Children suddenly find, as you, the reader, know from your own experience, that words you "never saw before" suddenly appear regularly in your reading once you become aware of their existence and their meanings.

6. Although incidental vocabulary development through wide reading is desirable and valuable, it must be accompanied by direct vocabulary instruction. Such planned instruction should be interwoven with lessons dealing with all facets of the curriculum.

[14] These principles are based on principles and other information suggested by: Helen M. Robinson, pp. 171–75, in *Reading and the Language Arts*, ed. H. Alan Robinson, Supplementary Educational Monograph No. 93, (Chicago: University of Chicago Press, December 1963); E. Brooks Smith, Kenneth S. Goodman, and Robert Meredith, *Language and Thinking in School*, 2nd ed. (New York: Holt, Rinehart and Winston, 1976), pp. 46–64; Thomas and Robinson, *Improving Reading*, pp. 13–14.

Isolated drills on lists of vocabulary words is of limited or no value for most learners.

7. If some words, phrases, or clauses are introduced to pupils before reading a particular selection (see chapter 4, pages 81–82), this introduction should not be considered or treated as a vocabulary lesson. Words, when introduced directly prior to reading, should be limited in number and discussed briefly as an aid to the reader for the reading of that given selection. Direct vocabulary instruction may follow but not immediately precede the reading of a selection.

8. Words that children are asked to study should come from the context of materials they are reading or they should be words the children bring up and want to know more about. Words that are relevant and pertinent have the best chance for retention, further recognition, and further use.

9. Context clues, discussed in the previous chapter and also in this one, are major aids for self-help in vocabulary development. Pupils ". . . . should become aware that words shift and change meaning and that the context of the moment determines the meaning of the moment." [15]

10. Pupils should become familiar, in contextual settings, with prefixes, suffixes, and roots that they can use to unlock the meanings of many words. These affixes and roots should not be taught through lists but as children gather a number of words containing the specific affix or root. Even as they become familiar with the meanings of a number of frequently used roots and affixes, they should always be tested out in conjunction with context clues.

11. Pupils should become independent dictionary users. In order to make the best use of dictionaries, most pupils need direct and sufficient guidance in all the dictionary skills. (See chapter 6, pages 173–75, and chapter 10, pages 278–82.)

12. As pupils proceed beyond the primary grades, vocabulary development for many individual pupils becomes a slow process—at least in relation to comprehension growth when measured on standardized tests. Time is needed to make the words their own. Time should be planned to have pupils review their personal banks of words and tie down those that remain hazy.

13. Teachers can help the acquisition of new vocabulary and new meanings of known words by using those words periodically in discussion. In addition, natural insertions of those words in materials they are reading will help children reinforce their recognition and meanings.

14. Encouragement of writing tasks using newly acquired words or word meanings is also a reinforcement technique that helps to cement the words for many pupils.

15. Teachers must be careful of overdosing with vocabulary games. A game here or there for motivation purposes will not harm anyone if attention is not placed on competition. On the

[15] Thomas and Robinson, *Improving Reading*, p. 13.

other hand, too many children tend to want to win the game and end up without mastery of the words that were emphasized.

DISCUSSION QUESTIONS AND ACTIVITIES

1. Ask pupils about some "common expressions" used in the world about them. You may find that they have not built up adequate concepts to fill in the words with appropriate meanings. For example: "launch a campaign," "hold up your end of the argument," "I pledge allegiance," "dish it out." Think about the words being used in the materials you are using and discuss some of those with pupils before asking them to "read and understand."

2. Extend pupils' knowledge of given words by investigating other meanings in other contexts. Select them from the materials the pupils will read and/or discuss in a given content-area unit. Prepare exercises to reinforce this knowledge. The exercise below can serve as a model.

Words Having More Than One Meaning [16]

Sometimes words which we use every day have entirely different meanings when used in science, geography, history, music, or mathematics. You will find some words of this type below.

| check | mouth | cape | bed | yard |
| bark | school | pole | bank | scale |

Read the definitions for number 1. Choose a word from the list that goes with these definitions. On your paper, write the word next to number 1. Do the rest of the page in the same way.

1. _____ Common use: The opening in our head through which we take food.

    In geography: The place where a river empties into a large body of water.

2. _____ Common use: A written order to a bank to pay money to someone.

    In mathematics: to test the answers to problems to make sure they are right.

3. _____ Common use: A tall, slender piece of wood to which telephone wires are attached.

    In geography: The point farthest north or farthest south on the earth.

4. _____ Common use: A piece of furniture on which to sleep.

    In geography: The bottom of a river.

[16] From BE A BETTER READER, Level A, Basic Skills Edition, by Nila Banton Smith, © 1977, 1968 by Prentice-Hall, Inc. Reprinted by permission.

5. _____ Common use: The short, sharp noise made by dogs.

In science: The outer covering of a tree.

6. _____ Common use: A small space in front of or in back of a house or other building.

In mathematics: A measure of length.

7. _____ Common use: A sleeveless garment worn around the shoulders.

In geography: A point of land extending into the water.

8. _____ Common use: A place where money is deposited.

In geography: Land along the edge of a river.

9. _____ Common use: A place of learning.

In science: A large number of fish traveling in a group.

10. _____ In science: A small, flat, hard plate forming part of the covering of fishes and reptiles.

Common use: A weighing machine.

3. Rauch, Clements, and Weinstein's *The World of Vocabulary Series* [17] is an example of the wise use of related vocabulary words reinforced in a variety of contexts. The material is suitable for the intermediate and middle-school grades. Each vocabulary unit deals with words highlighted in an interesting context and then has pupils use them in a variety of exercises culminating with a closure procedure. The exercise below is an example.[18]

Here are the ten vocabulary words for this lesson:

lunar	rover	craters	range	gravity
superstitions	data	creatures	diameter	astronauts

There are five blank spaces in the story below. Five vocabulary words have already been used in the story. They are underlined. Use the other five words to fill in the blank spaces.

Do you remember the name of the first man to walk on the moon? It was Neil Armstrong. He proved that many beliefs about the moon were _____, not facts. For example, he didn't find any strange moon creatures. He was very careful when he walked on the moon. Because of less _____, he didn't want to bounce up, lose his balance, and fall.

The Apollo 17 astronauts took a special moon car with them. It was called the lunar _____. It helped the astronauts to gather samples of lunar rock and soil.

We now have much data about the moon. For instance, we know it has many _____. These may range from a few feet to as large as 600 miles in _____.

[17] Sidney J. Rauch, Zacharie J. Clements, and Alfred B. Weinstein, *The World of Vocabulary Series* (New York: Globe Book Co., 1974–78).

[18] Rauch et al., *World of Vocabulary*, Book 1, p. 54.

Books and Pamphlets

BRIGHAM, BRUCE W., and JOHNSON, MARJORIE S., eds. *Reading in Modern Communication*. Proceedings of the Nineteenth Annual Reading Institute, vol. 1. Philadelphia: Temple University, 1962.

DALE, EDGAR. *The Word Game: Improving Communications*. Bloomington, Ind.: Phi Delta Kappa Educational Foundation, 1975.

——, and O'ROURKE, JOSEPH. *Techniques of Teaching Vocabulary*. Palo Alto, Calif.: Field Educational Publications, 1971.

DEIGHTON, LEE C. *Vocabulary Development in the Classroom*. New York: Teachers College Press, Columbia University, 1959.

GOODMAN, KENNETH S. "Behind the Eye: What Happens in Reading." In *Reading Process and Program*, edited by Kenneth S. Goodman and Olive S. Niles. Champaign, Ill.: National Council of Teachers of English, 1970.

HAYAKAWA, S. I. *Language in Thought and Action*. 3rd ed. New York: Harcourt Brace Jovanovich, 1972.

PETTY, WALTER T.; HEROLD, CURTIS P.; and STOLL, EARLINE. *The State of Knowledge about the Teaching of Vocabulary*. Champaign, Ill.: National Council of Teachers of English, 1968.

ROBINSON, H. ALAN, ed. *Reading and the Language Arts*. Supplementary Educational Monograph No. 93. Chicago: University of Chicago Press, December 1963.

Periodicals

AMSTER, HARRIETT. "Concept Formation in Children." *Elementary English* 42, no. 5 (May 1965), pp. 543–52.

COOK, JIMMIE E. "Teacher Survival Kit: The Dictionary." *Language Arts* 53, no. 7 (October 1976), pp. 755–57.

EISIMINGER, STERLING. "Using Name Origins in the Elementary Classroom." *Language Arts* 53, no. 7 (October 1976), p. 753.

FILLMER, H. THOMPSON. "A Generative Vocabulary Program for Grades 4–6." *Elementary School Journal* 78, no. 1 (September 1977), pp. 53–58.

LORENZ, ESTELLE K. "Excuse Me, But Your Idiom is Showing." *Reading Teacher* 31, no. 1 (October 1977), pp. 24–27.

TURNER, THOMAS N. "Figurative Language. Deceitful Mirage of Sparkling Oasis for Reading." *Language Arts* 53, no. 7 (October 1976), p. 758.

chapter 8

nurturing
reading
comprehension

What to Expect in This Chapter:
This chapter focuses on three aspects of comprehension: (1) the building of basic strategies for improving interactions between reader and author; (2) the large growth areas in comprehension; and (3) the roles of purposes and questions in nurturing comprehension. After discussing specific ways of developing comprehension strategies, four comprehension growth areas are described and explained: literal comprehension, interpretation, critical reading, and application of what is read. Techniques for working with pupils on strategies and in each growth area are suggested.

In the last section of the chapter, purposes and questions are discussed side by side because they are so interrelated and so central to developing comprehension. Cautions about the overuse and inappropriate use of questions are offered along with a variety of valid reading purposes.

Among the goals to meet the needs of our world today, perhaps none is more important than to improve literacy. One of the most urgent literacy needs of young people at present is that of learning to read in greater depth. One of the most urgent needs of teachers is that of recognizing in depth reading processes, and providing for their development. Because of this need for deeper reading in the present critical world situation and because of the shallow reading habits of many of our students, we should be deeply concerned about teaching children in school to read for greater depth. Knowing how to pronounce words or even knowing the meanings of individual words is not sufficient. To illustrate this point, an amusing example is given below.

Here is Lincoln's *Gettysburg Address* as read by a fifth grader adept at word identification and knowledgeable about certain meanings of words. The interpolations in parentheses express the thoughts that passed through the boy's mind as he perused this piece of literature.

Fourscore (a score is what we have after a baseball game is played) and seven years ago our fathers (this must mean the fathers of all the kids) brought forth on this continent (that's North America; we had that in social studies) a new nation (that's America or United States, I think), conceived (I wonder what that means) in liberty (that's what a sailor gets), and dedicated (that's what they did to the building on the corner) to the proposition (that's what they voted on to give the teachers more money) that all men (what about the women?) are created (we had something about that at Sunday School) equal (we use that in arithmetic problems). Now we are engaged (Marge is engaged to Bill and they're going to get married soon) in a great civil (civilians are people who aren't soldiers or sailors) war, testing (they say that when they try the microphone) whether that nation (I wonder which one this is), or any nation (I guess it doesn't matter which one) so conceived and so dedicated, can long endure (that's what the dentist said I'd have to do when he fixed my tooth). We are met (by whom?) on a great battlefield of that war. We have come to dedicate a portion (that's the amount of food I get for supper) of that field (like where we play games when we go home) as a final resting place (that's where we stop to rest when we go hiking) for those who here gave their lives that that nation might live (people live, but I didn't know that nations lived). It is altogether (everybody says it at once) fitting and proper (right) that we should do this (what?). But, in a large sense, we cannot dedicate—we cannot consecrate—(that means to think a lot about something) we cannot hallow—(nothing in the middle) this ground. The brave men, living and dead, who struggled here, have consecrated it far above (that means over the top of something) our poor (without money) power (electricity) to add (2 plus 2) or detract. The world will little note (on the staff in music) nor long remember what we say here, but it can never forget what they did here. It is for us, the living, rather, to be dedicated here to the unfinished work which they who fought here have thus far so nobly advanced (they got some money in advance). It is rather for us to be here dedicated to the great task remaining before us —that from these honored dead we take increased (that's what the cleaner did to dad's pants) devotion (part of a church service) to that cause for which they gave their last full measure (a ruler or part of music) of devotion; that we here highly resolve (to work a problem again) that these dead shall not have died in vain (a blood vessel); that this nation under God, shall have a new birth (a baby is born) of freedom (prisoners get that when they come out of prison), and that government of the people, by the people, for the people shall not perish (a district of the church) from the earth (the world or soil)

COMPRE-HENSION STRATEGIES

Reading comprehension means the understanding, evaluating, and utilizing of information and ideas gained through an interaction between reader and author. As Frank Smith has said, it is ". . . relating what we attend to in the world around us—the visual information of print in the case of reading—to what we already have in our heads."[1]

In order to comprehend reading materials successfully, most readers need help

1. To develop strategies for sampling and selecting graphic, syntactic, and semantic cues;

[1] Frank Smith, *Understanding Reading,* 2nd ed. (New York: Holt, Rinehart and Winston, 1978), p. 56.

2. To develop prediction strategies to anticipate meaning, syntactic patterns, and graphic features not yet seen;

3. To develop confirmation strategies to check predictions against subsequent cues;

4. To develop correction strategies when miscues occur which interfere with comprehension;

5. To develop flexible strategies for dealing with a wide variety of materials:
   a. Literature
   b. Nonfiction
   c. Instructions and directions
   d. Content area material
   e. Other materials

6. To develop critical strategies for judging validity of information in reading;

7. To develop flexibility in use of the reading process for different purposes:
   a. Pleasure
   b. Quick review
   c. Specific information seeking
   d. Other purposes.[2]

A Model

From the time pupils enter school and embark on learning how to read, emphasis should be placed on interacting with authors—always in search of meaning. Pupils should be helped to strengthen the knowledge and competence they already have in using language. Such instruction will stress the learners' integration of semantic, syntactic, and phono-

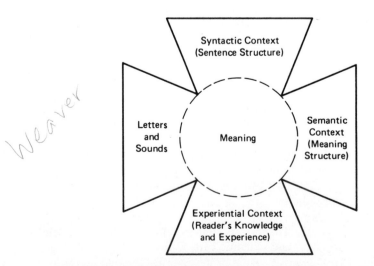

[2] E. Brooks Smith, Kenneth S. Goodman, and Robert Meredith, *Language and Thinking in School*, 2nd ed. (New York: Holt, Rinehart and Winston, 1976), p. 286.

graphological cues with their knowledge and' experience as they seek the authors' messages. The diagram on page 206 is a representation of such a model conceived by Weaver.[3]

> According to this model, meaning is the starting point of the reading process as well as its end-product; learning to read involves learning to bring meaning to the written page as well as learning to actively seek meaning from the written page. Instead of learning skills for proceeding from small units to larger or for dealing with words as if they occurred in isolation, children learn strategies for predicting what will come next, then testing and confirming or correcting their predictions.[4]

General Principles

These principles, among others, can guide growth in basic strategies.

1. Encourage risk-taking as pupils work at understanding messages, both through oral and written language. Let pupils know that it is better to try to communicate and understand the communications of others, and make errors, than not to try at all.

2. Give positive feedback when pupils make responses, even though some responses may be incorrect as you see them. Help the pupils learn to correct themselves.

3. Learn as much as you can about the cultural patterns of the group or groups in your classroom. You will better understand the contributions pupils can make as well as the misunderstandings they may have when trying to process material quite distant from their backgrounds.

4. Try to learn as much as you can about each individual in order to understand responses and behaviors. Each individual brings a different set of knowledges and experiences to the speaking, listening, viewing, reading, and writing situation.

5. Note differences in the speech patterns of each youngster and realize that this pattern will be brought to the speaking and reading situation. Pupils need time, without pressure, to add new patterns to their repertoires. Emphasis on accuracy of pronunciation in standard English may put a damper on the communication process.

6. Try to provide materials for discussion, both print and nonprint, which are interesting to pupils, and/or relevant and significant to them, and/or relevant to immediate school and societal needs.

7. Place emphasis on purposeful communication activity, particularly in reading. De-emphasize group oral reading as a drill activity, especially in round-robin fashion.

8. Encourage pupils to make use of all aspects of language as well as

---

[3] Constance Weaver, "Using Context: Before or After?" *Language Arts* 54, no. 8 (November/December 1977): 883. Copyright 1977 by the National Council of Teachers of English. Reprinted by permission.

[4] Ibid.

their own knowledge and experience when they meet a word, concept, or construction they are uncertain about. Have them look at context first before trying to analyze the word or words. Applaud reinspection of context both to the left of the unknown element as well as to the right. Purposeful regressions used to confirm meaning are positive, not negative, activities.

9. As long as pupils are understanding the authors' messages, do not direct them to correct mispronunciations (in terms of standard English) or substitutions. Place the emphasis on a meaningful interaction with the authors!

10. Provide a variety of the kinds of activities that follow so pupils receive conscious guidance in developing their basic strategies.

Activities for Developing Basic Strategies

The descriptions and examples of activities that follow may be used as both evaluative and instructional tools. In chapter 3, the topic of classroom evaluation of reading abilities was explored and some of the same types of techniques were cited. Evaluation and instruction are separated only for the sake of the teacher who must have some way of viewing each aspect of reading as a discipline; in practice, evaluation and instruction are inseparably tied together.

Closure Procedures. Closure procedures are prepared by deleting individual words or portions of words, phrases, or clauses from passages and then having pupils attempt to replace the words that have been deleted. The *cloze procedure*, originated by Taylor,[5] is the most commonly used. (See page 59 in chapter 3.)

In our opinion, although the evidence is by no means conclusive,[6] closure procedures are extremely valuable as instructional devices for helping pupils develop their strategies in processing written language. They are not the definitive ways of improving overall comprehension (what is?), but they appear to build strength in diminishing the distance between reader and writer. In all probability, although the use of closure activities may strengthen ability to "make connections" among ideas, success in filling in deletions does not always result in acquisition of the authors' main ideas. Closure activities should be thought of, essentially, as means of helping pupils strengthen their abilities to utilize syntactic and semantic cues in written language. (Note: A number of sources use the term *cloze procedure* to refer to all types of closure. We reserve the term for Taylor's specific use of closure.)

[5] Wilson L. Taylor, "Cloze Procedure: A New Tool for Measuring Readability," *Journalism Quarterly* 30, no. 4 (Fall 1953): 415–33.

[6] Eugene Jongsma, *The Cloze Procedure as a Teaching Technique* (Newark, Del.: International Reading Assn., 1971).

1. Introductory closure activities, especially for primary pupils.
Blachowicz indicated that most of the professional literature related to
the use of closure procedures and older readers, and that ". . . even the
most well intentioned teacher may wilt under the deluge of tears and
confusion when first and second graders attempt to deal with their first
cloze exercise." [7] She suggested a sequence of activities cited below with
minor adaptation. [8]

> *Oral.* Begin with oral closure by deleting selected content words
> (nouns, verbs, adjectives) from a high interest selection. One popular
> book that can be used is *Alexander and the Terrible, Horrible, No Good,
> Very Bad Day* (Viorst, 1972). [9] Because it is humorous and close to a
> young child's experience, it provides many passages such as the follow-
> ing which draw the children into supplying missing words. As the teacher
> reads aloud, s/he will substitute a pause for each of the words in brack-
> ets.

>> I went to sleep with gum in my [mouth] and now there's gum in my
>> [hair] and when I got out of [bed] this morning I tripped on the [skate-
>> board] and by mistake I dropped my [sweater] in the sink while the
>> [water] was running and I could tell it was going to be a terrible, horrible,
>> no good, very [bad] day.

> As the story is read by the teacher, the children supply possibilities
> for the words omitted. Student enthusiasm for the story makes the "con-
> tribution rate" high and provides many alternatives for discussion.
> The basic objective, introducing the students to the process of
> generating predictions, has been met while building enthusiasm for
> further prediction activities. More oral cloze, following a one-in-five or
> one-in-ten deletion pattern, can follow at a later time.

> *Zip.* One problem young readers frequently have when confronted
> with cloze exercises is a total loss of context some place in the passage.
> The "zip" procedure (so named by a second grade class with an innate
> sense of onomatopoeia) supplies constant feedback to the young reader
> while introducing the student to the first prediction task with a written
> stimulus.

> The story to be used can be in ordinary book or wall chart format,
> but the most effective technique involves putting the story or passage
> on an overhead projection transparency. Masking tape is used to block
> out the words which have been chosen for deletion. The children first
> skim for gist, then supply the masked words one at a time. As each pos-
> sibility is predicted and discussed, the tape is pulled (or "zipped") so
> that the readers receive immediate feedback from the text as well as be-
> ing given more of the context from which to make further predictions.

> Following a group introduction, the transparency can be used again
> with different words taped over. Children also enjoy preparing the taped
> selections for others and can follow a scheme given by the teacher to

[7] Camille L. Z. Blachowicz, "Cloze Activities for Primary Readers," *Reading
Teacher* 31, no. 3 (December 1977): 300.

[8] Ibid., pp. 300–302. Reprinted with permission of the author and the International Reading Association.

[9] Judith Viorst, *Alexander and the Terrible, Horrible, No Good, Very Bad Day*
(Hartford, Conn.: Aladdin Books, 1972).

increase their own awareness of certain word classes ("Tape over the nouns") or sentence elements ("Tape the verbs").

Maze. The vocabulary control that characterizes much primary material often produces reading material in which the content line is too meager to provide much of a context. The maze procedure (Guthrie and others, 1974) [10] can be used in such situations and provides a simple format for an individual cloze assignment.

In the chosen passage, words are not deleted. Rather, two distractors are supplied for each chosen item, providing a limited and manageable choice format for the young student. The first exercises should provide clear, unambiguous choices. For example:

The boy on the hill lived in a yellow
{ house.
  cat.
  umbrella.

The house had seven
{ stars.
  rooms.
  very.

Later, after the children are comfortable with the procedure, more sophisticated exercises can be structured to draw attention to specific word classes, pronominal reference, graphophonic features, and so on. This example focuses on a graphophonic distinction as well as that of form class:

The boy lived in the yellow
{ horse.
  house.
  harsh.

Using such "warm up" methods as [those] outlined above will provide practice in the prediction/confirmation processes so essential to fluent reading without overburdening or discouraging the young reader. They also provide a pleasurable framework for introducing the standard cloze procedure which can be used so effectively in the middle and upper grades.

Gove [11] reported introducing beginning readers to closure procedures by first deleting lexical items from experience stories. Pupils supplied "new" nouns and verbs for "old" ones. Passages were also taken from stories and articles. The passages were less than seventy-five words in length, and there were usually less than seven (and never more than

[10] John T. Guthrie and others, "The Maze Technique to Assess, Monitor Reading Comprehension," *Reading Teacher* 28, no. 2 (November 1974): 161–68.

[11] Mary K. Gove, "Using the Cloze Procedure in a First Grade Classroom," *Reading Teacher* 29, no. 1 (October 1975): 36–38.

fourteen) deletions. Three types of deletion systems were used: (1) every *n*th noun or verb (usually every third or fifth and no auxiliary verbs); (2) every *n*th word in systematic order (as each third or fifth regardless of type of word); and (3) portions of the words (deletion of all but initial graphemes, or terminal graphemes, or all vowels).

At the beginning of the year, the cloze passages were read to small groups of students by the teacher. Once the students were able to read the passages by themselves, they were given a short period of time to determine responses for each cloze blank. Near the beginning of the year this was done by encouraging them to "think to themselves" words they thought would be appropriate in the blanks. As their ability to write increased, they were given some time to jot down their ideas. Then, responses for each blank were discussed and the students were asked to verbalize reasons for responses. The teacher led these discussions by asking such questions as: "Why did you choose this word?"; "What word or groups of words indicate to you 'building' should be placed in the blank?"; "How does your word contribute to the meaning of the passage?"; "When your word is in the sentence, what does the sentence (or passage) mean?"; "How does your word contribute to the meaning in a different way?"; "When your word is in the sentence, does the sentence (or passage) have a different meaning?" Thus, the teacher led the students to understanding the process involved in selecting appropriate words for the blanks.

From these questions it is obvious that any response that was an exact replication of the deleted word, a synonym of the exact word, or formed correct language in the passage was considered as to its possibilities for contributing meaning to the passage. (However, when the deletion system was that of deleting portions of words, the students were almost always able to respond with an exact replication of the deleted word.) In this way, during these discussions of the process of choosing the "best" responses for the cloze blanks, the students were concerned with the meaning or the content of the passage.

Each group of children was involved in this type of discussion at least three times a week for a period of five to ten minutes. Each of the types of deletion systems was used approximately one-third of the time.

Teachers of beginning reading can easily incorporate the cloze procedure into ongoing programs. This is one means of focusing the beginning readers' attention on important aspects of reading that are often overlooked in beginning reading programs—the use of syntactic and semantic information to comprehend print.[12]

2. *Closure activities, especially for pupils beyond the primary grades.* Bortnick and Lopardo, who have pioneered in the use of closure procedures for instructional purposes in the upper grades, suggested using the conventional (every fifth word deleted) cloze procedure in this way:

As a group activity, or on a one-to-one basis or small group activity, the teacher instructs students to read silently an entire cloze passage

[12] Ibid., p. 38. Reprinted with permission of the author and the International Reading Association.

which has been specifically prepared for them. Reading the cloze passage in its entirety will help the students to make maximum use of redundant information and contextual cues *throughout* the passage when they later attempt to fill in the cloze blanks.

After the cloze passage has been silently read, it can be read aloud, sentence by sentence, either by the teacher or a student. Students can then suggest words which might fit into the blanks. All semantically and syntactically acceptable responses are taken but students are asked to offer reasons for their choices. Offering the reason is one of the most important aspects of the instruction since it encourages an understanding of the structure of the language and provides the teacher with a considerable amount of information on the instructional needs of students. For example, the student who replaces a noun in a verb slot or a present tense verb in a past tense verb slot is in need of particular type of instruction. Through examination of student responses, the teacher becomes sensitized to students' peculiar instructional needs.

Through discussion and direct instruction, the teacher helps the students decide on acceptable responses and to eliminate unacceptable ones. It is not necessary to discuss every item in a passage. The teacher may pick certain deletions for discussion which suit the purposes of the lesson and students.

The cloze passage with possible correct responses is then compared with the original, unmutilated passage. In this comparison, discussion and teacher guidance will focus on whether meaning is affected by the acceptance of certain responses. For example, it can be pointed out that the insertion of the word *automobile* for *car* does little or nothing to change the meaning of a passage. On the other hand, the substitution of the noun *bike* for *book*, although syntactically acceptable, most probably would affect the meaning of the passage. In using the cloze procedure to teach context, the teacher repeatedly points out the cues which immediately surround the blank as well as cues which may appear at the beginning, middle, or end of the passage.

Other kinds of information can be pointed out in the comparison of the cloze and original passages, depending upon the purpose of the instruction.

Certain words (noun, adjective markers) in the immediate environment of the deletion cue the reader.

The position of words in a sentence gives certain cues: a deletion that is the first or last word in a sentence limits the possibilities of choice.

The redundancy of language within the passage cues the reader: often a deletion at the beginning of the passage is clarified by later redundant information in the passage.

The teacher should lead students to understand that activities utilizing cloze passages involve strategies that will be of value to them in their independent reading. Reading strategies (such as those described above) need to be carefully delineated for students. Moreover, students will need many opportunities to apply and practice these strategies. Simply having students complete cloze passages does not teach the strategy but gives practice in what has already been taught.

After the comparison and discussion of the cloze and original passages, students can independently follow the same procedures on a different passage. Passages of different levels and length can be prepared to meet the reading needs of a wide range of students.

After the teacher sets the purpose for the particular cloze passage, the activity can be summarized in terms of directions to the students as follows.

Read through the entire cloze passage silently.

Reread the cloze passage, writing in words you think fit the blanks. If you can, try to offer your reasons for your choices for these blanks: (teacher selects certain items). "It sounds right" is a good reason in many cases.

Compare your choices with the original passage.

Be prepared to discuss both passages.[13]

Robert Pehrsson, Director of Language and Reading at the Lexington School for the Deaf in New York City, has devised a closure procedure (Op-In) in which clauses are omitted from every other sentence in a passage. He reports that he is able to help youngsters come closer to the authors' messages as they carefully think through their responses, which are focused on larger chunks of language than in typical closure procedures. In this procedure, all parts of the sentence are deleted following the complete subject. In the following example the portions that would be deleted are in italics.

Some animals use their teeth for protection. Dogs and wolves *have long, sharp teeth with which to defend themselves.* Rats, woodchucks, mink, and weasels also have sharp teeth. These animals *use teeth in attacking other animals.* The teeth of some animals have developed into large tusks. Elephants and boars *have tusks.* The tusks of an elephant or of a wild boar are greatly feared by their enemies.[14]

3. Closure activities, especially for pupils with demonstrated needs. Y. Goodman and Greene used a closure procedure in one of their "strategy lessons" for pupils who exhibited difficulty with such words as *as though,* *even though,* and *although.* The context of the material was familiar to the reader.

Use sentences like the following, including blanks where the target structures occur.

[13] Robert Bortnick and Genevieve S. Lopardo, "An Instructional Application of the Cloze Procedure," *Journal of Reading* 16, no. 4 (January 1973): 297–99. Reprinted with permission of the authors and the International Reading Association.

[14] Nila Banton Smith, *Be a Better Reader,* Level A, Basic Skills Edition (Prentice-Hall, Inc., 1977), p. 41. Reprinted by permission.

EXAMPLE:

Pat's mother said that milk was good for her and she should drink it _____ Pat does not like milk.

Tom played ball very well today _____ he isn't usually a good ball player.

Explore with the students what words or phrases can go into the blanks and the degree to which different choices change the meaning of the sentences. Point out to the students that they must read beyond the blank to the end of the sentence in order to decide which words or phrases are most appropriate.[15]

Lopardo suggested using a "language experience/cloze procedure technique" to focus on a specific need of a "disabled reader." [16]

Let us say that a teacher knows from testing that a child is in need of learning to recognize structural words such as *for, in, before, with,* and *by.* Such words are high frequency words which the reader needs to recognize instantly, since they appear in most material. Moreover, they are likely to be used by the child in dictating language samples, since such high frequency words give structure to the language. A cloze passage derived from the child's language sample is prepared; the selected structural words are deleted. The child is asked to fill in the missing words. He is told that the words are from his word bank (Stauffer, 1970),[17] that is, they are words, in his language-experience stories. After the child completes the passage, he compares his completed cloze passage with his original language sample. A discussion always follows the completion of the cloze passage. Discussions may center around (a) how the words function in our language; (b) visual aspects of words, along with their function, that might help in recognition; (c) "wrong" insertions and how meaning is affected; or (d) how these words were used in other language samples or in published materials. Only the particular goal of the cloze passage is discussed; in the preceding example, only structural words would be discussed.

Retrospection Procedures. When pupils are asked to think about their own reading strategies and the reasons for their successes and failures in coping with a particular passage, they are using retrospection—looking back at what they did and examining their own mental processes.

[15] Yetta Goodman and Jennifer Greene, "Grammar and Reading in the Classroom," in *Linguistic Theory: What Can It Say About Reading?* ed. Roger W. Shuy (Newark, Del.: International Reading Assn., 1977), p. 29.

[16] Genevieve S. Lopardo, "LEA—Cloze Reading Material for the Disabled Reader," *Reading Teacher* 29, no. 1 (October 1975): 43–44.

[17] Russell G. Stauffer, *The Language-Experience Approach to the Teaching of Reading* (New York: Harper and Row, 1970).

A number of investigators [18] have demonstrated the effectiveness of retrospection and introspection in learning about the reading strengths and weaknesses of pupils.

We feel that retrospection is a useful technique to develop. We realize that there is always the danger of the pupil not being able to verbalize or verbalizing what is thought to be expected, but we feel the value is worth the risk. Furthermore, the more experience pupils obtain in using the technique, with continuous positive reinforcement from the teacher, the more adept and honest they become.

There appears to be much merit in "consciousnessraising"—having the pupil become aware of strategies employed and not employed, of strategies employed well and not so well. Retrospection is urged as a vital part of the instructional sequence in using the closure procedures described earlier. It may also be used in other ways.

1. Miscus analysis (pages 60–62), described as an evaluative technique in chapter 3, may be used instructionally. Have a pupil read a short passage orally and record the miscues. Show the passage to the pupil again, after the initial reading, and point out a few of the miscues—one at a time. Ask the pupil why he or she thinks they were made. Guide the pupil in developing better strategies. An alternative is to record the reading on tape. Play the recording as the pupil looks at the passage again. Have the pupil spot miscues and attempt to give reasons for them.

2. Present pupils with a specific learning task involving reading. After they are finished, give them a duplicated answer sheet to check against their own answers. Allow time for them to think through the similarities and differences. (You might even have an intentional incorrect response and/or a response to a question which could be answered in several ways.) Now have them discuss the answers and challenge or defend. Get them thinking about *why* they responded in certain ways. Help them, over time, to generalize strategies for tackling certain types of problems.

3. Have pupils predict, either orally or in writing, (a) the next step in a sequence they have read; (b) the next event in a series of events they have read; or (c) the ending of a short story they have read or had read to them. Discuss the predictions and why they were made. Emphasize the fact that there is no right or wrong answer and do not supply one. Stress must be placed on the reasoning of the children. They are, of course, free to revise and question their own responses. Once pupils have established a good feeling about working together on predictions—without deprecating one another—then the teacher might introduce the next step or conclusion as written by the author. Now they must think

---

[18] These investigations have focused on the use of introspective-retrospective techniques among elementary and middle school pupils: Ahmed A. Fareed, "Interpretive Responses in Reading History and Biology: An Exploratory Study," *Reading Research Quarterly* 6, no. 4 (Summer 1971): 493–534; H. Alan Robinson, "Reading Skills Employed in Solving Social Studies Problems," *Reading Teacher* 18, no. 4 (January 1965): 263–69; Nathaniel Shapiro, "Critical Reading of a Short Story: An Introspective Study" (Doctoral dissertation, Hofstra University, 1974).

through the author's reasoning process and compare to their own. Again, right or wrong is not the issue!

Comprehension needs differ in terms of the goals of an individual, the nature of the reading material, and the purposes for reading. In order to be able to contend with the various types of comprehension needed across a school curriculum, pupils must be helped to develop and expand in four growth areas—literal comprehension, interpretation, critical reading, and application of what is read. Each is discussed separately in this chapter only so we may better understand the nature of each. Although, in some sources, a hierarchy is claimed and similarly stated growth areas are called "levels," there is no such intent here. Granted, frequently one must obtain literal meaning prior to interpreting, but such is not always the case. And, most often, the literal meaning and interpretation are so intertwined and almost simultaneous during the reading act that there is no need to be concerned about where one ends and the other begins. In addition, some people view evaluation (critical reading) and application of what is read as separate from comprehension—another step. And they may be right. On the other hand, the teacher concerned with comprehension must be responsible for development of those growth levels; hence, the four areas are considered here.

Literal Comprehension

Literal comprehension is getting the primary, direct, literal meaning of an idea in context. There is no depth in this kind of reading. It is the lowest rung in the meaning-getting ladder, yet it is the one on which teachers of the past have given the most practice, and on which many still are devoting the preponderance of their comprehension efforts. Teachers give practice in literal comprehension when they ask, "With what was Johnny playing?" and pupils answer, "With his red fire engine." These are the exact words given in the book; giving this answer requires no thinking. Such a question simply demands pupils to recall from memory what the book says, simply asks them to repeat parrot-like the words that are in the book.

Throughout the elementary grades and even in high school, practice in literal comprehension dominates practice on the meaning-getting skills because the following techniques are so widely used: (1) fact questions based directly on the text; (2) true-false statements; (3) completion sentences; (4) multiple-choice exercises. These objective techniques used in standardized tests, informal tests, discussions, and assignments give practice on literal comprehension, but they do little or nothing to develop the ability to use the thinking skills in obtaining deeper meanings.

Consider the paragraph below as the opening paragraph in a story:

The sun had sunk in the West. It was growing dusky. The car was filled with shadows.

If a reader did nothing more than to comprehend this paragraph *literally,* he or she would simply gather the "face" meaning from each sentence. In reading the first sentence, the pupil would understand that the sun had gone down in the West. If the meaning of *dusky* were understood, the import that would be gathered from the second sentence would be that it was growing sort of dark; and the child would understand from the third sentence that there were some shadows in the car. So far, the reader has been picking up apparent, surface meanings only; he or she has been engaging in "literal comprehension." But suppose that as a result of reading all these sentences the child gathers the impression that *night was falling;* then interpretation has taken place; the pupil has used the interpretation process in gleaning meaning not stated directly in the paragraph. The author did not say "night was falling" in so many words, but all the sentences combined were intended to create atmosphere, to convey the feeling of approaching nightfall.

In the example above, literal comprehension played a role in fully understanding the paragraph. The reader had to make a "cognitive leap" in order to interpret the overall meaning. Literal comprehension may be both, at different times and dependent upon purpose, a prerequisite to and a concomitant of higher-level thinking ability. Although the teacher will want to beware of overemphasis on literal comprehension, pupils do need to develop ability to respond to what they read with literal answers when reading purpose dictates such response.

A variety of literal comprehension responses may be called for in connection with the same selection. Samples of various types of responses used in connection with four different selections are presented below. In all cases, the answers were given directly in the text on which the activities were based.

1. Responses asked for in connection with a story in which two children visited a jungle country with their mother and father were:
   a. List the main characters in this story. You may use your book.
   b. Write the names of four foods that grew in the clearing.
   c. Write a sentence telling how far the talking drums could be heard.
   d. Copy the sentence that tells how tall the pygmies were.
   e. Complete the following:
      The monkey played two very funny tricks. She _____ to the top of the window blind and sat there chattering as though she were at home in the _____. Later she opened Mother's box of _____ and dropped a great deal on the floor.
2. Requested responses in regard to the experiences of a boy and his mother in Switzerland were:
   a. _____ and _____ were spending the summer in Switzerland.
   b. Write a sentence telling the names of the sounds they heard one night.

    c. Write on a paper summer, autumn, winter, spring. Under the name of each season, write some kinds of work done by Swiss farmers during that particular season.

    d. Write five ways in which electricity helps the Swiss people.

3. A series of factual questions based on specific sentences were asked in connection with a selection concerning Leif the Lucky:

    Find a sentence in the story that best answers each of these questions. Prepare to read each answer to the class.

    a. Where did Leif live?

    b. What did King Olaf ask Leif to tell the people of Greenland?

    c. Why did Leif call the country Vinland?

    d. Why didn't Leif go back to Vinland?

4. Practice in literal comprehension was given in connection with a selection dealing with dinosaurs through drawing activities as suggested below.

    a. Draw the dinosaur described in the story. Write a number above the dinosaur showing how many feet long it was.

    b. Draw four other animals that lived at the same time that the dinosaur lived.

Questions of this type require only slight mental activity on the part of the teacher and little or no thinking on the part of the pupils. Their responses undoubtedly give children practice in recalling and reproducing statements or facts and have a place in detailed factual reading. It is doubtful, on the other hand, whether this form of questioning helps children develop the ability to glean the types of meanings from reading that they need to enrich their lives to the fullest extent.

Interpretation

In literal comprehension, readers attempt to understand the words the author has written on the page as exactly as possible—in light of their experiential backgrounds. In interpretation readers "read between the lines," make connections among individual stated ideas, make inferences, draw conclusions, or experience emotional reactions. The readers probe for greater depth than in literal comprehension. They are concerned with supplying meanings not directly stated in the text.

In a third-grade classroom recently, such a discussion took place. The children had read a story about Fred. Here is the synopsis:

A boy named Fred visited his Uncle Bill, a sheepherder who lived in a covered wagon in the foothills. Two horses were eating grass beside the wagon. During the first few days of his visit, Fred was concerned with his uncle's shepherd dogs, who stayed out with the sheep at night, even in bad weather. One night, Uncle Bill took Fred out to the herd while a storm was raging. He called the dogs. They appeared from the midst of the herd of sheep, but they "did not want to leave their woolly hiding place." Fred said, "All right. I won't worry about them anymore."

The children and the teacher, Ms. Wolfe, discussed the story as they went along and also after they had finished. Everyone entered into the plot with interest and enthusiasm and relived the experiences of the characters. As all of this was taking place, the teacher kept uppermost in her mind the importance of stimulating children's thinking in working with meanings derived from their reading. Now and then, at appropriate times, she asked questions to which there were no answers directly in the text—questions that called for *thinking*, not just for a regurgitation of statements in the story.

"You have just read that Uncle Fred *lived* in his sheep wagon. What do you think the inside of the sheep wagon was like? Can you picture it in your mind and describe it?" (Reasoning about details not given.)

The children reasoned he must have had: a stove, probably fueled by wood that he picked up; cupboards; dishes; at least two bunks for beds; table and chairs.

"Of what use were the two horses eating grass beside the wagon?" (Inference.)

Answers volunteered were: "Uncle Fred needed them when he wanted to go to town and get groceries." "He used them to move his wagon when he had to take his sheep to a fresh pasture."

"Why do you suppose one of the dogs was called Taffy?" (Cause and effect.)

None of the children ever had seen warm taffy pulled or noted its golden-brown color when it is in this elastic state. The colors they associated with taffy were greens, blues, pinks, and yellows, which they found in the salt-water-taffy boxes that their parents had brought from the seaside. The children lacked the experience necessary for this concept; therefore, the teacher told them about taffy in its natural state and compared its color with Tom's sweater and Jan's hair. The children then easily decided why one of the dogs was called Taffy.

"Can you think of anything interesting that Fred might have done between the time that he arrived and the night of the storm?" (Supplying happenings between incidents.)

The leading character became a living boy, having real experiences, as the children speculated upon things that he might have done during the gap between events in the story: "Probably he went for a ride on one of his Uncle's horses." "Maybe he caught a rabbit to take home for a pet." "He might have met a bear and the dogs chased the bear away and rescued him."

"Compare the way that Fred felt at the beginning with the way he felt at the end of the story. Why did he change?" (Comparison, cause and effect.)

At no point in the story does the author tell how Fred felt, nor is there any statement in regard to why he changed. The children, however, were able to find telltale words and phrases that indicated how worried Fred was all through the early part of the story, and other words and phrases that revealed his satisfaction and peace of mind toward the end of the story. It simply required one major decision on their part to uncover the cause of this change in the boy—the dogs were happy out with the sheep.

"In what part of the country do you think this story took place?" (Generalization.)

The children examined the pictures, gathered bits of information here and there throughout the text, and after putting all these together decided that the story took place in the Rocky Mountains.

Some teachers appear to have the notion that poor readers or "slow learners" should not be asked to interpret; their responses should be limited to literal comprehension. Such a philosophy is not only dangerous to the development of thinking citizens, but the reasoning is fallacious. All individuals interpret, dependent upon the tasks, their backgrounds, their interests, their readiness, and the guidance given by others. All pupils should be helped to interpret ideas relevant and meaningful to them.

Critical Reading

In 1962, Ennis listed twelve aspects of critical thinking (defined in his terms as "the correct assessing of statements") that appear to have been applied to the reading processes over the years by a number of reading authorities.

1. Grasping the meaning of a statement.
2. Judging whether there is ambiguity in a line of reasoning.
3. Judging whether certain statements contradict each other.
4. Judging whether a conclusion follows necessarily.
5. Judging whether a statement is specific enough.
6. Judging whether a statement is actually the application of a certain principle.
7. Judging whether an observation statement is reliable.
8. Judging whether an inductive conclusion is warranted.
9. Judging whether the problem has been identified.
10. Judging whether something is an assumption.

11. Judging whether a definition is adequate.
12. Judging whether a statement made by an alleged authority is acceptable.[19]

For his own reasons, Ennis omitted "the judging of value statements," which is almost always included when critical reading is mentioned. Critical reading appears to be the use of critical thinking during and following reading.

Notice that as aspect number one Ennis listed "grasping the meaning of a statement," which we would consider to be a combination of literal and interpretive reading. Hence, literal and interpretive reading appear to be an essential foundation for, or prerequisite of, the other aspects of critical reading.

Critical reading demands that the reader evaluate and pass personal judgment on the quality, value, accuracy, and/or truthfulness of what is read. It ". . . requires the reader to develop a set of standards or criteria on which to base evaluation. It involves the withholding of judgment, the sorting of argument, the weighing of evidence, and the ability to be flexible."[20] The list of questions below should help teachers begin to guide learners in the development of criteria on which to base their critical reading.

1. Do students note the publication date and realize its importance in relation to events and attitudes of the writers?
2. Do they attempt to appraise the qualifications of the writers when feasible?
3. Do they ask, "What evidence supports this statement? Is it opinion? Are the writers trying to pass on opinion as fact?"
4. Do students ask, "Are the writer's implications reasonable in light of evidence presented? Are the writer's conclusions based on the information developed and supported within the piece of writing?"
5. Do students suspend judgment? Do they resist the impulse to accept the first plausible solution to a problem, holding on to that information, but waiting for other possible solutions?
6. Do they read widely and deeply, looking for and welcoming different points of view? Do they understand how to proceed when the viewpoints of authorities and/or researchers are in conflict?
7. Are students able to recognize writing designed to persuade—a conscious attempt on the part of a writer to get the reader to believe an idea, accept a fact, or buy a product?[21]

Critical thinking and critical reading can be cultivated in very young children. For example, Jean and other first graders were reading in

[19] Robert H. Ennis, "A Concept of *Critical Thinking*," *Harvard Educational Review* 32, no. 1 (Winter 1962): 157–87.
[20] H. Alan Robinson, *Teaching Reading and Study Strategies: the Content Areas*, 2nd ed. (Boston: Allyn and Bacon, 1978), p. 126.
[21] Ibid., pp. 126–27.

a preprimer. On the page, there was a picture of two chairs, backs toward each other and a space in between. A newspaper was spread over the tops of the two chairs to make a roof for a playhouse. A kitten was playing on top of the newspaper. Jean said, "There is something wrong here. A kitten couldn't stand on top of those papers. The papers would fall through with it." This was critical thinking at the preprimer level. It was the critical reading of a picture, to be sure, but the same mental process was used as would have been used had Jean passed judgment upon the content of printed text. Jean was praised for noting the flaw in the makeup of the picture.

Andres was reading in a second-grade arithmetic book which had been written several years ago. He read a problem that said, "Mary went to the store to buy two quarts of milk. If she paid 12 cents a quart, how much did the milk cost?" Andres said, "There is something wrong here. I went to the grocery store this morning and bought some milk for my mother, and it was 50 cents a quart." Critical reading you see; passing judgment! Critical reading can take place in arithmetic, or it can take place in literature or in any subject field. Incidentally, it should be added that Ms. Evans, the teacher, had the children find the copyright date in the book, and this explained the low price of milk in this particular case.

Some first-grade children were reading a story about some other children who used empty pea pods for boats. They sailed the boats in the bath. One of the boys made the boats go fast by splashing the water backward and forth with his hand. They supposedly played in this way all morning. "I don't think they sailed the boats all morning," volunteered Stephen. "If they splashed the water enough to make the boats go fast, they would have tipped them over." Stephen was questioning the author's statement. "Good thinking," reassured the teacher. "You probably have thought of something that the author didn't. Try floating some pea-pods in the bathtub at home. Splash the water and see what happens. Then you'll know whether you or the author of the story is right."

A group of third graders read a story in which grasshoppers were named as one of the foods that the Indians ate at a feast. "I don't believe they ate grasshoppers," said Susan. Several other children agreed with her. "How could you find out?" asked Mr. James. They searched through many books containing Indian stories to see if they could find any evidence of grasshoppers having been used for food. Mr. James finally brought in the IJ volume of Compton's *Encyclopedia*. The children found the section on Indians and "pored over it." Much of it they could not read. During the search through the pages, however, Sue ran across this statement, which she excitedly read to the class: "The Seed Gatherers ate quite a few things which many people would think unpleasant. These included crickets, grasshoppers, insect larvae, ants ground into flour, and certain lizards and snakes." The author of the story was right. The doubting third graders were wrong, but had learned from the valuable experience of checking a fact they had questioned.

Ruth, in the sixth grade, brought in a short article about Mars. It included a description of the canals on this planet. After she read the story to the class, Rob, another pupil, said, "I heard a woman say over the radio that scientists no longer believe that there are canals on Mars. This author evidently isn't up to date on his information." "Who is he?" asked Mrs. Steele. "Do you know if he is a scientist whose information could be trusted?" Rob did not know. Research followed making use of *Who's Who* references, a letter of inquiry to the publisher, science textbooks, periodicals, encyclopedias. As a result, the pupils concluded that the man who wrote the article was not a scientist but rather a freelance writer who wrote on many popular subjects. They found however, that most scientists at present do not believe that there are canals on Mars.

A Caution. Interpreters of Piaget's developmental stages as related to reading instruction [22] warn us that critical thinking involving concrete objects and ideas should precede critical reading. Teachers should plan informal experiences with materials and situations familiar to children. During the early primary grades, children will find it difficult to build solid, formal criteria on which to base judgments. Teachers need to give expert guidance in helping pupils move toward more objective judgments about more abstract ideas as they move into the upper intermediate grades and the middle school.

All of the evidence is not in, and it may be that Piaget's stages cannot be related on a one-to-one basis to reading instruction. On the other hand, carefully planned experiences moving from the known to the unknown are pedagogically and psychologically sound. The critical reading of propaganda, calling for rather formal logical operations, should *probably* be reserved for some pupils in the upper intermediate grades but largely introduced in the middle grades.

Propaganda. In this age of multitudinous attempts to influence our thinking through the use of printed material, much more emphasis should be placed upon detection and analysis of propaganda. Youth should be taught to look for slants and biases and tricks of propagandists so that they will be in a position to judge the validity of statements that they read in all printed material.

Propaganda may be defined as a deliberate attempt to persuade a person to accept a point of view or take a certain line of action. Propaganda always has been a strong force in shaping the affairs of human beings, and it still is. You will find propaganda in all types of reading material: billboard ads, handbills, pamphlets, newspapers, magazines, books, radio, and television.

Effective propaganda makes a strong appeal to human needs, in-

[22] Ronald J. Raven and Richard T. Salzer, "Piaget and Reading Instruction," *Reading Teacher* 24, no. 7 (April 1971): 630–39; T. Gary Waller, *Think First, Read Later! Piagetian Prerequisites for Reading* (Newark, Del.: International Reading Assn., 1977).

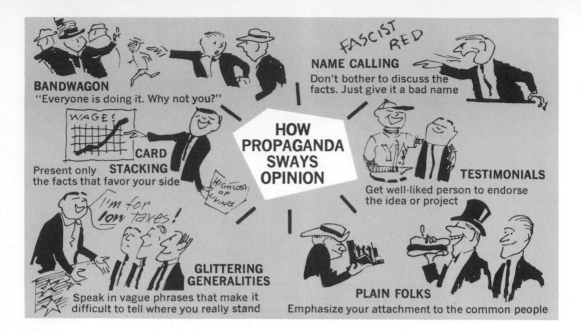

BANDWAGON
"Everyone is doing it. Why not you?"

CARD STACKING
Present only the facts that favor your side

GLITTERING GENERALITIES
Speak in vague phrases that make it difficult to tell where you really stand

HOW PROPAGANDA SWAYS OPINION

NAME CALLING
Don't bother to discuss the facts. Just give it a bad name

TESTIMONIALS
Get well-liked person to endorse the idea or project

PLAIN FOLKS
Emphasize your attachment to the common people

terests, curiosities, loves, hates, prejudices, fears, lusts, cupidities, or amusements. A first step is to identify the technique used in making the appeal. The six techniques portrayed above are generally recognized as basic.[23]

The recognition of these basic propaganda "tricks" can be initiated through the use of colorfully-pictured advertisements cut from magazines. The teacher explains one of the basic propaganda tricks, and then shows and reads (or has pupils read) several different advertisements to see if the pupils can recognize the "trick" in any of them. This continues, accumulatively, until all six tricks have been introduced and practice has been given in recognizing them. After children have had experience as indicated above, they may be invited to bring in advertisements themselves, show them to the class or group, and tell what trick or tricks they think have been used in each one. This approach may be extended to clippings of text (without pictures) from newspapers and magazines.

Another plan for providing practice in recognizing propaganda tricks is for the teacher to prepare or collect samples of text representing the different tricks, reproduce them, and then distribute a number at a time. Pupils study the sections of text, decide what tricks are used, and write the appropriate name above each sample. Follow-up class discussion may uncover healthy differences of opinion and multiple use of tricks for a given piece of text.

[23] From *Your Life As a Citizen, New Edition,* of the Tiegs-Adams Series, p. 290, © Copyright, 1976, 1967, by Ginn and Company (Xerox Corporation). Used with permission.

Planned Activities for Critical Reading. Although on-the-spot discussion is undoubtedly the most fruitful way of developing critical reading, some of the activities suggested below can be used effectively in the upper grades.

1. Ask the children to bring to class newspapers from different publishers; then, have them compare several reports of the same event and note the variations. Much worthwhile discussion will ensue. Guide them in evaluating the newspaper's reputation for containing "uncolored reports" and on the writer's reputation for presenting facts accurately. Encourage spirited discussion as the children pick out statements that they think are opinions and statements that they think are facts.

2. Invite the pupils to bring in articles from the various columnists, and discuss each one in terms of personal opinion versus facts, biases, radical ideas, and attempts at sensationalism. The same procedure can be used with magazine articles, pamphlets, and books.

3. Encourage a pupil to express an opinion on material read; then ask her or him to defend this opinion by showing how the material is related to it.

4. Find differing views on a subject and discuss which are most valid and why.

5. Develop an idea and have pupils find relevant and irrelevant information and valid information concerning the idea.

6. List authorities in specific areas and discuss whether their writing should be accepted or not. Determine why or why not.

7. Develop criteria with the class, such as author's background position, experience with the subject, prejudices, style of writing, and date of publication for use in determining the competence of the author.

8. Hold panel discussions with students presenting various views on the validity of different opinions.

Application

Almost all the reading we do is utilized and applied in some way at some time. In the case of some leisure and out-of-school reading, there may be a long delay between application and the act of reading. In most school reading activities, however, pupils are expected to read in order to satisfy a purpose (more about purpose in the concluding section of this chapter); they are then expected to demonstrate the satisfaction of the purpose to themselves and/or to a group and/or the teacher. Hence, application becomes an important part of the comprehension cycle. The reader attempts to answer a question, satisfy a need, or solve a problem. When the reader reorganizes the author's ideas or uses those ideas to create something new, application and utilization is called creative reading. Gray suggested that creative thinking (creative reading) involves ". . . the imaginative treatment of ideas in both inductive and deductive thinking . . . resulting . . . in new insights, fresh ideas, and new organizations or patterns of thought." [24]

Teaching Creative Reading. Creative reading in its higher form starts with a question or an inquiry that arises in the mind of the reader, personally, and is usually carried forward with high motivation, often a sense of urgency. We cannot expect this higher type of creative reading to happen in the classroom very often unless teachers do something to develop it. Because inquiry is the starting point of creative reading, teachers may ask questions that cause children to go beyond direct implications gathered from the text, at least calling for creative thinking; and they can encourage children, themselves, to ask questions. Once teachers develop the process of inquiry within children themselves, creative reading is apt to follow, and when it does follow it should be praised highly.

By way of illustration, one short and extremely simple example is given to indicate how a teacher might lead a group experience in using creative reading as they build on the other comprehension growth areas.

The children were reading a story about a little girl named Isabel who was left at home to take care of her younger brother while her mother went away somewhere. The youngster wanted a cookie to eat. The cookie jar was kept on the basement steps. Isabel opened the door to the basement and stepped down to get a cookie. At that moment, little brother slammed the door shut. It had a snap lock, so Isabel was locked in the basement when she was supposed to be upstairs taking care of little brother. She began to puzzle over her predicament. Finally, she asked little brother to take the receiver off the phone and say "16 Wood Street" over and over again. This he did. The operator, hearing a child's voice, repeating this address, suspected trouble, and sent a police officer who let Isabel out of the basement.

Literal comprehension:	"What did little brother want to eat?" (They are told that in the book).
Interpretation:	"Why do you think the cookie jar was kept on the basement steps?" (They are supplementing the author's text).
Critical reading:	"Did mother do the right thing in leaving the children alone?" (They are evaluating, passing judgment).
Creative reading:	"How would you have solved this problem?" (They are going beyond the author's text— thinking on their own).

[24] William S. Gray, "The Major Aspects of Reading," in *Sequential Development of Reading Abilities,* Supplementary Educational Monograph No. 90, ed. Helen M. Robinson (Chicago: University of Chicago Press, 1960), p. 19.

Purposes

Purpose plays a major role in comprehension. No reading occurs without purpose, even though that purpose may sometimes be almost unconscious or extremely general—to enjoy myself, to relax, to learn a lot about a topic. As purpose becomes more specific, we tend to gain more from the reading—at least in relation to that purpose. As Guthrie said,

> . . . purpose plays a selective role, increasing the learning of information within the focus and decreasing learning of information outside the focus. Clearly, a price must be paid for the benefits of purpose in reading, but that is probably justified since there are few of us who wish to learn everything about everything.[25]

Certainly when we use reading to unlock the multitudinous ideas across a school curriculum, reading purposes *must* be developed, or the reading assignments would be insurmountable. A reading purpose is really another way of saying, "What is the reading task?" Hence, purpose should include the *reason* for reading, the *mental processes* to be used in satisfying that reason, and the *material* to be read. Examples: (1) Teresa, who had recently read *Charlotte's Web,* wanted to learn more about how spiders create webs (reason), so she turned to volume S of *The World Book Encyclopedia* (material) to scan for the details about how spiders weave their nets (mental processes). (2) Mr. Morganstern, second grade teacher, asks the pupils in a reading group (reason) to reread and find what they consider to be the funniest part (mental processes) of a story they had read previously in their readers (material).

In number one above, the purpose was a cognitive one, initiated by the pupil. It is desirable, of course, that most reading purposes will be of such cognitive and/or affective value that pupils will want to turn to the reading—whether such purposes are initiated by the given pupil, classmates, or the teacher. On the other hand, the teacher will want to introduce certain purposes as part of an overall reading program that pupils might not consider independently, as in number two above. Here are a few other such purposes in which the teacher establishes the *reason* and presents the *material.*

1. Read to find out what an interesting title or picture means as the story unfolds.

2. Find and read the most exciting, most beautiful, and so forth, part of the story. (The group interacts and evaluates decisions.)

3. Read the selection silently and draw a picture to go with it. Then read the selection orally to the group. (The group discusses the picture in light of its representativeness.)

---

[25] John T. Guthrie, "Reading Comprehension Processes and Instruction," in *Cognition, Curriculum, and Comprehension,* ed. John T. Guthrie (Newark, Del.: International Reading Assn., 1977), p. 287.

4. Act out the part of one of the characters. Then read orally to the group that part which describes the role. (The group evaluates the match between description and performance.)

5. Read your paragraph in correct order. (The teacher has taken selections from old materials and cut them up into paragraphs. They have been passed out in random order. Pupils have read them silently and received help with the reading if necessary. Now the teacher asks for paragraph one, two, and so on. Others decide if the order is correct.)

6. Find parts of the story, without pictures, that you think would make the most beautiful pictures.

7. Find a more appropriate title for the selection.

8. In upper grades, read to find main points, verify statements, create headlines, organize an outline, write a summary, write a sequel.

Obviously, a number of the purposes above are suitable as meaningful rereading purposes.

Questions

Questions are, of course, the mainstay of teachers as they attempt to measure comprehension (see chapter 3), and they are usually vital parts of reading purposes. Used wisely by pupil and teacher, they can enhance understanding. Although a continuing goal of the teacher should be to help pupils learn to set their own purposes by creating their own questions, this cannot be done all at once or overnight. The teacher must learn to program questions that will guide readers into higher-level thinking processes as they are able to do so and in light of reading purposes.

The use of inappropriate questions or the use of questions when they cannot be coped with by the learner may defeat the very purpose for which they are intended—to develop comprehension. As Herber said, and has been implied here, "To be able to answer questions, one must be able to apply the reading skill or skills implicit in the relationship between the questions and the content." [26]

Herber went on to suggest:

> For students who do not have sufficient skill for independent responses to questions at the literal level, declarative statements are provided. These statements represent information which might be in the text. Students determine if it actually is included. The students accomplish two purposes as they decide if each statement reflects "what the author says": (1) they develop a sense of accuracy in sorting through information to determine what is actually presented; (2) they develop a sense of the relative importance among all the information presented by the author.
>
> Some statements do present information found in the text; some

[26] Harold L. Herber, *Teaching Reading in the Content Areas*, 2nd ed. (Englewood Cliffs, N.J.: Prentice-Hall, 1978), p. 193.

don't; some shade the information so that it is not exact and must be corrected to be fully acceptable. This process develops students' sense of accuracy and discernment.[27]

The following example is taken from Herber. Directions, of course, may be simplified for younger children or may be read to them. He suggested that the technique is most effective when a few pupils work together.

Directions: Listed below are three statements. Read the first statement with others in your group. Look in the following reading selection to see if it contains the same information contained in the statement. Place a check on the numbered line if the statement does so. It may use either the exact words or may paraphrase, as long as it says the same thing. You must be able to give evidence to support your opinion. If any persons in the group have a problem with words in either the statements or the reading selection, be certain to help them develop an understanding of those words. React to all three statements.

_____1. Seagulls have seriously damaged Swedish crops and gardens.
_____2. Seagulls laid eggs faster than the experts could destroy them.
_____3. Experts boil the eggs and the gulls keep trying to hatch them until it is too late.

For years millions of hungry seagulls have flown inland and seriously damaged Swedish crops and gardens. Experts at first tried to reduce the number of gulls by destroying their eggs but found that the gulls merely laid more eggs.

Now, armed with saucepans and cooking stoves, the experts boil the eggs and carefully replace them in the nests. The gulls, not knowing the eggs will never hatch, sit on them hopefully until it is too late to try again.[28]

Whether using Herber's technique or direct questions, teachers must be sure to fit the questions to the overall purpose for the specific reading. Reading purposes should be varied enough so pupils get much opportunity to move beyond the literal comprehension area. Guszak[29] and others have found that teachers tend to emphasize questions that call for simple recall and literal comprehension much more frequently than other types of questions. Two excellent books, one by Hunkins[30]

[27] Ibid., p. 194.

[28] Ibid., p. 39.

[29] Frank J. Guszak, "Questioning Strategies of Elementary Teachers in Relation to Comprehension," in *Reading and Realism*, Proceedings of the Thirteenth Annual Convention, vol. 13, pt. 1, ed. J. Allen Figurel (Newark, Del.: International Reading Assn., 1969), pp. 110–16.

[30] Francis P. Hunkins, *Involving Students in Questioning* (Boston: Allyn and Bacon, 1976).

and one by Sanders,[31] are extremely useful in helping the classroom teacher learn to pose questions that will move pupils through the comprehension growth areas—literal comprehension, interpretation, critical reading, application.

Types of Questions. Hunkins' questions of a cognitive nature (based on Bloom's "cognitive taxonomy"[32]) may be used in reading instruction with minor adaptations. The chart that follows represents our organization of those questions with examples related to reading instruction. Definitions are Hunkins' with limited interpretation by us. For Sanders' question types and examples related to elementary reading instruction, see Spache and Spache.[33]

QUESTIONS
AT VARIOUS
COGNITIVE
LEVELS
RELATED TO
READING
INSTRUCTION*

Knowledge Questions

1. **Knowledge of terminology**—Knowledge of individual word meanings.

   Examples: What does **gazebo** mean?
   Define **ecology.**
   What does **rabbit ears** mean in this sentence?

2. **Knowledge of specific facts**—recognition of details.

   Examples: Where did the dog go?
   What is the name of the building?
   Who fell in the hole?
   What happened to the elephant?

3. **Knowledge of sequence**—recognition of time order and steps in a process.

   Examples: List the five steps in doing the experiment.
   Which are the correct stages in the life cycle of a butterfly?
   a. larva, egg, adult, pupa
   b. egg, larva, adult, pupa

---

[31] Norris M. Sanders, *Classroom Questions: What Kinds?* (New York: Harper & Row, 1966).

[32] Benjamin S. Bloom, *Taxonomy of Educational Objectives: Handbook I. The Cognitive Domain* (New York: David McKay, 1956).

[33] George D. Spache and Evelyn B. Spache, *Reading in the Elementary School,* 4th ed. (Boston: Allyn and Bacon, 1977), pp. 455–57.

* Based on Francis P. Hunkins, *Involving Students in Questioning* (Boston: Allyn and Bacon, 1976), pp. 19–60.

c. egg, larva, pupa, adult
d. larva, egg, pupa, adult

4. **Knowledge of classifications and categories**—recognition of larger groupings of information.

   Examples: Place each of the animals in its proper family by writing it under the correct heading.

   The osprey is a hawk that
   a. eats fish.
   b. preys on other birds.
   c. feeds on rodents.

Comprehension Questions

1. **Translation**—translation or paraphrasing of the author's ideas (literal and interpretive).

   Examples: Tell in your own words about the habits of the gerbil.

   Draw a picture of the make-believe animal the author described.

   What did the author mean by "his room was as shiny as a new penny"?

2. **Interpretation**—based on translation and involves asking for major interrelationships.

   Examples: What does the graph on page 232 tell us?

   Compare the characteristics of the hare and the rabbit.

3. **Extrapolation**—conclusions and predictions made by the reader, based on what has been read.

   Examples: What do you think will happen when the spaceship finally lands?

   From studying the evidence about the cave, what conclusion can you draw?

Application Questions

1. **Application Questions**—solution of a problem through an integration of the ideas gained in reading.

   Examples: How can we be sure that some of the fish don't eat the other fish?

If Martha has only two days to spend in Copenhagen, what must she be sure to see and to do?

Analysis Questions

1. **Analysis of elements**—distinguishing among component parts of a discussion.

   Examples: What were two of the arguments presented in favor of "razing" the building?

   Is the main idea that dogs are helpful to human beings or that they make good pets?

   Is it fact or opinion that a lizard grows a new tail after losing one?

2. **Analysis of relationships**—based on analysis of elements and involves discerning relationships among them.

   Examples: How can you support your conclusion that dogs are helpful to human beings?

   Compare the arguments about "razing" the building. Do they help you make a final decision about the right thing to do?

3. **Analysis of organizational principles**—determining how the individual elements and the interrelationships relate to the total situation.

   Examples: "Dogs are better than cats." Tell how Timothy arrived at this conclusion. What do you think of this reasoning?

   What was the main idea the author was attempting to present?

Synthesis Questions

1. **Production of a unique communication**—creative reading.

   Examples: Write a poem to show how you feel about your country.

   Tell why you believe Lizzie Borden wasn't guilty.

2. **Production of a plan**—for solving a problem.

   Examples: What new exciting plan might get your fellow schoolmates interested in raising money for the Heart Fund?

Plan a better way of making use of the library corner.

3. **Derivation of a set of abstract relations**—generation of generalizations to explain or classify analyzed data.

   Examples: From your reading and then your experiment with magnets, what conclusion(s) do you reach?

   Was World War II a success or failure? Why?

Evaluation Questions

1. **Judgments in terms of internal evidence**—judgment of data based on logical accuracy, consistency, etc., of the writing.

   Examples: Did the authors present a sound argument for the settlers' treatment of the native Americans? Why or why not?

   Did you enjoy *Charlie and the Chocolate Factory?* How did the author's style or way of writing help you?

   Do you think the author of *Charlotte's Web* studied the habits of spiders?

2. **Judgments in terms of external criteria**—application of those criteria the reader has formulated to judge given situations.

   Examples: In what ways do you feel that **Charlie and the Chocolate Factory** is a wonderful story?

   Charlotte's Web has a sweet and sour ending. Should it have had a happy ending? Could it?

Without question, teachers cannot be expected to remember all of the question types above. All, however, should be programmed into lessons over time, building from one type of thinking task to the next. As teachers become used to considering questions carefully as viable tools for reaching the objectives of given lessons, they develop expertise in choosing appropriate questions. In addition, if the varied uses of questions for specific purposes are realized by pupils—brought to their level of consciousness—the pupils themselves will begin to improve in the use of questions they ask about what they have read and what they plan to read.

1. After having pupils become acquainted with closure techniques using very simple materials within their realms of experience, use the cloze procedure deleting each fifth word, but leave the first and last sentences intact. Have pupils work their way through the passage writing in the deleted words or telling you the words if the writing is too much of a difficult task. If they are writing, be sure they have erasers because making changes on earlier insertions, as they interact with the author, is commendable behavior that demonstrates a search for meaning. Discuss the final products with the group and ascertain *why* certain words were inserted. Synonyms and logical insertions, if appropriately defended, are fine. Although the goal is contact with the author, pupils need to learn how to make such contact through their trials and errors. A passage you use might look something like this:

> The settlers built homes like those they had lived in in Spain. So each house had _____ flat roof, balconies, and _____ courtyard in the center. _____ and cool shade trees _____ planted in this courtyard, _____ *patio*. Most rooms opened _____ to it. Since the _____ of Florida was usually _____, the family could use _____ patio all the year _____. Here they planted lovely _____ fruit trees which they _____ brought to the New _____ from Spain. Among these trees were figs, lemons, limes, and oranges.[34]

The precise deleted words, in order, are: *a, a, Flowers, were, or, on, climate, warm, their, round, flowering, had, World*. With this type of material the every-fifth-word deletion pattern gives pupils practice in thinking about both semantic and syntactic cues.

2. Try your hand at monitoring your own silent reading. McCullough [35] wrote about the nature of her experiences as she engaged in numerous silent reading tasks. One of her many examples related to a sentence she read in *Newsweek*, November 28, 1977, page 46:

> [The Israeli Government] put a full 10,000 police and soldiers on duty to provide security and told the Egyptian Government it was welcome to fly in as many of its own security agents as it wished.

McCullough reported:

> In the context of Sadat's sudden visit to Israel, and with the end of line 3, the reader anticipated *planes*, but accepted *security agents* with-

[34] Esther Crabtree with Ernest W. Tiegs and Fay Adams, *Understanding Your Country and Canada*, new ed. (Boston: Ginn and Co., 1968), p. 203.

[35] Constance M. McCullough, "A New Look at Reading," *Journal of Research and Development in Education* 11, no. 3 (Spring 1978): 54–60.

out incident, remembering that they had preceded Sadat by one day. In an oral reading test there would have been no hint of surprise or shift in meaning. However, to fly in security agents is to transport them as passengers; to fly in planes is to pilot them; to fly in planes is to be transported by them. This sudden successful shift by the reader left a feeling of satisfaction, even though the reader realized afterwards that the Israelis would not have invited an enemy to bring in as many planes as it wished.

Also encourage your pupils, with clear instructions and frequent feedback, to monitor their own miscues and successes.

ADDITIONAL READINGS

Books and Pamphlets

ALTICK, RICHARD D. *Preface to Critical Reading.* 5th ed. New York: Holt, Rinehart and Winston, 1969.

BEERY, ALTHEA. "Consulting Comprehension Skills to Solve Problems." In *Elementary Reading Instruction: Selected Materials,* 2nd ed., edited by Althea Beery, Thomas C. Barrett, and William R. Powell. Boston: Allyn and Bacon, 1974.

DAWSON, MILDRED A. comp. *Developing Comprehension/Including Critical Reading.* Newark, Del.: International Reading Assn., 1968.

ELLER, WILLIAM, and WOLF, JUDITH G. comps. *Critical Reading: A Broader View.* Newark, Del.: International Reading Assn., 1972.

GERHARD, CHRISTIAN. *Making Sense: Reading Comprehension Improved through Categorizing.* Newark, Del.: International Reading Assn., 1975.

GUTHRIE, JOHN T., ed. *Cognition, Curriculum, and Comprehension.* Newark, Del.: International Reading Assn., 1977.

HENRY, GEORGE H. *Teaching Reading as Concept Development: Emphasis on Affective Thinking.* Newark, Del.: International Reading Assn., 1974.

KING, MARTHA L., ELLINGER, BERNICE D., and WOLF, WILLAVENE, eds. *Critical Reading.* Philadelphia: J. B. Lippincott, 1967.

LEE, DORRIS; BINGHAM, ALMA; and WOELFEL, SUE. *Critical Reading Develops Early.* Newark, Del.: International Reading Assn., 1968.

SCHELL, LEO M. "Promising Possibilities for Improving Comprehension." In *Elementary Reading Instruction: Selected Materials,* 2nd ed., edited by Althea Beery, Thomas C. Barrett, and William R. Powell. Boston: Allyn and Bacon, 1974.

SMITH, E. BROOKS, GOODMAN, KENNETH S.; and MEREDITH, ROBERT. *Language and Thinking in School.* 2nd ed., pp. 284–320. New York: Holt, Rinehart and Winston, 1976.

SMITH, FRANK. *Comprehension and Learning.* New York: Holt, Rinehart and Winston, 1975.

SPACHE, GEORGE D., and SPACHE, EVELYN B. *Reading in the Elementary School.* 4th ed., pp. 438–61. Boston: Allyn and Bacon, 1977.

STAUFFER, RUSSELL G., and CRAMER, RONALD. *Teaching Critical Reading at the Primary Level.* Newark, Del.: International Reading Assn., 1968.

THOMAS, ELLEN L., and ROBINSON, H. ALAN. *Improving Reading in Every Class: A Sourcebook for Teachers.* 2nd ed., pp. 101–93. Boston: Allyn and Bacon, 1977.

TINKER, MILES A., and McCULLOUGH, CONSTANCE M. *Teaching Elementary Reading.* 4th ed., pp. 196–213. Englewood Cliffs, N.J.: Prentice-Hall, 1975.

ZINTZ, MILES V. *The Reading Process: The Teacher and the Learner.* 2nd ed., pp. 268–304. Dubuque, Iowa: Wm. C. Brown Co., 1975.

Periodicals

ARTLEY, A. STERL. "Reading Instruction and Cognitive Development." *Elementary School Journal* 72, no. 4 (January 1972), pp. 203–11.

BISKIN, DONALD S.; HOSKISSON, KENNETH; and MODLIN, MARJORIE. "Prediction, Reflection, and Comprehension." *Elementary School Journal* 77, no. 2 (November 1976), pp. 131–39.

BOYAN, CATHERINE S. "Critical Reading: What Is It? Where Is It?" *Reading Teacher* 25, no. 6 (March 1972), pp. 517–22.

CAMERON, JACK R. "Read Critically—or Join the Mob." *Journal of Reading* 12, no. 1 (October 1968), pp. 24–26.

CLARY, LINDA M. "How Well Do You Teach Critical Reading?" *Reading Teacher* 31, no. 2 (November 1977), pp. 142–46.

DURRELL, DONALD, and CHAMBERS, J. RICHARD. "Research in Thinking Abilities as Related to Reading." *Reading Teacher* 12, no. 2 (November 1958), pp. 89–91.

HAUPT, EDWARD J. "Writing and Using Literal Comprehension Questions." *Reading Teacher* 31, no. 2 (November 1977), pp. 193–99.

HERBER, HAROLD L., and NELSON, JOAN B. "Questioning is Not the Answer." *Journal of Reading* 18, no. 7 (April 1975), pp. 512–17.

JONES, MARGARET B., and PIKILSKI, EDNA C. "Cloze for the Classroom." *Journal of Reading* 17, no. 6 (March 1974), pp. 432–38.

KENNEDY, DOLORES. "The Cloze Procedure." *Instructor* 84, no. 3 (November 1974), p. 82.

LANIER, RUBY J., and DAVIS, ANITA P. "Developing Comprehension Through Teacher-Made Questions." *Reading Teacher* 26, no. 2 (November 1972), pp. 153–57.

LUNDSTEEN, SARA W. "Levels of Meaning in Reading." *Reading Teacher* 28, no. 3 (December 1974), pp. 268–72.

NEUWIRTH, SHARYN E. "A Look at Intersentence Grammar." *Reading Teacher* 30, no. 1 (October 1976), pp. 28–32.

SCHWARTZ, ROBERT M. "Strategic Processes in Beginning Reading." *Journal of Behavior* 9, no. 1 (Spring 1977), pp. 17–26.

SIMONS, HERBERT D. "Reading Comprehension: The Need for a New Perspective." *Reading Research Quarterly* 6, no. 3 (Spring 1971), pp. 338–63.

SMITH, RICHARD J. "Questions for Teachers—Creative Reading." *Reading Teacher* 22, no. 5 (February 1969), p. 430.

SULLIVAN, JOANNA. "Receptive and Critical Reading Develops at All Levels." *Reading Teacher* 27, no. 8 (May 1974), pp. 796–800.

TABA, HILDA. "The Teaching of Thinking." *Elementary English* 42, no. 5 (May 1965), pp. 534–42.

THORNDIKE, ROBERT L. "Reading as Reasoning." *Reading Research Quarterly* 9, no. 2 (1973–1974), pp. 135–47.

TURNER, THOMAS N. "Critical Reading as a Values Clarification Process." *Language Arts* 54, no. 8 (November/December 1977), pp. 909–12.

WHEAT, THOMAS E., and EDMUND, ROSE M. "The Concept of Comprehension: An Analysis." *Journal of Reading* 18, no. 7 (April 1975), pp. 523–27.

chapter 9

developing
fluency
and flexibility

What to Expect in This Chapter:

In this chapter, suggestions are made for laying the foundation for flexibility in rates of reading by focusing on getting meanings; developing habits of reading in thought phrases; breaking habits of bodily movements while reading; and encouraging wide, purposeful reading.

In discussing the intermediate grades and above, suggestions are given for making pupils aware of their various rates; developing the concept of reading in thought units; establishing habits of reading for purposes; and teaching the technique of previewing. Procedures are described for conducting timed reading exercises, but emphasis is placed on the development of flexibility. The special skills of skimming and scanning are treated, and suggestions are given for use in developing these abilities.

In a comparative analysis of the reading comprehension processes in good and poor readers, Golinkoff indicated that ". . . good comprehenders seem to use a scan-for-meaning pattern which can be flexibly applied to suit their varied purposes."[1] She suggested that poor comprehenders seem ". . . to read text in a word-by-word manner, with a minimum of text organization."[2] Golinkoff concluded that "inadequate reading comprehension seems to imply being somewhat of a slave to the actual printed word. It also implies a failure to extract structure and organization from text."[3]

Flexibility of reading rates is as important to develop in the elementary grades as basic fluency. In the past, this concept has been relegated to development in the upper grades (although infrequently implemented). Strategies for learning to suit rates of reading to the nature of the material and the purposes for the reading must be nurtured early in the development of a learner.

When high-school students and adults come to reading centers or labs for help, they invariably say: "How many words per minute should I read?" or "I hear that if I speed up my eye movements I'll become a good reader." or "I hear that people can learn to read over one thousand words per minute." All such questions and statements are indicative of prevalent fallacies. Eye movements can be "speeded up," but they are only reflections of the mental processes a person uses while reading. Understanding is both the process and the goal. Questions related to *how fast can I read* are based on the assumption that an individual has just

[1] Roberta M. Golinkoff, "A Comparison of Reading Comprehension Processes in Good and Poor Comprehenders," *Reading Research Quarterly* 11, no. 4 (1975–76): 654.

[2] Ibid., 655.

[3] Ibid., 656.

one reading rate that he or she uses in *all* situations. As a matter of fact, expert readers use many different rates as they accommodate their reading of different kinds of content for different purposes. Rates of reading are related to familiarity and complexity of material as well as reading purpose.

All of a person's rates can be improved, but improvement in speed alone should not be the goal; flexibility in adjusting speed to different situations is the achievement toward which learner and teacher alike should direct their efforts. Three different categories of rate are represented in the following diagram.

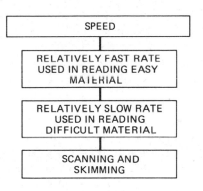

The diagram represents major *categories* of rate; no individual should have just one fixed speed for each category. There should be wide variations in each person within each category, again in terms of the material and the purpose for which it is read.

The relatively fast rate of reading material of average difficulty includes rate used in reading fictional selections and novels for recreational purposes, or in reading informative articles in popular magazines or nonfictional books for the purpose of pursuing a special interest or becoming broadly informed on some topic. Most of the reading material in the primary grades is of this type, and a considerable amount of the material in middle grade textbooks and supplemental books falls in this category.

A slower rate is used in reading or studying difficult material with a heavy burden of detailed facts. This is the kind of reading that a teacher does in reading and interpreting a technically phrased report of a scientific investigation, or in reading a technical article on space travel so that he or she can understand it well enough to relate its contents to the pupils. In the middle grades, pupils increasingly come in contact with material of this kind, which they study for the purpose of entering into class discussion, making a report, or taking a test. For example, in a science textbook they may encounter this kind of material in an explanation of how the telephone works, or in an arithmetic book they may work with such text in reading directions for dividing a whole number by a fraction. Examples in many other situations of this kind might be given.

Rate for use in the two categories described above is developed in the same general way but applied differently. The third category requires different techniques. Scanning and skimming are extremely fast rates of covering reading content; to be fully effective, these techniques should be taught and not left to chance.

The term *scanning* is generally used to designate the process of quickly locating a particular word, phrase, sentence, fact, or figure within a selection; *skimming* is used for the process of quickly passing over an entire selection or passage to get a general impression of it. A person scans when the eyes sweep over a list of items in a television schedule to find the time of a particular show. An example of skimming is glancing through a short article on "How to Increase Your Energy" to catch a few phrases now and then that give a general idea of what suggestions the article holds.

Scanning may be given incidental practice in the first grade and continued practice throughout the grades. Skimming should not be emphasized until a degree of fluent reading has been achieved; usually, pupils are ready for some work in skimming late in grade three or grade four.

FLUENCY FOUNDATIONS IN THE PRIMARY GRADES

We have evidence to the effect that rate in reading grows along with the other reading skills during the years in which the mechanics of reading are being mastered. As a child gains control over mechanics of reading, he or she is freed to cover the pages of print more rapidly. The cornerstones of speed are facility in: (1) recognizing words; (2) gathering meanings; (3) using study skills. Whatever a teacher does to improve these fundamental abilities will contribute also to an increase in rate.

In addition to efforts to improve these basic skills, however, there are many specific things that a teacher can do to develop faster rates of reading and flexibility in using them. Most authorities, however, are agreed that it is not advisable to have primary children undergo intensive speed pressure. Attention to comprehension—a search for meaning—should come first in reading skill. Also, intensive pressure to read faster might have unfortunate effects both on a child's physical and mental well-being.

Establishing Phrasing

Word-reading impedes speed. The teacher should try from the beginning to develop ability to read in phrases by doing some of these things:

1. In all chalkboard and chart work with primary children, divide runover sentences between phrases, as:

> The big black dog came running
> down the road.

2. In all chalkboard or chart work assist pupils to read in phrase units by sweeping a pointer or your hand under each complete phrase as it is read, rather than by pointing to each word separately.

3. When the children themselves are using a pointer, remind them to "keep the pointer sliding," thereby preventing the habit of pointing to and focusing on just one word at a time.

4. Ask children to read like they "talk" when reading orally, rather than reading one word at a time.

Breaking Habits of Bodily Movements

The mind of the good reader can leap far ahead of the rate at which physical movements can take place. Many children develop habits of using physical movements during beginning reading stages. If extreme and/or habitual movements continue unreined, an individual may be a slow reader throughout his or her life.

Lip-moving is natural at beginning stages when the child is making the transition from the use of oral language to the silent reading of printed symbols. Normally, it disappears at about second grade level. If it persists as a constant behavior, concentrated attention should be directed toward breaking the habit. However, vocalization (vibrations in the larynx, "mouthing of some words," or occasional lip movements) are always present in reading. Readers tend toward more lip movements when the material is complex or unfamiliar. Do not confuse occasional lip movements during silent reading with a persistent habit.

Here are a few ways of helping learners break the habit. Some techniques will work with some pupils and not others. The first two suggestions, however, are the most useful for most learners.

1. Provide materials, and help children select materials, that will be of interest to them. Encourage wide reading of materials that help to solve problems, stimulate interest, and satisfy curiosities.

2. Provide materials, and help children select materials, that are not too difficult for them to read. Particularly for pupils with the persistent lip-moving habit, encourage lots of easy reading for specific purposes.

3. Make children themselves conscious of the desirability of eliminating lip movement as a means of helping them to become better readers.

4. Watch the children during study periods and frequently remind the lip-readers to "read with your eyes."

5. Place printed slogans around the room, such as "Fast readers use their eyes, not their lips." "Eyes are for reading; lips are for talking."

Finger-pointing holds some readers down to reading one word at a time so that only a very slow rate of reading can be attained. The first two suggestions made for those who use their lips during silent reading apply here, too. In addition, some pupils might benefit from:

1. In first grade, provide pupils with a cardboard marker, about an

inch wide and as long as the width of the page. Have them place this marker under the first line of print and move it down line by line as they read. (As a rule, do not continue the use of markers beyond first grade.)

2. Ask pupils to hold each side of the book with one hand. If they keep both hands in use holding the book, they will not have a free finger with which to point.

Head-moving prevents fast reading. Some children (and many adults) move their heads from left to right and back again from right to left each time they read a line and return their eyes to the beginning of another line. Have children with head movements place their chins in one of their hands while reading. Instruct them to "make your hand keep your head from moving."

Setting Purposes

Adults and children read more rapidly when they are motivated by a well-defined purpose. Try to work out purposes with the children for reading selections in their daily work. It is by no means too early in the primary grades to discuss the nature of reading assignments and the approaches that may be used to complete the assignments.

Some possible pupil purposes and ways of reading to accomplish the purposes are:

1. Read the weather report in the newspaper. Then write the information you think is important for the class to know on the chalkboard. (Approach—Careful reading of the whole thing. Picking out certain facts for writing on chalkboard. Use of judgment. Need for some thinking time.)

2. Read the directions for playing a new game. Then explain the directions to your group so they will be able to play the game without reading the directions themselves. (Approach—Read all the information first to find out about the game. Read again to understand each direction. List the directions, in order, on a piece of paper. Use the directions you wrote down to help you as you explain to the group.)

3. Read the short story to yourself. Then read it out loud to the group. (Approach—Read through the story to understand it. Then reread to be sure you can pronounce the words accurately; get help if you need it. Read it out loud, alone, to be sure you are able to read it smoothly and in an interesting way. Now you are ready to read it to the group.)

Wide Reading

One of the best ways to promote growth in reading fluency at the primary level is to encourage wide reading of easy, interesting material. As indicated earlier, a purposeful search for meaning and enjoyment will tend to keep the reader's attention on larger units of thought rather than on each individual word. See chapter 11, Developing Interest and Taste in Literature, for some techniques useful in the encouragement of wide reading.

Scanning

Children who have begun with a language-experience approach and a feel for unlocking ideas, rather than a concentration on the accurate pronunciation of *every single word*, are ready for scanning early in the primary grades. During a lesson on a language-experience story, for example, Ms. J. might explain that "when you are looking for one particular thing in a story, you don't have to read every single word." She might demonstrate by showing how quickly she can find a specific word in the language experience story. The children may then see how quickly they can find other words named by the teacher.

Throughout the primary grades, many functional opportunities will arise to give practice in scanning. Usually such practice should be given *during rereading* rather than during the first reading of a selection.

Here are a few scanning activities that children can do appropriately at this level:

1. Find a word or phrase in book text that has previously been discussed and placed on the chalkboard.
2. Find a sentence, phrase, or word to answer a specific question.
3. Find a phrase or sentence giving specific information.
4. Prove or disprove a statement as indicated in a particular sentence given orally or written on the chalkboard.
5. Find the page on which a chapter or story begins, first from chalkboard, later in table of contents.
6. Find a sentence that gives a word picture.

INCREASING RATES IN GRADES FOUR THROUGH EIGHT

Conscious effort should be made to help upper-grade pupils continue the training begun earlier. Among the practices used in the primary grades, the following should be continued and emphasized: (1) copious reading of easy material; (2) *purposeful* reading; and (3) discontinuance of any bodily movements that persist while reading. In addition, the activities that follow seem particularly useful.

Develop an Awareness of Personal Rates

At the beginning of the year, the teacher may give the pupils an informal test of speed and content. Prepare for this test by making up ten questions on the content of three or four pages of a story they have not read.

Have the children find the page on which the story begins, keeping a finger in the place and immediately closing the book. Provide yourself with a stopwatch if one is available; if not, use an ordinary watch with a second hand. When the second hand is at 12:00 or 6:00 (for convenience in time-keeping), give the children the signal to start reading. Allow them to read silently for three minutes, then give them the signal to stop. Children may make a faint pencil dot (which later can be erased) at the point they reached when the "stop" signal was given.

Place on the chalkboard the ten questions that you had prepared. Ask the children to write the answers to the questions with their books closed.

After the answers are written, pupils check their own papers as you give the answers orally. A score of ten should be allowed for each correct answer.

Following the checking of the answers, ask the pupils to count the number of words they read and divide the number by three. This will indicate the number of words per minute that they read. Have this number written on the answer paper along with the score on questions relating to the content.

Gather up the papers and, without giving the names of the pupils, write the rate scores on the board, ranging from the highest to the lowest, with the question score to the right of the rate score in each case.

Use the scores as the basis for discussion. Point out the variation in both speed and grasp of content. Call attention particularly to the relationships between speed and grasp of content. Some scores will show that pupils read very fast and still answer all the questions correctly. This should be held up as a desired standard, but one that can still be improved in speed. Others will have a high speed score but a lower content score. This may mean that these pupils were reading too fast and also that they need to give more attention to getting meanings. Some will have read slowly but have high scores on understanding of content. They should be encouraged to read faster. Some probably will have low scores both in rate and content. They probably should work harder on grasping content, before trying to read faster.

Following the discussion, return the papers so that each child may place himself or herself in the total distribution.

Develop the Concept of Reading in Thought Units

Everyone agrees that fluent reading relies upon reading in thought units. Everyone does not agree, however, that one way to develop this is through marking off the thought units that appear to be the writer's, as suggested below. Although the goal is to help pupils "take in" their own chunks or groups of words as an idea and not to necessarily hold them to one way of doing it, we believe there is merit in putting emphasis on the thought units that appear to be those of the writer.

The teacher may give the pupils information similar to that presented below.

"Investigations of eye movements have shown that the rapid reader's eyes move fleetingly across the lines, pausing briefly two or three times on each line, picking up an 'eyeful' of words at each pause, while the eyes of the poor reader pause on every word or on small word units.

"It is the mind, of course, that controls the eye movements. The great value of eye-movement investigatons is that they furnish us a picture of the different ways in which the mind works in perceiving reading symbols. They tell us that the mind of the poor reader loafs along, picking up very small units at a time, while the eyes of the excellent reader race over the lines, gathering an entire, meaningful idea at a glance.

"Cultivating the habit of reading for *ideas* not only increases speed but also increases understanding. A person who reads one word at a time thinks in terms of the meanings of these separate words and thus 'can't see the woods for the trees.'

"The first and most important instruction is, 'Read for Ideas!' If you can cultivate the habit of rapidly picking up one complete thought unit after another, the eye movements will take care of themselves."

This explanation may be followed by writing a paragraph on the chalkboard, dividing it into logical thought groups, and letting the children try to read it for ideas. An example of a paragraph so marked is as follows:

OLD BET
The pioneer elephant in our country/was imported by a sea captain./She was named "Old Bet,"/and she arrived in New York/about 1815./ She was sold/to a Mr. John Sloat./ He sold her again/to a man named Bailey. The big old elephant/was transported on a sloop/to Ossining-on-the-Hudson./She was driven from there/back into the country,/where she was exhibited/in a barn./ [4]

Write other paragraphs on the chalkboard. Ask the children to mark them into thought units that seem sensible. All responses will not be the same.

Reproduce paragraphs or short selections and give them to the class to divide into thought units.

Continuously remind the children to read in thought units.

Develop Habits of Reading for a Purpose

The teacher may inform children of the desirability of setting up purposes for reading. Perhaps the advice below will be useful in making such suggestions.

[4] Adapted from George S. Bryan, "The First American Circus," *The Mentor*, April 1922, p. 34.

"In increasing your speed, and in fact in developing all the other skills in reading, decide upon your purpose for reading a selection *before* you start to read it. Is it to get information about some special topic that you will need in class discussion? To find out how something works? To get an answer to some problem? To find out how to do something? To review for a test? To gather news about what others are doing? To find out how to improve yourself personally? To be entertained by some light reading? To follow the plot of a story? Or what?

"Phrase your purpose concisely, and keep it uppermost in your mind throughout the reading of the entire selection. A well-defined purpose pulls your eyes along more rapidly, and it gives you something to tie to in selecting and organizing ideas gathered from the text. In fact, your purpose hastens your eyes along and acts as a pilot that guides you over the sea of print and leaves you with a well-filled dragnet of ideas at the end of your reading journey."

Discuss with the children the possibility of a purpose for their next assignment. Work with them to set up a definite purpose, and urge them to try to keep the purpose in mind while they read.

Frequently set up a purpose for reading a selection or ask the children to do so. Help them to develop the habit of setting up their own purposes. See page 227 and Discussion Questions and Activities at the end of this chapter.

Develop the Preview Technique

The technique of previewing a selection or a chapter before reading it is a valuable one for middle-grade children to learn. Skillful previewing contributes both to increased rate and comprehension.

There is a basic reason why people "window shop" before buying a garment or a car or a new gadget. They want to "size up" certain characteristics of articles that interest them as a whole. If it is a coat, they first evaluate it in terms of material and color. Then they look at the style of the garment and note the cut of the collar and the flare of the cuffs. No doubt, they compare this piece of merchandise with others in price. In short, they gather as much information as possible about characteristics that are important to them before they actually buy. Likewise, it is possible and advisable to glean as much information as possible about an article, a chapter, or a book before reading it.

A preview aids pupils by whetting appetites, arousing interest in the subject, and strengthening personal motives for reading about it. It acquaints readers with the general subject matter of the text to be read and its structure or organization. When pupils actually begin to read after previewing, they find that prereading insight has paved the way for speedier and more comprehensive coverage of the printed page.

Introducing Previewing. The steps that follow are usually used in previewing. As students become accustomed to the procedure, they will alter some of the steps to the nature of the material. Steps are directed toward the student.

1. *Study the Title.* The title holds a world of information for you. It tells you concisely what the selection is about. It gives you a quick cue as to the topic of discussion. It provides you with advanced information in regard to the subject to be discussed and enables you to read in terms of the promise that the title holds out to you.

2. *Examine Visual Aids.* When they are present, look at pictures, maps, graphs, charts, and diagrams carefully. Read captions and labels when present. Your advanced study of visual aids will give you a quick grasp of some important ideas and relationships that will be introduced or discussed in the printed material.

3. *Read the First Paragraph or Two.* Most of the time, the first paragraph or two will introduce you to the topic of the total selection. They sort of set the stage for you and may raise questions in your mind that you will want to answer when you read the material carefully.

4. *Read All the Headings.* Next, glance through the selection to see if headings are used. If so, you will find that a quick survey of these headings will be very valuable to you. You should consider each one for the information that it actually gives or which it implies. These headings are the major topics in the author's outline.

5. *Read the Last Paragraph or Two.* Very often, the author "wraps up" or concludes the selection with some type of summary that highlights the important points. An advanced reading of this helps you to understand the main points and to think about further explanation you need when you read the material carefully.

When you're reading material that has no visual aids, or material without headings, adjust your preview plan to the material. There will be occasions in reading easy articles when a preview of headings will tell you all you want to know. At other times, especially when studying in the content subjects, they will serve as interest leads to reading the different sections, and as door openers to better understanding of the text that follows.

After the preview technique has been explained, the children should be asked to try it out step by step in reading a chapter or a section of a chapter in a science, geography, or history textbook.

Following the preview, the teacher may give a test based on information that could be gotten alone from the title, visual aids, first and last paragraphs, and headings. The pupils will be surprised to find how much information they have gotten solely from previewing.

The habit of previewing should be firmly established during the intermediate grades. Repeated experiences similar to the one described above, together with frequent reminders, should accomplish this goal.

Practicing Previewing. Here is a preview test slightly adapted from Level B (fifth grade) of Nila Banton Smith's *Be a Better Reader* series, 1977. Similar tests can be constructed for other grade levels.

CORAL THROUGH THE AGES [5]

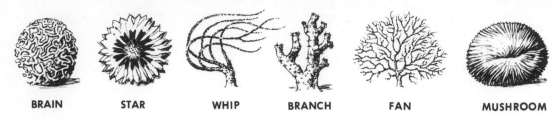

BRAIN   STAR   WHIP   BRANCH   FAN   MUSHROOM

DIFFERENT SHAPES OF CORAL

Throughout the ages coral has been highly prized. It is one of the wonders of nature.

Coral has beautiful shapes. Coral grows in several different shapes. Some corals build stone-like structures that look like the tendrils of climbing plants. Some types are shaped like vases or fans. Others build structures that look like the brain or like feathers.

Coral grows in many beautiful colors. It can be as white as snow or the color of flesh. Deep red coral is very beautiful. There are also purple, violet, yellow, and black corals. Yellow coral is the most rare, and the black is especially prized. White, pink, and red coral are quite common.

Polyps produce coral. For many years it was thought that coral was produced either by plants or insects. In 1723, a French doctor discovered a small sea animal, now called a polyp. The polyp when born is a tiny, jelly-like oval which is only a fraction of an inch long.

Polyps increase like plants. Many young polyp buds spring from a parent polyp. The coral polyp fastens itself to rocks and stones by means of a disk-shaped foot which each polyp has. The stone-like structures that polyps build around themselves remain after the polyps die. They often form islands or large reefs.

The coral industry is largely carried on in Italy. The Italians get most of the coral that we have from the sea by "fishing" for it. This fishing is done by large boats which dredge the ocean. In addition to getting the raw coral from the sea, it is the Italians who do most of the work in preparing the coral for market. There are over sixty shops in Italy, with a total force of 6,000 expert coral workers.

There is a legend about coral and a disappointed lover. According to this legend, there was a Chinese maiden who mourned her lover who had been killed by her cruel brothers. One morning she found a rose growing in her garden. She knew at once that this flower was her lover who had returned to life in the form of a rose.

Day by day the petals fell until nothing remained but the heart. This the maiden plucked and held in her hand. It was a pale-pink bead of coral. The rose blossomed again and again. Each time the maiden plucked out the heart and hid it near her own. Then she strung the hearts of the rose on a golden chain and called it her "necklace of endless sighs."

PREVIEW TEST

1. What does the title tell you that the article is about?
2. Is a short period or a long period of history covered in the article?
3. What are the names of the different shapes of coral shown in the picture?
4. What can you say about the various shapes and colors of coral?
5. What produces coral?
6. In what country is the coral industry largely carried on?
7. What is the legend of coral about?

[5] From *Be A Better Reader*, Level B, Basic Skills Edition by Nila Banton Smith, Copyright © 1977, 1968, pp. 78–79. By Prentice-Hall, Inc. Reprinted by permission.

Timed Reading Practice

From about the fifth grade level and up, pupils who are working at about grade level or beyond may be given systematic timed practice to increase their rates of reading.

Materials. Materials used for timed reading practice may be either commercially prepared or they may consist of selections that the teacher chooses from readers, textbooks in the content areas, or trade books with which the children are working.

Easy material should be used while pupils are breaking their old tempo and establishing new habits. Later, they may try increasing their rate in reading more difficult material.

Instructions for Giving Timed Practice. Instructions for giving timed reading practice with commercially prepared materials usually accompany the material itself. The procedures suggested below are provided for the use of teachers who use the regular reading materials available in the classroom.

Timed reading tests may be given from two to five times per week. Three minutes per period is a desirable length for a practice period at the beginning of timed reading practice. Two or three repetitions of practice periods of three minutes each may take place at one sitting, with time being allowed between each practice period for scoring speed and grasp of content. The length of the practice period may be increased when in the judgment of the teacher it is desirable to do so.

Comprehension questions should, of course, be prepared in advance of each practice period. Checking speed without comprehension is quite valueless.

Ascertaining Rates and Grasp of Content. Comprehension questions should *always* follow timed reading practice. Each pupil should check his or her own answers to questions, as the teacher reads the answers to the questions orally. If ten questions have been used, a score of ten should be given for each correct answer, the total being the sum of all of the correct answers scored.

Speed is ascertained by counting the number of words read during a given time and dividing this number by the number of minutes or number of minutes plus seconds consumed in the reading.

For checking purposes, it is not necessary to count each word on the page individually. An estimate of the number of words on one page of the total number of pages covered may serve as an estimate for all pages in the same selection. In making such an estimate, the number of words in six or seven lines are counted. As a result, three or four of the lines may turn out to have the same number of words, let us say thirteen. If this does not happen, then words may be counted in several lines and the average number found by dividing the total number of words by the number of lines in which words are counted.

Once the average number of words in a line has been ascertained, then pupils can quickly count the average number of lines covered during a practice period and multiply by the average number of words per line, as:

$$75 \times 13 = 975 \quad \text{Total number of words}$$

This number divided by the number of minutes used in the practice yields the number of words per minute read, commonly designated as WPM. As an example, if three minutes were used for the practice period, the computation would be:

$$975 \div 3 = 325 \text{ WPM}$$

The suggestions apply when the teacher holds the time of the practice period to the same number of minutes for all pupils. The time is constant, but the number of words read by each individual varies within that time. An alternate procedure is one in which all pupils start reading at the same time and each one keeps a record of the time at which he or she individually finishes reading an entire selection or section of a selection that has been assigned for practice purposes. Such a practice period may be conducted by having the teacher write time intervals on the chalkboard, or better, by flashing time cards for the pupils' use in recording their respective finishing times.

File cards, $3'' \times 5''$ in size, may be used for timing. A number is written on each card. This number should be large enough in size so that all children in the group can see it easily from where they are sitting. India ink or strong black crayon strokes should be used in making the number easily legible.

Usually, 60 is used as a beginning number; then five is added for the number on each additional card, as 65, 70, 75, 80, 85, 90, 95, 100, and so on. The cards are held up at intervals of five seconds, beginning with the number that represents the number of seconds that have elapsed since the students started, until all have finished reading.

As in the other timing procedures described above, the teacher makes sure that all pupils wait to start reading until he or she gives the signal. It is easier for the teacher to keep time if the signal is given when the second hand is either at 12 or at 6.

When some of the students have nearly finished with their reading, at the expiration of each five seconds the teacher should flash a card with a figure on it representing the total number of seconds that have elapsed since they began reading. As soon as a student finishes, he or she looks up at the card the teacher is holding and writes down the number on the card as representing the number of seconds that it took him to read the selection. For example, if the number on the card is 125 when Tom finishes, he makes a note of 125, which indicates that it took him 125 seconds, or two minutes and five seconds, to read the article.

When computing rates involving seconds as well as whole minutes, the following formula is useful:

$$\frac{\text{No. words}}{\text{No. seconds}} \quad \frac{a}{b} \times 60 = \underline{\hspace{2cm}} \text{ WPM}$$

If a pupil read 320 words in 140 seconds, his or her completed formula would be:

$$\frac{\text{No. words}}{\text{No. seconds}} \quad \frac{320}{140} \times 60 = 138 \text{ WPM}$$

Keeping Personal Records. A strong motivating force in rate and content improvement is that of keeping records of personal progress. Individual records are better than group records in which students compete with each other for gains in spite of personal limitations. Trying to beat one's own record is the best kind of competition.

Various kinds of graphs, charts, and tables may be used for this purpose. In keeping records of growth, it is very important that material of comparable difficulty be used for each successive recording. Growth in grasping content should always be recorded along with rate growth.

One sample of a graph that can be used for recording growth in rate is presented on page 254 along with one for recording growth in understanding of content.

Controlled Reading. Several mechanical aids are on the market for use in regulating the rate at which reading content is exposed. These instruments are useful as motivational and pacing devices for readers who need to be "pushed" into developing faster reading abilities. Selections used with such devices should vary in complexity beginning with material at rather easy levels for given readers. Emphasis must be placed on helping children maintain these "pushed" rates when they are reading in natural reading situations. Instruments are by no means a cure-all for children who are not doing well in reading, nor as a substitute for a complete, well-rounded developmental program for average or high achievers.

There are, primarily, two ways of controlling reading. *Pacers* utilize any type of reading material. A metal arm or shadow can be moved down over the reading material covering a line at a time, and the reader has to read fast enough to read the line before it is covered. Rate can be regulated to different speeds. *Instruments using film strips* are also available for rate practice. One of these appropriate for use at the elementary level is the Controlled Reader (Educational Developmental Laboratories, McGraw-Hill).

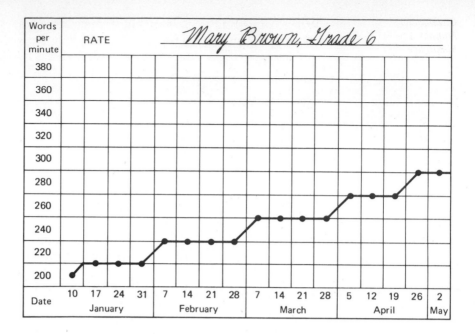

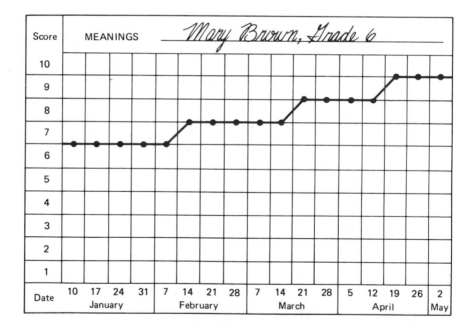

Emphasis on Flexibility

At the beginning of the year, the teacher may give timed reading tests to pupils in reading different types of material for different purposes: a story to follow the plot; a geography or history selection to get general information; a science selection to get detailed facts. The pupils should read for a period of three to five minutes in each case, and then each should determine his or her average rate per minute. In every case, the teacher should test comprehension with questions designed to check the kind of information for which the pupils were reading. All three speed scores and all three comprehension scores by subjects for a few of the pupils should be placed on the chalkboard and used as a basis for discussion. Many needs may be pointed out by examining these sample scores. Some pupils may have used the same rate in three situations and gotten poor comprehension scores in the science and geography tests, indicating that they were reading too fast in these subjects for the purpose assigned. Some may have used the same rate for all three and gotten perfect comprehension scores, which would indicate that they probably could have read the story at a rate that was much more rapid, and that they might be able safely to improve their rate in the other two fields. Some might have adjusted their rates, reading the story very rapidly, the geography or history material less rapidly, and the science materials more slowly than either of the others—making high comprehension scores in all of them. Such a set of scores should be held up as an example of the desirable thing to do.

After background discussion, pupils should compare their own scores and arrive at conclusions in regard to how they can develop flexibility. Such practice in the flexibility of rates of reading may be given periodically throughout the year, and records of improvement may be kept.

It is useful, occasionally, to list purposes for which pupils might read and to determine the possible rate of reading for each purpose. (See pages 227–28, and page 259.)

The social studies example below calls for a preview first, and then a careful reading. The material is difficult (about grade seven), although its subject matter is pertinent and suitable for good readers in grades five and six.

Step A: Preview the material and answer the preview questions.

Step B: Read the material carefully to get more details about the problems, to find out why they exist, and to learn about some possible solutions.

PROBLEMS OF AMERICAN CITIES [6]

[6] From *Be A Better Reader*, Level D, Basic Skills Edition, by Nila Banton Smith, © 1978, 1969, 1963, 1958, pp. 59–61. By Prentice-Hall, Inc. Reprinted by permission.

The first count, or census, of Americans was taken in 1790. At that time nearly all people lived on farms or in small villages. Even one hundred years later, two-thirds of our people lived in the country.

Since 1890, however, many changes have occurred. Because of new farm machines and improved farming methods, fewer farmers were needed. People in the country moved to towns to find work. During the nineteenth and twentieth centuries, great numbers of people in Europe moved to the cities of America to seek a better life. Now, over two-thirds of our people live in cities or large towns. This rapid increase in the number of people living in cities has been the chief cause of many city problems.

School Buildings are Outdated. Many school buildings still in use in cities today were built 50 or more years ago. These buildings lack playgrounds. They don't have large libraries, gymnasiums, or assembly halls. These schools often do not have enough classrooms.

New schools are being built to replace the old ones. However, they cost a great deal. Also, the land needed to build large schools and playgrounds is often hard to find. So sometimes changes take place very slowly.

School Populations Are Not Balanced. It is desirable that people of all races and backgrounds live and work together peacefully. We know that everyone benefits when people understand and help each other.

At the present time, certain sections of a city may be settled largely by people of one race or national background. Some sections may be inhabited mainly by black people; Spanish-speaking people may live in others. In certain neighborhoods, most of the people are of Japanese or Chinese origin. In still others, most of the people are of European origin. Because of this, children with different backgrounds may not get a chance to work and play together.

Various programs are being tried to bring children of different races and backgrounds together in school. If these programs are successful, all the people in our cities will benefit.

The Air Is Impure. Factories and furnaces pour poisonous gases into the city air. Cars probably do more than factories to make the city air impure. Thousands of people now drive to their city jobs. As a result, the air is becoming polluted.

Scientists are studying this serious problem to find ways of solving it. Devices have been attached to car engines to cut down on the exhaust fumes. It is even possible that some day electric cars that produce no exhaust fumes will be used. In addition, people are being encouraged to come into the city by subway, bus, or railroad.

Many City People Have Poor Housing. As factories sprang up and thousands of people came to cities to work, there was a need for more homes. Apartment houses were built in which many families could live. Often these apartment houses were built in rows joined together. They were several stories high. Each floor of these buildings was divided into three or four apartments of small rooms. These apartments are often cramped and crowded.

Many such buildings of this type, as well as other kinds of old houses, are still standing. The living quarters in many of these buildings are small and dark. Sometimes, they are without heat except for an oil or gas stove.

Cities are trying to make these old living quarters more comfortable and modern. They are also destroying many old houses and building new apartment houses in their places. This, however, takes time and money.

Poverty Is a Problem. Many people in our cities have not been educated or trained to do work that pays well. Some of them are out of work a good part of the time. As a result, they have little or no money to buy the things that they want.

There are also many families who don't earn enough money to rent or buy a good home. They don't earn enough to buy the food and clothing they need, either.

Attempts are now being made to offer unemployed men and women more education and to teach them new skills. By offering such programs, cities hope to get rid of poverty and to ensure a better life for all.

Crime Is a Problem. Throughout the nation the crime rate is high, especially in cities. Often crime and lack of education go together. Some people who didn't get a good education are now unable to get a job. Sometimes these people break the law to get the things they want.

Schools are trying to prevent young people from "dropping out." Youngsters are encouraged to finish their high school education. Special programs are offered to teach adults who cannot read and write how to do so. Aiding people to become successful and useful in their neighborhoods should help reduce the crime rate.

Preview Questions

1. What does the picture tell you?
2. What does the title of the article tell you that you are going to read about?
3. What is the chief cause of problems of American cities?
4. What is wrong with many school buildings?
5. What is another problem in schools?
6. What is the problem about air?
7. What kind of housing do many city people have?
8. Does poverty still exist?
9. Name another serious problem.
10. Six major problems were stated in the headings. On your paper, write the six major problems of American cities.

Questions after a Careful Reading—

Three phrases are provided as possible answers to complete each sentence below. On your paper, write the letter of the phrase that properly completes each sentence.

1. In 1790 practically all people in the United States lived
   a. in big cities.
   b. in apartment houses.
   c. on farms or in small villages.
2. Two-thirds of our people now live in
   a. cities or large towns.
   b. the country.
   c. the South.
3. Many school buildings
   a. cost very little.
   b. were built 50 or more years ago.
   c. can be built in a short time.
4. Certain sections of a city may be inhabited by
   a. schoolchildren.
   b. people of one race or national background.
   c. scientists.
5. City air is becoming impure because
   a. so many people are breathing in a city.
   b. people have so much garbage.
   c. factories and furnaces and cars pour poisonous gases into the air.
6. The problem of impure air is
   a. being overlooked.
   b. being studied.
   c. not important.
7. Many old, run-down apartments are
   a. not occupied.
   b. large and airy.
   c. still standing.
8. Cities are
   a. doing nothing about shabby, old homes.
   b. renting old apartments at very high prices.
   c. rebuilding old apartments or building new modern ones.
9. Cities hope to get rid of poverty by
   a. refusing to get people jobs.
   b. moving people somewhere else.
   c. educating people so they can get better jobs.
10. These two often go together
   a. prosperity and crime
   b. lack of education and crime
   c. good homes and crime

SKIMMING
AND
SCANNING
IN GRADES
FOUR
THROUGH
EIGHT

Skimming

In our opinion, the claims of some commercial "reading schools" about increasing ability to *read* thousands of words per minute are misinterpretations of the reading act. To attempt to read all types of material at breakneck speed is foolish and probably impossible—if reading is synonymous with understanding. To preview material as a prelude to more careful reading or study or to obtain just an overview of some material for particular purposes—at very fast rates—makes sense.

Being able to **skim—to look over material rapidly for given purposes without** *reading* **every phrase**—is a great asset for a reader to possess. Skimming enables people to select content that they want to read and to discard that which is inconsequential for their purposes. Skimming permits people to gain a general idea about material when that is their purpose, rather than to read all material in detail.

Grades four through eight are none too early a time to make pupils aware of the skill of skimming and its uses and advantages. Informal, functional practice in skimming can be given safely to children in the fourth and fifth grades who are not having serious basic problems in reading. Good readers in the sixth grade and above may be given timed practice in skimming. Children should be guided to skim (1) as a prelude to careful reading and study (preview); (2) to obtain just the major ideas; (3) in review for a quiz or test; (4) to develop an outline; (5) to write a summary; and (6) to decide whether or not to read a book.

Scanning

Being able to scan—to search through material rapidly, with a given purpose in mind, in order to find a specific fact or an answer to a particular question—plays a large role in much of a youngster's reading. Scanning enables people to locate specific information without reading all the material around it. Scanning permits people to use a variety of sources with economy.

Scanning actually never exists by itself as a reading rate. Once the specific fact is located or it seems as though the answer to a question is being given, the reader shifts into a slower pace, reading that particular information carefully to be certain the purpose for reading has been met.

Scanning begun in the primary grades should be continued throughout the elementary-school program. The activities below are just a few possible scanning suggestions. Pupils should be asked to see how quickly they can:

1. Scan a table of contents to find out on what page a chapter begins or a topic is treated.
2. Scan parts of an article in an encyclopedia to find a particular bit of information.
3. Scan to find a word in the dictionary.

4. Scan an index to find an entry pertinent to a certain topic.
5. Scan a selection to find one particular bit of information.
6. Scan a table to find one particular statistic.
7. Scan to find and read orally the most exciting part of a story or the part that describes the prettiest picture.
8. Scan to find the answer to each of a series of questions that the teacher writes on the chalkboard, placing at the end of each question the page number on which the answer may be found.
9. Scan to find sentences that portray the character of a person in a story.
10. For those ready to do so, scan several sources in search of supporting or conflicting evidence about a specific point.
11. Scan to find a particular name in a telephone directory.
12. Scan to find a specific program in a television guide.
13. Scan to find a certain movie in the newspaper.
14. Scan to find a time on a subway, train, bus, or plane schedule.

Numbers 11–14 above were suggested by Evelyn B. Spache in the second edition of her *Reading Activities for Child Involvement* (Boston: Allyn and Bacon, 1976), p. 214.

DISCUSSION QUESTIONS AND ACTIVITIES

1. Ask pupils to name purposes for reading. They will differ in different classrooms, at different grade levels, and in different socio-cultural situations. Some children will have to do a great deal of thinking to come up with any purposes at all. Keep the conversation and thinking going, however, for they will surprise themselves when they view the list you have written on the board. Such a list might be:

> To enjoy a story.
> To find out how to take care of an animal.
> To read about a person.
> To read a shopping list.
> To study for a test.
> To learn about something in science.
> To solve a mathematics problem.
> To find out the time of a television program.
> To find out what happened next in a comic strip.

After the list is complete for the time, ask pupils to think about how they might read to satisfy each purpose. Lead them to consider the need for purpose in determining strategies in reading, particularly flexibility of rates. You might want to indicate suggested rates on the chalkboard next to each purpose.

To enjoy a story   Fairly fast

To read a shopping list   Fairly slow

To study for a test   Slow

Pupils may want to add more detail to both the purpose and the suggested rate after discussion. For example, when they consider the purpose "to study for a test," they may want to discuss the nature of the test, the kinds of tests the teacher gives, the nature of the material to be studied. Their decisions may then affect the rate. They could decide that for the purpose "to find out how to take care of an animal" that they are interested in taking care of a dog. If the book is about a number of animals, they will read fast—scan—until they reach the information about dogs; then they will read slowly for the specific information.

Such discussions held periodically will help to develop flexibility of reading rates.

2. Evelyn Spache suggested an interesting scanning activity for pupils beyond the primary grades:

> Upper-grade children enjoy this news activity. Choose five news categories, such as local politics, national politics, sports, theater, science. Assign a committee to each category. Each committee chooses several prominent people associated with their category. Daily, for a week, students search through the local newspaper and keep a tally as to the number of times their VIP's names appear in the news.[7]

3. Thomas and Robinson, although writing for secondary-school students, presented some skimming activities suitable for intermediate- and middle-school pupils. Obviously, pupils must learn some basic skimming techniques prior to engaging in the suggested activities.

A. Have pupils turn to an unexplored textbook chapter or magazine article and say: "How much can you learn about this chapter (or article) in just three minutes? Use your skimming techniques to hit the high spots and then let's talk about your results."

B. When pupils have found a book or magazine article they think they may want to read but are not sure about, suggest: "Skim it! See if you want to read it by just hitting the high spots! If it doesn't suit you, or doesn't seem to answer questions you want answered, don't read it. Turn to another piece of material and skim it. Eventually you'll find what you want."

C. Help students to skim newspaper articles. They should read the headlines, other headings, and then turn to the first paragraph or two. The "lead" paragraph(s) ". . . is dense with the answers to key questions—the five *w*'s and sometimes *h*: who? what? when? where? why? how? The content of the rest of the news story tapers off in im-

[7] Evelyn B. Spache, *Reading Activities for Child Involvement*, 2nd ed. (Boston: Allyn and Bacon, 1976), pp. 214–15.

portance. Against a time limit, students skim the headlines, the sub-heads, and the lead for the gist of front page stories." [8]

ADDITIONAL READINGS

Books and Pamphlets

BERGER, ALLEN, and PEEBLES, JAMES, comps. *Rates of Comprehension.* Newark, Del.: International Reading Assn., 1976.

HARRIS, THEODORE L. "Flexibility: A Neglected Aspect of Reading Instruction." In *New Horizons in Reading*, Proceedings of the Fifth IRA World Congress on Reading. Newark, Del.: International Reading Assn., 1976.

RANKIN, EARL F. *Measurement of Reading Flexibility.* Newark, Del.: International Reading Assn., 1974.

Periodicals

AHRENDT, KENNETH, M., and MOSEDALE, S. "Eye Movement Photography and the Reading Process." *Journal of the Reading Specialist* 10, no. 3 (March 1971), pp. 149–58.

CARVER, RONALD P. "Speed Readers Don't Read: They Skim." *Psychology Today* 6, no. 3 (August 1972), pp. 22–30.

GLUCK, H. ROBERT. "If Comprehension Comes Can Speed Be Far Behind?" *Journal of the Reading Specialist* 8, no. 4 (May 1969), pp. 176–81.

GROFF, PATRICK. "Subvocalization and Silent Reading." *Reading World* 16, no. 3 (March 1977), pp. 231–37.

KATZ, LEONARD, and WICKLUND, DAVID A. "Word Scanning Rate for Good and Poor Readers." *Journal of Educational Psychology* 62, no. 2 (April 1971), pp. 138–40.

MARCEL, TONY. "The Effective Visual Field and the Use of Context in Fast and Slow Readers of Two Ages." *British Journal of Psychology* 65, no. 4 (November 1974), pp. 479–92.

MENDELSOHN, LEONARD R. "Jetting to Utopia: The Speed Reading Phenomenon." *Language Arts* 54, no. 2 (February 1977), pp. 116–20.

PAUK, WALTER. "Can the Mind Speed Read?" *Journal of the Reading Specialist* 10, no. 1 (October 1970), pp. 14–18.

SINGER, HARRY. "A Developmental Model for Speed of Reading in Grades Three Through Six." *Reading Research Quarterly* 1, no. 1 (Fall 1965), pp. 29–49.

SWALM, JAMES, and KLING, MARTIN. "Speed Reading in the Elementary School." *Elementary School Journal* 74, no. 3 (December 1973), pp. 158–64.

[8] Adapted from Ellen L. Thomas and H. Alan Robinson, *Improving Reading in Every Class: A Sourcebook for Teachers*, 2nd ed. (Boston: Allyn and Bacon, 1977), p. 224.

chapter 10

developing study strategies in the content areas

What to Expect in This Chapter:

In this chapter the focus is on specific aspects of reading instruction related to reading in the content areas. Five major areas of study strategies are described and explained: selection and evaluation; organization; recall; locating information; following directions. Samples of activities are presented for both primary- and upper-school children. Patterns of writing in the various content areas are discussed, and specific patterns for each area are enumerated. Four types of specialized vocabulary are illustrated: technical vocabulary; overlap words; multi-meaning words; function words.

Reading programs in the elementary grades have depended traditionally on basal reading materials for reading instruction, with some inroads made by trade books in individualized reading programs. But a reading program in a school or school district cannot be left to just the basals or the selected trade books or a combination of both. The reading program should span across the total curriculum so pupils learn how to unlock ideas in print—wherever they find them. And they will find many in content-area textbooks and supplementary materials.

Relatively little attention has been given to helping pupils become proficient readers in the varied content areas. Talk about doing it has been more prevalent than action! Such reading should begin in the primary grades—as soon as pupils consult content area material to learn. Content-area books become increasingly difficult as children proceed through the grades. It stands to reason that we should be preparing them in organized fashion.

In this chapter, we have chosen to concentrate specifically on several aspects of reading instruction that grow in significance as pupils cope with the demands of the curriculum as well as the needs for reading outside of the school. In reality, most of the other chapters in this book deal also with aspects of reading instruction vital to reading in the content areas.

STUDY STRATEGIES

Successful reading in the content areas depends upon the acquisition of study strategies, often called study skills. We have chosen the term study *strategies* rather than *skills* in an effort to suggest that a strategy is an overall plan of attack for a given purpose; a skill is usually looked upon as just the ability to do something competently. We wish to highlight the fact that a study strategy includes purpose, thinking process or skill, and product.

Study strategies involve comprehension, retention, organization, and location of information. They are used to unlock ideas and obtain information in the various content areas. Different authorities give different

EXAMPLE:

(Skill)   *Morris has learned to read for details.*
(Strategy) *Morris has learned to pay careful attention to the details in word problems in math and is able to demonstrate his ability to do this by using the details accurately in the solution of the problem.*

names to the major areas of study strategies or skills. In this book, we have grouped them into five major areas: *selection and evaluation, organization, recall, location of information,* and *following directions.* All overlap; the categorization is to help the teacher. In most study situations, clusters of study strategies will need to be used in order to satisfy the varied purposes for dealing with particular material. All study strategies are used in each content area, often in different ways dependent upon the nature of the material and the nature of the assignment.

Selection and Evaluation

The skills of *selection* and *evaluation* team up together to make one important, composite study strategy. This strategy is significant because of the frequency with which it is needed and also because it is basic to other study strategies, particularly *organization* and *recall.*

In using the selection and evaluation process, the child needs to select a certain item from many other items in context and evaluate it in terms of some condition imposed in a question or direction; in other words, the child must pick out some item and judge its worth in meeting the specifications of an activity that he or she is asked to carry forward. For example, the child may be asked to find the answer to the question, "In what way do bees help farmers?" The chapter in the science text in which this answer can be found contains many statements about the helpfulness of bees, several of which pertain to their helpfulness to people in general, some to flowers and plants, and one in particular to the farmer. In finding the answer to this question, the child finds and reads several statements, mentally evaluating the pertinence of each to the farmer and his needs, and through this process finally selects the one that answers the question.

Examples from Textbooks. The popular technique of finding the main idea in a paragraph involves a selection and evaluation study strategy. When, for example, children are attempting to develop some major ideas about the sun during science period, they can be asked to *evaluate* all the ideas in the following paragraphs and *select* the one that.

is most important in each case. An ensuing discussion can further help them develop the ability of *evaluation* through thinking about the answers of others and verifying their own responses.

The Fascinating Sun [1]

1. The surface of the sun looks like a sea of white-hot clouds. These clouds are not made of water vapor. They are made of copper, iron, calcium, sodium, and other substances. These substances, however, do not exist in solid forms on the sun. Because of the hot temperatures, they are gases. That's why the sun appears to be covered with bright clouds.
   a. The sun is hot.
   b. These clouds are not made of water vapor.
   c. The surface of the sun looks like a sea of clouds.

2. The surface of the sun appears rough and flaky. When astronomers look at it through a telescope, they see something that looks like snowflakes on gray cloth. These flakes are from 400 to 600 miles in diameter. They appear in many different shapes and change continuously. Old ones go out of sight. New ones come into view. But always they cause the surface to look rough.
   a. These flakes are from 400 to 600 miles in diameter.
   b. The surface of the sun appears rough and flaky.
   c. Old ones go out of sight.

3. Dark spots, called sunspots, can be seen on the sun at times. Sunspots are really whirlpools in the gases on the surface of the sun. These sunspots have a dark central portion and a lighter outer portion. Many of these sunspots last for only about 24 hours. Very few can be seen for longer than a week.
   a. They have a dark central portion.
   b. Dark spots can be seen on the sun at times.
   c. Many sunspots last for only about 24 hours.

All selection and evaluation strategies do not include a search for main ideas; many times, pupils must select details that they feel will answer the question or satisfy the reading purpose. The questions below, from social studies and mathematics, focus on both major ideas and details for specific purposes.

Social studies.

1. What two words tell about summer weather near the coast of Ireland?
2. After several activities of Columbus have been mentioned, children are asked, "Which of all these things were most important?"
3. What useful trees are found in Southern forests?
4. Find on page 40 a sentence telling one way in which control of the Mississippi River helped Pioneers in the Ohio Valley.

Mathematics

1. Find the number that you need in working this problem. Find the one that you do not need.
2. How many parts does this problem have?

[1] Nila B. Smith, *Be a Better Reader*, Level C (Englewood Cliffs, N.J.: Prentice-Hall, 1977), p. 23. Copyright 1977, 1968. Reprinted by permission.

Development of Selection and Evaluation Strategies. In order to meet study situations adequately, children should be given experience in using the selection and evaluation process at all levels of the elementary school. The teacher, of course, should not depend solely upon textbook exercises to develop these strategies. Many occasions present themselves during discussion periods for giving instruction and practice. The alert teacher will sense and take advantage of opportunities to have children select pictures, words, phrases, sentences, paragraphs, stories, informative selections, and so on, as needed in meeting the prerequisite of evaluation for some particular purpose.

Teachers may follow up class discussions and activities by providing materials of their own preparation. These may consist of oral, chalkboard, or duplicated instructions or exercises prepared in connection with the subject matter being studied. Such supplemental activities are particularly valuable in giving practice to children who are especially in need of help in the use of these study strategies. Those listed below may be adapted for use in most content areas. They should always be attached to a meaningful purpose.

First grade. During the first-grade period, children may work both with pictures and with reading symbols. They may engage in activities of the following types:

1. Select from several pictures on the chalk ledge one that represents a word, phrase, or sentence held up by the teacher.
2. Select, upon request, specified words and phrases in context in their books.
3. Select words and phrases to answer questions and complete sentences.
4. Select statements on the basis of whether they are true or false.
5. Select from given lists the correct answers to riddles.

Second and third grades. As children go on to the second and third grades, they are capable of participating in selection and evaluation experiences at higher levels. They may continue to select phrases, sentences, paragraphs, and stories of increasing difficulty in terms of a variety of specific purposes. In addition, they may participate in activities of the types indicated below.

1. Select portions of context that express a specific idea.
2. Select a paragraph in terms of its importance.
3. Select the most important thought in an informative selection.
4. Find answers to specific questions in informative articles.
5. Select and read materials pertaining especially to certain problems or interests.

Upper grades. In the fourth, fifth, sixth grades, and above, children should continue to have many selection and evaluation experiences of all the types previously mentioned in connection with the reading that they do in all of their subjects. In addition, they are now ready for, and should have specific development of and practice in, more complex types of selection and evaluation, such as indicated below.

1. Find the main idea of a passage together with supporting details.
2. Select and evaluate statements that:
   a. support a conclusion or generalization.
   b. prove a point.
   c. answer a leading question requiring judgment.
   d. lead to a decision in regard to statements of fact versus opinion.

Organization

Another study situation frequently encountered calls for organization of information gained through reading; that is, putting together systematically those things that belong to a whole. Grouping or listing items that belong to one classification or that occur in a certain order, outlining, and summarizing are the procedures most often used in making organization responses. The preview technique applied to an article, chapter, or book (described in chapter 9) is primarily one of organization.

All the organizing strategies require selection and evaluation as a first step—to pull out the items to be organized. Here are two examples of the use of organization strategies that clearly indicate their dependence on the strategies of selection and evaluation.

In grade three, after reading a chapter in their science textbooks about butterflies, the children were asked to give the life cycle of a Monarch Butterfly. Because there was no one place in the chapter in which this information was given, they had to assemble the information by picking out pertinent bits here and there and organizing them into the entire life cycle.

In fourth-grade geography, the children were asked, "What are the land features of the Atlantic Coastal Plain?" In order to answer this question, they had to turn back to several paragraphs of text that discussed climate, land features, occupations, crops—and out of it all, they sorted out those things that had to do only with land features and pieced them together to make a total "picture."

Examples from Textbooks. Responses calling for organization appear very frequently in subject matter textbooks and workbooks. A small sampling of different types of textbook responses calling for organization is given below:

Science.

1. Pick out all the names of trees. Make a list of the trees.
2. Write the names of all the animals that sleep all winter.

3. Make a list of things that change the earth's surface.
4. Study the outline below and see if the items under each heading are correct. If not, change the items to come under the headings to which they belong.

Social studies.

1. Choose a scene from the experiences of Columbus to act. Plan what the characters should do and say.
2. List facts that prove the statement: "When the Pilgrims first came to America, they knew very little about living in a new, wild country."
3. What are the advantages of an ocean-front location for Korea? Write these advantages in one paragraph.
4. Outline the selection, "Jet Lag." Select the main points and include as subtopics under each main point any statements you think important in the story.

Mathematics.

1. In a first-grade mathematics book: Draw a line from a big candy bar to each of the small candy bars. How many small candy bars are there all together?
2. Divide this list of numbers into two groups. Put all the 10s in one group and all of the 100s in another (list of numbers followed).
3. Make a list of the clothes in the picture on page 8, and write the price of each. Put the things that cost most first on your list and those that cost least at the end of the list.

Development of Organization Strategies. Although exercises in textbooks frequently call for organization responses, teachers are not relieved of the responsibility of *developing* these important strategies and helping children to apply them in connection with their daily reading. If teachers are keenly aware of these strategies and their significance, many opportunities will be found to discuss them and to have pupils make use of them.

Practice in the strategies of organizing what is read may be given in some of the ways suggested below, adapted by teachers, of course, to meet their own situations.

First grade.

1. Pupils at this stage may arrange sentences in the wall chart in the order in which the events in a chart or reader story took place.
2. They may group together words representing a given classification, such as *toys, animals, people*.
3. They may classify ideas; for example, after reading about a park, the teacher may place on the chalk ledge the words birds, train, girls,

baby, doll, boats, Mother, store, tree, chair, boys. Then he or she may write on the chalkboard, "In the Park," "Not in the Park." Pupils classify the words.

4. After reading an easy science book, children may classify living things or objects, such as "Animals that Have Fur" and "Animals that Do Not Have Fur."

5. In addition to classifying words, phrases, and sentences for a variety of purposes, first-grade children may retell science or social studies text they have read, being careful to observe the exact sequence of processes or events, as: "Tell just what the children did in their experiment in planting beans in the order in which they did the different things," or "Just how did the Indians make their headbands?"

6. They may search for as many selections as they can find about *boats* or *rabbits* or some other topic of interest.

Second and third grades. In second and third grades, experiences in organizing reading content should take on forms and purposes that are even closer to those found in study situations in content fields.

1. Children at this stage may select and organize simple bits of information under a specific heading or in answer to a question.

2. They may organize in sequence steps, events, and incidents selected from increasingly difficult content.

3. They may select and organize in a written list all items in a given selection that belong under a particular heading.

Intermediate grades and above. If the organization strategies have been nurtured all through the primary grades, then children in the middle grades should have no trouble in taking several advanced steps of the type that will be needed in their future study activities. During this period, the teacher should develop and give practice in such organizing activities as indicated below.

1. Listing in sequence the steps leading up to an event, climax, undertaking, or preparation of a finished product.

2. Placing events in the right sequence when reading historical materials.

3. Classifying products, industries, and land features in regard to certain locales when reading geographical material.

4. Organizing facts to support a conclusion.

5. Finding and bringing together information from several sources as it has a bearing on some specific topic or problem.

6. Taking notes and organizing them to give the gist of a selection.

7. Reading, making, and using outlines of material read.

8. Summarizing a selection in a paragraph or in a sentence.

9. Organizing facts gleaned from reading in tabular form, graphs, and charts.

Recall

Recalling what is read, fixing content in mind so that it can be brought back when wanted, involves study strategies needed in all content areas. The present emphasis upon learning how to locate facts we need at the time they are needed, rather than memorizing a multitude of items, is excellent.

Examples from Textbooks. Responses calling for recall of facts in subject-matter texts and workbooks are exceedingly numerous. The questions and directions used for this purpose are almost wholly of the type used in literal comprehension: questions based upon a statement in the text, true-false, multiple-choice, and completion exercises. The responses following, however, differ from the checking of literal comprehension and the strategy of selection and evaluation in that the fact that what is being checked must be *remembered*. The child is supposed not only to understand the statement but also to fix it in mind for recall purposes.

In all the examples given below, the *responses were to be given without reference to the text*.

Science.

1. How does sleeping all the time help some animals to live all winter? Answer this question without looking it up.
2. Do you remember some of the plants that are used for making clothing? Write their names.
3. What did the book tell you about the way in which electricity is carried to our homes?

Social studies.

1. Do you remember what is done with much of the milk sold by farmers in the Netherlands?
2. Can you recall where the first successful oil well was drilled?

Mathematics.

1. Learn this multiplication table. Repeat it until you can remember all answers correctly.
2. Write the table for measurement of weight on a paper. Check with your book. Learn the correct number to any part you missed. Repeat until you remember all parts of the table.

Development of Recall Strategies. As in the case of the other study strategies, learning how to remember what one reads should not be left to chance. Just because children are frequently asked to give memory responses in textbooks does not necessarily mean that they know the best ways of fixing in mind the facts called for. Here are some suggestions for elementary school children.

First grade.

1. The too-frequent practice of questioning children verbally in order to check their remembrance of content may be supplemented by other interesting activities that serve the same purpose. One way to vary the question-answer response is for the teacher to place words or phrases in the wall chart that answer questions based on the selection. The teacher then asks the questions one by one and requests different children to answer different questions by finding and reading the appropriate word or phrase on the wall chart. Cards may contain the words *swim, fly, run, crawl*; the pupils are asked to hold up the right card in answer to such questions as, "What do fishes do?" To add variety, the teacher may write the answers on the chalkboard and call upon different children to underline the correct answer to each question asked.

2. Children may be given help in selecting and remembering items in a short section of content in this way:

> You may draw pictures of all the things that Curtis got for his birthday. Glance through the story to find the names of all of the different presents (selection and evaluation) and tell me the names as you find them. Now close your books and see if you can tell the names of all of the presents. All right, now draw pictures of all of Curtis' presents.

3. Pupils may draw pictures to show how well they have understood and remembered concepts. After reading a section on *Wind* in their first-grade science book, discussion might take place in regard to how wind affects trees, bushes, leaves on the ground, kites, people, and other things mentioned in the text. The teacher may then suggest that the pupils draw a picture to show how the wind affects people and all the objects mentioned. Reference to the text may be necessary for practice in recalling the items before drawing the picture.

4. Recall the events of a social-studies story as the teacher writes the sentences that they dictate on the chalkboard.

5. Recall directions for carrying out some class activity.

The directions may be written on the chalkboard, the children being asked to fix them in mind, and then to carry them out after the directions have been erased.

Second and third grades.

1. Recalling factual details, of science, social studies, or health information, by answering questions and making multiple-choice, completion, or true-false responses.

2. Recalling information needed in furthering a class project or needed in solving a class problem or in giving an oral report to the class.

3. Writing short, informative reports based on something they have read.

4. Verifying exact recall of facts. After making recall responses, they should frequently be asked to reread and check the accuracy of their statements.

Intermediate grades and above. Give children directions such as these:

1. Reread the selection. Prepare to report to the class facts about "The Railroad Track." Try to pick out these facts as you read and memorize them.

2. Take notes on this selection. Use them to guide you as you practice reproducing the information in the selection. Do this until you can give an account of the information accurately and well.

3. Reread the selection on Hawaii and prepare to report to the class facts you have learned about a *luau*. Take notes, and underline the important words as an aid in memorizing points you wish to report.

Location of Information

The reader no doubt has heard of such incidents as the one in which the college librarian announced that she and her staff had to spend most of their time during the first month of the fall semester in teaching freshmen how to find things in the library; or of the social-studies teacher who had to stop teaching his own subject for a week while he taught his high school students how to use the location strategies. Much evidence of inadequacies at higher levels point to the fact that a better job could be done in teaching the location strategies in the elementary grades.

In this day of wide reading, both the prospective teacher and the teacher in service are well aware of the fact that authors of books in all content fields, as well as present-day teachers themselves, frequently ask pupils to search for information in many different sources. No examples are needed to reinforce this point.

The study-strategies area of locating information is very complex. The constellation of location strategies embraces many items, such as those enumerated under the headings below. And all these items need to be developed and practiced.

Primary Grades. Foundation should be laid in the primary grades for the use of all location strategies. The strategies listed below are appropriate at this level. Many advanced third graders, however, will be able to participate in some of the activities suggested for children in the later grades.

Finding page numbers. Location strategies should be introduced functionally and given functional practice as much as possible. The need for finding page numbers usually occurs several times each day and is the easiest of the location strategies to introduce. In beginning first grade, the teacher may write the number of the page to be found on the chalk-board as he or she says it, and then ask the children to match the number in their books. This procedure may also be used later when the number of the page is of a higher denomination than the children are able to read.

While in the early stages, pupils enjoy seeing how quickly they can find each of a series of numbers that the teacher reads orally and if necessary writes on the chalkboard for matching purposes.

In second and third grades, a variation in practice may be provided by writing on the chalkboard several numbers, which the children then write in a column on the left side of their papers. The class or group is then asked to see how quickly they can find and write on their papers the name of the story that begins on each of these pages.

Finding specific phrases or sentences in context. A specific phrase or sentence may be found quickly to prove an answer, to settle a disagreement, to emphasize a particular fact, or to take a quick look again at something to be remembered.

Children enjoy the activity of finding a word or phrase in answer to "Who, What, and Where" questions, as "Who was Happy?" (A little black dog.) "What did Judy give to Happy?" (A bone.) "Where did Happy bury the bone?" (Behind the garage.)

Using titles. The concept of titles may be introduced during chart work. Sometimes before, sometimes after reading a chart, the teacher may say something to this effect, "Let's give this story a title. What would be a good name for it?" Thus, children may have opportunities to compose titles before reading them in a book. After a selection has been read, the teacher may take time occasionally to discuss the appropriateness of the title, and to ask the children if they can think of a better one.

Recognizing chapters. Learning to recognize chapters or units in a book should be introduced as early as these subdivisions occur in books with which the children are working. Early readers, science books, and social-studies books often mark the introduction of a new topic by an entire introductory page, a double-page illustration, or a page of colored paper bearing the title of the new topic. In all such cases, it is advisable for the teacher to take time to have the children read the name of the new topic and to explain why it is so marked.

Using tables of contents. The table of contents may be introduced when the children meet a new topical division in a book they are reading. After having pupils read the title of the new unit, the teacher may have them turn to the table of contents, find the title there, and then read the names of the selections that come under the title. They may check the page number given for the title and some of the selections by turning to the pages indicated to see if the selections really are on the pages as stated.

Whenever the children are about to read a new chapter or unit, they may be asked to examine the section heading, discuss what they might expect to find under this heading, turn back to the table of contents, and read the titles under the heading. The table of contents should also be used whenever pupils are searching for stories or informative selections about a topic.

Reading illustrations. Children in the primary grades should be helped to read the pictures, diagrams, tables, and graphs in their content area books as they begin to meet them. Pupils' attention should be focused on the importance of finding out what the illustration has to say as well as what the words on the page tell them. They should be guided to inspect the illustration carefully, read the caption and/or labels when present, and relate the illustration to the words they are reading on the page.

For example, pupils might be asked to read the caption and labels and look at the pictures in the diagram following.[2]

Growing Corn

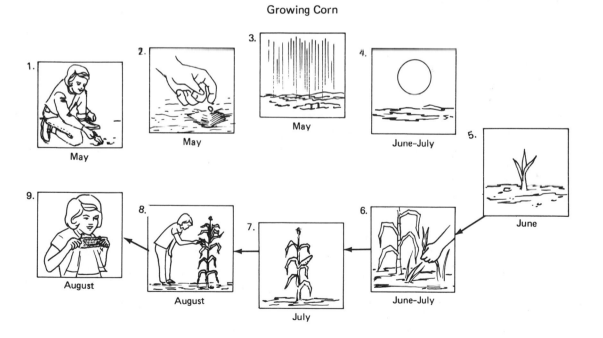

Then pupils can be presented with a group of nine sentences that also tell the steps in raising sweet corn. Pupils will be told that the

[2] This activity is drawn from the EDL Study Skills Library, Level C, 1978. Reproduced with the permission of EDL-McGraw Hill.

sentences are not in the right order. They need to refer to the diagram in order to put the sentences in the correct order. Such an activity insists that the pupils "read" the diagram.

Alphabetizing. The first-grade and kindergarten teacher usually have pupils who are at different stages of development in their familiarity with the alphabet. Some know the alphabet in order. Others do not even know the names of the letters.

The sequence of letters in the alphabet must be taught as a readiness activity for dictionary work. Perhaps some functional situation can be used in introducing sequence. For example, the teacher might ask help in preparing an alphabetical list of the names of children absent during the past month to send to the principal. As they have difficulty, the teacher may ask a pupil who knows the alphabet well to say it in order. The teacher will then write the letters in order on the chalkboard. The names of the children who have been absent are then arranged through reference to the alphabet on the chalkboard. The teacher may show the children a telephone directory, a dictionary, the classbook, and so forth, and explain the use of an alphabetical arrangement.

Skill in using an alphabetical arrangement requires a variety of competencies, and much practice. If pupils can locate words in a dictionary quickly and easily, they will use a dictionary freely. If they have difficulty in finding words, they probably will not bother to look them up. The most basic and most important dictionary skill is that of using an alphabetical arrangement rapidly and accurately. This requires much practice throughout the elementary grades. A few activities for primary-grade use are suggested below.

1. Working with sections of the alphabet in order: "Who can tell me what the first six letters are?" Write the letters *a*, *b*, *c*, *d*, *e*, and *f* on the chalkboard. Have children who need the practice read the letters. Erase and rearrange the letters. Ask children to tell in what order to put the letters. Erase one of the letters. Ask what letter goes in that space. Repeat with variation.

2. Children may find all the words in a mixed list that begin with *b*, all that begin with *f*, and so forth.

3. Arrange a mixed list of letters alphabetically; similarly, a mixed list of words. Have the children tell you the order in which to write them.

house, boy, apple, fat, dog, cat, go, every

4. Crossing out those words in a list that are not in alphabetical order.

and, big, hat, can, do, man, eat, long

5. Filling blanks with words in alphabetical sequence. Children may select from several words a particular word needed in filling in a blank space in lists of words alphabetically arranged, as:

animal	errand	ignite
bake	_____	_____
cobweb	garden	_____
_____	_____	lantern

feather, join, hustle, kind, drug

Contacts with reference materials. Picture dictionaries, classroom-prepared or commercial, are useful tools for children in the primary grades. (See pages 173–75 in chapter 6.) They permit realistic use of alphabetical order and introduce many dictionary basics as readiness for beginning dictionaries—format, entry words, definitions. Some third, and even second, graders may begin working with beginning dictionaries with much guidance from the teacher. No formal dictionary training need take place in the primary grades, but for those who are turning to the dictionaries teachers may make them aware of guide words and varied definitions.

Children at the primary level are not usually expected to make direct use of encyclopedias, atlases, or almanacs. On the other hand, some may be eager to use these sources; if so, teachers must take great care that they turn to parts of these references they can handle. No recognized encyclopedia on the market today is below fourth-fifth grade reading level, and even that designation is "stretching it." (See pages 284–85.) Although teachers may want to discourage the direct use of most references for most primary pupils, they will want to have pupils become acquainted with the nature of such references and with their respective uses. Contacts with these references frequently may be provided through teacher demonstration when a need arises. For example, Tom brought in an amphibian that he said was a frog. Some of the children said it was a toad. Miss Drake borrowed two encyclopedias from an upper-grade classroom, one with *F* on the shelfback and the other with *T*. She explained the function of encyclopedias, demonstrated how she could find *toads* and *frogs*, respectively, read the information to the children, showed them the pictures, and let them arrive at their own conclusion in the light of the encyclopedic information. Frequent contacts with atlases and world almanacs may be given in a similar fashion.

Grades Four and Above. All the skills and strategies developed in the primary grades should be used with increasing proficiency as pupils move from grade four through eight. In addition, pupils should learn at this time to use with ease all location strategies that are needed by high-school and college students, and to develop permanent habits of using these strategies whenever they may serve a purpose.

Using parts of books. The use of parts of books, usually taught in the intermediate grades, embraces recognition of copyright data, preface, introduction, glossary, and index.

With the present emphasis upon critical reading the *date that a book was copyrighted* often is an important item to know.

1. When the occasion arises, show the children where the copyright date can be found in a book. Follow with practice in which they find and report orally or in writing the latest copyright date of several books. They may also report the name of the individual or company who holds the copyright in each case.

2. When a new book is used for the first time, call attention to the *preface* or *foreword*. Explain that if a preface or foreword is written by the author its purposes usually are to give an overview of the book, to set forth its objectives from the author's viewpoint, and, sometimes, to give acknowledgments. If the preface is written by the editor or a person other than the editor, it usually presents an evaluation of the book.

Have the children read the preface or foreword at hand to check and discuss the information given above. Practice may follow by using a similar procedure with other books.

3. The use of the index, a complex skill, should follow after most of the other basic location strategies have been developed. (See pages 282–84).

Using dictionary and glossary skills. The most extensive achievement in location strategies to be realized at this level is the thorough establishment of the entire constellation of dictionary skills. These skills should be introduced through functional situations, if possible. Each different skill, however, should be given planned practice.

Alphabetizing. Alphabetizing skills should be extended to include: (1) locating a letter quickly by its position in the alphabet, rather than by going through the alphabet one letter at a time; (2) locating words by examining the total alphabetical arrangement within the word.

After the children have had some practice in finding words by the use of the initial letter, the next step is to develop the short cuts of (first) the ability *to find a word in glossary or dictionary by use of the first two letters*, and (later) by the *use of the first three letters*, and so on, until the alphabetical arrangement within an entire word is noted. For example, in looking up the word *guitar*, the children should be told not to search all the way through the *g*'s but to look at once through the section where *g* is followed by *u*.

Following this—as with a word like *strait*—the children may be told to turn immediately to the section of *s* words in which *s* is followed by *t* and then to turn quickly to the section of *st* words where the *st* is followed by *r*.

After introduction, practice activities may be used. Teachers will, of course, use these suggestions merely as examples for preparing activities of their own based on content with which the children are working.

1. Write the letters from *l* to *o*. Write the letters from *p* to *t*. Write the letters from *d* to *k*. Write the letters from *v* to *z*.

2. Write *Before* or *After:*
    a. Does *m* come before or after *l*?
    b. Does *t* come before or after *u*?
    c. Does *k* come before or after *r*?
    d. Does *s* come before or after *r*?
    e. Does *e* come before or after *f*?

3. Write in the blanks the letters as they come in the alphabet:

```
_____ _____t
_____d_____
w_____ _____
a _____ c
g h _____
_____ _____g
```

4. Pupils may be asked to see how quickly they can find words in the dictionary by looking for the first two letters in each of a group of words written on the chalkboard. Such words as these may be used: *Africa, emery, guariba, maniac, serpent, triple, shear, giraffe.*

This activity may be repeated as children locate words by examining the first three letters, the first four letters, and so on.

Children may carry out directions with words similar to those in (5) and (6) below.

5. Which word of each pair of words should appear first in the dictionary:

dilute	scientist	chuck	claw	western
den	stampede	chance	clean	wait

6. Arrange these words in the order in which they would come in the *d* section of the dictionary:

delegate	dynamite	dinosaur
double	dyspepsia	Darwin
Diesel	dabble	diction
donate	destroy	duct

Using guide words. It is usually advisable to introduce guide words in connection with the glossary of one of the textbooks that the children are using and then transfer the skill to dictionary practice.

As an example of an introduction, consider that *ridge* and *Sweden* are guide words on a glossary page of a book that the children are using. The teacher may call the children's attention to the guide words at the top of each page in the glossary. Finally, the teacher may pause to discuss a certain page with *ridge* at the top of the left-hand column and the word *Sweden* at the top of the right-hand column. Through discussion, children are led to discover that the left-hand guide word represents the first word that appears on a page, and that the right-hand guide word represents the last word that appears on a page. They may then check this information by examining several pages.

Here are some possible practice activities.

1. Here are the guide words on page 471 and page 472 of your glossary. Write the number of the page on which each word in the list appears.

Guide Words

Page 471	abyss carbon
Page 472	Canute Egypt

_____	bazaar	_____	dense
_____	anaconda	_____	custom
_____	chariot	_____	eager
_____	bridle	_____	Cabot

2. The guide words on a certain page are *damp* and *dead*. What words from the following list would be on that page?

dinosaurs, dying, darkness, dad, dashed, den, discovery, daylight, divide, discovered

3. The guide words on page 230 of your glossary are *Egyptian* and *Gritti*. Follow these directions in working with these guide words.

First, list those words found on preceding pages
Second, list those words found on the same page
Third, list those words found on later pages

fiber, iceberg, coyote, hurl, English, afford, guitar, ivory, gamoose, bow, estate, hare, flute, current, graze

Using pronunciation aids. See pages 174–75 in chapter 6 for a discussion of pronunciation key and other pronunciation aids to be considered in using a dictionary.

Finding definitions. Children need to be given considerable practice in choosing the right definition of a word as used in a certain context. They need to develop the concept of bringing the sentence, paragraph, or paragraphs in which the word is embedded *to* the dictionary as they search for the appropriate definition. A good time to introduce this skill is when confusion arises about a multiple-meaning word met in an immediate reading situation. As an example, the pupils in one group read, "The Colonists used candles to illuminate their homes." There was disagreement in regard to the meaning of *illuminate*. The teacher, in this case, explained that several definitions of a word are often given in dictionaries, and that they need to select the one that best fits the sentence or paragraph in which it is used. The children then were asked to turn to the dictionary definitions for *illuminate*, where they found five numbered definitions. All the definitions were read, discussion followed, and the definition "to make light" was selected as the most appropriate one.

Activities to use in practicing the selection of the right definition are suggested below.

1. The teacher may have the pupils locate and choose the appropriate dictionary definitions for several words selected from pages of text with which they are working. Oral discussion should accompany or follow this activity.

2. Pupils may be asked to write the appropriate definition for each of several words as each appears in the context of a certain sentence.

3. They may also write the number of an appropriate dictionary definition on a blank line placed before a sentence containing an underlined word that is to be looked up, as indicated below:

_____a. Judith thought the new movie was very *tame*.

_____b. Mr. Fowler grew some *tame* blackberries in his back yard.

_____c. Sam had a pet owl that was very *tame*.

_____d. After a long and bitter fight, the inhabitants became quite *tame*.

4. Pupils may be asked to number their papers with all the definitions for a certain word, then to write a sentence using the word appropriately for each definition.

Finding synonyms. Locating and understanding synonyms in the dictionary might be introduced by the teacher in some such way as this: "Frequently, you will find the abbreviation 'Syn.' following the definitions of a word. This abbreviation stands for 'Synonym,' or another word or words that mean the same or nearly the same as the word being defined. It will help you to build your vocabulary if you note these synonyms." (See also pages 190–92 in chapter 7.)

The teacher may have the children look up a word such as *fortunate* and find its synonym, *lucky*. They may then be asked to give a sentence containing *fortunate*. The sentence is written on the chalkboard. *Fortunate* is erased and *lucky* is written in its place. The teacher has the sentence read and discussed in terms of meaning when one word has re-placed another.

A useful and interesting activity is to have the children copy several sentences, each of which contains a word that has a synonym, and then proceed as follows.

Directions: Find a synonym for the underlined word in each sentence. Cross out the word and write the synonym above it. Then read the sentence to see if there has been any noticeable change in meaning.

The tree surgeon put an application on the trunk of the
     retard
tree to   its decay.
    delay

            strong
The plant had a   stalk.
           sturdy

               bear
Mr. Jones could hardly   the pain in his leg.
              endure

          smart
Jocko was a very   seal.
          clever

Using an index. This is a rather complicated skill. Its introduction should probably be delayed until most of the other skills discussed so far have been initiated and practiced.

In introducing this skill, the teacher might use an index in the back of a textbook that the children are using, showing them the index and giving an explanation of this sort:

"Most textbooks have an index. If you are looking for information in a textbook, you will save yourself a lot of time by using the index. You will also be able to find much more information through the use of the index. Usually, not *all* the information about a topic is given in any one chapter. Bits of information may be found here and there throughout the book, and only the index will tell you where."

Following this explanation, the children may be asked questions in regard to different sections of the index that call their attention to its nature and use.

The activity below is an example of practice with index skills.[3]

Use the index to find the correct page number for each blank on page 283. Write the number of the line on your paper and write the page number next to it.

[3] Smith, *Be a Better Reader*, Level C, pp. 140–41.

INDEX

Backbone, 287
Bacteria, 200–209
  broth culture, 208–209
  control of, 207
  food destroyers, 204
  harmful, 203
  microscope and, 206
  types of, 200–201
  uses of, 205
Bacterial diseases, 301
Ball bearing, 421
Balloons, 220
Bar magnet, 425
Barometer, 310–314
  aneroid, 314
  mercury, 313
  ship, 310
  water, 314
Bats, 161
Batteries, 342
Bears, 87
Beavers, 88
Bees, 129
Beetles, 134
Birds, 172–188
  care of, 34
  description of, 173–175
  eggs, 176
  harmful to man, 340
  how they fly, 183
  insect-eating, 135
  laws protecting, 209
  uses to man, 341

Black widow spider, 131
Blindness, 321
Blood, 264–283
  circulation of, 275
  oxygen in, 280
  types of, 264
Bloodstream, 295
Bluejays, 151
Brain, 269
Bulbs, 21
Butterflies, 137

Cactus, 25
Calcium, 408
Calories, 298
Camels, 92
Canned foods, 301
Carbon, 37
Carbon dioxide, 38
Caribou, 79
Cells, 250–262
  body, 257
  nerve, 261
  plant, 29
  retina, 291
Cereals, 293
Chipmunks, 51
Climate, 240–247
  clouds, 246
  rain, 241
  snow, 243
  sun, effects of, 417
  winds, 244

1. Do you want to know about bats? Page _____ is a good place to be.
2. How does sun affect climate? Turn to page _____ to see.
3. To find out how to plant bulbs, page _____ is a good place to look.
4. If you want to know about birds' eggs, turn to page _____ in the book.
5. Birds can be harmful to man. Turn to page _____ to see why.
6. Look on page _____ if you want to know how birds fly.
7. Are you interested in balloons? Page _____ is the place to turn.
8. What are the types of blood? Page _____ is the place to learn.
9. You'll find out about black widow spiders if you turn to page _____.
10. Find out about beetles on page _____, and now this game is done!

Finding key words. A more advanced skill in using an index is to select key words under which to look for information about a topic. The teacher may introduce this skill by writing a topic such as the following on the chalkboard: "How is cheese made in Switzerland?" He or she may then ask the children to find two words under which they might look to find the information asked for. Explanation may follow to the effect that words in a topic, such as *cheese* and *Switzerland,* that lead to information are called *key words.* The pupils should follow through by actually searching for information under these heads.

Dictionaries for grades four through eight. If feasible, every classroom should be equipped with one unabridged dictionary that catalogs all the words and their important uses in the English language. It is also advantageous for every pupil to have in their possession one of the abridged dictionaries prepared for the intermediate and middle grades. In classrooms with youngsters who are bilingual, there should be at least one copy of the simplest dictionary available in that language and English.

At first, it is advisable to use a dictionary from the same publisher because dictionaries differ in the way they handle pronunciation keys. Once the children become used to using the pronunciation key, however, the introduction of other dictionaries offers a good opportunity for them to learn how to use any pronunciation key.

Some of the several abridged dictionaries appropriate for elementary- and middle-school grades are:

> *Harcourt Brace School Dictionary.* New York: Harcourt Brace Jovanovich. Grades 4–8.
>
> *Holt Intermediate Dictionary.* New York: Holt, Rinehart and Winston. Grades 4–9.
>
> *Macmillan School Dictionary.* New York: Macmillan Co. Grades 4–6.
>
> *Thorndike-Barnhart Beginning Dictionary,* 2nd ed. Glenview, Ill.: Scott, Foresman and Co. About 3–5.
>
> *Thorndike-Barnhart Intermediate Dictionary.* Glenview, Ill.: Scott, Foresman and Co. Grades 4–8.
>
> *Webster's Intermediate Dictionary.* New York: American Book Co. Grades 4–8.
>
> *Webster's New World Dictionary,* basic school ed. Englewood Cliffs, N.J.: Prentice-Hall. Grades 4–8.

Encyclopedias for grades four through eight. Traditionally, it has been suggested that reference work with formal encyclopedias begin at about fourth-grade level. In light of the complexity of reading in even the simplest of the "high quality" encyclopedias, it would seem that children need to be reading at least fifth-sixth grade levels in order to obtain information of any significance to them. Dohrman found that "approximately two-thirds of the topic-articles evaluated. . ." in her study of eight encyclopedias were "above the grade level ranges for which they were intended." She questioned the use of such encyclopedias for children reading below high fifth-grade level.[4]

Dohrman used two readability formulas (see chapter 3) that may not always be a valid indicator of whether or not given children can read certain material. Certain aspects of language and the motivations of children are not considered in these formulas. Nevertheless, it would seem advisable to delay introducing formal encyclopedia research until at least the time when certain pupils are able to read beginning fifth-grade materials independently. Even then, the introduction should be carefully structured. Using encyclopedias can be a lifetime tool that should not be turned off by initial frustrations. Certainly, teachers cannot expect pupils to read material in an encyclopedia and then write a report in their own words without a great deal of help in learning how to select and evaluate, organize, and paraphrase.

The best time to introduce and give practice on encyclopedia skills is at a time when information that an encyclopedia contains is needed. At such a time, some such procedure as the one described below may be used.

The teacher may show the children a set of encyclopedias and explain somewhat as follows:

> "An encyclopedia, like the dictionary, is a book of facts. But whereas the dictionary or a glossary gives facts about *words*—their pronunciation, meaning, and so on—the encyclopedia gives facts about *topics*—that is, about the things we talk about and need to know about. Encyclopedias are very valuable sources of information that you will need to use all your lives.
>
> In the encyclopedia, as in the dictionary, the topics are arranged in alphabetical order. To find out about anything, one must know under what topic to look for it. The work you have done in finding the key word in a sentence or question will help you in using the encyclopedia."

Children can, of course, be introduced to some of the skills used in encyclopedia work through the use of the less-formal reference books especially printed for primary grade pupils. This kind of preliminary work should be used as readiness for the more formal and demanding work of the traditional encyclopedias.

Following this preliminary experience, expanded practice should be given in finding and using information needed in furthering individual and group interests.

The index in the back of encyclopedias should be introduced and practice in its use given after children have had some experience in using an index in some of their textbooks.

To provide practice in deciding upon a volume in which to look for

[4] Mary H. Dohrman, "The Suitability of Encyclopedias for Social Studies Reference Use in the Intermediate Grades," *Journal of Educational Research* 68, no. 4 (December 1974): 151.

a given topic, the teacher may draw a diagram of a set of volumes and ask children to locate lists of topics as indicated in the figure that follows.

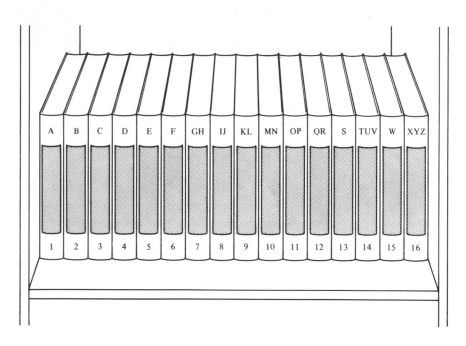

Directions to children: See how quickly you can find the right volume for each of the topics below. Write the letters of the volume in which you think the topic would be discussed in the space to the right of each topic.

a. soil _____

b. England _____

c. forests _____

d. diet _____

e. shells _____

f. navigation _____

g. fish _____

h. oranges _____

i. zinc _____

j. weather _____

k. soap _____

l. boats _____

m. Daniel Boone _____

n. Jonathan Chapman _____

Several encyclopedias are intended for intermediate- and middle-school youngsters and appear to contain articles that start out at about fourth grade level but quickly become more complex. Assignments in these encyclopedias should refer, at first, just to the beginning paragraphs. As pupils become accustomed to using them, and/or as reading ability increases, teachers can have pupils read further into the articles for limited and specific information. Reading encyclopedia articles for comprehensive understanding should not be expected for most readers in the intermediate grades.

Here are a few excellent quality and "easier" encyclopedias:

The World Book Encyclopedia. Chicago: Field Enterprises Educational Corp. Some introductory paragraphs in articles about fourth-grade level.

The New Book of Knowledge. New York: Grolier. Introductory paragraphs seem to be simple.

Compton's Encyclopedia. Chicago: Encyclopaedia Britannica. For those at upper fifth- and sixth-grade reading levels.

Britannica Junior. Chicago: Encyclopaedia Britannica. For those at upper fifth- and sixth-grade reading levels.

Reading illustrations. The reading of graphs, charts, diagrams, and tables begun in the primary grades needs heavy emphasis in the intermediate and middle grades when pupils meet many important illustrations in their textbooks. Teachers should take the time to help pupils learn to read each type of illustration when first confronted. Of particular importance in these grades is the interpretation of maps and globes. The type of exercise below, taken from *Be a Better Reader,* Level B (1977),[5] helps to focus pupils' attention on the reading of maps while learning important information that can be transferred to subsequent map-reading demands.

These are three maps of Mexico. Map No. 1 is a physical map showing mountains, plateaus, and plains. Map No. 2 shows where there is light rainfall, medium rainfall, and heavy rainfall. Map No. 3 shows where there are natural resources of gold, silver, lead, copper, coal, and oil. Study these maps as you answer the following questions on your paper.

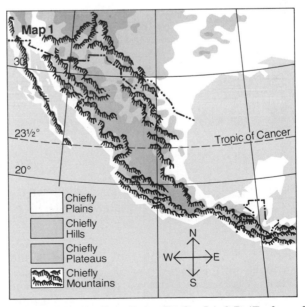

[5] Nila B. Smith, *Be a Better Reader,* Level B (Englewood Cliffs, N.J.: Prentice-Hall, 1977), pp. 142–43.

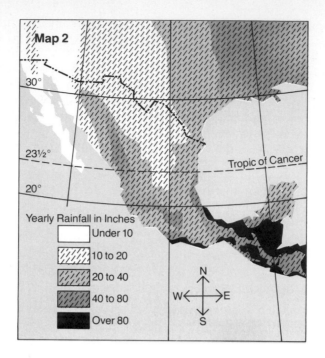

Map 2

30°

23½°

Tropic of Cancer

20°

Yearly Rainfall in Inches

Under 10

10 to 20

20 to 40

40 to 80

Over 80

N
W E
S

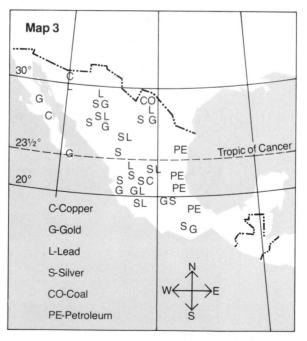

Map 3

30° C

G
L
S G
C
S
SL
G
CO
L
S
G

SL
G
S
PE
Tropic of Cancer

23½°

20°
L
S SL
S SC
G GL
SL
GS
PE
PE
PE
S G

C-Copper

G-Gold

L-Lead

S-Silver

CO-Coal

PE-Petroleum

N
W E
S

1. Look at Map No. 1. Does the high central plateau make up the largest part of Mexico?

2. Next look at this plateau in Map No. 2, the rainfall map.

a. Is the rainfall light or heavy in the entire northern part of this plateau?

b. Do you expect many people in this section to be farmers?

3. Look at Map No. 3.

a. Is there any gold, silver, copper, lead, or coal in this plateau?

b. What kind of work would you expect people who live on the plateau to do for a living?

4. Look at the rainfall map again.

a. Does more rain fall in the southern part of the plateau?

b. Would you expect that plants would grow well there?

c. Do you think many people might be engaged in farming there?

5. Now in Map No. 1, look at the range of mountains that border on the plateau in the west.

a. According to the rainfall map, are these mountains in the northern part mostly in a dry area?

b. Look at Map No. 3. Might mining be done in these mountains?

6. Look at Maps No. 1 and 2. Note the small plains along the western coast that receive rainfall. Would you think any crops might be grown there?

7. Now find the eastern mountains and coastal plain on Map No. 1. Look at Map No. 2.

a. Do the eastern side of these mountains and the coastal plain receive more rain than the northwest coast?

b. Would you suspect that grass for grazing might grow on the lower slopes of these mountains?

c. If so, how might some people make their living in this area?

8. Look at Map No. 3. How do people on the east coast make a living?

9. Look at the plains in the south as shown in Map No. 1.

a. Referring to Map No. 2, do these plains receive a good rainfall?

b. Would this be a good or a poor place for growing crops?

c. How would most people in this section make their living?

Library skills. Organization of books. Children should learn early that books are grouped in libraries. Some activities directed toward this end follow.

1. They may group books in their own classroom by topics, such as fairy stories, true stories about people, animal stories, science books, history books, health books, and so on.

2. They may prepare labels for the different classifications.

3. They may draw a floor diagram of their school library or the children's room in a public library and show where different kinds of books are kept.

4. They may read and discuss the Dewey Decimal System and its function from a listing of numbers representing ten classes of this system, which the teacher writes on the chalkboard or on a chart.

000–099 General Works	500–599 Science
100–199 Philosophy	600–699 Useful Arts
200–299 Religion	700–799 Fine Arts
300–399 Social Science	800–899 Literature
400–499 Language	900–999 History

(Note: Some school and public libraries use the Library of Congress classification system, but the majority of them and almost all college libraries use the Dewey Decimal System, so children may as well become acquainted with it in the elementary grades.)

5. Perhaps advanced children can label groups of books in their classrooms with appropriate designations.

Card catalog. The teacher may find a chalkboard diagram, similar to the one following, useful in introducing a card catalog.

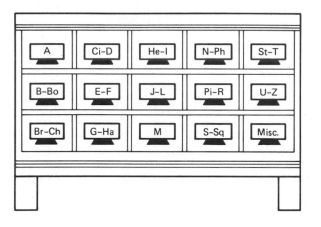

The nature of the card catalog and its use may be described in some such way as this:

"You might think of a card catalog as a huge encyclopedia, each drawer representing a volume. Instead of containing pages, however, each drawer contains cards. Instead of giving you the information itself, the cards tell you in what book you can find the information.

The letter or letters on each of the drawers shown in the diagram tell you in which drawer you can find cards with names of authors, books, or topics beginning with the letter or letters shown.

If you wish to find the names of some books on the topic of *atoms*, you would of course look in the A drawer. If you wish to look up the names of books on *opossums*, you would look in the drawer marked *N–Ph* because the letter O comes between N and P, and cards representing that letter would be included in the *N–Ph* drawer. If you are looking for the name of a person, you look for the first letter of his or her last name; for example, if you were looking for John Bakeless, you would look in the second drawer which contains cards falling between B and Bo."

The teacher should have the pupils write the letter or letters of the drawer in which they would find cards having to do with certain topics or persons as:

a. lumber _____   c. Panama _____

b. conservation _____   d. humus _____

e. sugar _____
f. Sam Houston _____
g. desert _____
h. furs _____

i. glaciers _____
j. weather _____
k. David Crockett _____
l. Daniel Boone _____

Cards in the card catalog. This skill may be introduced through the use of a chalkboard diagram representing the three types of cards to be found in a card catalog.

Author Card	Title Card	Subject Card
532:4 Putnam, John A.	532:4 Cosmos rays.	532:4 Science
Cosmos rays	Putnam, John A.	Putnam, John A.
Holton 1954	Holton 1954	Holton 1954

The teacher may explain each type of card and call attention to the name of the publisher and the date. Then erase the content of all three cards and have the pupils tell what to write on each card using information given for other books, such as:

Library number—921.3; author—Mary Louise Strong; title—The Second World War; publisher—Southwick; date 1948.

Additional activities in reading cards in a card catalog are as follows:

1. Take the children to a library. Show them a card catalog. Give them turns in finding the different types of cards for several books whose titles and authors are given to them.

2. Have the pupils write the different kinds of cards for certain books selected from the class supply.

3. Have the pupils catalog the library-type books in their classroom.

Following Directions

Reading to follow directions consists of a group of fundamental strategies needed in studying the content of all subjects. In mathematics, children must follow detailed and intricate directions for performing new processes, checking answers, and doing various things with examples and processes. In science, they must read and carry out experiments and observations with high accuracy. In geography and history, they are given directions for finding locations, tracing routes on maps, preparing time lines, reading graphs, and so on. In addition, practically all assignments in all subjects are given in the form of directions, many of which are printed.

In the early primary grades, the teacher may frequently write directions for classroom work on the chalkboard, have the children read the directions orally, and tell in their own words exactly what they are going to do. At other times, the pupils themselves may make up directions that the teacher writes on a chart. In either case, decision should be made later through group discussion in regard to how well the directions have been carried out.

As children encounter more complicated directions in textbooks, it is often advisable to have the directions read orally and discussed before carrying them out. If some children are having considerable trouble in carrying out directions, the textbook directions may be written on the chalkboard and read and discussed before the pupils read and follow the directions in their textbook itself.

In all situations in which children follow printed directions, it is of the utmost importance that the work resulting from reading these directions be checked carefully, often through discussion and evaluation by the group. Children who have persistent trouble in following directions should have special practice in reading and carrying out sets of directions prepared by the teacher in keeping with their level of reading ability. Here is one possible approach.

1. Point out to pupils the value of reading the *entire* set of directions first to obtain a general understanding of purpose and method.

2. Require the pupils to number the consecutive steps when reading directions.

3. Discuss the reasons for the particular sequence indicated.

4. Require the pupils in the second, more deliberate reading of the directions to determine how the steps in sequence, if followed, will achieve the purpose.

Survival Strategies

Mattleman and Blake [6] wisely suggest that study strategies are best learned as survival strategies—application in functional settings. Here are a few of their suggested activities suitable for upper-intermediate and middle-school youngsters:

1. Using last evening's newspaper, select gifts for your three cousins (all girls under six years old) that would cost no more than $10.00 altogether. (Skills: skimming, evaluating material, locating information)
2. Using the television page of your local newspaper, place the shows from six p.m.—nine p.m. in four different categories that you select. (Skills: recalling, following directions, organizing material)

[6] Marciene S. Mattleman and Howard E. Blake, "Study Skills: Prescriptions for Survival," *Language Arts* 54, no. 8 (November/December 1977): 925–27.

3. If your roof started leaking in the middle of the night how could you use your telephone book to get fast emergency help? (Skills: selecting material, evaluating material, skimming, locating information)

4. Using a local train schedule, find out how long it takes to get from the main terminal to the station nearest your school. (Skills: following directions, locating information)

5. Using yesterday's newspaper, find the highest and lowest temperatures of the cities listed. What was the range in the country for that day? (Skills: locating information, selecting material, skimming)

6. Using a menu from the nearest luncheonette, choose a dinner that a vegetarian could buy for less than $3.50. (Skills: evaluating material, organizing information, skimming)

7. How would you instruct a stranger to get to your City Hall or Courthouse from your present location? (Skills: following directions, recalling information, organizing material)[7]

PATTERNS OF WRITING

In addition to learning the study strategies needed for unlocking ideas, pupils need to be aware of the patterns of writing used by authors in the various content areas. Different patterns of content intermixed with varied purposes call for different approaches and strategies. Let us examine a small sample of text from four content areas to note evidence of contrasts between them.

First, let us consider the strategies that are necessary when a child reads narrative stories in readers and trade books just for pleasure, not mastery of content. In working with story content, for enjoyment, the child reads text something like this:

> The warm spring sunshine was coming in through the window of Sandy's room. Sandy opened his sleepy eyes and looked around.
> He heard his father and mother talking downstairs. Then he heard his father get a pail of water from the well.

The story goes on to tell that it is Sandy's birthday. He is getting gifts. The reader is held in suspense about one gift, which is kept a surprise until the end of the story.

With such content, all the child has to do is to read on continuously, pleasantly, just for the fun of following the plot. The sequential story pattern is an experience similar to the listening experiences children have had since the age of two. The mental processes involved are comparatively simple. Children can get the sense of the story even if there are several words or phrases they do not understand or cannot pronounce.

In science, a different kind of reading is required. Let us examine a typical sample from a third-grade science textbook.

[7] Ibid., p. 926.

Air Has Pressure

This experiment will show that air has pressure.

Put one-half cup of water into a syrup can.

Heat the water until steam comes out of the opening for about a minute.

Remove the can from the stove.

Quickly put in the cork.

Set the can in a stream of cold air. What happens? Can you explain why it happened?

The child reads the text to find out how to conduct an experiment. The section requires exact, detailed reading. The pupil must recognize the meanings of most every word. If *steam* and *stream* should be confused, for example, this error alone would throw out the experiment.

The pattern is sequential again, but each step must be understood—precisely—and linked to the next one. Also, the pattern calls for action: children must hold the meaning of each direction in mind while performing it. And then, when all the directions are both read and carried out, the pattern asks for further involvement; the pupils must review, reason, summarize the results, and find an explanation of the results.

Let us next examine a sample of geography text.

Southwest of Philadelphia, areas of dense population are centered in two cities, Baltimore and Washington. You can see these cities best on the map on this page. Like the other great cities you have studied, Baltimore is a seaport. On page 62 is a picture of part of its harbor, which is the wide mouth of a little river flowing into Chesapeake Bay. It is an old city, started by a group of early settlers who came from England. Turn back to the map on page 45 and look at the land that had been settled in this region by the year 1700. There was a fringe of settlement all around the shores of Chesapeake Bay.

Even this limited sample indicates that geography text has its own characteristics insofar as reading is concerned. Whether a child is reading this kind of material in geography as part of activities carried on as a class problem or unit, or as an assignment, the basic reading purpose presumably is to obtain information about Baltimore and Washington. The child must not only grasp detailed facts as he or she goes along but must frequently turn from the text to carry out a direction to examine a map or a picture elsewhere in the book. These examinations, in turn, involve skills needed for picture-reading and other skills needed for map-reading. To complicate the situation further, a time concept enters into the situation. In each case, the child finds the reference, uses the skills required to examine it, and contrasts information obtained in terms of two time settings. After all this, the child must return to the text originally read and fit newly found ideas into the total import of the paragraph.

In mathematics the writing patterns are typically quite different from those in other content areas. Let us examine a sample from a mathematics text.

In mathematics, the word *line* means a straight line. Below is a picture of a line. The line is made up of a countless number of points or locations. This set of points extends in both directions forever.

On the line shown above, we have named two points, A and B. We may call the line AB. The arrows show that the line never stops.

The set of points between A and B is called a *line segment*. Segment means *part of,* so a line segment is a definite part of a line. A line segment has a beginning point and an end point. This is line segment BC.

1. Draw a picture of a line that includes Point P, below. (Remember that in mathematics a line means a straight line.)

P
•

2. Does the line really end where you have ended it on the paper? _____

3. Draw a picture of a line segment in the space below. Name the beginning point D and the end point E.

Here a child reads explanations and directions, reasons, makes applications of the abstract concept of a line in mathematics, and works with letters of the alphabet—not within words but as separate symbols to mark off the mathematical construct of line, segment, and point.

Just a glance at this one example is convincing in regard to the hypothesis that reading present-day mathematics requires strategies that are quite different from those needed in reading the content of readers, trade books, or other books in the subject fields.

Specific Patterns

The major patterns found in elementary textbooks in content areas are mentioned below. Patterns are not exclusive to certain content areas—just more prevalent in one than another. In addition to helping pupils develop their study strategies for unlocking the ideas in the content areas, teachers should help pupils identify the major patterns and learn to adjust to them. As pupils begin to recognize patterns when they survey or preview material, they will find themselves able to set reading purposes for themselves.

Literature.

Reading short stories

Reading novellas or novelettes

Reading poems of different types: lyric, elegiac, ballads, light-verse, free-verse

Reading drama

Reading biographies and autobiographies

Reading trade books that deal with informative material: travelogs, how-to-do-its, real-life adventure

Reading essays

Reading the varied types of materials in newspapers and news magazines

Science.

Reading the enumeration pattern in which the reader is told to look for a certain number of factors (There were three main causes for the earthquake.)

Reading the classification pattern in which certain likenesses and differences are pointed out in regard to certain things classified by scientists under one heading (rocks, animals, minerals, and so on)

Reading the explanation of a technical process (How the telephone works, for example)

Reading and interpreting diagrams

Reading and carrying out directions for an experiment

Reading content giving several examples leading up to a principle or generalization

Reading problem-solving information to find out how a problem was solved scientifically

Reading detailed information heavily packed with science facts

Social Studies.

Reading primary sources

Reading information about a particular topic

Reading the enumeration pattern

Reading bits of information and examples that lead up to a generalization

Reading questions and then seeking the answers

Reading pictures

Reading maps, globes, atlases

Reading cause-and-effect content

Reading content in which comparisons are made

Reading content in which sequence of events is given

Reading content in which dates are associated with events

Reading critically material in which (a) different viewpoints are expressed; and (b) facts are mixed with opinions

Mathematics.

Understanding the relationships among a number of concepts

Putting concepts together to understand a generalization in the form of a principle

Reading numbers

Reading mathematical symbols

Reading graphs

Reading tables

Interpreting detailed explanations of new processes

Following directions for using a new process

Reading problems for the following purposes: (a) to visualize the setting; (b) to answer the question, "What am I to find?" (c) to answer the question "What facts am I given to work with?" (d) to answer the question "What process or processes do I need to use?"

VOCABULARY

Although many aspects of vocabulary development have been discussed in chapter 7, the four types of specialized vocabulary related to content area reading are presented here.

Technical Vocabulary

Every subject has its own technical vocabulary, which all of us would agree have special significance; for example, probably no one would dispute the fact that *magnets, terrarium, velocity* are peculiar to the subject of science; that *abolition, fortress, proclamation, allies* belong particularly to the field of history; that *fraction, cancellation,* and *divisor* are definitely mathematics words; and that *hemisphere, continent,* and *equator* are special geography words. Special subject words of this type are not ordinarily met by children in stories or simple expository materials. One reason why many children find reading in some subject fields difficult is because of their lack of concepts for these specialized words. Large numbers of children would profit by guided class discussion of such words in connection with their reading and study.

Overlap Words

Another type of special vocabulary word is the overlap word, the one that may be claimed in two or more subject fields. "Rain" and "rainfall" for example are very important words in geography, yet they also belong to the weather vocabulary, which is definitely in the realm of science. "Group" is important in social studies referring to a social group of people. "Group" may also be claimed in the mathematics vocabulary because of its significance in giving the concept of an assemblage of numbers. These overlap words, which do not vary too much in their fundamental meaning from one subject to another, give very little trouble to the average reader.

Multi-Meaning Words

The real troublemakers are the polysemantic words that mean something entirely different when used in different subject contexts. For example, consider the word *check*. In mathematics, *check* may mean a blank form that one fills in and presents at the bank to draw some money from an account. In science, children may be told to "check their experiment," meaning to prove it. In history, they read that a certain group of soldiers were able to "check the enemy," meaning that they were able to stop the progress of an oncoming attack. In geography, they may read that the fields on a hillside look like "a great checkerboard"; and in literature, they may read about a girl with "a checked gingham dress." Although many children pick up these changed meanings incidentally as they occur in different subject contexts, others do not. Teachers who cultivate a sensitivity in themselves to shifts of word meanings from one subject to another and who take the trouble to inquire into pupils' understanding of these words in different contexts will discover that much confusion exists in their pupils' minds, and that it is very worthwhile to help them to understand these distinctions.

Such work is particularly needed with multiple-meaning words whose meanings range from something very concrete to something very abstract. The word *bar* may be used to illustrate this type of word. Perhaps the first time the child encounters the word *bar* in print is when reading a mathematics problem such as this: "Mary bought a candy bar for 5 cents, and Sue bought a candy bar for 5 cents. How much did the girls pay for the two bars of candy?" The pupil has no difficulty in understanding this meaning because of personal experience with candy bars, and, in this instance, *bar* to the child means a long, narrow piece of candy.

Next the child may read a story in which a boy put a basket on "the handle**bars** of his bicycle" and used the basket as a receptacle for carrying his puppy. Again, the child will have no trouble with the word *bar*, for "handlebars" are concrete objects that he or she has seen and probably used. In reading a selection on farming, the pupil may have first contact with the primary meaning of the noun *bar* when reading that "the farmer pried up a large rock with a long iron bar." As a result of first-hand experiences, pictures, and context, the child arrives at the generalization that a bar is a piece of material that has greater length in proportion to its breadth and thickness, and easily grasps the meaning of *bar* whenever reading text in which the word is used in this way.

Children may even understand the term "bar of music" when encountered in a book, particularly if they have been well instructed in the subject of music. A "bar of music," however, is a bit less concrete than "a bar of candy" or "handlebars." Finally, as children progress through the grades, they read in geography about a "sand bar"; in science, about a "bar magnet"; in mathematics, about "a bar graph." In all these instances, *bar* is becoming farther and farther removed from its most concrete meaning.

Finally, in social studies the child reads that someone was "behind bars"; that a certain group "was barred because of religious prejudice"; that a thief was brought "to the bar of justice"; and eventually in literature at higher levels he or she reads Tennyson's "When I Have Crossed the Bar."

Who is going to help the pupil make the transition from one level of abstraction to another if not the teacher—the teacher who is on the lookout for these different levels as they occur in all subject fields?

Function Words

Function words make up a significant amount of the words used in all content-area writing. They ". . . are the articles, auxiliary verbs, prepositions, and conjunctions of traditional grammar. Often they have only two or three letters." [8] These are the words that pupils often find difficult to remember because they can attach no meaningful experience to them. On the other hand, sometimes these words do carry a type of special meaning in a content area. For example, consider *and* and *are*. In a story, primary children may read that "Tom and Nan are in the car." In such common usage *and* is used as a simple connective and *are* means that the children exist in a certain place at that time. But when these same primary children turn to arithmetic text, they are immediately confronted with sentences like this: "2 and 2 are 4." In these arithmetic sentences *and* means "plus" and *are* means "equal."

Most of the time, they serve as signals or markers that provide cues to the reader about meaning. The articles—*a, the, an*—are noun markers that tell the reader that a noun comes next or soon after. E. Brooks Smith, Goodman, and Meredith use this example: "If the reader mistakes *monkey* for *money*, he would be likely to realize he had made an error, because *a* does not precede a noun such as *money*." [9]

Words such as *are, is, did, what, where*, and *who* with initial capital letters and at the beginning of a sentence signal that the sentence is a question well before the young reader may see the question mark. Prepositions, and they are plentiful in the content areas, are important in help-

[8] E. Brooks Smith, Kenneth S. Goodman, and Robert Meredith, *Language and Thinking in School*, 2nd ed. (New York: Holt, Rinehart and Winston, 1976), p. 273.
[9] Ibid.

ing pupils identify the location or spatial orientation of a situation or action.[10] They are particularly important in science and mathematics when detailed and precise understanding is crucial. Understanding the exact meaning signaled by prepositions often is particularly difficult for bilingual learners.

Connectives that join clauses, particularly subordinate clauses, are often not understood by elementary-school learners. Rodgers found the following connectives in grade-six science and social-studies texts and. listed them in order of frequency of use:

1. but	11. although
2. if	12. while
3. when	13. for example
4. because	14. since
5. as	15. yet
6. then	16. so that
7. even	17. such as
8. also	18. too
9. perhaps	19. until
10. however	20. whether [11]

Although pupils may understand the functions of some of these connectives and use them to advantage, there are probably a number they skip over or do not understand. Help is needed by many elementary-school pupils in developing strategies that focus their attention on connectives and the other function words as aids to comprehending the ideas presented in content-area materials. The best way to help is to look over the content material with pupils and ask questions about their understanding. For those that appear to be obstacles, a closure technique is useful. (See the example in chapter 8, pages 213–14.)

The context of social studies, science, arithmetic, and even literature abound with specialized word meanings of these types. The skillful teaching of reading in the various areas demands abundant explanation of the meanings of words that are specialized in their primary meaning, and also of those that suddenly become specialized when they appear in different subject contexts.

**DISCUSSION
QUESTIONS
AND
ACTIVITIES**

1. For most first and second graders, the ability to recall what has been read may be developed through the drawing of pictures as suggested in

[10] Charles J. Fillmore, "Verbs of Judging: An Exercise in Semantic Descriptions," in *Studies in Linguistic Semantics*, eds. Charles J. Fillmore and D. Terence Langendoes (New York: Holt, Rinehart and Winston, 1971), pp. 273–89.

[11] Denis Rodgers, "Which Connectives? Signals to Enhance Comprehension," *Journal of Reading* 17, no. 6 (March 1974): 466.

the chapter. An activity especially suited to the early primary grades is to have pupils draw a picture to answer a question. For example: "What kind of a boat did the Indians use?" Such a question gives practice in recalling details, and the resulting pictures indicate how well details have been grasped and retained. For those pupils who like to draw, this strategy can also be used all through the grades from time to time.

2. The list of specific writing patterns in the four major content areas on pages 296–97 is quite voluminous. They should serve as a remainder about the necessity of focusing in on each specific pattern at some time in order to make pupils aware of all of them. For guidance in "teaching" these patterns as well as accompanying study strategies, you can turn to two commercial products written by the authors of this volume:

   a. H. Alan Robinson and others, *EDL Study Skills Library*. Each kit, C-I (grades three through junior high), focuses on study strategies in science, social studies, and on reference or locating information skills. They are published by Educational Developmental Laboratories, Mc-Graw-Hill, 1978.

   b. Nila Banton Smith, *Be a Better Reader*. Each text, A-E (grades four through eight), focuses on patterns of writing and study strategies in literature, science, social studies, and mathematics. They are published by Prentice-Hall, 1977 and 1978.

3. Both direct and incidental instruction is needed in vocabulary development in the content areas. The technique of having pupils develop their own content-area word banks is useful for both purposes. Pupils can collect their own content-area terms and keep them filed in a small box for future reference, in alphabetical order for easy retrieval. The illustration below is an adaptation of Thomas and Robinson's content-area vocabulary slip.[12]

SCIENCE VOCABULARY TERM

Term _____

Sentence in which you found it _____

_____

Meaning _____

Your use of it in a sentence _____

_____

---

[12] Ellen L. Thomas and H. Alan Robinson, *Improving Reading in Every Class: A Sourcebook for Teachers*, 2nd ed. (Boston: Allyn and Bacon, 1977), pp. 64–65.

ADDITIONAL READINGS

Books and Pamphlets

CARLSON, KENNETH L. "A Different Look at Reading in the Content Areas." In *Help for the Reading Teacher: New Directions in Research*, edited by William D. Page. Urbana, Ill.: National Conference on Research in English and ERIC Clearinghouse on Reading and Communication Skills, 1975.

CHEYNEY, ARNOLD B. *Teaching Reading Skills Through the Newspaper*. Newark, Del.: International Reading Assn., 1971.

DULIN, KENNETH L. "Teaching and Evaluating Reading in the Content Areas." In *Views on Elementary Reading Instruction*, edited by Thomas C. Barrett and Dale D. Johnson. Newark, Del.: International Reading Assn., 1973.

EARLE, RICHARD. *Teaching Reading and Mathematics*. Newark, Del.: International Reading Assn., 1976.

FAY, LEO, and JARED, LEE ANN, comps. *Reading in the Content Fields*. Newark, Del.: International Reading Assn., 1975.

HERBER, HAROLD L. *Teaching Reading in the Content Areas*. 2nd ed. Englewood Cliffs, N.J.: Prentice-Hall, 1978.

KARLIN, ROBERT. *Teaching Elementary Reading*. 2nd ed., pp. 249–315. New York: Harcourt Brace Jovanovich, 1975.

ROBINSON, H. ALAN. *Teaching Reading and Study Strategies: The Content Areas*. 2nd ed. Boston: Allyn and Bacon, 1978.

SMITH, RICHARD J., and JOHNSON, DALE D. *Teaching Children to Read*. Pp. 247–63. Reading, Mass.: Addison-Wesley Publishing Co., 1976.

SPACHE, GEORGE D., and SPACHE, EVELYN B. *Reading in the Elementary School*. 4th ed., pp. 275–312. Boston: Allyn and Bacon, 1977.

THELEN, JUDITH. *Improving Reading in Science*. Newark, Del.: International Reading Assn., 1976.

THOMAS, ELLEN L., and ROBINSON, H. ALAN. *Improving Reading in Every Class: A Sourcebook for Teachers*. 2nd ed. Boston: Allyn and Bacon, 1977.

Periodicals

BONENFANT, RICHARD G. "Map Reading: A Language Arts Approach," *Elementary English* 50, no. 4 (April 1973), pp. 581–82.

CHANCE, LARRY L. "Reading in the Content Areas: Some Practical Approaches." *Middle School Journal* 7, no. 1 (March 1976), pp. 6–7.

COLLIER, CALHOUN C., and REDMOND, LOIS A. "Are You Teaching Kids to Read Mathematics?" *Reading Teacher* 27, no. 8 (May 1974), pp. 804–8.

CUNNINGHAM, DICK, and SHABLAK, SCOTT L. "Selective Reading Guide-O-Rama: The Content Teacher's Best Friend." *Journal of Reading* 18, no. 5 (February 1975), pp. 380–82.

DOHRMAN, MARY H. "The Suitability of Encyclopedias for Social Studies

Reference Use in the Intermediate Grades." *Journal of Educational Research* 68, no. 4 (December 1974), pp. 149–52.

DUSCHER, RAYMOND. "How to Help Social Science Students Read Better." *Social Studies* 66, no. 6 (November/December 1975), pp. 258–61.

ESLER, WILLIAM K., and MERRITT, KING, JR. "Teaching Reading Through Science Experience Stories." *School Science and Mathematics* 76, no. 669 (March 1976), pp. 203–6.

LEES, FRED. "Mathematics and Reading." *Journal of Reading* 19, no. 8 (May 1976), pp. 621–26.

ROBINSON, H. ALAN. "Reading Skills Employed in Solving Social Studies Problems." *Reading Teacher* 18, no. 4 (January 1965), pp. 263–69.

RUPLEY, WILLIAM H. "Content Reading in the Elementary Grades: An ERIC/RCS Report." *Language Arts* 52, no. 6 (September 1975), pp. 802–7.

SMITH, NILA B. "Patterns of Writing in Different Subject Areas: Part I." *Journal of Reading* 8, no. 1 (October 1964), pp. 31–37.

———. "Patterns of Writing in Different Subject Areas: Part II." *Journal of Reading* 8, no. 2 (November 1964), pp. 97–102.

TURNER, THOMAS N. "Making the Social Studies Textbook a More Effective Tool for Less Able Readers." *Social Education* 40, no. 1 (January 1976), pp. 38–41.

VACCA, RICHARD T. "The Development of a Functional Reading Strategy: Implications for Content Area Instruction." *Journal of Educational Research* 69, no. 3 (November 1975), pp. 108–12.

What to Expect in This Chapter:

The development of interest and taste in literature are treated as interlocking and integrated factors. Such important topics as personality development through literature and the stimulation of interests are discussed. Some emphasis is placed on enrichment of the curriculum and an indirect contribution to skills through the use of literature in the classroom. The reading interests of today's children are summarized, and interest-inducing activities are discussed extensively. Suggestions are made for selecting, recording, and reporting. The concluding section of the chapter focuses on library activities in three locales—classroom library, school library, and public library.

The development of interest and taste in reading is a growth area of great importance. Of what value are all our efforts to establish proficiency in the skills and strategies of reading if children do not make the fullest use of them to enrich their lives, at present and during the adult years? Permanent carry-over interest in and the utilization of reading have long been stated as the ultimate goals of reading instruction. These goals are more urgent now than ever before because of the many competing communication agencies with which reading is confronted.

In addition to the goal of developing permanent interest in reading per se, we need to develop desirable attitudes and habits in reading *selectively*. Our concern should not be simply to develop interest in reading anything and everything. We need to develop discriminating readers; readers who will choose to read those things that will contribute most to their lives culturally, socially, and informatively. Bettelheim stated, "The acquisition of skills, including the ability to read, becomes devalued when what one has learned to read adds nothing of importance to one's life." [1]

PERSONALITY DEVELOPMENT

Personality is an integration of social, emotional, and behavioral characteristics. These characteristics emerge as qualities that interact with experience. Literature provides an inexhaustible well of human experience, from which children may take deep draughts of life and living. It follows, then, that one of the most important functions of literature is to help children relive the experiences of others and thus to deepen and broaden their own personal experiences.

Literature affords an opportunity to participate sympathetically in the viewpoints, problems, and difficulties of others. It helps children to understand culture patterns, both those that are current and those of the

[1] Bruno Bettelheim, *The Uses of Enchantment: Meaning and Importance of Fairy Tales* (New York: Alfred A. Knopf, 1976), p. 4.

chapter 11

developing interest and taste in literature

past. It enables them to interpret personal needs for security, love, companionship, success.

In addition, literature aids therapeutically in solving personal problems. As children read literary selections, they are bound to encounter characters who have had problems similar to their own and who have successfully solved these similar problems. *Bibliotherapy* is the term used by teachers who consciously, but obliquely, direct pupils toward literature that may help them solve personal problems.

Literature also contributes to the improvement of attitudes and behavior toward people, animals, cultures, creeds, beliefs, occupations, institutions, country. Here is an opportunity to discuss sexism and ethnic stereotyping reflected in some publications. Children and staff should be involved in selecting contemporary literature that attempts to eliminate such inequities and misconceptions.

> Few people would seriously suggest rewriting the classics or historical fiction, or discarding them altogether. Teachers, librarians, and parents can, however, make available to young people materials which explain the limitations of books with stereotyped depictions, why they were written, and how and why society used to be different. They can speak to students about perceived differences between cultural conditioning and genetic inheritance.[2]

As evidences of some of the personality values heretofore mentioned, the writers submit a few quotations from a study entitled "Some Effects of Reading on Children."[3]

Cynthia, Grade 6, wrote:

> The story of *The Blind Colt* impressed me very much. I never thought that blind animals could get around or play tricks. I thought they should be killed. But now I know that with patience some blind animals can be taught to do the things they need in order to get along in life. They must have companions, though, who are interested in helping them.
>
> Animals are something like people.

Janice, Grade 7, in writing about "America For Me" said simply:

> This poem made me realize how nice it is to be an American.

Richard, Grade 8, wrote:

> I didn't realize very much what my country meant to me or what it meant to other people until I read *The Man Without a Country*.

[2] Zena Sutherland and May Hill Arbuthnot, *Children and Books*, 5th ed. (Glenview, Ill.: Scott, Foresman and Co., 1977), p. 604.

[3] Nila Banton Smith, "Some Effects of Reading on Children," *Elementary English Review* 25, no. 5 (May 1948): 271–79.

When I read this, I realized that I was lucky to live here in this free land and am thankful that I don't have to live on a boat.

Roger, Grade 6, wrote:

> I had always heard that Sitting Bull was a terrible Indian and that he was always killing people. Then I read the book *Sitting Bull*. It told how he had held back from fighting as long as he could but at last he had to fight and when he did he was a terror. After he made a treaty someone accused him of trying to start a war and he was killed in a cowardly way.
>
> I learned that Indians have honor and now I have a greater respect for them than I did before.

Cynthia changed her attitude and behavior toward blind people. Janice and Richard developed a deeper love for their country, and Roger came to have better attitudes toward another race. Surely, literature greatly helped these children to improve their personalities.

Creative self-expression, which often buds out of communication with literature, is a salutary agent in developing personality. Two important elements of creativity are, first, uniqueness, inventiveness, making something new and different; and second, integration, weaving personal feelings, attitudes, and generalizations into some form of expression. Creative experiences involving these elements lead to discovery of dormant powers, draw upon reserves of untouched artistic emotion, develop a capacity for clarifying concepts and for arriving at basic generalizations. These new powers summoned to the surface through the medium of literary experiences release tensions, bring satisfactions, and induce personalities to unfold and to bloom.

As children derive pleasure from reading literary materials, they naturally feel compelled to prolong this pleasure through other arts closely akin to literature. For instance, they may wish to dramatize a story. They may want to draw, paint, or sculpture characters and scenery. They may want to write other stories and poems of their own, and even to set their poems to music.

The reading of literature in itself is a creative experience. Even so, however, it serves as a springboard for creative activities expressed in several other forms of symbolization.

THE STIMU-LATION OF INTERESTS

One of the most important areas of growth in reading is the area of interests.

As Giovannini said:

> Each storyline provides a means of encompassing the written word within the scope of each child's life, bringing with it those things that he or she has already experienced or adding a new dimension to the child's learning process.[4]

[4] Gail M. Giovannini, "Children's Literature and More," *Elementary English* 49, no. 7 (November 1972): 981.

Without interests, all the laborious work of developing reading skills would be of no avail. Unfortunately, many children and adults *can* read but never *do* read. Radio, television, and movies almost completely satisfy many persons' desires for entertainment and information. If reading is to continue to function as a valuable means of tapping our inexhaustible supplies of printed communication, then we must put forth far greater effort than ever before to establish abiding interests.

One of our best allies in achieving this goal is literature. Literature is entertaining. Entertainment is enjoyable. That which is enjoyable is interesting. When children first experience pleasure in literature, their appetites are whetted for more literature. Providing them with stories and poems geared to their interests, chronological maturity, and reading ability is one of the surest ways of encouraging them to delve ever more deeply into their literary inheritance. For example, the magnificent picture story book, *Come Away from the Water, Shirley* by John Burningham (Crowell, 1977) is bound to interest beginning readers to look for more of the same. Geoffrey Household's *Escape into Daylight* (Atlantic-Little, 1976, and Archway, 1977) brings together the modern and the ancient in a spellbinding mystery that will have older readers on the edges of their chairs.

Interests developed through literary experiences are likely to continue throughout elementary school, secondary school, college, and even throughout life. If literature had no function other than helping a person to establish life-time interests in reading, this value alone would place it close to the apex of curricular offerings.

Providing Functional Information

Children have many intellectual curiosities. Their quest for knowledge leads them to seek information about bugs, snakes, birds; stars, sun, moon; seaweed, shells, fish. They want to know about airplanes, rockets, trains, boats, and automobiles. They are eager for enlightenment about human beings, events, relationships, occupations, ways of living, castles, heroes, battles, and wars. This thirst for information is satisfied in many ways through the medium of literature.

One of the unique characteristics of literature is its diversity of content. It does not confine itself to one specialized area of knowledge. The writers of literature do not pour their stories and poems into subject-matter compartments. They write about things that touch them deeply at the moment, things that they feel impelled to share with others.

Authors write on topics as broad as life itself—as all-inclusive as children's searches for knowledge. In view of this fact, children find literary content a very satisfying source of information to answer numerous questions that prompt them to read.

Literature does far more, however, than provide information in the factual sense. It presents information in meaningful situations, rather than in organized subject-matter categories. For this reason, it has a special advantage in broadening concepts, deepening insights, clarifying human relationships, arriving at social and philosophical truths. In other words, it provides knowledge far beyond facts—it enables facts to live and to function.

Another informative value inherent in literature is that knowledge is presented in interesting, dramatic, and colorful settings that appeal to children's interests. Many children, who are reluctant to read books designed to provide direct instruction, become completely absorbed in stories and poems that indirectly provide information and insights. Trickling interests born in these integrated situations, if carefully guided, may well lead to the purposeful reading of textbooks or encyclopedic materials.

Thus literature serves in many ways, not only to provide facts, but also to stimulate and satisfy the child's quest for knowledge and wisdom.

Curricular Enrichment

Some of the literature available for children may be used for teaching subject matter directly, although most literature serves admirably to supplement, extend, and reveal content in the various curricular areas. Social studies and science receive particular benefit through the integration of literature and materials designed for instruction. The subject matter of literature is the subject matter of life, and life's subject matter lies almost entirely within the content areas of social studies and science. Consequently, literature, social studies, and science have a great deal in common.

Let us examine briefly how literature may serve to enrich the social-studies area. Literature deals with people, their work and recreation, their sorrows and joys, their relationships and individual problems. Consider Mother Goose, for example. In listening to or reading Mother Goose, young children learn about planting and reaping, grinding flour, milking cows, shearing sheep, tending garden, making cheese and butter, and many other activities. They visit farms, villages, cities, markets, mills, fairs, and shops. They meet kings, queens, farmers, fishermen, shepherds, blacksmiths, and milkmaids—all as these people laugh or weep, talk or sing, work or play together in harmonious interpersonal relationships.

Mother Goose, of course, occupies but one tiny niche in the great world of literature. Many different types of literary materials—folktales, legends, modern fanciful tales, realistic stories, poetry—all have potentialities for social-studies enrichment.

Children studying the lumber industry, for instance, gain invaluable insights by reading about legendary Paul Bunyan and his blue ox. Children studying about the beginning of the American Revolution gain rich understandings by reading the easy-to-read, informative story, *Sam the Minuteman,* by Nathaniel Benchley (Harper & Row, 1969). Young people concerned with contemporary Black history, and particularly the roles of women, will find Olive W. Burt's *Black Women of Valor* (J. Messner, 1974) very informative and readable. Children studying city life certainly should have an opportunity to read the delightful poem, "The Buildings," by Rose Fyleman. One could go on endlessly in giving such examples. Perhaps enough has been said to establish the point that literature is an inexhaustible source of enrichment for the varied subject-matter areas in the social-studies curriculum.

Science is equally fortunate in having strong reinforcements in literature. Consider Mother Goose again. In listening to or reading Mother Goose, children make repeated visits to farm, lane, field, sea-shore, and stream. They meet and learn about bird life and barnyard fowl, fish and turtles, spiders and flies. They witness a fascinating procession of farm animals, such as lambs, sheep, colts, horses, calves, cows, and donkeys. Truly, Mother Goose may be called the child's first "Natural History."

The whole world of literature, of course, is pregnant with possibilities for enriching science. Children may learn about space stations and space vehicles of the present and future in Benjamin Bova's *Workshops in Space* (Dutton, 1974), and basic concepts about ecology in Jeanne Bendick's *Place to Live* (Parents' Magazine Press, 1970). Those interested in the processes of communication and insects can choose a book perfect for them, *How Insects Communicate,* by Dorothy H. Patent (Holiday House, 1975). Young people interested in getting answers to questions about snow and who like to do simple experiments will want to take a *Walk in the Snow,* written by Phyllis S. Busch (Lippincott, 1971). These, of course, are merely selected samples of the abundant and fruitful materials that literature affords to supplement and enrich the area of science.

Three extremely useful annotated book lists that are published annually relate directly to the use of literature in content areas.

1. *Classroom Choices: Children's Trade Books,* published in a fall issue of *The Reading Teacher.* Books are selected by book-selection teams under the administration of an International Reading Association-Children's Book Council joint committee.

2. *Notable Children's Trade Books in the Field of Social Studies,* published in a spring issue of *Social Education.* Books are selected by social-studies educators under the administration of an International Reading Association-Children's Book Council joint committee.

3. *Outstanding Science Trade Books for Children,* published in a spring issue of *Science and Children.* Books are selected by science educators under the administration of an International Reading Association-Children's Book Council joint committee.

Free copies of each list may be obtained annually from the Children's Book Council, Inc., 67 Irving Place, New York, New York 10003. (Enclose a stamped, self-addressed business envelope with your request.)

The more children enjoy the reading they do, the more proficient they become in using reading skills. Teachers will not use literature solely as a basis for teaching reading skills, but literature should be used frequently as a medium for utilizing skills in joyful, purposeful reading. Care must be taken, however, to make certain that all literature falls within the "readability levels" of the children for whom it is provided. Although children will read different things at different levels, the frustrating experience of trying to read literature that is "too hard" may discourage a child from making attempts to read at all. Any literature that interests children, but that is too difficult for them to read, should be read or told to them by the teacher.

Interest is especially conducive to fluency and speed in reading. Even word-by-word readers forget to loiter over each symbol when they become absorbed in a story. Instead, such readers race over the pages to find what will happen next, and in their eagerness they take in whole meaningful groups of words.

Folklore is particularly valuable for reluctant readers. Repetition of phrases, simplicity of characterization, swiftness of plot make for easy reading. Also, the simple conversation in folklore helps to bridge the gap between oral reading and silent reading, a gap that the inexperienced reader often finds difficult to bridge.

Thus, literature services children in inestimable ways. Many people today, realizing the intrinsic worth of literature in this mechanized and troubled era of history, are combining their efforts to make the beneficent influences of literature more widely available. Educators are urging more abundant supplies of literature for classrooms and more skillful use of literature by teachers. Publishers are making available excellent story books for children and graded anthologies filled with fascinating selections for classroom use. Trained librarians, literary people, and childhood specialists are cooperating wholeheartedly in advancing and disseminating literary values. All these efforts are evidence of a growing realization of the unlimited values of literature.

Primary Grades

In a summary of research related to children's interests, Helen Robinson and Weintraub [5] reported that investigations indicated that young children are particularly interested in "animals, make-believe, and children's activities." They reported some interest in contemporary scientific events and phenomena, but pointed out that there are many individual differences in reading interests even among the very young. They also suggested that ethnic and socioeconomic factors might influence reading interests.

[5] Helen M. Robinson with Samuel Weintraub, "Research Related to Children's Interest and to Developmental Values of Reading," *Library Trends* 22, no. 2 (October 1973): 81–108.

Kirsch, Pehrsson, and Robinson,[6] in an international study of the expressed reading interests of first- and second-grade pupils, found more similarities than differences among the more than two thousand pupils from ten countries. The top choices of over two-thirds of the first graders for the entire sample were (1) fairy tales and fantasies; (2) stories about children; (3) stories about real animals; and (4) information about animals. In grade two, the choices were the same, but information about animals moved to second place. More of the second graders than first graders preferred nonfiction, and second graders' choices were generally more diverse.

Grades Four through Six

The range of reading topics and media increased from the primary grades. Students in grades four through six turn to comics, magazines, and newspapers as well as "story" books. Sex differences become more pronounced. "Boys tend to prefer adventure and action as well as historical and scientific topics. Girls often enjoy realistic and fanciful stories, mysteries, and humor." According to Helen Robinson and Weintraub ". . . it appears that pupils' comprehension is enhanced by a strong interest in what is read."[7]

Grades Seven and Eight

Although many of the students in grades seven and eight continue interests in the reading they did in grades four through six, some expand their interests into adult themes. Helen Robinson and Weintraub, in reporting on both junior and senior high school, indicated that the boys like books that focus on ". . . action, sports, crime and war, historical novels and mystery. Girls' interests lie in books about people and social relationships, romance, humor, and mystery without violence."[8]

It would seem that sex stereotypes are still evident in the reading interests of young people. Perhaps the studies of reading interests yet to emerge will reflect some of the breaking down of rigid sex roles now evident in our society.

INTEREST-INDUCING ACTIVITIES

Setting the Stage

Interest is the touchstone to reading achievement, reading enjoyment, and reading usefulness. It is the generator of all voluntary reading

[6] Dorothy I. Kirsch, Robert S. V. Pehrsson, and H. Alan Robinson, "Expressed Reading Interests of Young Children: An International Study," in *New Horizons in Reading*, Proceedings of the Fifth IRA World Congress on Reading, ed. John E. Merritt (Newark, Del.: International Reading Assn., 1976), pp. 302–17.

[7] Robinson with Weintraub, "Research Related to Children's Interests," p. 92.

[8] Ibid., p. 94.

activity. Everyone is acquainted with students and adults who possess the skills of reading but who rarely ever do any reading unless they have to as a result of some extraneous pressure. Lack of interest in reading prevents these people from capitalizing fully on the skill assets that elementary teachers have striven so arduously to build in them.

Attitude toward reading lends itself to development as truly as do other aspects of reading achievement. Teachers have to work at it though, as hard as they work at developing word recognition skills, comprehension strategies, or study strategies. Interest in reading must be nurtured by the substance of appropriate content and guided by a teacher with tact and understanding. Materials and guidance when skillfully in-

314

tegrated by enthusiastic teachers can tap dormant springs of interest and keep them flowing in ever-widening streams of reading enjoyment and usefulness.

Several studies have shown that a teacher's enthusiasm for literature is contagious. These studies indicate that in nearly every class children prefer the same book that the teacher is enthusiastic about. This is true of poems also. The teacher's influence upon the literary taste of pupils is exceedingly strong.

Cappa [9] reported reactions to storybooks read by their teachers to kindergarten children. The responses in rank order were: desire to look at the book the teacher had read (38.2 percent), request to have the story read or told again by the teacher (27.3 percent), drawing (10.7 percent), and block play (2.2 percent). Other lesser responses were dramatic play, painting, clay modeling, and so on. This study gives evidence of the teacher's influence on interest insofar as actual contact with the book, or having an opportunity to hear the story again, is concerned.

Because teacher enthusiasm is such a potent factor in developing children's interest, this is a quality that teachers should cultivate in themselves. Many teachers already possess this quality. They are fortunate, and so are their pupils. For those who would like to become more interested, appreciative, and enthusiastic about children's literature, it is suggested that they *do* something about it. Take courses in children's literature, in appreciation of literature at the adult level, and perhaps in the appreciation of art or music. Furthermore, acquaint yourself thoroughly with books in the whole realm of children's literature and read widely in this area. Several good sources for annotated listings of literature for children are:

Adventuring with Books (new ed., 1977). National Council of Teachers of English, 1111 Kenyon Road, Urbana, Illinois 61801.

Best Books for Children (annual). R. R. Bowker & Co., 1180 Avenue of the Americas, New York, N.Y. 10036.

Bibliography of Books for Children (New ed., 1977). Association for Childhood Education International, 3615 Wisconsin Avenue, N.W., Washington, D.C. 20016.

Bulletin of the Center for Children's Books (monthly except August). University of Chicago Press, 5801 Ellis Avenue, Chicago, Ill. 60637.

Children's Books (annual). Superintendent of Documents, U.S. Government Printing Office, Washington, D.C. 20402.

Interracial Books for Children Bulletin (eight times a year). Council on Interracial Books for Children, Inc., 1841 Broadway, New York, N.Y. 10023.

Notable Children's Books of . . . (latest edition). American Library Association, 50 East Huron Street, Chicago, Ill. 60611.

[9] Dan Cappa, "Kindergarten Children's Spontaneous Responses to Storybooks Read by Teachers," *Journal of Educational Research* 52, no. 2 (October 1958): 75.

Reading Ladders for Human Relations (5th ed.). American Council on Education, 1 Dupont Circle, Washington, D.C. 20036.

Permit yourself to escape real life and live in fantasy as when you were a *child*; let tears moisten your eyes at sad parts and chuckles come to your throat at funny parts; identify with realistic heroes and heroines as they surmount obstacles and solve problems; give yourself freely to the emotions of sympathy and admiration as animal characters bear suffering and emerge triumphant; *feel* the beat and music of a poem and *see* the pictures that the poet paints with his or her words. Do these things frequently as you delve into the wonderful storehouse of children's literature—and lo—you soon will be an enthusiast! The glow that you feel will become infectious, and your pupils will begin to feel that way, too.

Recommending Books

Teachers must be cautious, however, about recommending books. Teacher recommendations are very effective *if* given at the right time and under the right conditions. Teacher recommendations should be backed up with knowledge about the book and about the child to whom the recommendation is made. Of course, teachers will be sure to take the greatest care not to say, "Here is a book for you to read, John." For John's reading of the book, then, would not be voluntary; it would be *assigned* reading. Teachers should observe pupils' interests and listen to their requests and have such complete knowledge of the books at hand that they are in a position to say without hesitation, "This book has a chapter in it about engines, John, that would answer the question you just asked"; or, "You enjoyed that book about Colonial transportation so much, Lucille, you might like to read another one about Colonial times. There are two very good Colonial books on that shelf over there if you would care to look at them before choosing your next book to read." Thus, in several indirect ways the teacher may recommend books to meet individual interests and needs, but *never* should teachers press recommendations because to do so might blight rather than excite the interest that they are striving to cultivate.

Counseling Parents

Another strong factor in the development of interest in reading is concerned with the situation in the child's home. Keshian [10] studied the characteristics of good readers and found, as one would expect, that the

---

[10] Jerry G. Keshian, "The Social, Emotional, Physical and Environmental Characteristics and Experiences of Children Who Learn to Read Successfully," Paper presented at the Annual Meeting of the Educational Research Association, Atlantic City, New Jersey, February 20, 1962.

best achievers in reading read the most books. What is especially pertinent to the discussion of the home as a factor are two other conclusions of this study: (1) the parents of good achievers read to their children often during early childhood; and (2) the children came from homes where there was a great variety of reading materials.

Teachers might contribute to home influences, which affect reading interests, in the following ways:

1. Encourage parents to supply their child with an abundance of books selected in terms of the child's interests and levels of readability.

2. Encourage parents to read aloud often to their children.

3. Encourage parents to work out a time budget with children that allows for physical recreation, studying (if the child is at the age at which he or she has homework), television viewing, and *reading*.

4. Suggest to the parents that they devote a stated period each evening to their own reading, with the child also participating by reading in *his* or *her* books and magazines at the same time.

Making Materials Available

Children's reading interests vary in terms of age, sex, intelligence, home influences, and teacher influence. Also, reading-achievement levels of children in most classrooms vary from three to as much as ten or twelve grade levels. Because of the extensive scope of interests and abilities within any one classroom, the best assurance of nurturing reading interests is to make available to children a wide enough variety of reading materials so that each pupil can find something to pique her or his curiosity, challenge interest, and be suitable for the pupil's reading ability.

Every classroom should have a collection of books covering a wide range of subjects. A school library and a nearby public library are strong assets, but in addition, classrooms should have their own library collections. It is fortunate if a school budget will permit the purchase of a large variety of books and some children's magazines for classroom use. In addition, some school systems have bookmobiles, which go from school to school and lend books to teachers and children. This is an excellent provision.

There are many schools, however, in which the supply of classroom books is extremely limited, and that are not served by bookmobiles or other facilities of this type. Nevertheless, teachers in such schools often find ways of providing their pupils with a variety of books. Some teachers invite children to bring their books from home for other children to share. Sometimes, principals are able to find a small amount of money to help toward the building of a classroom collection. Teachers may prepare order sheets of desired paperback books beginning as low as 95 cents and suggest that parents might like to contribute to the collection. One teacher we know had much success with the plan of having parents contributing books on their children's birthdays and inscribing the books with the names of the birthday children.

The teacher may increase and contribute to an ever-changing supply by getting as many children's books from the public library as an individual is permitted to check out on a personal library card. Pupils should be encouraged to take out library cards in the public library and bring the books to class. Parent-teacher associations, upon the appeal of the principal or the teacher, frequently conduct coat-hanger or newspaper drives or candy sales as money-raising projects for the purpose of buying more books for the school. Children of individual classrooms often exercise their ingenuity in contriving ways to raise money for a book fund.

Ingenious teachers will think of other ways of supplementing the school's supply of books in case the school cannot supply the abundance and variety in reading materials that are desirable. In order to keep the variety fresh, the classroom supply of books should have some of the old titles replaced with new ones at intervals throughout the year.

Classroom Activities to Stimulate Interest

Any appreciation experience is deepened by sharing with others. If we see a beautiful sunset, we call others in the family to come and share its beauty with us. If we have just procured an exquisite recording for our stereo and a friend drops in, we say, "Sit down a minute. I want you to hear this beautiful recording." Appreciation of literature, in common with other appreciation experiences, is deepened through sharing.

Reading Orally and Telling Stories. Oral reading and storytelling are the most natural mediums for sharing enjoyment of literature at all grade levels and for all ages. For example, children in any grade will feel the melody and understand the issues in Theodora Kroeber's *Carrousel* (Atheneum, 1977), a good book for reading aloud. So many books are enhanced for the readers by exciting and sincere oral renditions.

The amount of oral reading by the teacher will decrease to some extent as children pass through the grades because the goal, of course, is to develop permanent interests in children to seek enjoyment and satisfaction through their *own* reading of literature. But even in the upper grades, a very effective interest-arousing technique is to tell the children a little about a story or read a preliminary part from the book—not enough to give away the climax, but just enough to serve as a "teaser" of interest. If the members of the Swiss Family Robinson are left in a despairing predicament on their wrecked ship after the crew has shoved off in the last life boat, few children can resist the desire to find out more about this story, which promises to be so adventuresome; or, hardly more than a mere suggestion of the fascinating life of the butterfly need be told by the teacher to stir within a child a desire to discover the untold wonders of its full life story.

Planning for Specific Periods of Sharing. Extending reading interests is such an important objective in the elementary and middle grades that definite periods should be set aside for group activities in connection with voluntary reading. Many teachers use the last hour on Friday afternoons for this purpose. Others devote a little time at the beginning of morning sessions, two or three times a week, to discussion of school, library, and home books that have been read.

Different arrangements and frequency of times for sharing voluntary reading will vary from teacher to teacher. The important consideration is to plan definitely for periods of sharing and to be sure that other subjects and activities do not encroach upon these planned times.

An example of the use to which a weekly sharing period was put is described below.

The teacher of one fifth grade class wished to develop library habits in her pupils and to link up school, home, and library reading. She wished also to develop new tastes for different types of reading content, as well as to aid her pupils in reading along the line of already established interests. In order to provide for such growth, some library activity was sponsored each year. This particular year it took the form of a Reading Club. As several of the pupils received books for Christmas, the Reading Club was organized in January for the purpose of sharing books and interesting some members of the class who did not care for reading. It was decided that the qualifications for admission to the club would be twofold: (1) Candidates must have read and reported on four books and satisfactorily answered the questions put to them on the books by the group. (2) They must take a prominent part in contributing news items and discussing such items during the weekly period devoted to current events.

The Reading Club conducted all its own activities. It had a president and a secretary. At its weekly meetings, reports on reading were given, and other matters were discussed.

During one of these meetings, it was decided that the books in the school library were stale, and that new books were needed that were wider in variety of content and more attractive in form. The teacher told the club that the principal would not be able to provide any new books that year. The group then decided to earn enough to buy some books. This plan resulted in preparations for a fair. The children made favors, tea towels, clown's suits, grab bags, and so on, and planned various forms of entertainment. The fair was successful and netted the sum of forty-five dollars.

The next problem was that of selecting books. In class discussion, the children decided that they would like to have books of the following types: stories about other countries, interesting history stories, stories about great persons of our day, and stories of adventure. They immediately began to bring in book catalogs and reviews from the Sunday newspapers all of which were read and discussed with a view to selecting suitable books for their class library. Many of the pupils also read books in the children's department of the city library and wrote reviews, which were read to the class in order to acquaint the other children with the books found there so that they might decide if they wished to buy any of these.

Although teachers want to be available to pupils who wish to confer with them during voluntary reading periods, teachers must also serve as visible models to emulate. Teachers should carry a book they are reading to class with them and take time to do some reading during the voluntary reading time. When appropriate, teachers will also want to share events from what they are reading with the class or a group.

Some pupils may not want to share what they are reading with the group or the teacher. They should not be forced to do so. Gradually, and/or under certain conditions, given pupils may be nurtured to share with others. Voluntary reading time is not enforced book-report time!

Using Table or Shelf Arrangements. One successful device for awakening interests in new books may be found in arranging attractive displays. Two or three new books may be placed on a table against a novel tapestry or wallpaper panel. The new books may be casually laid on a table with colorful bookmarks indicating particularly alluring pages or illustrations. Perhaps new books may be placed in a background setting suggestive of the subject matter of the books, such as a small serape utilized as a hanging behind the table that displays new books on Mexico, and at the side a sombrero and a figurine of a burro carrying its pack. One teacher had a shelf placed on the wall of his classroom. He then prepared several miniature three-wing screens, each wing about $12'' \times 6''$. Each screen was covered with wallpaper of an attractive design taken from a page of a discarded wallpaper sample book. When he wanted to stimulate interest in a new book, he would place it on the shelf with one of the colorful screens behind it. A different screen would be used each time a new book was displayed.

Using Bulletin Board Displays. The resourceful teacher will recognize the value of the bulletin board in displaying materials to stimulate an interest in free-choice reading. On one occasion, a brilliant illustration of Chinese boys participating in a kite festival aroused such curiosity that the five books that the classroom library contained on the subject of Chinese customs were in constant demand until everyone in the class had read them. A magazine reproduction in colors depicting Long John Silver, with his wooden leg and black patch cocked over one eye and a parrot obviously screeching over his shoulder, caused an instant demand for *Treasure Island*.

Colorful book jackets of new books usually create a number of inquiries on the day they are displayed. Interest persists if they are changed often and displayed well. Large straight pins permit the jackets to be

pushed out toward the heads and a three-dimensional effect is gained. Colorful poster paper, turned at angles in back of book jackets, add to the attractiveness and stimulate interest. Flyleaves can be shown at times and not at other times.

Sometimes, teachers place lists of new books on the bulletin board and children ask for books whose titles appeal to them. Comments and reviews about books when placed on the bulletin board disclose elements of interest that are not apparent to the children from a mere title. Beautiful poems placed on the bulletin board now and then may spur some pupils to voluntary reading of poetry.

If displays on the bulletin board are changed frequently, the teacher will soon find that the children glance eagerly toward the board each morning to see what new interests it may reveal. Children also enjoy contributing to and arranging the bulletin board display themselves, and such responsibility should frequently be given to them.

Preparing for Assembly, Television, or Community Programs. Searching for appropriate content to use in preparing for an assembly program motivates wide and discriminating reading. The program may be a dramatization of a series of scenes from one book or one scene each from several books. In either case, one or more children may give the titles of the books, the names of the authors, and tell why they recommend the book or books to others.

Many schools are now making it possible for children to dramatize stories over a closed television circuit. This is a splendid medium for developing interest in literature.

Preparing to participate in a community activity, such as a "Book

Week" program, offers a motive for reading many stories in order to find appropriate ones to review, describe, re-enact, and discuss.

Selecting

If teachers are to develop children's interest in literature, then the children should be allowed to select the books they want to read during voluntary reading activities. If pupils are to be guided toward the development of criteria on which to evaluate the quality of the books they read, it is essential that they be given a free rein in choosing materials. They can establish valid criteria for evaluating the literature they read only by reading a large variety of materials. Sincere and logical discussions with children about book choices can be held once children have had varied reading experiences; critical analysis cannot be based on external standards set by the teacher, parents, or the community.

Children often do need guidance in regard to the difficulty of the reading content. If certain children should make the mistake of choosing books upon two or three successive occasions that are too difficult for them to read with enjoyment, they may become frustrated and give up. Some guidance is often desirable, but it should be given in subtle ways, still leaving the children free to make their own choices. Some suggestions for guidance in the selection of books have already been given in the section, "Interest-Inducing Activities," but there are additional and more direct ways of meeting the problem of content difficulty.

One way to meet the problem is to place the responsibility on the readers for deciding whether books are easy enough. If the teacher suspects that a book chosen is above a given child's reading ability, the teacher might say, "I wonder if this book is easy enough for you to enjoy reading it. Why don't you try out parts of it and see? Read a few paragraphs here and there and see if you know most of the words and can understand what the author is trying to say." The child may then try reading a few paragraphs silently (or orally to the teacher) in two or three places in the book. If it is too difficult, the pupil no doubt will come to realize this and will decide to choose another book. Furthermore, the child is learning a technique that can be used in deciding upon difficulty before taking a book away to read.

Some teachers meet the problem of difficulty by placing together books that are at about the same readability level. Books of fifth-grade level may be placed on one shelf or table, those of fourth-grade level on another, those of third-grade level on another, and so on, in as many groupings as there are readability levels in the class. The children are not told the grade level of the books in any of the groups.

Bands of colored paper are sometimes attached to book covers to indicate their levels of difficulty. Pink bands, for example, may be attached to books of second-grade level, blue bands to those of third-grade level, and so on.

Keeping Records

Some children are strongly motivated by keeping a record of their voluntary reading and watching how they progress through the school year. Teachers will want to emphasize the concept that the record keeping is done for and by the individual; it is not a contest. Some suggestions for record-keeping follow:

1. In the primary grades, pocket charts are favorites with pupils. The teacher may prepare a pocket chart using as its base a strip of tagboard three to four feet long and twelve to fourteen inches wide, which is to be hung vertically on the wall. To this base, the teacher attaches pieces of tagboard to make a series of pockets.

Such pocket charts can be used in various ways. One way particularly liked by first graders is as follows: The teacher writes a number on each pocket, such as 1 to 3 on the lowest one, 4 to 8 on the next-higher pocket, and so forth. Each child places a picture of himself or herself in a pocket that represents the number of books read, and moves the picture to a higher pocket when more books are read than is indicated by the highest number on the pocket in which the picture currently sits. The pictures may be snapshots that the children bring from home, pictures that they have found in magazines or catalogs that they think resemble themselves, or a paper doll that each child makes to represent himself or herself.

2. In classes in which children are able to write, the teacher may prepare a large pocket chart with a pocket for each pupil with his or her name written upon it. As each pupil finishes a book he or she places a card in the pocket on the chart, bearing the title of the book, author, and a sentence or two, perhaps a paragraph in higher grades, telling a personal reaction to the book.

3. In later grades, it adds to interest and helps develop balanced reading tastes if colored cards are used for the pocket charts, each card representing a certain type of literature, as: pink for fiction, blue for poetry, red for science, green for biography, and so on. A glance at the colors of cards in the pocket will tell a pupil to what kind of books most time is being devoted and what kinds are being neglected.

The cards in various pockets may be used also to aid children in selecting books to read. A child may read the cards in the pockets of several other children in deciding which book he or she will choose to read next.

4. Individual reading charts or booklets are effective. An individual record chart may consist of a piece of brightly colored paper for a foundation; or if it is to be developed into a booklet, several pieces of colored paper may be bound together and confined in an attractive cover. "Books I Have Read," or some other appropriate title may then be placed on the chart or booklet. In the case of either a chart or booklet, the child may write on a foundation sheet of paper the name of each

book read, and then paste above or below the name a picture that he or she has made to illustrate some scene in the book.

5. In the intermediate and middle grades, keeping a simple reading diary is an interesting reading activity for most children. In this case, the pupils buy or prepare a small notebook. Upon completing the reading of each book, they write in the notebook the date, the name of the book, and the name of the author. Then they make a note of anything personal that they wish to say about the book. Many children keep these diaries as prized possessions in later years.

6. A personal file may be kept by each child. Such a file may consist of an ordinary box, perhaps a shoe box or a cheese box, or a small file case bought at a ten-cent store. As a pupil completes a book, he or she writes on a file card the name of the author and book, together with a note giving personal reactions to the book. The cards are then arranged in the file box in alphabetical order.

7. A large class notebook may be used for record keeping. This notebook should be placed somewhere near the classroom supply of books. It should contain as many pages as there are books available. The title and author of each book should be written at the top of one of the pages. When a pupil finishes one of the books whose title is in the notebook, this pupil writes his or her name in the notebook under the title. He or she then prepares a card for the teacher giving the title and author of the book, a brief summary, and personal reaction. Both the class notebook and the cards serve as records of personal reading. A second class notebook may be prepared for use in recording library books read, the titles being added cumulatively as pupils finish the books.

8. Preparing bibliographies for other children to use may become a record-keeping activity as well as a valuable reading experience. A bibliography on Alaska, for example, might be prepared on 3″ × 5″ cards. Each pupil may write the title and author of each reference read on a card, adding the pages if the reference is a part of a book, and then write a summary telling what kind of information the book contains and whether the pupil thinks the reference is worthwhile. The child then signs his or her name to the card. The bibliography may be given to another class of pupils who are or soon will be studying the same subject, or it may be left for the next class that will occupy the classroom in which the bibliography was prepared.

Reporting

One of the problems most frequently voiced by teachers in regard to voluntary reading is how to *check* children on reading done to be sure they have read the books and understand them. It is neither desirable nor feasible to report formally on each book read. Formal book reports can kill interest and appreciation in one fell swoop. Pupils will, however, frequently want to talk about or report on books they have read and teachers can think of a multitude of ways of learning about the reading of their young charges without having each book read orally and/or asking a series of corresponding questions about the book.

Granting that it is often desirable to check voluntary reading, we must think of pleasant ways to accomplish this, ways that will give the teacher the information needed in determining how much of the book the child has assimilated, but ways that are not terribly distasteful to the learner. We, as adults, would not enjoy a novel if we knew that someone was going to give us a comprehension test after we were through reading it. Children feel the same way. Their voluntary reading should be motivated entirely by their personal interests, curiosity, pleasure, and satisfaction, with no thought of testing activities. Here are some suggestions for having children report on what they have read.

1. Carry on an informal discussion about the book or story with the child. It is not necessary to check on the understanding and retention of every detail, but rather to learn if the book or story was generally comprehended and enjoyed. Reactions usually pour out quite naturally in such an informal situation.

2. Ask a pupil to show two or three pictures in a book and tell what was happening in each one of them.

3. Have the reader draw pictures or maps to illustrate some scenes from the book.

4. Suggest, or agree to, the giving of an illustrated talk on certain books, such as a "travel talk."

5. Let pupils make posters with drawings and brief quotations from a book or story.

6. Encourage a child to tell something about a book to other children in order to "sell" it to them.

7. Have one child read aloud for the other children's enjoyment the funniest parts of the book, or the parts describing the most beautiful scenes, and so forth.

8. Allow several children to join together in a "quiz show," in which different children take turns in quizzing each other about books they have read.

9. Suggest that several pupils who have read the same book rewrite or give interpretations of their reading in dramatic form, pantomime, or tableau, depicting characters or scenes. Children enjoy questioning each other about the reasons for varied interpretations.

10. Encourage those children who are interested to construct mobiles by choosing important events in the story or book.

11. Permit one or more pupils to tell a story through the use of puppets. If the enterprise does not become too long and drawn out, they could construct the puppets to represent characters in the book.

12. Encourage children to think of their own ways of reporting on books or stories. Suggest that they develop their own ideas.

Library experience is an essential part of a well-rounded instructional program in reading—essential to skill development, refinement of tastes, and establishment of permanent, carry-over interests and habits in reading. Library activities may take place in three different locales—classroom library, school library, and public library.

The Classroom Library

The favorite setting for a classroom library seems to be a corner of the room. Around the wall in this corner there usually are low shelves filled with books. Two or more tables surrounded with chairs are set in the corner space. In case there is not a central school library to loan books, the library corner may contain a child's desk in which library cards and files are kept.

Reading Materials. Some teachers prefer to arrange books and magazines in two groups, either in two separate sets of bookcases or on two different sets of tables.

In one group are placed all books and other materials that pertain to a center of interest or unit topic that the pupils are pursuing as a group. Assuming that the center of interest is pioneer life, in this group there might be readers and trade books containing Indian stories, the life of Daniel Boone, tales of the covered wagon; a pamphlet of songs and dances of the pioneers; informative material, such as "How to Make a Loom," "Preparation of Flax for Spinning"; perhaps colored illustrations depicting pioneer subjects, such as the operation of a spinning wheel, the pony express, and so on, mounted on cardboard and bound into book form; puzzles and question games utilizing pioneer vocabulary; magazines and newspapers with marked pictures or articles on pioneer subjects.

The second group of tables or bookcases should be given over to a great variety of materials that have nothing to do with the center of interest and that may be used by the children in forwarding their individual preferences. The materials on this table should cover a wide range: magazines and newspapers of various kinds of interest to the children; picture books, paperbacks of numerous types, and hardbound volumes of varied shapes, sizes, and content; stories of animal life, stories of make-believe, biographies, science books, books of adventure, books of travel, books about history; and books of poetry and prose. Colorfully bound stories written by pupils can be included. On the table, or adjacent to it, should be a wide range of audio-visual materials that introduce children to literature; these materials should be available for use during voluntary reading time and at other logical times during the day. This second group of materials, print and nonprint, acts as a supplement to the center of interest table or bookcase, both in variety and in literary value.

The teacher should be sure to include in the classroom library materials that represent several different levels of reading difficulty. In a fourth-grade classroom, for example, there should be some books easy enough for a second-grade child to read and possibly others difficult enough for a seventh-grade pupil to read. Such an assortment makes it possible to provide reading that will meet the individual abilities of all children in the class.

Use of the Classroom Library. The classroom library may be used in several different ways. A committee or individuals may do research reading to obtain information about a group topic being studied. Individual children may be prompted by a desire to walk over to the library, take down a book whose cover, perhaps, has attracted them, and sit down and browse solely for pleasure. At another time, children may go to the library for the definite purpose of referring to an article on the trajectory of a spaceship, for example, in order to make sure of accuracy in completing a painting on space travel. Upon other occasions, pupils may utilize these classroom facilities in true public-library fashion by "taking out" on a library card a chosen book, either to carry home or to keep at a seat until the book has been finished. In classrooms using individualized instruction as the central feature of a reading program, books chosen from the classroom collection usually serve as the basic materials of reading instruction.

The School Library

There is little doubt about the salutary contribution made by a central library or media center in the elementary school. Faculty and parents together must fight vigorously for this vital force in the development of reading interests and tastes as well as lifelong utilization of reading. In times of economic downturn and diminished school populations, it is tempting to cut the budgets of, or even cut out, elementary-school libraries. Such an act contributes toward deprived schools and certainly does not make for the development of thinking citizens who will use library facilities for the good of society and themselves.

Value of the School Library. The school library serves many worthy purposes. It is closer to the life situation, insofar as libraries are concerned, than is the classroom library. It contains card catalogs and reference materials that facilitate children's research reading. It contains the wide range of reading materials necessary to meet the interest and ability levels of all children in the public school.

If adequately conducted under the guidance of a skilled librarian, activities will be planned so that within the library many services may

be rendered. Reading materials will be made easily accessible to a child who comes to the library looking for an answer to a question raised in the classroom. The librarian can artfully assist the pupil in making the transition from supervised to independent reading by arousing genuine interest so that the child will voluntarily seek out reading as a pleasurable pastime in later life. The librarian can help develop the skills needed in making the best use of a library.

The librarian can render a great service in helping to build tastes for good literature by showing children that the simplest way to satisfy natural curiosities is through reading, and by giving them an attractive, inviting atmosphere in which to enjoy it. Many a child has lost earlier tendencies toward reaching for a book of hair-raising comics by the surprised discovery in the library that "thrillers" of a much more satisfying quality than that depicted in comics can be found in real literature. (Make suggestions from Kennerly's *Mysteries Too Good To Miss* (The Children's Book Council, 67 Irving Place, New York, N.Y. 10003. Att: Current Brochure.)

And last, but by no means least, such library activities develop in children a knowledge and appreciation of the valuable services that a library and a librarian can offer, sources of assistance that can be extremely valuable throughout life.

Use of the School Library. The central library should become an integral part of the child's daily living in school. The most common plan of scheduling is one that provides for a daily allotment of time in the library for each class. This time may be used for research, pleasure reading, or for working rather directly with a librarian. Librarians' activities with pupils include storytelling, discussions of books, instruction in library skills, supervision of reference reading, stimulation of recreational reading, guidance in regard to readability levels and in raising tastes to higher levels, and the extension of interests to a greater variety of subjects and literary types.

Individual children use the library, also. In most schools, individuals may go to the library at any time for special work. Children are also permitted to borrow books to take to their respective classrooms or homes for study or recreation.

Cooperation between Teachers and Librarians. Classroom teachers and librarians need to work together closely. Classroom teachers should give information to librarians about the reading needs and the reading abilities of different children. They should also keep librarians informed concerning group interest or unit topics being pursued in the classroom.

Librarians should promptly fulfill requests from the teachers for supplies of books relating to certain topics. They should keep classroom teachers informed concerning the interests, habits, and needs of children as observed in the library. Librarians should become familiar with all courses of study used in the school in order to choose books for the library that have to do with topics studied and in order to have these books available at appropriate times. Occasionally, librarians will go into a classroom to show new books or magazines and to tell something about them.

Public Library Activities

Whether or not a school has a central school library, children should have opportunities to engage in some activities in connection with the local public library or with one of its branches. Becoming acquainted with the public library and its services is one of the best assurances of promoting lifetime usage of books.

Some suggestions are given below of activities in which children may participate in a public library. If the school does not have a central school library, then such activities should take place frequently at the public library. If the school does have a central library, contacts with the public library may be much less frequent, but they should still take place on occasion.

Taking Excursions to the Library. An excellent way to acquaint children with the services and benefits of a public library is to take them on excursions to the nearest library. The librarian should be notified in advance when the class will pay its visit to the library, and the teacher should also give the librarian some advance information about the children's grade levels, reading levels, and interests.

During visits to the library, the librarian may show the children

330

certain books that may be of special interest and where different kinds of books may be found on the open shelves; may acquaint them with the card catalog and teach them how to use it; and may encourage them to apply for a library card and to take out books for home reading. Most librarians in public libraries are very cooperative in working with teachers to further such activities as those mentioned.

Story Hours. The children's department in many libraries regularly holds a "story hour." This event is usually scheduled for some period in the late afternoon or Saturday. These storytelling activities are conducted by a librarian who enjoys and understands children and their needs. The group usually is held enthralled by the unfolding of a tale dear to their hearts, told or read in a delightfully realistic manner, and accompanied by the showing of cleverly characterized illustrations that are found in the book containing the story.

Reading Clubs. Very successful reading clubs are conducted by some librarians. At the beginning of a semester, notices are sent to schools in the vicinity of the library, inviting the children to join the club and to help plan its program for the semester.

With the guidance of the librarian, the plan usually includes one meeting each week. Each meeting is concerned with a different field of interest that is agreed upon in advance by the members of the club.

In arriving at the subject to be reviewed, the children are usually influenced by some recent happening or outstanding contact that has impressed them. For example, Henry had recently seen in a museum one of the earliest models of phonographs, and his inquiries had disclosed that it was invented by Thomas A. Edison. In relating this experience for the enlightenment of the club, it was suggested by one of the members that information about Edison be the subject of their next meeting.

It has been found that in the late spring when attention is turned toward approaching vacations, travel stories usually are the most popular subjects brought up for discussion.

Often a specific event in history is chosen. A varied collection of poems dealing with a certain topic is decided upon if there is a sufficient number who are interested in poetry or who can be carefully guided by the librarian to become interested in having a poetry hour. Sometimes, stories are taken from the old but ever-new treasures of literature and dramatized by a group; or demonstrations of puppet shows, artcraft, and so on are shown to accompany discussions.

Certain committees of children are made responsible for planning the entertainment at each meeting. Because reading must be done on the subject in order to present it, these clubs accomplish much toward exciting the interest of many heretofore dormant-minded readers.

School-Representative Clubs. An excellent medium for bringing about a closer relationship between the classroom and public library is a school-representative club. In organizing such a club, a child from each room in the school is asked to represent his or her class at a series of monthly meetings in the library. One activity of this type that met with encouraging results is described below:

Jackie was chosen to be the representative of the A–5 class. During the course of the first meeting in the library, she was asked to inform the group of the special reading activities, discussions, programs, or other book projects that her own class at school was carrying on at the time. Her report disclosed that her classmates were now deeply engrossed in a study of desert life. She told briefly a few of the most interesting aspects of the study and gave the names of some of the books the children had been reading as their needs developed.

When Jackie came back to her classroom, she in turn brought with her a report consisting of items that representatives from other classrooms had contributed to the group regarding the reading activities, book reviews, and so on, in which their respective classmates had participated. She also had included in her notes news about recent books that the librarian had introduced to the club by giving a brief but enticing synopsis, as well as telling about books she had noticed on display and reporting other items of information that she had gained at the meeting.

Through the medium of such a club, the librarian may assist the teacher in many ways. Knowing, for example, that the A–5 class is studying desert life, the librarian may prepare and send to the teacher a list of references that are available at the library that pertain to various forms of desert plants, desert animals, climate conditions of the desert, information on attempts made to reclaim certain portions, old desert tales, and so on; the list branching out from any one of these topics is endless.

Supplying Teachers with Book Lists. As another service, the librarian may send to the teacher at the beginning of each month a list of new books accompanied by comments concerning their content, grade placement, and interest features. Likewise, the librarian may provide the teacher with lists of books and appropriate comments for distribution to the children in order to arouse their interest in summer reading.

In these and various other ways, the librarian of a public library and teachers in nearby schools may cooperate. Such cooperation will contribute much to laying a foundation in childhood for a lifelong reading enrichment through the use of public library facilities.

DISCUSSION QUESTIONS AND ACTIVITIES

1. Raise the question, "Is reading necessary in our society?" and discuss the varied answers. Pupils often think of valid reasons that have never occurred to their teachers. For example, one youngster (in re-

sponding to such a question) said that she could not foresee the time when talking tapes could or would take the place of print on merchandise in a store.

2. Ask pupils if they have ever been deeply affected by something they have read or had read to them. Share your own experiences. For example, one of the authors of this book found himself in tears while sharing the reading of *Charlotte's Web* with his daughter.

3. Explore the interests of individuals in the class. Discuss how and why interests change. The incomplete sentence technique is often useful for ascertaining interests:

I like to read about ＿＿＿＿＿＿＿.
I am bored by stories about ＿＿＿＿＿＿.
My favorite animal story is (or is about) ＿＿＿＿＿＿.
Poetry is ＿＿＿＿＿＿.

4. Conduct a session with pupils comparing textbooks with literature. Help children to note the values of each. A collection of materials that include both trade books (literature) and instructional media assembled to help them solve a given problem (what makes airplanes fly, for instance) helps learners realize the need to use varied sources.

5. Send for the current book lists suggested on page 311. Have pupils choose those that, on the basis of the annotations, sound particularly interesting and/or that will fit into units being studied in class. Try to purchase or borrow those books that seem most pertinent and interesting for the children in your situation.

6. Obtain some of the current book lists suggested on pages 315–16. Have pupils each choose one book they would really like to read. Try to purchase or borrow as many of the choices as possible.

7. Build a written list of techniques for trying to motivate children to read gathered from this chapter, your own experiences and ideas, and successful techniques used by colleagues. Read the article by Johns and Lunt listed in Additional Readings for a variety of ideas contributed by teachers. Having the written list, and referring to it as well as adding to it from time to time, ensures variety.

8. Build a written list of methods for reporting on books read. In addition to the suggestions in the chapter and the methods you and your colleagues may have developed, refer to Johns and Lunt again as well as Criscuolo's "Book Reports: Twelve Creative Alternatives" cited in Additional Readings. Ask pupils to add to the list.

9. When asking questions about what your children have been reading, find out whether or not they are conscious of sex and ethnic stereotyping

or prejudice reflected in the writing or the story line. Have them cite examples. Ask how they might change some of the writing.

ADDITIONAL READINGS

Books and Pamphlets

HILLERICH, ROBERT L. *50 Ways to Raise Bookworms.* Boston: Houghton Mifflin Co., n.d.

HUCK, CHARLOTTE S. *Children's Literature in the Elementary School.* 3rd ed. New York: Holt, Rinehart and Winston, 1976.

LARRICK, NANCY. *A Parent's Guide to Children's Literature.* 4th ed. New York: Doubleday, 1975.

MONSON, DIANNE, and PELTOLA, BETTE, comps. *Research in Children's Literature.* Newark, Del.: International Reading Assn., 1976.

SEBESTA, SAM L., and IVERSON, WILLIAM. *Literature for Thursday's Child.* Palo Alto, Calif.: Science Research Associates, 1975.

SUTHERLAND, ZENA, and ARBUTHNOT, MAY HILL. *Children and Books.* 5th ed. Glenview, Ill.: Scott, Foresman and Co., 1977.

THOMAS, ELLEN L., and ROBINSON, H. ALAN. *Improving Reading in Every Class.* 2nd ed., chaps. 15–17. Boston: Allyn and Bacon, 1977.

Periodicals

BILLIG, EDITH. "Children's Literature as a Springboard to Content Areas." *Reading Teacher* 30, no. 8 (May 1977), pp. 855–59.

CRISCUOLO, NICHOLAS P. "Book Reports: Twelve Creative Alternatives." *Reading Teacher* 30, no. 8 (May 1977), pp. 893–95.

ENGEL, ROSALIND. "Literature Develops Children's 'I's' for Reading." *Language Arts* 53, no. 8 (November/December 1976), pp. 892–98.

FEELEY, JOAN T. "Interest Patterns and Media Preferences of Middle-Grade Children." *Reading World* 13, no. 3 (March 1974), pp. 224–37.

JOHNS, JERRY L. "Reading Preferences of Intermediate-Grade Students in Urban Settings." *Reading World* 14, no. 1 (October 1974), pp. 51–63.

———, and LUNT, LINDA. "Motivating Reading: Professional Ideas." *Reading Teacher* 28, no. 7 (April 1975), pp. 617–19.

NATIONAL COUNCIL OF TEACHERS OF ENGLISH. *Elementary English* 52, no. 4 (April 1975).

———. *Language Arts* 52, no. 7 (October 1975).

———. *Language Arts* 53, no. 5 (May 1976).

———. *Language Arts* 54, no. 1 (January 1977).

———. *Language Arts* 54, no. 5 (May 1977), pp. 522–66.

O'DONNELL, HOLLY. "Trade Books in the Classroom." *Reading Teacher* 31, no. 1 (October 1977), pp. 118–21.

Post, Robert M. "The Reading Teacher as Oral Interpreter of Literature." *Reading Teacher* 31, no. 3 (December 1977), pp. 303–7.

Rupley, William H. "Reading Interests: Motivating Students to Read for Personal Enjoyment." *Reading Teacher* 30, no. 1 (October 1976), p. 118.

Stewig, John W. "Storyteller: Endangered Species?" *Language Arts* 55, no. 3 (March 1978), pp. 339–45.

Troy, Anne. "Literature for Content Learning." *Reading Teacher* 30, no. 5 (February 1977), pp. 470–74.

CHAPTER 12   CLASSROOM INSTRUCTION

Differentiated Grouping and Individualization

THE CLASS AS A READING GROUP

TEMPORARY INSTRUCTIONAL GROUPS

INTEREST GROUPS

SOCIAL GROUPING

THE INDIVIDUAL

OVERALL PLANS
Open School or Classroom
Nongraded Primary

Organizing Instruction

INDEPENDENT ACTIVITIES
Directions
Agendas

LEARNING CENTERS IN READING
Using Technological Devices

Teaching and Learning

PLANNING

READING TO CHILDREN

READING BY CHILDREN

DIRECTED READING LESSONS

DIRECTED READING-THINKING ACTIVITY

Advising Parents

PRESCHOOL READING

AFTER SCHOOL READING BEGINS

WHAT PARENTS CAN DO
Responding, Listening, and Encouraging
Reading to Children
Selecting Books

Concluding Statement

Discussion Questions and Activities

Additional Readings

CHAPTER   13   READING IN GRADES FOUR THROUGH EIGHT

Organizational Plans

THE JOPLIN PLAN

DEPARTMENTALIZATION

IN-CLASS ORGANIZATION

SECTION D
CLASSROOM INSTRUCTION

Nature of the Materials

   BASAL READERS

   OTHER READING DEVELOPMENT MATERIALS

   CURRICULUM MATERIALS

Instructional Plans

   STEPS IN THE DRTA

   JUNIOR GREAT BOOKS REFLECTIVE ACTIVITIES

   ALTERNATE PLANS

Independent Reading

   STUDY-READING

   STUDY GUIDES
      Process Guide
      Content Guide
      Individualized Guides
      Alternative Guide Formats

   INDIVIDUAL READING

Oral Reading

Complexities in Language Processing

   ANAPHORA

   IDEA COMBINING

   VOCABULARY

Discussion Questions and Activities

Addtional Readings

CHAPTER 14 A FOCUS ON SPECIAL NEEDS

"Divergent" Language and Culture

   BUILDING POSITIVE CONCEPTS

   "INTELLIGENCE" AND ENVIRONMENT

Dialects and Reading

   THE ROOTS OF DIALECTS

   INFORMATION ABOUT BLACK ENGLISH

   DIALECT INTERFERENCE

   TRANSITION ACTIVITIES

Bilingualism and Reading

   LEARNING PATTERNS AND CULTURE

   LEARNING TO READ
      The Value of Context Clues
      Approaches and Activities

Discussion Questions and Activities

Additional Readings

chapter 12

reading
in grades one
through three

What to Expect in This Chapter:
Various ways of grouping for reading instruction are discussed, plus a brief discussion of overall school organization.
Emphasis is placed on both how the teacher organizes the classroom for instruction and on specific teaching and learning procedures. Suggestions are also offered for advising parents in regard to their roles in preschool reading activities and in support
activities once their children enter the primary grades.

In the United States during the 1600s and 1700s, schooling was
largely selective and individualized. In the early 1800s, the English
"monitorial system" was utilized to divide the larger groups of pupils
coming into our schools into smaller groups. A teacher directed instruction with the help of able students or monitors who led the small groups.
In the 1840s, rumblings came from Germany that children should be
grouped in classes according to age and ability, a single teacher to a class.
The idea was accepted, the graded system evolved, and children were
taught in large groups by grades. The American lockstep approach was
upon us!

The years 1870 to 1910 were characterized by new schemes, new
groupings, new plans. As a result of these efforts, the three-group plan
was born. In the traditional three-group plan, the teacher divides the
entire class into groups according to reading ability (often based on a
range of reading levels established through testing): the fast, the average,
and the slow group. Each group is taught as a whole during one period
each day, usually working at a certain place in a basal reader.

This traditional plan is being criticized by many educators. One of
the arguments advanced against it is that there is wide variation in
achievement, rate of progress, and motivational drives among the pupils
in any one of these three groups and that individual needs cannot be
met to the best advantage by simply labeling three groups as high,
average, or low. Another argument leveled against this plan is that it is
undesirable from the psychological and social points of view. Those in
the average group seem to feel that they are doing as well as ordinarily
can be expected. Those in the higher group, however, seem to feel that
they are there because they are smarter than the others, and many of
those in the lower group believe they are there because they are stupid.

Attempts have been made to conceal from children the ability level
at which they are working by labeling the groups with such names as
"Bluebirds," "Cardinals," and "Robins," or "Brownies," "Elves," and
"Pixies." This pseudo-nomenclature simply does not serve its purpose.
Aside from the fact that such labels—particularly for those in the *low*
group—lower self-concepts, children are well aware of what group they
are in regardless of the name used for each classification.

This point was neatly illustrated in an incident described by Mrs. White, a visitor at a certain school, who went out on the playground at recess time to chat directly with the children about their work. Walking up to Tommy, she asked, "What grade are you in?" "The second grade," replied Tommy. Then he added, "I'm with the 'Busy Bees.'" What are the 'Busy Bees'?" asked Mrs. White. "They are the low group. We don't know anything in that group," replied Tommy. "Did your teacher tell you that the 'Busy Bees' are in the low group?" asked Mrs. White in shocked amazement. "Oh, no," explained Tommy, "She doesn't want to hurt our feelings." "Why don't you tell her that you know that you are in the low group?" persisted Mrs. White. "We don't want to hurt *her* feelings," was the surprising answer.

Another criticism of the traditional three-group plan is that the same children are sometimes kept in the same three groups during several successive grades. The second-grade teacher continues on with the same three groups established by first grade, and so on.

DIFFERENTIATED GROUPING AND INDIVIDUALIZATION

What should a primary-school teacher do then in order to avoid static, labeled groups? There are several alternatives open that can be intermixed as the teacher becomes comfortable with the class and the varied organizational plans. During the beginning days of school, the teacher may want to work with the class as a total group striving to establish principles of class behavior, procedures for work and play, and ways of helping pupils to work independently. Experience charts should be developed with the pupils, to be placed on large visible sheets of paper, that outline procedures and principles adopted by the group for particular activities. For example, the following headings would have easy-to-read points listed under them: Leaving the Room; Using the Library Corner; Using the Science Table; Things to Do By Myself. Once pupils new to a teacher and a classroom learn to understand the varied activities open to them and learn to work with each other in orderly fashion, differentiated instruction can begin for parts of the day.

The Class as a Reading Group

There may be times when the entire class becomes a reading group. All the children in the room may meet with the teacher while preparing and reading plans for an excursion, questions in connection with a center of interest, for slides, a television show, or movie, and so on. There will also be sharing occasions in which all the children will participate: when they share the stories in books they are reading independently; when one child reads to the entire group something of interest; when one group enacts a dramatization of a story; when one group has done research reading and shares its findings with the entire class. In addition to motivating reading, such total-group situations develop a sense of togetherness, of social give and take, of being a worthy member of a larger whole.

Temporary Instructional Groups

Groups formed for particular purposes for a session, a day, a week, or even a month should be named for the activity (alligator research), a temporary group leader (changed daily), or a concept (the think tank). These groups may be reading a common book, studying a common or group of related topics, planning a project, and so forth. They may be called together by the teacher for specific emphasis on a strategy or skill of reading. For example, ten children may need help in using the pronunciation key of the dictionary, and these children work with the teacher in a group while the rest of the children do something else. Or the teacher may want to develop a whole lesson or series of lessons with the group based on their basal readers or individual trade books. Or the teacher may want to meet with them for a given amount of time in order to cement some ideas and instructions before turning them loose as a group working independently or as individuals turning to their own assignments.

Interest Groups

Pete, Edith, Maria, and Guy, a group of children from Mr. Gray's third-grade room, were strolling along together on their way to school on a bright sunny morning when Guy spied a "shining stone." Small particles in this rock glistened in the sunlight. The other children gathered around to examine the find. "Does it have gold in it?" "Maybe the glistening parts are diamonds." Thus, they speculated, and interest was still high at the opening of the morning session. The children wanted to identify the composition of the stone. Mr. Gray said that they might sit in one corner of the room, which he designated, and work on their problem. Incidentally, it might be added that as the children worked with this problem they extended their interest in rocks in general.

Maria, a very good reader, checked out two juvenile encyclopedias from the library. Edith and Pete, relatively average readers, surrounded themselves with all the different science books in the classroom. Guy was not a good reader and could not manage to read any of the information in the materials available. However, Mr. Gray managed to obtain a trade book on rocks from the librarian. Guy could not read much of the information, but, with Mr. Gray's help, he managed to get information from the detailed captions that accompanied the well-done illustrations. Mr. Gray helped Guy to write his notes, which he read to the other three children and subsequently in a report to the class.

Social Grouping

Social grouping deserves consideration. There are many occasions in which children may be grouped on the basis of social choice, those children being permitted to work together who want to be together or who want to work with a certain leader. This type of organization best lends itself to such activities as finding a suitable story to dramatize or pantomime, to use in a puppet show or mock radio or television show; to plan and write down the steps for a particular project; to carry on research as background for undertaking a construction project, such as making the moat and drawbridge in a model of a castle or preparing the miniature trees to be used in a diorama of a South American jungle.

As small groups are organized on the basis of self-selection of working companions, there may be two excellent readers and two poor readers in the same group. The good readers will probably read independently, but at the same time stand ready to give individualized help to the poor readers—and all will proceed happily because of it.

The Individual

Individualized reading instruction as an approach was discussed in chapter 5. Here we are considering individualization as one means of organizing a classroom for instruction. There are obviously times when it is useful for children to work on their own, on their own with a helpful adult (paraprofessional or volunteer tutor), on their own with the help of an able peer, or on their own with the teacher. The nature of the task should shape the situation. If a given child keeps having trouble with a particular aspect of reading, the teacher will want to work directly with that one pupil or assign an able assistant. Pupils could need help with a specific concept, cementing the strategy of using context to understand words, understanding directions for conducting an experiment, and so on.

There are other times when a pupil wants to, or is asked to, work independently on a reading assignment. Certainly, all pupils must master independent activities if teachers are to work with the many pupils and group formations in a classroom. Independent activities are discussed later in this chapter.

Overall Plans

In an attempt to break down regimented grade levels and static groupings in the primary unit, some schools and school systems have tried a number of organizational plans. The open school or classroom and the nongraded primary are used most often. In such overall plans, the individual teacher's structure for teaching reading is pretty much dictated by the plan.

Open School or Classroom. Borrowed from the British, this plan is based on individualization of instruction with no set program. Plans change as they evolve from children's interests and activities. The school has few internal walls, and children are free to work on the variety of experiences available in the building. Teachers interact with pupils as individuals or in self-organized groups as needed.

In the United States, some buildings have been constructed as open schools, but frequently existing buildings have been renovated. In other cases, teachers have taken the concept and applied it to contained classrooms. Most of the time, planned attention is paid to reading instruction, using the individualized approach. Children read self-selected books, ask for help when needed, and have scheduled conferences with teachers.

A number of teachers use a modified open-school philosophy and include in it the flexible types of planned groups discussed earlier.

Nongraded Primary. On a July day in 1935, Robert Hill Lane [1] tossed an educational bomb into the midst of a group of listeners in Denver during the Annual Convention of the National Education Association. Lane, District Principal in the public schools of Los Angeles, proposed to establish a school unit that he called the "Junior School." In this unit, there would be no grades. Reading would be the major problem attacked; children would be "passed" only once, and that would be when they made the transition to the "Upper School." Some children would be in the Junior School three years, others four years, or two years, or whatever period of time it was necessary for them to achieve such ability as would enable them to move into the "Upper School." Several years elapsed before the idea took hold, but recently a number of school systems have adopted the plan and extended it (in some cases) to the intermediate grades.

Ideally and theoretically, the plan is highly desirable because it can relieve tensions aggravated by yearly promotions and permits each child to progress at her or his own learning rate. All grade labels are removed from doors, and thinking in terms of grade levels becomes obsolete. Children can still move in groups, but periodic evaluations are given, and they are shifted from one group to another as often as necessary to ensure continuous growth. The chief drawback to the nongraded primary is that it is difficult to administer. Many are criticized on the grounds that about all they have done is to remove grade labels and that the sound concepts suggested for the program are not being applied.

McLoughlin said, "As long as schools seek practices designed to group away differences they are *not* nongraded. The nongraded school never held this as a goal, for it is impossible. Rather, nongrading says: 'Accept children as they are, with all their differences, and teach to these differences. Don't try to eradicate them!' Until educators develop instructional programs that will meet this challenge they are not nongrading. They are simply masking their old egg-crate schools with a new facade." [2]

---

[1] Robert H. Lane, "The Junior School—Its Plan and Purpose," *Addresses and Proceedings of the National Education Association* (January 1935), pp. 381–83.

[2] William P. McLoughlin, "The Phantom Nongraded School," *Phi Delta Kappan* 49, no. 5 (January 1968): 250.

ORGANIZING INSTRUCTION
The primary reading program works best when the classroom structure provides for rich experiences, a multitude of resources, organized activities, and opportunities for engaging in meaningful, purposeful, independent tasks. Teachers who take the time to build such a structure and share its organization with their pupils have the greatest opportunities for helping to develop successful readers. How marvelous that a reading program can incorporate the materials from all disciplines so that a science table and a math corner may and do involve pupils in the processes of reading!

Independent Activities

Primary teachers are always searching for independent activities—meaningful reading and writing tasks that children can execute on their own. They are essential if the teacher is to devote instructional and listening time to individuals or small groups. All independent activities should be instructional activities before they become independent, or the teacher should be certain, through appraisal, that given children are capable of handling specific activities on their own. For example, if a simple crossword puzzle is to become an independent activity, the teacher must be sure that the children who will turn to it, understand it—that they have had experiences with crossword puzzles. Uncertainty and confusion at the independent level can turn to disinterest, boredom, and misconceptions.

Directions. The directions pupils are to follow for independent activities must be simple and clear. Sentence structure should be within the experience of the reader. One, and certainly never more than two, specific directions should be in one sentence. When ideas are combined in one sentence, clauses should contain conjunctions pupils can handle. Pronouns should be avoided when possible. Pikulski and Jones [3] provided an example of an original set of instructions rewritten in order to facilitate independent reading and action.

Original Directions

Hold the following up to a light or window: Take the yellow slip and put the blue one on top and what color do you see? Then take the red one and put it on top of the blue one. Now take the yellow one and put it on top of the red one. What do you see?

Revised Directions

1. Put the yellow paper against the window. Put the blue paper on top of the yellow paper. What new color do you see?

[3] John J. Pikulski and Margaret B. Jones, "Writing Directions Children Can Read," *Reading Teacher* 30, no. 6 (March 1977): 599–60.

2. Put the blue paper against the window. Put the red paper on top of the blue paper. What new color do you see?
3. Put the red paper against the window. Put the yellow paper on top of the red paper. What new color do you see?

Pikulski and Jones suggested that for some readers, particularly first graders, the teacher might substitute a colored bar for each color word and use the language of an equation.

$$\boxed{\text{yellow}} \quad + \quad \boxed{\text{blue}} \quad = \quad ?$$

Agendas. Beginning with day one of the first grade, pupils should become used to the concept of specific planning. The results of oral planning sessions should be printed on the chalkboard daily. If the results of the planning are important for future activity over days, weeks, or months, the list of activities or actions should be transferred to chart paper and posted in a convenient place. Such agendas should be on display at the centers of interest in the classroom—spelling out their use.

Personalized agendas for the day or week are extremely useful. Pupils should list the activities they want to or must accomplish individually and/or with one or more groups. The top of the agenda should feature priority activities; the bottom, subject to change, may list optional activities that can be dealt with at will.

EXAMPLE:

My Agenda
Tuesday   Ann Sloane
1. *Finish the last chapter in* Charlotte's Web.
2. *Fill out a reaction card and file it.*
3. *At 10:30 meet with Ms. Lambert to discuss the whole book.*
4. *At 11:00 meet with the party group to plan our class party.*
5. *At 1:30 meet with Gene's group and Ms. Lambert for help with the science book.*
6. *Pick another book from library corner.*
7. *Show myself the filmstrip about pollution.*

Agendas, of course, do not include every detail of the school day. They feature only independent activities and specific group obligations.

EXAMPLE:

Agenda for March 6–10
Harvey Epstein

1. *Choose a picture from the picture pocket and write a story about it.*
2. *Meet with my group for a half hour each day to work on the play.*
3. *Correct last week's story to hand in to the newspaper.*
4. *Do the science experiment on food coloring.*
5. *Write a report on the experiment.*
6. *Whenever there is time, work on the frieze.*

The teacher will probably have many other activities planned for groups or the whole class.

Learning Centers in Reading

Dependent upon space and creativity, learning centers may be organized in many different ways. Tables surrounded with chairs or desks may be pushed together, seat side outward, to make sets of separate, flat-top surfaces. Children may gather around these tables or flat-top desk areas to engage in a variety of reading and reading-related activities. A rug is desirable for individual children to sit on or lie on to read, or for groups of children who are reading for the same purpose or who meet for discussion and sharing.

In its simplest form, the "reading center" activities consist of children selecting books from the shelves and sitting around the tables or desk-top surfaces and reading them. In a "Reading Learning Center," provisions are made for practice on specific activities to serve different learning purposes. The learning activities as commonly provided in a reading learning center are briefly indicated in the following paragraphs. The materials used in the activities mentioned are usually prepared by the classroom teacher. This extra work is often alleviated, however, with the help of paraprofessionals or aides, who under guidance can do a good job in preparing such material, and it is excellent experience for them.

A large box may be placed on each table or desk top. In each box, the teacher has filed information relating to a special activity. If abilities differ widely, three boxes may be provided at different levels of complexity.

On one table or set of desk tops, the box or boxes may be prominently labeled "Stories to Read" and, if desired, further subdivisions into "Animals," "Boats," "Ships," and so on, may be made. This box contains references to stories in books on the book shelves.

On another table or desk surface, the file box may be labeled "Games." On this surface, there also are sheets of paper, pencils, scissors, glue, crayons, or possibly ballpoint pens.

The "games" are sets of directions to the child for doing the types of activities described in chapters 6 through 10.

The study strategies may be given practice through sets of directions for reading and doing accompanying activities in connection with different subareas. One box may be labeled "Reading Interesting Articles in Science," another "Interesting Articles in History." To provide practice in reading in mathematics, the teacher may prepare sets of problems and files in a box titled "Solving Problems." The problems should of course be suitable for the grade level and organized around problems close to the children's lives, such as "Food You Eat," "Clothes You Wear," "Your School Books," and so forth.

Using Technological Devices. The increasing use of technology is an advantage to learning reading centers. Records, slides, films, film strips, transparencies, cassettes, and computers all have contributions to make to reading. All can be used by individuals or groups in a learning reading center, and many classrooms now have several of these devices available and in use in their learning-reading centers.

TEACHING AND LEARNING

Chapters 1 through 11 have focused on teaching and learning applicable to the primary grades, but we have placed little attention on specific methodology. Contemporary manuals and guidebooks for basal series and other instructional materials usually supply detailed suggestions. Nevertheless, teachers should have useful, existing procedures in mind in addition to creating their own. The aspects of the primary program, as well as the methods or procedures that follow, may be used in different ways at different times with different individuals or groups. The approach is eclectic—choosing and selecting what seems best in given situations. But the approach is not unplanned. Too often *eclectic* is considered *incidental*. A sound program must be carefully thought through and planned, but it does not have to follow one particular system— nor should it.

Planning

Whether the teacher is working in a team with another teacher or alone (sometimes with aides), a great deal of preplanning must go into the first, second, or third-grade program. Teachers should plan their rooms and activities during the summer months with their new pupils in mind. Plans, of course, are subject to change, and planning will be part of the instructional cycle throughout the school year. But the first days and weeks are of great importance; these plans should be especially specific. Smith and Johnson presented some very detailed plans for the first days and weeks of school in their book, *Teaching Children to Read.*

Time	Objectives, Materials, Motivation, Procedures, and Followup		Notes
8:50–9:00 (10 min.)	*Opening:*	Welcome children, help them find places, note calendar and weather	Name cards in manuscript-writing are taped on desk tops
9:00–9:20 (20 min.)	(Whole class) *Objective:*	Welcome and introduction	
	Materials:	Name tags to pin on children	Cutouts of leaves, animals, etc.
	Procedures:	Call names, child tells something of self, family, pet	Note shy child and do not force speaking
9:20–9:30 (10 min.)	(Whole class) *Objective:*	Chance for listening and oral expression	
	Procedure:	Discuss expectations for school year—need for cooperation, good listening habits, room rules	Teacher guides discussion, rather than lectures
			Children may state that they *expect* to learn how to read
9:30–9:40 (10 min.)	(Whole class) *Objective:*	Provide motivation for experience story	
	Materials:	Classroom pet, food, name card, felt-tip pen	
	Procedure:	Gather class around pet cage, encourage comments, choose name and print name on tag, attach to cage	Make note of verbal children, watch for child who appears disinterested
9:40–10:00 (20 min.)	(Whole class) *Objective:*	Record group chart story in manner outlined in Chapter 6	Teacher needs to prod class with leading questions if children are hesitant to contribute
	Materials:	Chart tablet, felt-tip pen, pet cage on table near chart	Place chart tablet at level visible to everyone
	Procedure:	Explain task, encourage free expression, record comments	Teacher comments on a few letters and words while recording; remind children to watch carefully
10:00–10:10 (10 min.)	(Whole class) *Objective:*	Reread story, note individual abilities	Let the children get up and stretch a bit; rhymes and songs can be found to use at times such as this and
	Procedure:	Teacher reads story, using normal intonation, and sweeps hand along lines;	

Time	Objectives, Materials, Motivation, Procedures, and Followup	Notes
	volunteers read story with teacher's help, identify a word or letter they know	are good to have in "bag of tricks"
10:10–10:30 (20 min.)	**(Whole class)** *Objective:* Draw pictures to reinforce theme of story; provide something for children to carry home to show parents	This activity provides a worthwhile project to show parents
	Materials: 9″ × 18″ manila paper folded in half, crayons	Provide extra boxes of crayons, as children do not bring all supplies on the first day
	Procedure: Discuss what may appear in picture related to chart story, demonstrate how to use top half of paper for picture, instruct children to put name on top of paper, collect papers	Some children will finish in a couple minutes and do not want to work on picture any more; circulate and talk to these and other children, print any words child requests on picture
	Followup: Use any time remaining for children to show their pictures and tell about them	Some may still be working
Later in day	Pass out pictures with story stapled to lower half of manila paper, reread story as group, suggest that children show story to parents, and tell them about class pet	Teacher or aide will have used the break time to type and mimeograph the chart story Solves dilemma in many households when anxious parent asks about the school day and child has little to say

Comments

First-grade children come into the classroom expecting to learn how to read. You have provided them with a positive step in that direction on the first day of school. Children want to carry something along home with them to show to their families. The illustrated chart story satisfies this need in a meaningful way. You may wish to send a brief note (pinned to each child's collar) which explains to the parents that the child is not expected to be able to "read" the story in total. It may be worthwhile to explain this program to the parents during a PTA meeting or parents' visiting night.

After thinking about the day's activities, make note of children who seemed especially interested in the story development or who seemed to know a few words or letters. Note those who were easily distracted and the ones who were unable to contribute to the activities. Divide the class into two groups (A and B) for tomorrow's work. Include a few "contributors" in each of the groups.

The plan for week one–day one of grade one is reprinted with their permission.[4] It was designed by an experienced first-grade teacher, Sandra Dahl.

Reading to Children

Teachers should read to children daily. The material should be close to the interests of the children and in language that they can easily process. Hearing the sounds and sense of language read well with emphasis on meaning encourages them to read in the same way. They should hear different kinds of materials and be asked to listen for differing purposes. It is fine to continue the reading of Maurice Sendak's *Seven Little Monsters* (Harper & Row) over a few days, but during that time period children should listen to a newspaper report, a science paragraph, and so on. Whenever material lends itself to it, listeners should be encouraged to predict what will happen next rather than always be asked to relate what happened. Developing prediction power is most valuable for their own reading. McCormick pointed out the research that supports reading aloud to children:

> Research now provides evidence of the direct relationship between reading aloud to children and reading performance, language development, and the development of reading interests. The evidence indicated that reading to children is an activity that should be scheduled regularly.[5]

Reading by Children

As soon as children are able to read—beginning with picture books and experience stories—short periods each day should be set aside for sustained silent reading. The time can increase as pupils' attention spans and reading interests and maturities expand. This reading should be of their choice—guidance given only when desired. Reports are not necessary or desirable unless children are eager to share what they read with the teacher and others. The teacher should be available to interact when pupils so desire but, more important, the teacher should also be reading at that time. Pupils also need models to emulate. Such sustained reading increases interest for most pupils, proclaims the importance of individualized reading in the school curriculum, and contributes to improved reading ability.

We are speaking here of *silent* reading. Group oral reading in different materials, of course, is chaos and serves no real purpose. We are also not speaking of the practice in some individualized reading pro-

---

[4] Richard J. Smith and Dale D. Johnson, *Teaching Children to Read* (Reading, Mass.: Addison-Wesley Publishing Co., 1976), pp. 294–96.

[5] Sandra McCormick, "Should You Read Aloud To Your Children?" *Language Arts* 54, no. 2 (February 1977): 143.

grams of "hearing" a child read for a few minutes each day just to see how he or she is coming along. Oral reading is an important aspect of a primary program but children must consider it to be meaningful and purposeful. Oral reading should rarely occur without preparation; that is, reading the material silently first. The usual exception is sight reading for the purpose of learning more about the reader's strategies (pages 60–62 in chapter 3).

Oral reading is not a game of accurate pronunciation. Unless meaning is distorted by pronunciations or substitutions that deviate from the expected response, pupils should not be corrected. The major goal in oral reading, as in silent, is the reconstruction of meaning. Each story in a reader does not have to be read silently and orally. Oral reading should be selective—for meaningful purposes. Here are some:

1. Putting on a play.
2. Interpreting poetry.
3. Reporting on something (the weather, a funny incident to be shared, information from a meeting everyone did not attend).
4. Reading directions for people to follow.
5. Sharing a story, a riddle, a joke with others.
6. Finding a section in a passage that verifies a point.
7. Reading and explaining an experiment, a model, or the way to construct something.

Directed Reading Lessons

Pupils will read on their own for a multitude of purposes—enjoyment, problem solving, gathering information about a topic, and so forth. At times, the teacher will interact informally, and at times the teacher will not be involved at all. But there will be many times when the teacher will want to direct the lesson in order to help pupils learn to handle varied literary genres, writing styles, thought processes, strategies, and skills. Teachers use a number of different procedures. One of the most common is the directed reading activity (DRA).

The DRA consists of the following steps:

1. *Focus the attention of pupils on a topic in advance of reading about it.* Try to interest them by raising questions, having them raise questions, using a variety of visual or audio-visual aids, and capitalizing on their background experiences. This process is usually carried on with a small group of pupils about to read the same selection. For example, a visit to the zoo interested the group in learning more about the differences between lizards and snakes. The teacher knew in advance that a story in their books dealt with the similarities and differences. The discussion came from their experience and also acted as readiness for reading the selection.

2. *Clarify important difficult words or concepts in advance of the*

reading as long as the author does not do so; if the author does, do not spoil the story; let the pupils discover for themselves. The teacher will have preread the material and selected the appropriate words for the group—not just because they may be listed in a guidebook as new words. As much as possible, the words or phrases should be worked into the discussion begun in number 1 above and then written or printed on the chalkboard in context. Isolated words do not trigger memory or even give many cues to pronunciation. The sentences should be left on the chalkboard for pupils to refer to as they read. For example, in discussing the similarities and differences between lizards and snakes, the teacher was able to introduce *natural habitat*, which was important to understanding but not explained well in the selection. This sentence left on the board, among a few others, helped pupils as they read: Usually the *natural habitat* of the lizard is a warm country.

3. *Establish purposes for reading the selection.* The discussion should quite naturally lead to reading purposes. In the example above, the preliminary discussion could result in a list of similarities and differences left on the chalkboard and subject to confirmation and extension during the reading. For immature readers, it may be best to read a story in sections for specific purposes. Do not break the story up into such small parts, however, that readers are not able to depend on the redundancy of language to comprehend fully. Short pieces of writing are not usually comprehended as well as longer pieces of writing that take the time to develop the plot, the characters, the incident. (Even with such expository material as that about lizards and snakes, the natural redundancy of language assists the reader.) Pupils should be helped to develop their own reading purposes. In the case of the lizards and the snakes, this is easy. In other instances, the teacher may need to give more direction.

4. *Pupils should read silently for the purposes they developed.* For younger readers, as suggested above, the reading may be stopped at natural breaking points and a given purpose or purposes discussed. Then the reading continues. More mature readers in any primary grade should be allowed to finish the entire selection keeping one, two, or three purposes in mind. The purposes may be listed on the chalkboard.

5. *Readers may discuss the selection as a group (with or without the teacher) or may answer questions in writing.* Whichever format is utilized, reading purposes should be satisfied first. Additional questions may probe other aspects of the selection. The lizard-snake selection, for instance, could result in an altered and extended chalkboard comparison, or each pupil could be asked to list similarities and differences on a piece of paper. Additional questions might be: Do all lizards have legs? Which island has no snakes? Which would you rather have as a pet?

6. On the same day or another day, if time does not permit, *pupils can reread parts silently and sometimes orally* to verify answers, to refute someone else's argument, to support their feelings.

7. On the same day, or another day (if time does not permit), the

teacher may *conduct a lesson on a particular skill or strategy linked to the selection*. The skill or strategy lesson is usually in response to a need demonstrated by the group and noted prior to the reading or during it. For example, the teacher might have noted that pupils were able to ferret out similarities much more easily than differences—both prior to and during the reading of the selection. The teacher then might work with paragraphs related solely to the differences among certain kinds of animals. After the pupils seem to understand contrasts, the teacher will take them back to the selection to be sure they comprehend the major differences between lizards and snakes.

8. *Follow-up activities should focus on skill, strategy, or content.* For example, as a primary independent activity for the group, at the top of their agenda might be:

1. Pick any of these pairs of paragraphs from the animal box: turtle-lizard, rabbit-hare, alligator-crocodile. Write down all the things that are different about them.
2. Find out about the two poisonous lizards: Where do they live? What do they look like? How dangerous are they to human beings?

Directed Reading-Thinking Activity

As an important alternative to the DRA, Stauffer's Directed Reading-Thinking Activity (DRTA) [6] contributes a somewhat different approach that the teacher will find particularly useful for strengthening reading strategies. Although the DRTA employs some of the same steps, the responsibility for setting purposes is always the pupils'. Pupils are to make predictions about what they will read, and they constantly confirm or reject their predictions. The teacher assists by raising questions to help pupils set their own purposes, helps them question their predictions, and insists on proof. Stauffer stated that a view of DRTA processing might be outlined as follows:

I. Pupil actions (PRP)
   A. Predict (set purposes)
   B. Read (process ideas)
   C. Prove (test answers)
II. Teacher actions (WWP)
   A. What do you think? (activate thought)
   B. Why do you think so? (agitate thought)
   C. Prove it! (require evidence) [7]

[6] Russell G. Stauffer, *Directing the Reading-Thinking Process* (New York: Harper & Row, 1975), pp. 31–72, 225–60.
[7] Ibid., p. 37.

(The DRTA is described in somewhat more detail on page 371 of chapter 13.)

Although all aspects of comprehension are part of the teaching-learning process in the primary grades, and those aspects have been discussed in chapter 8 and elsewhere, we wish to stress the need for the kind of critical reading highlighted in the DRTA. Pupils must learn from the inception of reading instruction that they may question what is written, that there is more than one right answer to a question, and that their teacher does not believe that there is only one right answer to a question.

ADVISING PARENTS

Preschool Reading

Many preschool children at the present time show an interest in learning to read. This interest may be initiated by the child in requesting the parent to tell what a word on a grocery package says, or what a recurring word on the television screen says. Or some children may begin to pick out a word here and there in one of the story books from which their parents read to them. If preschool children show an interest in reading in such ways as these and ask for help, then the parents should by all means provide it.

Although responding to the child's requests for help with reading is desirable, the *systematic teaching* of reading to young children is questionable. If the preschool child is not interested in reading and resists or responds negatively to learning to read, the chances are strong that the child is not sufficiently mature to have any reading instruction at all. Under such conditions, the parent may do harm in persisting in attempts to teach him or her to read.

When young children are not ready to even begin thinking about reading, it is far better to provide them with an abundance of rich, happy experiences, to let them have opportunities for abundant physical activity out of doors, to surround them with a wealth of picture books, and to read to them frequently. Eventually, children will ask: "What does it say on that package?" or "What does that flashing off-and-on sign say?" It is fine and highly desirable to answer such questions. But for a parent to take a book, while the child is still too immature to read, and sit down and make a job of teaching him or her is another matter and one that can promote anxiety, boredom, and a distaste for reading.

After School Reading Begins

Another critical period of parent teaching often occurs when the parent discovers that a child is having trouble with reading as the child progresses through the grades. In his or her anxiety, the parent then attempts to teach the child to read.

Very frequently, parent teaching is highly charged with emotion on the part of both the parent and the child. The parent often is in a definite state of worry because the child is not getting along well. He or she is annoyed because the child does not learn to read like other children in the neighborhood and impatient because the child does not "remember the words" after being told once or twice. The child, on the other hand, probably comes to the situation with a distaste for reading, inferiority feelings, and fear of failing to respond in the way the parent desires. Under these conditions, "the lesson period usually blows up," and both parent and child are worse off than if the teaching attempt had not been made. So in the interest of developing sound emotional health and desirable attitudes toward reading, it is not advisable for an overanxious parent to attempt to teach reading to a child who is having difficulty.

Another reason many parents should refrain from actually teaching reading to underdeveloped readers is because they have not been trained in modern methods of teaching reading. For example, a parent was heard to say, "I had him memorize all the words in the word lists in the back of his reader, but he still can't read in the book at all. He doesn't know these words when he comes to them in sentences."

This parent was using the wrong approach. Teachers who have had recent training in reading wouldn't think of teaching a child to read by forcing him or her to memorize a list of isolated words. Teachers found out long ago that having children memorize isolated lists was no assurance that they would be able to read these words when woven together in sentences.

When parents attempt to teach reading, they usually confine their instruction to word recognition. There is a lot to the teaching of reading these days, and one has to be trained to do this job well. Parents should be advised to leave the technical aspects of teaching reading to teachers who have been trained in this specialized field, just as they leave their child's health problems to a physician and dental problems to a dentist.

What Parents Can Do

"What can I do to help John with his reading?" "Nothing. Don't try to teach him at all. It will interfere with the method I am using in school." Such a conversation occurred very frequently between parents and teachers not too many years ago. Parents went away feeling helpless and frustrated because they were blocked from doing something that might contribute to the well-being of their children.

Nowadays, teachers answer such questions in some such way as this: "Yes, Mrs. Brown. There are some things you can do to help. Studies have shown that growth in reading depends upon many aspects of child development. My job is concerned largely with *teaching* your child to read, but you have a major role to play in developing him in many other ways that will help my teaching to be successful. He is with me only five or six hours a day. He is with you or under your supervision seventeen or eighteen hours a day, so you have a better chance than I do to develop him in many important phases of his growth, which in turn will contribute to his ability to learn to read. You have a very great contribution to make to Tom's reading success."

Responding, Listening, and Encouraging. Parents should be advised to take advantage of every functional situation that offers children opportunities to use reading. If the child receives a toy that must be put together and is inclined to try to read the directions, parents should refrain from reading them. The child should read the directions with as much help as he or she wants. Parents should encourage the child to carry out instructions one at a time as each is read. If children want to know the name of a picture on a movie marquis or on the television screen, they should be encouraged to figure it out, but helped as they desire help. If children ask what the words on an ad in a bus, train, or subway says, the reply might be, "You know many of those words. The first one is *remember*. What's the next one?" So, parents have many ways of responding to requests and help directly with reading instruction without attempting to enter into the technical process of actually *teaching* reading.

Parents should also listen attentively to children who wish to read from books. If the child cannot figure out a word, the parent should say, "Skip it and go on. Maybe you'll figure it out." If the child does not want to go on or does go on and still needs the word, the parent should tell the word immediately. The parent should not interrupt enjoyable reading for analysis of words. Rather parents should listen with interest, enter into an enjoyable discussion of content, and find a way of praising the child for figuring out words, reading smoothly, and understanding what was written. The parent should not force a child to read but should reinforce the child's wanting to read. Overanxious parents who cannot refrain from constant correction should be encouraged to help through experience building, not reading. If a parent insists that a child must somehow and somewhere learn the words missed during reading, the parent can be told to jot down the words and give them to the teacher for further analysis.

Reading to Children. Parents should read to children; they should read whatever children want to hear. They should select books and other materials for reading that they feel children will enjoy. Such reading should be done with enthusiasm and interest. (They should also serve as models and let their children view them reading a multitude of materials.) With such activity, children soon become aware of the fact that books, magazines, and newspapers contribute to their lives through providing needed information and through making contact with their feelings. They come to realize that such an enjoyable experience, locked within black and white symbols, can be unlocked when one knows how to read.

Selecting Books. Usually, parents who buy books for a child go to a bookstore preceding Christmas, the child's birthday, or similar occasions and choose a book that they think the child would like or which they think the child should read because of its cultural, exemplary, or informative value. A book chosen in this way often proves to be of little or no interest to the child and frequently is too difficult. Instead of being read and enjoyed, it becomes just a permanent fixture on the bookshelf.

It would be well to suggest to parents that they take their child with them to the bookstore and frequently to the library. Upon these occasions, let the child pick out his or her own book but give some guidance if necessary. Parents might suggest that pupils "try a book on for size" prior to purchase or borrowing by reading a few paragraphs. If the situation is a comfortable one, the children might read a paragraph or so orally to the parents. Parents and children might then look for other books on a related topic if the book is too difficult.

If the children do not know what books they want, the parent might show and discuss several books, calling attention to the characters and their vicarious experiences in some of the appealing pictures. In such situations, the parents' enthusiasm often becomes contagious and the children suddenly decide, "This is the book I want." Once the book is brought home, enthusiasm should continue, and reading can be shared by parents and pupils. Children should have their own bookcase or set of low shelves on which the books are placed, with plenty of space for adding more.

CONCLUDING STATEMENT

In this chapter about reading in the primary unit, emphasis has been placed on classroom organization because this is usually an area of concern, particularly for the inexperienced teacher. A reading program with sound principles and practices can be destroyed if young children are not helped to structure the way they go about their activities. As indicated in the chapter, no one type of organization should be used; individualization and different kinds of groups should be organized on the basis of need and desire.

Independent activities should be meaningful and purposeful while keeping learners occupied when the teacher is not working with them. Directions for independent activities must be clear. The agenda approach is useful as an organizational technique and also as a way of having pupils learn to plan for themselves. Learning centers promote communication activities and aid in structuring the classroom environment for active, independent learning.

If classroom instruction is to allow for the completion of many reading tasks—including those that are creative, the teacher must plan carefully, especially during the early weeks of instruction. The primary reading program should feature all the areas discussed in chapters 1 through 11. The ways of doing this are to read to children, to have children read orally and silently for specific purposes, and to teach directed reading lessons at times in order to help pupils learn to read with purpose and to help them with certain strategies and skills.

Primary teachers should involve parents in the program in the ways described. Parents have many contributions to make; they should be helped to make them in positive directions.

**DISCUSSION
QUESTIONS
AND
ACTIVITIES**

1. Which grouping or individual organizational pattern would you use for the following? Why?

a. Explain to the youngsters and discuss with them the behaviors to be observed when checking materials in and out of the classroom library collection.

b. Five children demonstrate a need to become more proficient in using tables of contents.

c. Three children express an interest in putting on a television show related to a topic being discussed in class.

d. Jack wants to do some further reading about pollution; Beatrice would like to complete an experiment; Chuck and Randy are interested in building a store.

2. Some independent activities are suggested in the chapter. Here are a number of others that you will want to try out, and to evaluate, in relation to your situation and the pupils with whom you are working. Many of the activities require your preparing materials in advance. They can be used individually or grouped in learning-center units. Whatever you do, if they turn out well, save them for the next year, the next group, or the next individual.

a. Place interesting pictures from magazines in an envelope or box. Have children write titles and/or stories about what they see. They can be asked to answer such specific questions as: Who are the characters? What are they doing? Why?

b. Place interesting paragraphs or very brief stories or incidents in an envelope or box; they can be clipped from old workbooks or readers, newspapers, and magazines. Have children draw single pictures or a comic strip sequence to explain or describe what they read.

c. Cut the endings off stories and other kinds of writing taken from old workbooks, texts, and so on. Have children write the endings.

d. Have children compose riddles for other children to solve.

e. Encourage children to build personal dictionaries containing the words and meanings they have learned.

f. Prepare closure activities that children may pick from a wall pocket. Two children may be permitted to interact and review the reasons for each of their responses.

g. Permit children to make peep boxes. They draw scenes or characters from books they have read. They set such drawings up in shoe boxes with a hole in them for others to see. Such activity often encourages wide reading.

h. Permit children to prepare movies. They recreate a story by drawing illustrations of it. They paste them in succession on a roll of paper that may be wound on a stick.

i. Story jigsaw puzzles may be figured out by children if the teacher will cut up stories from old materials, mix the parts up and stick them in envelopes. Children piece them together and read them.

j. For any of these independent activities and the ones you will find and generate, pupils can be allowed a free choice. They can pick a card or activity that says, SURPRISE—DO YOUR FAVORITE THING!

ADDITIONAL READINGS

Books and Pamphlets

AUKERMAN, ROBERT C., ed. *Some Persistent Questions on Beginning Reading.* Newark, Del.: International Reading Assn., 1972.

CUNNINGHAM, PATRICIA M.; ARTHUR, SHARON V.; and CUNNINGHAM, JAMES W. *Classroom Reading Instruction, K–5: Alternative Approaches.* Lexington, Mass.: D.C. Heath, 1977.

LARRICK, NANCY. *A Parent's Guide to Children's Reading.* 4th rev. ed. New York: Doubleday, 1975.

LLOYD, DOROTHY M. *70 Activities for Classroom Learning Centers.* Dansville, N.Y.: The Instructor Publications, 1974.

MCKEOWN, PAMELA. *Reading: A Basic Guide for Parents and Teachers.* Boston: Routledge Kegan Paul, 1974.

NYQUIST, EWALD B., and HARVES, GENE R. *Open Education: A Sourcebook for Parents and Teachers.* New York: Bantam Books, 1972.

STAUFFER, RUSSELL G., and CRAMER, RONALD. *Teaching Critical Reading at the Primary Level.* Newark, Del.: International Reading Assn., 1968.

Periodicals

BURLANDO, ANDREW A., and FARRAR, NANNETTE L. "Teaching Primary Children to Read Critically." *Language Arts* 54, no. 2 (February 1977), pp. 187–88.

CRISCUOLO, NICHOLAS P. "Parents: Active Partners in the Reading Program." *Elementary English* 51, no. 6 (September 1974), pp. 883–84.

GOODMAN, YETTA, and WATSON, DOROTHY J. "A Reading Program to Live With: Focus on Comprehension." *Language Arts* 54, no. 8 (November/December 1977), pp. 868–79.

HARRIS, BEECHER H. "No Labels, Please!" *Language Arts* 53, no. 8 (November/December 1976), pp. 906–10.

HEINRICH, JUNE S. "Elementary Oral Reading: Methods and Materials." *Reading Teacher* 30, no. 1 (October 1976), pp. 10–15.

LAMME, LINDA L. "Reading Aloud to Young Children." *Language Arts* 53, no. 8 (November/December 1976), pp. 886–88.

McCormick, Sandra. "Should You Read Aloud To Your Children?" *Language Arts* 54, no. 2 (February 1977), p. 139.

Page, William D. "Are We Beginning to Understand Oral Reading?" *Reading World* 13, no. 3 (March 1974), pp. 161–70.

Wallen, Carl J. "Independent Activities: A Necessity, Not a Frill." *Reading Teacher* 27, no. 3 (December 1973), pp. 257–62.

Weiner, Roberta. "A Look at Reading Practices in the Open Classroom." *Reading Teacher* 27, no. 5 (February 1974), pp. 438–42.

chapter 13

reading in grades four through eight

What to Expect in This Chapter:

Some attention is paid to organizational plans utilized for reading instruction in grades four through eight. The nature of the materials and instructional plans for using them are highlighted. Specific and detailed explanations of study techniques are provided. The role of oral reading is explored. The chapter concludes with a discussion of some of the complexities pupils encounter as they try to process difficult material.

Children *arrive* in grade four as different people with different strengths and different needs. Sometimes, they need help normally relegated to the primary unit; sometimes they need review of earlier concepts. Teachers of grades four through eight might want to turn to chapter 12 in this book to read about or review some of the concepts, techniques, and structures that may be applicable for their pupils.

A great part of this chapter focuses on reading as a tool of study because upper-grade youngsters are expected to use reading to gain information about many disciplines.

ORGANIZA-TIONAL PLANS

Some organizational plans cause problems and complexities when teachers try to view the reading program in its entirety across all the curricula in which printed materials are used, particularly when departmentalization and interclass grouping systems are in operation. Unless careful planning and evaluation takes place in a team situation encompassing all the teachers of a given group or given pupil, no one really knows all the reading strengths and needs of the pupils. And much too often, though the teachers may want to work in a close partnership arrangement, the logistics are complex.

The Joplin Plan

This plan, which originated in Joplin, Missouri, was quite popular in the late 1950s and early 1960s. Modifications of it are used in a number of schools today. In this plan, pupils went to specific classrooms, "homogeneously" grouped for reading level, during the reading period daily. Teachers would teach a mixture of youngsters from fourth through sixth grade but considered to be reading (usually on the basis of a standardized reading test) in a given range.

Many felt that this arrangement cut down the planning for a teacher and allowed time for planning better lessons. Some liked the interaction of all the intermediate grades; others did not. Research was far from definitive.

Our objection (in agreement with Miller [1]) is that teachers, other than the teachers who happen to have children in their groups from their own classrooms, tend to know these youngsters only as *readers* of specific materials and not as *children* with special strengths and needs. They cannot view the child's total interaction with the reading materials in use throughout the school or classroom program.

Departmentalization

One can see the organizational advantages of departmentalization—different classes for each subject—but, as the Joplin plan, it has distinct disadvantages. Normally, two things can happen to reading in a departmentalized setup: (1) It becomes part of the English class and little attention to reading instruction goes on elsewhere. In fact, little reading instruction sometimes goes on in English class, and often the diet is overwhelmingly the reading of literature. (2) A separate reading class is scheduled—often à la Joplin—and reading is taught as though it were a subject. Often, the teacher uses only skill-oriented materials because the teacher is never sure of what the children should be given to read.

Here again, the *whole* child in relation to reading ability can never be viewed and integrated. In theory, departmentalization is probably best put off until the learner becomes a rather effective reader in the varied disciplines of the overall curriculum.

In-Class Organization

In-class groupings for varied reasons have as many benefits in intermediate- and middle-school classes as they do in the primary grades—special skill work, common interests, research, and so forth. In addition, teams and tutorial situations in which a pupil expert in an area helps one or two others are particularly useful in these grades for both the tutor and tutees—provided the teacher helps tutors in their planning and in their evaluations.

Teachers who help pupils learn to work in flexible groupings and as individuals, in addition to ongoing work with the total class, have established the means of differentiating assignments and caring for individual needs. The use of agendas (pages 348–49) described for use in the primary grades may be put to more detailed use, including assignments done at home.

Agenda—Week of April 7–14
Miriam Sirgado

1. Finish the report about the use of the zodiac in astrology. Finish the drawing of the zodiac. Put the bibliography together.

---

[1] Wilma H. Miller, *The First R: Elementary Reading Today*, 2nd ed. (New York: Holt, Rinehart and Winston, 1977), p. 214.

2. Ask Mr. Ross for two appointments: (1) to discuss *A Dream for Addie;* (2) to figure out some ways to read and better understand the organizational chart about the UN.
3. Schedule two meetings with Albert to help him read the math problems. Spend some time planning the help. Give Mr. Ross my plan the day before so he can make suggestions.
4. Use the learning center on patterns of writing and find the unit on cause and effect. Do the work and then go back to the textbook and see if I can find the other two effects I couldn't seem to find before.
5. Pick a new book from the classroom library and plan at least ten minutes each day for reading it.

NATURE OF THE MATERIALS

Each classroom should house material to be read, listened to, and viewed that centers on units being studied, units to be studied, and related topics. A variety of materials should range from levels easy enough for pupils having problems with the processing of print through materials that challenge the top readers. Materials for listening (listening-post setups, cassettes, tape recorders, and so on) and for viewing (specialized instruments, television, slide projectors, movies, and so forth) should be accompanied by materials that will both enhance and clarify some of the concepts in the written materials. No classroom should be without a classroom library collection that is changed from time to time to suit the changing demands of the pupils and the learning environment.

Basal Readers

Some teachers will want to continue a basal program. If this is done, it should be considered only one very small part of the total reading program because pupils' reading needs are largely not met by the selected readings in basals. In addition, if a basal is used, selections and skills should be chosen in relation to the group rather than the sequence sometimes suggested in the guide. A useful procedure is to turn to that part of the basal which deals with a skill area children are demonstrating problems handling in content-area materials.

Other Reading Development Materials

A multitude of materials, in addition to basal readers, are available today to help children improve their reading abilities. The teacher can find kits, workbooks, supplemental texts, and a variety of materials using an intermix of modes. Some of these materials are helpful in giving pupils specific kinds of assistance they may need at a given time. They are best used in that way.

As with basals, when problems occur involving certain strategies or skills that do not seem cemented well enough as pupils tackle cognitive problems in content-area materials, these other materials can be utilized.

They are best used in this way: (1) Pupils demonstrate some needs in using certain skills or strategies to unlock ideas in the materials they are reading. (2) The teacher develops a lesson to help pupils with the skill or strategy. (3) Following the lesson, the teacher directs pupils to materials that focus attention on the skill or strategy and help to reinforce the teaching. (4) The teacher observes as pupils reapply what they have learned to the materials where the problem was first encountered. Sometimes, through assignments, the teacher is able to put renewed emphasis on the skill or strategy.

Curriculum Materials

Pupils must learn to read and study the content-area materials for each of the disciplines represented in the overall curriculum. This reading cannot be left to chance. Reading instruction with basals and other supplementary materials do not constitute *the* reading program; only incidental applications can be expected. Content-area reading needs a direct and frontal attack. (See chapter 10 for specific suggestions.) Pupils should be helped to preview textbooks and learn how to contend with the structure of the books as well as the language patterns of the books. Teachers should pay careful attention to unusual constructions and inserts—such as primary source material in history.

In addition, children should be helped to read, and to do the necessary writing, with everyday tasks that are important to them. Such tasks may include: reading directions for constructing or putting something together; reading labels on medicine bottles; following recipes; writing accurate business letters; writing informal letters of application for jobs; drawing a map to help someone get to their house; reading timetables. These tasks should not be left to chance; they should be given priority, and pupils should feel free to ask for help in completing such tasks as they arise in life situations.

There is little doubt that we live in a television-mass media world. For many pupils the habitual reading of books, in spite of our encouragement and enthusiasm, will not develop. This does not mean we should not keep trying to stimulate youngsters to read and acquire a wonderful lifetime activity. But, for many, it will not occur. The reading activities that most of them will engage in as they develop into adults will be essential reading—for college or job, the reading of sections of a newspaper, utilitarian tasks for life needs, and in some cases the reading of sections of magazines.

Pupils should have many opportunities to read newspapers and magazines; in fact, instruction in reading them should occupy a central place in the curriculum. Teachers should guide pupils in learning about the sections of a newspaper and in how to read each section—in relation to their purposes. Particularly, pupils should recognize the differences between reporting the news and writing editorials and columns about the news. They should be encouraged to compare the way news has been written in more than one newspaper. Actually, aside from the reading of certain aspects of literature and long textbook passages, pupils can meet all the kinds of writing they will ever encounter in the pages of a newspaper. They certainly can put all of their reading strategies to use as well as all the skills they will ever need to use. Magazines, depending on the type, offer various kinds of reading and the use of varied skills and strategies. Pupils can be helped, in the intermediate- and middle-school grades, to become intelligent users of such mass media.

It is our opinion, also, that the school should be making more use of commercial television. There are some excellent programs that can introduce ideas in ways that printed materials cannot. There are also excellent programs that can extend, enrich, and reinforce both the content of what has been read and the skills that need to be taught. There are also poor programs and misleading commercials that pupils need guidance in evaluating. Their education is being neglected in a most important area if television is not brought into the classroom.

INSTRUCTIONAL PLANS

The directed reading activity (DRA) and the Directed Reading-Thinking Activity (DRTA) described on pages 354–57 in the last chapter both feature what is probably the most important step in a reading lesson—readiness (pages 78–87 of chapter 4). The activities engaged in *before* the eyes hit the page may be more significant than what happens *when* the eyes hit the page. In both activities, the pupils' background experiences, interests, and linguistic abilities are considered in advance of the reading assignment. In both activities, emphasis is placed on developing specific readiness for the reading, although in a DRA the teacher is more involved with the content than in the DRTA. For some pupils, the steps of motivating or focusing attention, developing concepts, and setting purposes led by the teacher are necessary, particularly for some reading tasks. Generally speaking, however, the DRTA is more productive of useful reading strategies for intermediate- and middle-school children. The DRTA is closer to the strategies readers may take as they read independently, and it encourages both divergent and convergent thinking. Convergent thinking, a major goal of the DRA, means "coming together" with the authors—finding out what they have to say and accepting it or agreeing with it. Such thinking has a role to play for certain kinds of reading and for certain kinds of purposes. But divergent thinking is significant because it is the birthplace of inventions, solutions to complex problems, and new ideas. Divergent thinking, as Guilford put it, is the production of a diversity of ideas that are logically probable. The ideas are possible considering the limitations of the facts available.[2]

[2] John P. Guilford, "Frontiers in Thinking That Teachers Should Know About," *Reading Teacher* 13, no. 3 (February 1960): 176–82. Cited by Russell G. Stauffer, *Directing the Reading-Thinking Process* (New York: Harper & Row, 1975), p. 43.

Steps in the DRTA

1. Pupils look at the title of a selection along with its subtitles and any other headings. (This step, as others, may vary with the nature of the material.) Pupils, sitting in roundtable fashion, speculate about the nature of the selection.

2. Pupils look through the selection inspecting all the illustrations and giving them some thought. They each attempt to integrate their present thinking with their thoughts after reading the headings.

3. The teacher asks pupils to consider which speculations might be those that get closest to what the selection is about. They discuss their predictions in this light and then decide to read a given amount of the selection to find out.

4. They stop reading at an agreed-upon page and discuss the validity of the earlier predictions. Predictions are evaluated on the basis of convergence and also on the basis of the divergent ideas that might be possible under certain circumstances.

5. Pupils speculate further about the rest of the selection or a part of it. They read again to try to confirm their speculations.

6. Pupils, with the teacher's urging rather than direction, are asked to prove their answers. Proof must be established in terms of what the author says as well as the pupils' interpretations and evaluations.

Note that the skilled teacher acts as leader but only to encourage, activate thought, keep the thinking processes going, require proof. A significant byproduct of this "teaching" procedure is its transfer to independent study, which is discussed later in this chapter.

Junior Great Books Reflective Activities

Biskin, Hoskisson, and Modlin [3] cited studies based on a comparison of the DRTA and the Reflective Reading-Thinking Activities of the Junior Great Books Program. They concluded that for specific retention of content, the Reflective Reading-Thinking Activities were more effective than the DRTA. In the Great Books Program, a purpose or problem to be solved is initiated by the leader. Pupils read to solve the problem by shifting, relating, and ordering the flow of ideas. They consciously hold back evaluation; they suspend judgment. The leader challenges unclear, incorrect, or contradictory statements, but offers no answers. In the end, facts are called for along with interpretations and evaluations.

[3] Donald S. Biskin, Kenneth Hoskisson, and Marjorie Modlin, "Prediction, Reflection, and Comprehension," *Elementary School Journal* 77, no. 2 (November 1976): 131–39.

Alternate Plans

Kachuck and Marcus [4] suggested that overuse of directed reading activities might not be productive in terms of children learning how to apply and extend their own reading strategies. They suggested something akin to readiness steps in directed reading activities followed by independent, self-directed reading.

1. Begin with material about a topic familiar to the readers.
2. Develop some type of advance organizer with the children. (See pages 82–87 in chapter 4.)
3. Have the pupils search for answers related to the advance organizer on their own.

For example: A group has become interested in finding out more about the 1977 track and field events held in West Germany. They are especially interested in the records made by men and women from the United States. The teacher provides them with an adapted account from the *1978 Britannica Book of the Year*. Before reading the material, they talk about the possibilities and develop this advance organizer on the chalkboard:

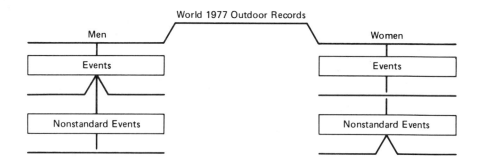

From prior knowledge, previewing the selection, and discussion, they establish the fact that the men and women won three events each. The men won two of the standard events and one of the nonstandard; the reverse was true for the women. They read on their own to confirm the advance organizer and obtain the relevant information.

Other teachers, as Charnock,[5] feel that the DRA with reading groups is too time consuming for harassed teachers. Charnock suggested

[4] Beatrice L. Kachuck and Albert Marcus, "Thinking Strategies and Reading," *Reading Teacher* 30, no. 2 (November 1976): 157–61.

[5] James Charnock, "An Alternative to the DRA," *Reading Teacher* 31, no. 3 (December 1977): 269–71.

that teachers preread selections and write out thought-provoking questions to give to pupils in advance of the reading. Pupils must then read to answer the questions and write their answers. The teacher limits her or his involvement to offering clues and encouragement if assigments are difficult. The teacher reads the answers to the questions and returns the papers with comments. Pupils must redo their papers—and correct their errors—if the teacher is not satisfied with the response. At times, pupils convene in groups and discuss the selections and the responses to the questions.

INDEPEN-DENT READING

Without question, in the intermediate- and middle-school grades the goal is to guide pupils toward independent reading and study. The instructional plans reported above begin to move pupils in that direction, but specific attention should be placed on the development of independent study strategies as well as on turning to reading as a source of individual enjoyment and problem solving.

Study-Reading

Artley [6] listed four steps in study reading: (1) awareness and understanding of the existence of a problem to be solved or a question to be answered; (2) securing and marshaling the facts and information in order to solve the problem or answer the question; (3) evaluating and weighing of each piece of information in order to put all of it together effectively; and (4) resolution of the problem or answering of the question. In order to help pupils do this, teachers should wean them away from teacher-directed activities to pupil-directed activities. Individual study plans will differ for different pupils, but teachers should introduce all pupils to the possibilities.

Francis P. Robinson,[7] working with college students a number of years ago, arrived at a successful study plan that has since been modified and applied to study reading in the high school, the middle school, and the intermediate grades. The steps are Survey, Question, Read, Recite, and Review (SQ3R).

1. *Survey*. Pupils examine the title, subheadings, and illustrations in a chapter or selection. They should devote thinking time to what they examine and think about what they might find out when they do study the material. It is also helpful to read the introductory paragraph or paragraphs and the concluding ones. If a selection has no subheadings and few or no illustrations with captions, it is useful to read the first sentence of every other paragraph or so to get an idea of what the material contains. This step has been introduced already, as *preview*, on

[6] A. Sterl Artley, "Effective Study—Its Nature and Nurture," in *Elementary Reading Instruction: Selected Materials*, 2nd ed., ed. Althea Beery, Thomas C. Barrett, and William R. Powell (Newark, Del.: International Reading Assn., 1974), p. 449.

[7] Francis P. Robinson, *Effective Study* (New York: Harper & Row, 1961).

pages 248–50 of this volume. Pupils should be urged to develop their own techniques for using survey to establish purposes for reading.

2. *Question.* Pupils will need teacher guidance for a while in learning how to change headings into questions, which is the essence of this step. Sometimes, pupils will also formulate questions growing out of their study of the illustrations and captions, and the reading of introductory and concluding paragraphs. These questions should be written down and used as a guide for study. The greatest danger in this step is that questions will not probe deeply enough or will concentrate on a narrow area. (Some of the question-type headings in existing content-area materials suffer from narrowness and lack of depth.) Teachers should work with pupils long enough to help them gain competence in question formulation and to help pupils realize that looking for the answers to questions does not eliminate discovering other important ideas.

3. *Read.* Pupils read silently to satisfy the questions raised and obtain any other information they deem significant.

4. *Recite.* Recite means to give an account or organize the answers in some way. Pupils need to be guided to this step over time because it requires note-making ability. In this step, pupils organize notes—often in informal outline form—that appear to answer the questions and deal with other important and pertinent information. Francis Robinson's original plan called for the reading of a chapter, section by section, with note-making following each section. Some pupils like to make notes as they proceed through a section. In some cases, teachers may indicate the structure of the recite step by calling for the filling in of an outline, replacing the words in a cloze passage, and so on. This step seeks variety dependent upon the individual pupil's style, the nature of the material, and the nature of the task.

5. *Review.* Here, the pupil reads through the chapter once again and reviews the notes that have been made. This is an opportunity to view the whole and correct any errors made during the notemaking process. Thomas and Robinson suggested the cover card, an index card used to conceal parts of the selection or the notes as pupils try to recall specific information. We suggest a 3×5 card; the cover card illustrated on page 375 is broadly adapted from Thomas and Robinson.[8]

There are a number of variations of SQ3R. Many pupils will find parts useful and others not so useful. The teacher's goal should be to help pupils establish procedures for themselves that will allow for effective, independent study. (See chapter 10 for a variety of ways of helping pupils unlock ideas in content-area materials.)

Study Guides

Study guides are structures that teachers or authors create to help pupils get the most out of their reading when they are engaged in inde-

[8] Ellen L. Thomas and H. Alan Robinson, *Improving Reading in Every Class: A Sourcebook for Teachers,* 2nd ed. (Boston: Allyn and Bacon, 1977), p. 158.

A COVER CARD TO HELP YOU REVIEW

You will find this card very handy for review purposes.

Use it to cover parts of your book or your notes. You can cover all the information under a single heading in your book and see if you can remember the important ideas. Then lift the cover card and check. Or you can cover an important diagram and see if you can remember the important parts and what they do. Or you can cover one part of your notes and see if you can remember the next part. You will think of many other ways to use this card.

You will find this cover card a useful way of helping you to remember what you read. It is a powerful tool!

---

pendent study. They help pupils establish purposes for reading, and they help to facilitate study—particularly of complex aspects of the text. Study guides created by teachers take time to develop, and especially when they are somewhat individualized, wise teachers will file them for use in subsequent years. There are several types of study guides that can be organized.

Process Guide. As viewed by Karlin, this type of guide "... provides children with a 'teacher' who offers suggestions on how to read the material. It calls their attention to the skills they might need in order to resolve difficulties and makes them aware of skills they might otherwise ignore." [9]

For example, in this paragraph about chimpanzees (only a small portion of the text children might ordinarily study), Karlin suggested duplicating questions and comments on strips of paper that could be lined up with the text.[10]

> You may have seen chimpanzees on television or at a zoo. These primates are taught many tricks and are very smart. Chimpanzees are not monkeys but are apes. Apes do not have tails, but monkeys do. Apes   a contrast have larger brains and are smarter than monkeys. There are four kinds of apes, two from Asia and two from Africa. The chimpanzee is from Africa. Chimpanzees live in bands of as many as 30. They are good climbers   Who are *they?* and can swing from limb to limb, but spend most of

[9] Robert Karlin, *Teaching Elementary Reading: Principles and Strategies,* 2nd ed. (New York: Harcourt Brace Jovanovich, 1975), p. 264.

[10] Ibid.

their time on the ground. They build nests in trees to spend the night. Chimpanzees mostly eat plant foods, but will eat smaller animals, termites, and eggs. In one part of Africa, chimpanzees have been seen to hunt, kill, and eat colobus monkeys.[11]

important details

The word *but* is a signal. What does it tell you?

Content Guide. Karlin suggested that another broad type of study guide could be called the content guide. This type of guide focuses attention on the content and establishes purposes for reading. It could also be used in place of teacher-directed discussion following a reading. "In that case, children would respond to the items in the guide after they have read the chapter or section." [12] Or, as Karlin demonstrated in a discussion of such a guide, the guidesheet could have purpose-setting questions *as well as* response questions following reading.

For a selection about chimpanzees and other apes, the guide might read like this:

> *Read question number one, answer it on your paper, and then go to number two, three, and four. The page and paragraph numbers for each question are in parentheses.*
>
> 1. How are chimps similar to and different from human beings? (page 271: paragraphs two, three, and seven)
> 2. How do apes communicate? Is there a chimpanzee language? (page 272: all paragraphs but the last one)
> 3. Compare the orangutan, the chimpanzee, and the gorilla. (pages 272–74: last paragraph on p. 272 through first paragraph on p. 274)
> 4. What makes you think chimpanzees are intelligent? (page 271 through first paragraph on page 274)
>
> *After reading the selection and answering the four questions, do one of the following:*
>
> 1. Draw a picture of the chimpanzee accompanied by a paragraph describing the chimpanzee. Make sure the paragraph includes any details you couldn't manage to show in the picture.
> 2. Write a newspaper article with the headline, *Chimps Talk!* Be sure you are perfectly clear so your reading audience knows exactly what you mean.
> 3. Organize a chart with four headings: Human Beings; Chimpanzees; Orangutans; Gorillas. List the characteristics of each in detail. You may need to use some of your own knowledge about human beings.

Individualized Guides. In this type of guide, the types of questions suggested for content guides may be used, but they are not directed

---

[11] Neal J. Holmes and others, *Science: People, Concepts, Process,* Level 5 (New York: Webster Division, McGraw-Hill, 1974), p. 172.

[12] Karlin, *Teaching Elementary Reading,* p. 265.

toward the content of a given selection or book. The teacher suggests a number of references at a range of readability levels that contain similar information. Pupils may refer to one or more books or magazines, suggested by the teacher, which may be found in the classroom or in the school library. Teachers may want to suggest to some pupils that they try certain references suited to their abilities. Pupils are at liberty to find additional references that speak to the questions.

Alternative Guide Formats. Most guides feature specific questions for pupils to answer, as above. There are several interesting alternatives.

A study guide may be introduced through a closure technique:

You are going to read about three types of apes.
The chimpanzee is most like the _____ being.
Chimps seem to "speak" a _____ and appear to be quite _____ . Learn about the _____ and its closeness to humans. Then learn how the orangutan and gorilla _____ differ from the _____ and from human beings.

The closure technique may also be used effectively as a response procedure following the reading: Example—The chimp shows its _____ by learning many tasks and by learning how to communicate through a type of _____ .

In chapter 8 on pages 228–29, Herber decried the use of direct questions for pupils who did not have the experience to bring to the material. For such pupils, the types of statements suggested by Herber might be utilized in a study guide prior to reading. For example:

Read each of the three statements below. Then read the material about chimpanzees and apes. Check each statement you believe to be true according to what the material stated. Defend each answer on your paper—those you believe to be true according to the material and those that you do not feel are true.
_____1. Chimpanzees and monkeys are the same.
_____2. Chimpanzees eat smaller animals, termites, and eggs.
_____3. Chimpanzees eat colobus monkeys.

Teachers will think of many other techniques for helping pupils set purposes and respond to the material. Study guides stimulate the interest of able readers and help less-able readers over some of the hurdles. The ultimate purpose is to assist pupils in becoming independent learners who understand, organize, and retain what they need from their reading.

Individual Reading

Aside from the specific study assignments made in class, pupils should be permitted to read materials in class that interest them, that may provide background for the more difficult textbook reading, that may help them acquire information they desire, and/or that may help them solve problems. Just as their counterparts in the primary grades, these pupils should be encouraged to read on their own—silently—in a sustained fashion daily. Time must be planned in the class day for the class, a group, or individuals who schedule themselves on their agendas. Everything individuals read does not have to be reported back to teachers. Pupils need to learn to satisfy their own reading purposes. When pupils want to report on what they have read, they should be given freedom to choose the method they like best. The teacher will have offered several alternatives in the past, although creative reporting on what has been read should be valued and encouraged.

There are legitimate times when teachers will want children to report on what they have read: to cement concepts related to aspects of literature; to help a pupil learn to organize what he or she has read; to evaluate comprehension of certain kinds; to share with others; to present plans for solving certain types of class problems. Book, magazine, or newspaper reports should not be stereotyped. They can be travelogs, radio or television reports, pantomimes and other kinds of dramatizations, straight storytelling, series of pictures, and so forth. Fennimore [13] suggested *projective* book reports where pupils were given the opportunities to extend their books in expressive ways that suited their personalities. Fennimore first presented several such projective reports to pupils as models before they were let loose to "project" on their own. Reports were not *given* at one time during the day *en masse*; pupils could give them whenever they were ready, even if other classroom activities were interrupted.

ORAL READING

Oral reading has a role to play in the intermediate- and middle-school grades. But, other than when individual reading appraisals are taking place, it should not be done at sight or in round-robin fashion. Oral reading should always be purposeful; it should always be prepared by having silent reading precede it.

Sometimes teachers who work with many poor readers feel that assigning paragraphs or sections and having them read out loud one after the other at least exposed the poor readers to the material. Unfortunately, it does not work that way. As Curry and Geis [14] indicated, little is gained by the listener or the reader; poor reading habits are reinforced;

---

[13] Flora Fennimore, "Projective Book Reports," *Language Arts* 54, no. 2 (February 1977): pp. 176–79.

[14] Robert L. Curry and Lynna Geis, "Fallacies in Oral Reading Instruction," *Language Arts* 54, no. 2 (February 1977): 188–90.

poor models are provided; poor listening habits are created; boredom sets in; and, for those who do not read well, self-esteem is further lowered.

Here are some suggestions for oral reading in class:

1. Pupils have read some common material and disagree about certain points. They should look back to verify and then support their points of view by reading a particular section from the material.

2. Pupils have read some common material about a specific problem that they wish to pursue in class through a simulation technique—a courtroom trial, a kitchen scene, a plane ride. They help each other decide on the parts to develop by reading parts aloud. They may also want to cite particular quotations during the simulation.

3. Pupils decide to put on a dramatization and assign roles. They probably go through many oral readings.

4. One or two pupils would like to read a selection to the class. They rehearse and get as much help as possible prior to their rendition because they must hold the listeners' interest. (Listeners will not maintain much interest, or listen well, or improve their own reading by reading along in the book. Listeners should concentrate on listening.) Pupils who are doing the oral reading should set purposes for their listeners.

Teachers will establish many other purposeful and meaningful oral reading situations. And, in addition to the oral reading by the children, the teacher should read to the class often. Materials should be chosen with great care in regard to relevance and interest. Teachers should prepare for oral reading in advance so their renditions are of high quality. There is much competition from television and other media. Oral reading by the teacher serves three vital functions: (1) Pupils keep contact with the wonderful world of literature. (2) They hear good oral reading. (3) They realize that some adults are interested in reading a variety of things, in addition to the necessary reading in school and life.

COMPLEXITIES IN LANGUAGE PROCESSING

Although the other chapters in this book deal with concepts, skills, and strategies directly related to reading instruction in the intermediate- and middle-school grades, there are some aspects of processing written language that begin to become especially critical in the intermediate grades. We need to look carefully at the nature of the written language, which becomes more and more complex as pupils proceed through the grades. Teachers should examine new materials and try them on for size with youngsters. They may not necessarily be discarded because of some difficult language structures if they have many other saving graces, but teachers must know what kind of help pupils will need in reading the material.

Anaphora

Anaphora is the use of a word or words to substitute for a word or words used previously and sometimes later. The simplest form of anaphora is the pronoun and its antecedent: *Lil is a lovely girl. She is bright too.* (*She* is the pronoun substituted for *Lil.*) Most pupils do not have difficulty processing this type of simple anaphoric relationship.

Content-area reading—including literature—appears to be replete with many more complex anaphoric relationships. Look at the brief example below, typical of such writing.

> Between the coastal mountains and the Rockies is a dry region, as you have learned. Here summers are often hot and winters very cold. The trees of this region are much thinner than those along the coast. In some places it is too dry for trees to grow.[15]

Note the anaphoric relationships above:

1. The clause "as you have learned" carries the reader back to an antecedent that may be distant in space and time. The reader will be helped in processing the information to come if he or she recalls the facts and feelings about the dry region.

2. The first word at the beginning of the second sentence—"Here"— refers back to the dry region.

3. In the third sentence, "this region" refers back to the dry region.

4. In the same sentence, "those" refers *back* to trees but also *forward* to along the coast.

5. "In some places" in the last sentence refers back to the dry region but also refers to only parts of that region.

6. The indefinite pronoun "it" in the last sentence reinforces the concept of parts of the dry region.

Teachers should examine the materials pupils are to read and help them become conscious of the referent-antecedent relationships used by the authors. Such assistance also helps pupils to realize that one does not read a passage word by word or sentence by sentence; reading must involve intersentential thinking. Study-reading, in particular, involves frequent regressions in search of meaning.

Idea Combining

Much of the material in the primary grades consists of simple sentences expressing one idea or two simple sentences combined with such coordinate conjunctions as *and, but, or.* They are relatively easy to process, although some youngsters need help in realizing that each of the coordinate conjunctions signals a different kind of message. *And* says "go on and read the additional idea." *But* says "read this exception to the idea you've just read." *Or* says "this next idea is a possible alternative."

In the intermediate grades and beyond, as authors consider the complex ideas they wish to express, they frequently cannot help embedding several ideas in a single sentence. Because the relationships to be ex-

[15] Esther Crabtree with Ernest W. Tiegs and Fay Adams, *Understanding Your Country and Canada,* new ed. (Boston: Ginn and Co., 1968), p. 488.

pressed are complex, pupils sometimes have difficulty untangling the ideas. They need assistance with the types of embeddings the authors use and the words they use to signal the varied ideas. Authors and publishers of modern instructional materials often consciously try to simplify the surface structures of the sentences pupils read, but the nature of the relationships to be expressed permits only limited simplification. For example:

> *When workers are happy in their jobs, production is usually good.*

In the sentence above, pupils often need help in realizing that they must hold the conditional statement introduced by *when* in short-term memory, while they read the independent one. Then they put the two together, understanding that one situation is dependent upon the other.

> *When workers are happy in their jobs, they usually produce better work.*

In the sentence above, the same thinking process takes place, except pupils must also be aware of the anaphoric unit—*workers–they*—as they process the information. Such ideas, as expressed in the example above, are often better understood if the independent clause precedes the dependent clause.

The most frequently used connectives are listed on page 300. Pupils should understand their functions in introducing different kinds of ideas.

Dependent upon their own use and recognition of linguistic structures, different pupils may have different needs in untangling ideas. The following constructions are examples of those that sometimes need discussion, when and if they appear to get in the way of understanding.

> *On the ocean side was the English fleet.* (prepositional phrase at the beginning of the sentence and the subject of the sentence following the verb)
>
> *The frontier, that edge of settled land where the wilderness began, was being moved west of the Appalachians.* (two embedded clauses in apposition to explain the meaning of *frontier*)
>
> *Since the mold could be seen clearly, and the material had turned color, they could be pretty sure that, the experiment begun only yesterday, was successful.* (several connected ideas expressing different relationships within the one sentence)

Vocabulary

As more technical material is introduced and ideas become more complex, pupils will need guidance with the changing meanings of known words and the host of "new" words. Chapters 6 and 7 contain a variety of suggestions for helping intermediate- and middle-school pupils with the processing of these words.

DISCUSSION QUESTIONS AND ACTIVITIES

1. Have pupils discuss the activities they would like to complete during a week in addition to those you feel must be accomplished. Guide them in producing a trial agenda to be evaluated at the end of the week. Ask pupils how they like the idea of planning their own activities.

2. Have pupils try to find subtle differences in reporting the news in news magazines, newspapers, television, and/or radio. Discuss the differences in class. Try to develop objective criteria for reports.

3. Try the closure technique as an introduction to a project and as a response technique. Pupils like the approach and learn many things about processing language while they are completing their assignment. For example:

Today you're going to learn about the stars other than our _____ . Here is a _____ of books that can help you. You will find _____ in our classroom or in the school _____ . Pick one _____ and find the _____ to any two of the questions. You may work by yourself or with one _____ if you like. On Thursday at 10:30 we'll have a class _____ to learn what you have _____ .

(Following this paragraph on the chalkboard appears a short list of books that the teacher has studied earlier. The following questions might be on the chalkboard following the list of books.)

1. How _____ away are the _____?
2. Why are some _____ called dwarfs and _____ called giants?
3. How many _____ are there in the _____?
4. Where did the _____ get their names?
5. How _____ do _____ travel?
6. Why are some _____ brighter than _____?

4. Ask pupils about the various anaphoric relationships in their reading material. We usually think of anaphora as related to subjects and objects rather than verb forms. Pupils in these grades often see infinitives and verbs that refer back to larger concepts. Many times, they need guidance in realizing that the verb or verb phrase stands for something that was discussed earlier. For example:

Heat is conducted by metal. *To test this,* place one end of a. . . .

or

Timothy likes chocolate soft ice cream better than the frozen kind. Lisa *does too.*

Time spent in raising the consciousness of pupils about anaphoric constructions is worthwhile because they are inadvertently also learning how to plot the development of the discourse.

ADDITIONAL READINGS

Books and Pamphlets

HEILMAN, ARTHUR W. *Principles and Practices of Teaching Reading.* 4th ed., pp. 501–49. Columbus, Ohio: Charles E. Merrill Publishing Co., 1977.

LYNN, BONNIE. *Anaphora: A Cross Disciplinary Survey.* Report no. 31. Urbana, Ill.: Center for the Study of Reading, 1977.

NIELSEN, DUANE M., and HJELM, HOWARD F., eds. *Reading and Career Education.* Newark, Del.: International Reading Assn., 1975.

SPACHE, GEORGE D., and SPACHE, EVELYN B. *Reading in the Elementary School.* 4th ed., pp. 275–312. Boston: Allyn and Bacon, 1977.

Periodicals

CUNNINGHAM, DICK, and SHABLAK, SCOTT L. "Selective Reading Guide-O-Rama: The Content Teacher's Best Friend." *Journal of Reading* 18, no. 5 (February 1975), pp. 380–82.

FILLMER, H. THOMPSON. "The Middle Schoolers' Reading Program." *Language Arts* 52, no. 8 (November/December 1975), pp. 1123–26.

SAWYER, DIANE J. "Linguistic and Cognitive Competencies in the Middle Grades." *Language Arts* 52, no. 8 (November/December 1975), p. 1075.

VACCA, RICHARD T., and VACCA, JOANNE L. "Consider a Stations Approach to Middle School Reading Instruction." *Reading Teacher* 28, no. 1 (October 1974), pp. 18–21.

chapter 14

a focus on special needs

What to Expect in This Chapter:

In this chapter, we treat the historical perspective for some of the problems related to dialect and bilingualism. The importance of self-concept is reintroduced and restressed. Suggestions are made for helping pupils develop intellectually through rich interactions with the environment and through careful programming of instruction and the instructional situation.

Dialects and reading are considered with special attention given to the roots of dialects, information about Black English, and the present conclusion that dialect probably does not interfere with the reading processes. Some activities are suggested for helping pupils cope with transitions to regional standard English.

Bilingualism and reading are discussed with special emphasis on learning patterns and cultures. Activities are suggested for particular groups and for teachers who need help with a variety of bilingual individuals in their classrooms. Learning to read is considered as learning to read in two languages and specific examples of procedures are offered. The value of utilization of context clues in bilingual reading instruction is highlighted. Approaches and activities for promoting the reading of English are suggested.

Instruction should, of course, always consider individual differences among children. But, in addition, group patterns that differ from the "norm" must be taken into consideration. This concept of "norm" is a difficult one to deal with. It is easier to view when a minority group exists within a majority group, but very difficult to view and understand when the "minority group" *is* the school population. What we really seem to be talking about when we speak of "divergent learners" and "culturally different learners" are those children who do not fit into the mold of school life as the mainstream society has shaped it. When we find this happening, we counteract with *remedial, corrective,* and *intervention* as well as *prevention* programs. In recent years, we find ourselves organizing *bilingual* programs. These programs may be necessary, but they become insertions into the overall curriculum rather than integral parts of it. Ideally, our curriculum should be organized on a developmental continuum where all children progress as rapidly and as well as they can without any of them being labeled *divergent,* or *different,* or *remedial.*

Now having taken such a stand, we too must fall into the trap of using labels in order to discuss those groups who do not at this time *blend* into the existing school curriculum. Our discussion centers on two groups: (1) those who communicate in a dialect other than standard regional English, or mixtures thereof; and (2) those who speak another language or who are at various stages of becoming bilingual. These children frequently come from homes where circumstances force pragmatic goals largely related to existence rather than enrichment.

"DIVERGENT" LANGUAGE AND CULTURE

Life in the United States changed when the new independent nation was established; it changed again when the immense western frontier was being settled; it changed again when its great agrarian society became urbanized and industrialized. The most startling change that has come, however, is the one attending the present technological revolution. This drastic and sweeping change made helpless many who did not have the skill to run the new machinery, the managerial ability to produce and market new goods, the education to hold the rapidly increasing jobs that require high-school or college educations.

This change struck its first devastating blows with the great black population of the deep South; later, it had similar effects with Mexican Americans in the great expanses of the Southwest, Indians on their secluded reservations, Puerto Ricans on their green island, and whites, many more whites than minorities, not only in the hills of Appalachia but on small farms and towns all over the United States. Some of these people have stayed in their native locale; thousands, in fact millions, have moved on to larger towns and cities in the hope of finding work and a better life, only to discover in too many cases that this hope was just a shining chimera that vanished as days passed in the new location.

The situation for these people is improving, but many still do not have jobs. As teachers, we have pupils whose parents may have jobs now but who bear the scars of suffering from poverty in their earlier years; and we also still have those suffering from living in poverty at present. How can we help these children retain pride about, and knowledge of, their backgrounds and cultures while also inducting them into the mores and behaviors of "mainstream" America? We have not done a very good job of implementing this goal as yet. We do seem to be making some progress. It is hoped that the suggestions in this volume, and particularly in this chapter, will aid teachers and future teachers in making contributions to this progress.

Building Positive Concepts

The role of self-concept in reading instruction has been mentioned directly or indirectly several times in other chapters of this book. It is of prime importance when speaking of learners with special needs that teachers help them build positive self-concepts. In classes where certain groups are in the minority, it is essential that teachers help "majority" pupils build positive concepts about those in the "minority." Both goals can be implemented by:

1. Listening to or reading stories or poems involving persons of different ethnic groups, or composed by authors from these groups.

2. Reading about the contributions made to American life by individuals or groups of individuals in different ethnic groups.

3. Reading and discussing general information about different ethnic groups in supplemental books and in subject matter textbooks, especially in the social-studies area.

4. Visiting schools and/or sections of the city inhabited chiefly by one ethnic group, guided at the time and afterward with discussion by a skillful, sympathetic, unbiased teacher.

5. Responding through skillful handling by the teacher of spontaneous expressions of prejudice that arise in the classroom.

This last situation is the one in which the teacher probably will most often have opportunities to modify undesirable attitudes. Children carry over attitudes formed at home. Besides, younger children usually consider ways of living which differ from their own as "strange" or "funny." Their expressions of prejudice are spontaneous and frequent. A skillful teacher can use these expressions to great advantage in changing attitudes. This has to be done with extreme tact, however, and often not on the spot. It takes careful thought and planning in some cases to devise a strategy for combating prejudice in a subtle but effective way. The example that follows illustrates this point.

> The children were to study about native Americans. Recognizing their need for the concrete, the teacher had the usual wigwam and Indian dress available. Aware that the children were unconsciously building attitudes toward native Americans in the process of their studies, the teacher planned to use this to help them build a better perspective.
>
> During class discussion, the teacher mentioned that the tribe being studied regarded the length of fringes on the dress as a sign of the individual's importance or status. The children burst out laughing. Resisting her impulse to raise the question, "How would you feel if someone laughed at you?"—because her purpose was not to make them feel guilty—she set about doing some homework. She realized more concrete experiences were needed if the children were to see native Americans as equals and not as "funny" or "odd." So she brought in pictures of diamond rings and models of different-sized cars and reintroduced the fringe variations, reminding the children of their original response to them. The children were given an opportunity to see that the social significance of rings and car sizes might seem "funny" to others. Without putting either negative or positive value on status symbols, she provided the children with materials that permitted them to expand their thinking and extend their feelings about such symbols.
>
> The teacher was not sure at the time how this affected the children because she carefully avoided phrasing their conclusions for them, knowing that they would mouth her words. Interviews prior to the experience showed that these first graders had many

negative concepts, apparently derived from television. But it is interesting that in her interviews with individual children following the experience she found a marked change of attitude in a positive direction toward native Americans.[1]

"Intelligence" and Environment

For many years, it was thought that intelligence was fixed by heredity. The changing view that now has wide acceptance is that intelligence is something that grows with stimulation, and that the early childhood years are critical years for this growing to take place. One *may* be born with a particular intellectual capacity, but the development of that capacity depends upon the interaction of the individual with environment.

It would appear that the role of the school is to supplement the life of the child with rich experiences continuously interwoven with a stream of language expression, and withal offering a multitude of opportunities to think, inquire, and find solutions to situations. Some suggestions for classroom activities follow.

1. Take children *out* of the school, into the community, and *beyond* the community. At first, take them on walks around the block or down the street, perhaps to see a bird's nest in a nearby tree, then eventually to the bakery, post office, zoo. Then, take trips to such places as a newspaper printing press and office, airport, automobile factory, railway depot and yard, sections of the city occupied by different cultural groups. When they are sufficiently mature to profit by such trips, take them to visit historical scenes and monuments, museums, art galleries. Always provide and/or develop purposes for learning prior to the visits and discuss outcomes following them.

2. Provide for thought-provoking, problem-solving, creative activities in the classroom. In the early years, such materials as the following are desirable: blocks for building purposes (or orange crates or empty cartons); a cooking corner with pots and pans; sewing materials; balance scales with small objects to weigh; materials for sorting according to color, shape, and size; a "feel box" to use in guessing what an object is just by feeling it; puzzles of many kinds to be solved; practical math materials; materials for creative activities in modeling, painting, drawing, woodwork.

3. Throughout the grades, encourage careful problem-solving in all classes but especially in the areas of social studies, science, and mathematics. Provide abundant creative opportunities in English, art, and music.

4. Surround the children with books. Let them live in an atmosphere of interest-compelling, concept-forming, information-giving books. At ear-

[1] Margaret Yonemura, "The Rights of Young Children," *National Elementary Principal* 51, no. 1 (September 1971): 57–63.

liest ages, provide attractive picture books with a minimum of text. Later, increase text gradually until in the upper grades there may be several pages of solid text. At all levels, let the content consist of subject matter dealing with information in science and social studies as well as stories from literature. In all cases, also, have the book collection represent several different races and cultures.

The Roots of Dialects

Dialects are indigenous to America. They are part of our heritage. Even standard English, the language usually used by people with many years of education, is called a dialect by some because there are so many regional differences. These regional differences, as explained by McDavid, have been shaped by geography and history.

> In the Middle West, settlers from New England followed the shores of Lake Erie westward and did not cross the swamplands of the Maumee and Kankakee, while settlers from the upland South moved north along the tributaries of the Ohio, taking up holdings in the bottom lands; today, despite subsequent industrialization, the speech of Ohio, Indiana, and Illinois is split between Yankee and Southern highland.[2]

Shuy pointed out

> . . . that social layers exist *within* regional dialect areas. That is, well-educated, partly-educated, and uneducated people may all live within the boundaries of a well-defined dialect area. In one sense, they all speak the same dialect. However, they speak different varieties of this dialect. Certain aspects of the dialect are shared by all social levels; others are used by only one or two of the groups.[3]

Information about Black English

Teachers who work with pupils who speak a distinct dialect or intermix of a dialect and regional standard English (SE) should become well acquainted with the nature of the dialect. The dialect that many urban teachers—and an increasing number of suburban teachers—hear is called Black English (BE) by most researchers. Many black children appear to speak this dialect of English, ". . . which is as highly structured as, but

[2] Raven I. McDavid, "Historical, Regional, and Social Variation," in *Culture, Class, and Language Variety*, ed. A. L. Davis (Urbana, Ill.: National Council of Teachers of English, 1972), p. 11.

[3] Roger W. Shuy, *Discovering American Dialects* (Champaign, Ill.: National Council of Teachers of English, 1967), p. 3.

linguistically at variance with, that which is used and taught in the schools." [4]

The chart below is reprinted with the permission of Harber and Beatty and the International Reading Association. It is taken from their excellent booklet, *Reading and the Black English Speaking Child*. The booklet is called an annotated bibliography, but it is more than that. It brings together important information clearly and succinctly.

MAJOR DIFFERENCES BETWEEN STANDARD ENGLISH AND BLACK ENGLISH [5]

Phonological Differences

Feature	Example (SE - BE)
Simplification of consonant clusters	test - tes, past - pas, went - win
th sounds	
voiceless *th* in initial position	think - tink or think
voiced *th* in initial position	the - de
voiceless *th* in medial position	nothing - nofin'
voiced *th* in medial position	brother - brovah
th in final position	tooth - toof
r and *l*	
in postvocalic position	sister - sistah, nickel - nickuh
in final position	Saul - saw
Devoicing of final *b*, *d*, and *g*	cab - cap, bud - but, pig - pik
Nasalization	
ing suffix	doing - doin'
i and *e* before a nasal	pen - pin
Stress—absence of the first syllable of a multisyllabic word when the first syllable is unstressed	about - 'bout
Plural marker *	three birds - three bird or three birds
	the books - de book or de books
Possessive marker *	the boy's hat - de boy hat
Third person singular marker *	He works here - He work here
Past tense—simplification of final consonant clusters*	passed - pass, loaned - loan

* Some authorities include these under syntactical differences.

---

[4] Jean R. Harber and Jane N. Beatty, comps., *Reading and the Black English Speaking Child: An Annotated Bibliography* (Newark, Del.: International Reading Assn., 1978), p. 3. Reprinted with permission.

[5] Ibid., pp. 46–47. Reprinted with permission of the authors and the International Reading Association.

Syntactical Differences

Feature	SE	BE
Linking verb	He is going.	He goin'. or He is goin'.
Pronomial apposition	That teacher yells at the kids.	Dat teachah, she yell at de kid (kids).
Agreement of subject and third person singular verb	She runs home. She has a bike.	She run home. She have a bike.
Irregular verb forms	They rode their bikes.	Dey rided der bike (bikes).
Future form	I will go home.	I'm a go home.
"If" construction	I asked if he did it.	I aks did he do it.
Indefinite article	I want an apple.	I want a apple.
Negation	I don't have any.	I don't got none.
Pronoun form	We have to do it.	Us got to do it.
Copula (verb "to be")	He is here all the time. No, he isn't.	He be here. No, he isn't. or No, he don't.
Prepositions	Put the cat out of the house. The dress is made of wool.	Put de cat out de house. De dress is made outta wool.

NOTE: The inventory of differences between SE and BE is far smaller than the inventory of similarities.

Although the rules of other dialects are usually not as clear or as carefully spelled out, teachers of children who speak other dialects should also become familiar with them. Familiarity with the details of a dialect will enable the teacher to better understand the difference between a miscue in reading related to dialect and one related to lack of—or partial lack of—comprehension. The "rules" of the dialect are not stated for expression but impression; teachers should be able to understand the dialect; they do not have to learn how to speak it.

Dialect Interference

Rupley and Robeck stated: "A sampling of studies found in the ERIC system . . . suggests that Black dialect has minimal, if any, effects on Black children's reading achievement." [6] Harber and Beatty said:

> Research has shown that BE speaking children often translate into their own dialect parts of what they read aloud. The important question, still unanswered, is whether this translation negatively affects comprehension of SE materials.
> Numerous studies report that BE speaking children are bidialectical, their use of SE increases with age, and they use SE in classroom

---

[6] William H. Rupley and Carol Robeck, "ERIC/RCS: Black Dialect and Reading Achievement," *Reading Teacher* 31, no. 5 (February 1978): p. 598.

situations. A few studies have examined the influence of vocabulary knowledge and nonstandard orthography on the acquisition of reading among lower SES black children, but the evidence is scanty and inconclusive.[7]

The authors of this book, in agreement with a number of theoreticians and teachers, believe that dialect does not normally interfere with reading comprehension. Misunderstandings about the nature of communication, inadequate teacher-training programs, and negative attitudes toward dialects appear to be the important interfering factors. When pupils read silently, no problems exist in relation to dialect; problems arise in the minds of some teachers when pupils read orally. If the purpose of written language is for communication purposes, and if the dialect-speaking child receives the messages with adequate comprehension, there is no problem. The goal of oral reading is not 100 percent in word pronunciation; it is understanding the message. Hence, the child who uses a dialect or an intermix of dialect and SE to read orally with comprehension should not have teachers interfere by insisting on accurate (SE) pronunciation. Yes, the school probably has the obligation of helping all dialect speakers to also learn regional SE well as a vehicle for upward mobility. But, it cannot be done all at once and at the risk of "turning off" communication. Emphasis must be placed on *what does it mean* not *how should it be pronounced*.

Transition Activities

It requires a great deal of thinking, listening, and emulating for children who speak dialects to learn how to speak and read orally in regional SE. It also requires knowledgeable, sympathetic, and patient teachers who make the children realize that learning SE is just another way of communicating with a broader audience; it is not a replacement for the dialect, which is still necessary for many kinds of communication. The three types of activities below, although related to Black English, may be utilized in connection with any dialect.

1. *Choral Reading.* After children have gained some proficiency in reading SE, let them do some choral reading of easy, melodious selections. This activity has two values: (1) Pupils who use their own dialect at times will discover that they are out of sinc and can self-adjust. (2) The flow and rhythm of the language encourages transitions to SE.

2. *Conscious Listening.* Once pupils have become aware of the differences between certain constructions in dialect and in SE, directed listening activities stressing those constructions in meaningful situations often cements learning. Giving a set of directions involving the accomplishment of a task where the *to be* verbs are emphasized in the directions and the task can be helpful. For example: Here are two things. One is a pencil. One is a piece of chalk. Tell us the color of each one.

[7] Harber and Beatty, *Reading and the Black English Speaking Child*, pp. 5–6.

Recording what is said or read on tape and then playing it back—individually—provides a strong lesson for some pupils.

3. *Closure Tasks.* Presenting pupils with passages where the parts that have been deleted represent SE is useful as fun and as a way of raising the consciousness level of the dialect speaker.

EXAMPLE:

Max and Hazel _____ goin_____ to see the show. Max _____ a car so he _____ goin_____ to call for Hazel.

In the example above, only three types of differences were focused on. Larger spaces were deleted to indicate words; smaller spaces indicated letters. Emphasis was placed on *is-are*, *has-have*, and the *g* ending. Children may also be given words to choose from if leaving the space blank is too frustrating.

In general, with emphasis on meaning and a solid rapport between the child and the environment, these changes will take place without putting such conscious attention on them. On the other hand, as long as rapport is present and meaning is not sacrificed, some children will move along more rapidly in learning SE with such planned activities.

BILINGUALISM AND READING

In its true sense, bilingualism means to be able to communicate effectively and efficiently in two languages; to communicate in this context means to speak and understand oral language, to read, and to write. Few pupils in the elementary or even middle school grades in the United States are bilingual; most are at a variety of stages along a bilingual continuum. Some who enter day-care centers, nursery schools, kindergartens, or grade one are just developing oral language proficiency in their native language, or the native language of their parents. They are no different in this development than the young native speaker of English with one *big* exception: except when interacting with their culturally similar peers, they often find themselves in an alien environment. Their familiar, warm cultural backgrounds are, of course, intermixed with language; suddenly, they are thrown into not only a world of strange noises but a world of strange behaviors and reference points. Much depends on the reception given to this child by the school environment, the peers in school, and the teacher. The teacher is possibly the most important variable of them all.

If communication is to take place, children must be able to use their language, the language they know. If the teacher does not understand and speak the language, problems must arise. That is why in many places with large groups of pupils who speak the same language and share similar cultures the school has been urged, and often ordered, to employ teachers who speak the language. These teachers must also be proficient in English because it is their job to help the pupils become bilingual.

Learning Patterns and Culture

Because cultural background and language are so integrated, teachers must learn as much as possible about the specific culture of the children in addition to the specific language. This is difficult even for the teacher who speaks the language and shares the general culture. Important language differences and specific cultural rites must often be added to this teacher's knowledge. For the teacher who does not share either culture and/or language, the task is especially complex. As Ching pointed out, dissimilar cultural values may be responsible for many misunderstandings between teacher and pupil. The levels of aspiration, value orientations, and social amenities of the pupils may differ widely from the expectations of the teacher who is a part of the "mainstream" culture.[8]

As a result of cultural background and experiences, the learning styles of children from particular ethnic-language groups sometimes differ from the learning styles featured in the classroom. For example, Dixon listed these classroom activities for Mexican-American children, based on an analysis of some existing research:

1. Activities which emphasize the improvement of the skills of all the members of the group instead of merely self-improvement may be more successful than those activities which place emphasis only on individual improvement.

2. Activities which require cooperation rather than competition will reflect the cognitive style of Mexican American children.

3. Mexican American children will profit from educational experiences which allow them to interact with the teacher or other students, so that activities involving the use of books, or paper and pencil tasks may be most effective if human interaction is also included, and if the affective comfort of the child is a consideration in the instructional design.

4. The use of other children in authority roles may be viewed as natural and desirable in the classroom as a result of the generalization from the use of other children as authority figures in the "home" culture.[9]

[8] Doris C. Ching, *Reading and the Bilingual Child* (Newark, Del.: International Reading Assn., 1976), pp. 2–3.
[9] Carol N. Dixon, "Teaching Strategies for the Mexican American Child," *Reading Teacher* 30, no. 2 (November 1976): p. 143.

Still other learning patterns may be dictated by necessity as well as the culture. Migrant children, who are poor and most often from minority groups speaking another language or dialect, must learn to cope with "continual disruption of their classroom studies" and "repeated adjustments to new environments." [10] After reviewing pertinent studies in the ERIC system, Reed recommended:

> The focus of the educational program for migrant children must be on individualized instruction. Each child must be tested and then given activities that will help him or her become an independent learner —a must for any child who continually moves from one school to another—and that will give the child a feeling of achievement. Curricula designed for these children should be multifaceted with emphasis in four areas. 1) a language-oriented program to bridge the gap between home and school oral language, 2) a task-oriented program to increase the child's ability to solve problems at his or her particular stage of intellectual and motor-skilled development, 3) an experience-oriented program to assure opportunities for effective relating to school and the larger community, and for expanding knowledge beyond the immediate home environment, and 4) a social-emotional development program conducive to growth in self-esteem.[11]

And still other learning patterns and activities need to be developed when a teacher is confronted by one or just a scattering of youngsters speaking another language(s), seated in the classroom, and waiting to see whether their education may begin. As Allen indicated: "How do you help a child with whom you cannot communicate? Where do you begin?" [12] Allen [13] reported that many of these children are placed in grade levels below their age group, receive English primers to read even though they may be reading fluently in their language, and may be considered remedial reading or speech problems. Allen suggested several alternatives for the classroom teacher when a bilingual teacher or program is not available.

1. The child needs time to adapt to a new culture and to develop an oral language base in a new language.

2. There are many "teachers" to help the child learn English. Every child in the room is a "native informant" and can provide the oral language input that the non-English speaking child will need.

3. In order to find out how well the child understands English, a series of questions can be asked. The child responds by an action or by pointing to an object or a picture.

4. In order to find out how well the child speaks English, first ask a

[10] Linda Reed, "ERIC/RCS: The Migrant Child in the Elementary Classroom," *Reading Teacher* 31, no. 6 (March 1978): p. 730.

[11] Ibid., pp. 730–31.

[12] Virginia G. Allen, "The Non-English Speaking Child in Your Classroom," *Reading Teacher* 30, no. 5 (February 1977): pp. 504–5.

[13] Ibid., pp. 504–8.

series of short-answer questions. If the child can respond, go on to those that call for longer answers.

5. After ascertaining the language performance of the child, organize "exchange" lessons. Here, a trained peer or aide works on establishing language patterns. For example:

Tutor: Show me the white paper.
Pupil: Here is the white paper.
Tutor: Show me the yellow paper.
Pupil: Here is the yellow paper.

6. To help raise the self concept of the learner and also to strike a blow for bilingualism, the exchange lesson may be followed by one in the native language of the learner. Both the tutor and the classroom teacher, as well as interested peers, might take part.

Tutor: Muéstrame el papel blanco.
Pupil: Aquí está el papel blanco.
Tutor: Muéstrame el papel amarillo.
Pupil: Aquí está el papel amarillo.

7. As the child grows more proficient, opportunities for simulation lessons should be capitalized on: everyday dialogues using puppets, playing store, talking on the telephone, and so forth. Peers should think of special situations for developing pragmatic language skills.

8. Allow the children to use varied materials to express ideas. Classifying actual objects and then entering them on a chart is a useful experience. Explanations of procedures can be bolstered through the use of visuals—cuisinnaire rods, markers, geometric shapes, measuring cups, drawings, slides.

9. Provide a listening table with records and tapes and storybooks accompanied by records or tapes. Children can listen and answer by drawing or by building up scenes and objects on a flannel board.

10. Physical education classes and recess provide many opportunities for the child to develop an understanding of important prepositions. For example: "Crawl through the tunnel. Climb up the rope. Skip around the circle."

11. Children's picture books as well as all the supplies they need to express themselves should be easily accessible.

12. Learn as much as possible about the cultures and languages of the children in the classroom.

13. Bring double language dictionaries into the classroom for the use of the children speaking a language other than English, for the English-

speaking children so they may learn to communicate, and for the teacher's reference.

14. Prepare materials that introduce the culture of the bilingual children in the classroom to the rest of the class.

15. As English proficiency grows, prepare well-structured and success-oriented material for the youngster to work on independently.

16. Read aloud to the children daily. Use books and other materials that use pictures wisely so children may use the pictures to help with language concepts they may be uncertain about.

17. Above all, realize that these children can think. They may have difficulty expressing their thoughts. Encouragement and patience will go a long way.

As Allen concluded:

> What happy opportunities there are for sharing language and customs, for learning that differences are fascinating and similarities are many! **These children bring to all of us a rare and special gift.**[14]

Learning to Read

Step number one for the "bilingual" child is to become *reasonably* proficient in her or his native language—speaking, reading, and writing. The word *reasonably* is the key word because there is not enough evidence as yet for any of us to be sure what that means. We do know that native English-speaking youngsters appear to fare best in reading and writing when they have facility in speaking and listening; the same adage seems to hold true in any language. For the child who must learn to handle the English language as well as the home-community language, it seems *reasonable* to encourage the child to do his or her thinking in the language interrelated with the culture. Communication tasks in the English language should not be offered until the child has cemented those concepts in the native language. This principle is particularly important for the beginner. Once the learner is able to do a lot of code switching (moving back and forth from one language to the other), more complex concepts can be offered in both languages.

Because the goal of reading is meaning, more attention should be placed on ideas than on the sounds and shapes of individual words. Learners should be searching for meaning rather than for similarities and differences in sound and syntax. Granted, some graphemes and constructions will pose problems that need attention. But learning should be focused on gaining the message rather than endless patterning. Once in a while, translations are useful but not as a frequent diet. Teachers who translate every word, phrase, or sentence from one language to another

---

[14] Ibid., p. 508. In addition, the seventeen points related to classroom activities were largely contributed by Allen, plus a few points she stimulated the authors to generate.

as the major means of helping pupils read are encouraging rote learning. Example: El perro es peligroso. The dog is dangerous. Ella es génera. She is kind.

It is more conducive to developing the realization that reading is a purposeful, meaningful act to develop readiness for reading something and then to have pupils read for a purpose—even at a very simple level.

EXAMPLE:

Talk with Juan about the things he likes to do. When he highlights swimming, tuck that away in mind and later, or the next day, write this sentence on the chalkboard—Juan swims. Here is an opportunity to have Juan predict what swims means as he tries to think, in response to the teacher's question, "What is Juan doing?" Here, too, is an opportunity to develop the concept of a sentence, a subject, a verb, and a verb ending. When Juan also says he likes to jog, here is an opportunity to read for two purposes and to cement concepts of capitals at the beginning of sentences as well as anaphoric relationships (see pages 379–80). In addition, Juan will be able to predict the meaning of the word also from his own knowledge—both experiential and linguistic. Juan swims. He jogs also.

EXAMPLE:

Present a simple riddle for Takahiko to solve. He breathes fire. He is very big. He kills people. He walks on houses. He lives in the ocean. He is a ＿＿＿＿＿＿＿. Japanese children, as other children, usually love monster stories, and with some help they will search for the answer to this riddle. Along the way, they get help in **sentence patterning, anaphora, prepositional phrases,** *and the noun marker* **a.** *If Takahiko guessed the name of a particular monster, the teacher can have him read the sentence out loud to see how* **a** *is the marker for a generic term rather than a specific name.*

The Value of Context Clues. For many years, the contention that the reading process was one of decoding symbols to sounds and sounds to words, particularly in languages more "phonetic" than English, remained unchallenged. The assumption was that children had to, therefore, learn the sounds of English (with a little attention to syntax) and they could "read" in English. Oh, they might have to contend with some of the exceptions to phonics rules, but mastery of pronunciation would do the trick. Today that contention *is* challenged. Reading is considered a search for meaning and, hence, attention should not be placed on each letter, or syllable, or word. In oral speaking, as in oral reading, accurate pronunciation is not the primary goal; carrying on a meaningful dialogue with the author is the goal.

Research evidence shows us that children attempt to use the same strategies while reading Spanish.[15] In a study of seventy-five Spanish speaking children in grades two and three who were receiving reading instruction in Spanish texts, pupils made use of context clues. Words pronounced incorrectly in an isolated list were pronounced correctly in the selections:

Preprimer—54.7 percent
Primer—71.4 percent
First Grade—82.5 percent
Second Grade—91 percent
Third Grade—80.3 percent [16]

López, who conducted the study cited above, offered the following instructional implications—among others—based on her findings:

- Strategies for giving children practice in using context should be included in a Spanish reading program. Even young readers are able to use context to predict missing words—this should be encouraged. Contextual exercises should be built into a Spanish reading program, so that children increase this skill.
- Children should be allowed to make a few errors when they read, without having to go back and correct these errors. As has been demonstrated, many of these errors illustrate that children make substitutions that fit the context. This ability should be encouraged and trained rather than discouraged.
- Teachers do not need to focus on or correct every word recognition error a child makes. Rather, they should focus only on those errors that change the meaning of what is being read.[17]

For both the reading of English and other languages, "bilingual" youngsters should be helped to develop strategies for developing word recognition and word approximation abilities. (See chapter 6.) These strategies should emphasize the use of context—both syntactic and se-

[15] Sarah H. López, "Children's Use of Contextual Clues in Reading Spanish," *Reading Teacher* 30, no. 7 (April 1977): 735–40.
[16] Ibid., p. 737.
[17] Ibid., p. 739.

mantic; phoneme-grapheme correspondences should be taught when essential but always interrelated with context.

Approaches and Activities. Language-experience approaches (pages 100–105) should be used at the beginning stages of instruction and throughout instruction in both languages. As Ching pointed out, such approaches do the following: (1) They build self-concept because they are so personal and individualized; they tend to set up positive relationships between pupil and teacher. (2) They interrelate the language arts, a very important concept for "bilingual" children. (3) They deal with meaningful content pertinent to the child.[18]

Of course, "bilingual" children must move on to reading in varied materials and become acquainted with new vocabulary and patterns of writing. They will need much guidance from the teacher. Chapter 4 on readiness for reading (particularly pages 78–87) presents ideas essential for helping pupils read materials that deal with concepts distant from their experiences. (See also chapter 10 dealing with reading in the content areas.)

The suggestions that follow are aimed at promoting the reading of English in interesting ways for young children. They are simple and may be used between continuing projects. Teachers will undoubtedly think of many more.

1. A calendar is useful. Children read the name of the month and the numbers while marking off the days as time passes.

2. A large imitation clock with movable hands is useful in learning to read numbers. Children enjoy having turns in moving the hands to represent different times of the day.

3. A concentric circle designed with several layers is of interest to children in learning to read personal names in English. In the first circle, the child's name is written; in the next one, the names of brothers or sisters; in successive circles going outward may be written the name of a pet, name of the town where the child lives, street and number, and state. The teacher may work out two or three of these on the chalkboard. If the children have learned to write, they work out their own circles and read them to another child, the teacher, a group, or the class—dependent upon their feelings of security.

4. After children have achieved some proficiency in reading in English, they enjoy reading to each other in pairs. It is desirable to pair one of the best readers with one who is not reading so well. This activity provides practice both in reading and in listening.

5. An object box may be used to advantage in helping to establish an initial vocabulary. Decorate a box attractively. Place several objects in the box representing several common nouns. Hold up one of the objects and ask "What is this?" The children probably will answer in their native language. You may replace their answer by saying "Yes, it's a ball.

[18] Ching, *Reading and the Bilingual Child*, p. 34.

What is it children?" Then give a child a chance to hold up the ball and ask the question in English with the other children answering in English. Continue in the same way with the other objects. Pictures, instead of the objects, themselves, may be used in conducting this activity. The names of the colors may be used by having objects of different colors in the box and asking "What color is this?"

Later on when the children are more advanced, a guessing game may be played by having a child pull out pictures of objects representing different colors and say, "I have a picture of something brown. Guess what it is." Other children ask, "Is it a coat?" "Is it a dress?" "Is it a shoe?" and so on. The child with the picture then holds it up for the others to see and says, "It is a coat." Continue in this way with the other pictures in the box.[19]

Encourage children to write their sentences on cards—as they become more confident. Then have a child pass a card to another child for him or her to read.

In addition to the specific suggestions made in this chapter, the teacher of "bilingual" children should refer to the procedures suggested in chapter 12, "Reading in Grades One through Three," and/or chapter 13, "Reading in Grades Four through Eight." Many of the other chapters, as well, will provide ideas that can be adapted for classroom use in bilingual settings.

DISCUSSION QUESTIONS AND ACTIVITIES

1. If you are teaching, invite pupils who come from cultural backgrounds that differ from the majority group to describe and explain special holidays, rites, and beliefs. Set the stage first by discussing the importance of varied backgrounds and the richness they bring to the learning situation. Experience stories, individual and group, can grow out of these experiences.

2. If you are not teaching now, choose a minority group and find resources that will help you better understand the language and the culture of the group. Some of the materials listed in the bibliography of this chapter will help you, but if you want to study a particular group intensively, use the subject index in a good library. For example, should you want to learn about the customs of children from the Dominican Republic, look under that topic for the book or pamphlet which might provide the information.

3. If you are working with youngsters who appear to speak Black English, do a mini-study and see if the differences listed on pages 390–91 of

---

[19] Object box activities were suggested by Nina Phillips, *Conversational English for the Non-English-Speaking Child* (New York: Teachers College Press, Columbia University, 1968), pp. 19–28.

this chapter hold true with your group. Some of them may not because children may be at different transition places and Black English may differ slightly from region to region.

4. Try doing a miscue analysis (pages 60–62) with children who speak a dialect other than regional standard English or who speak in a native language as well as English. Note the nature of the miscues and see if and why comprehension is influenced by them.

ADDITIONAL READING

Books and Pamphlets

CHING, DORIS C. *Reading and the Bilingual Child*. Newark, Del.: International Reading Assn., 1976.

CONDE, DAVID. "Bilingualism, the School, and the Chicano: A Point of View." In *Literacy for Diverse Learners: Promoting Reading Growth at All Levels*, edited by Jerry L. Johns. Newark, Del.: International Reading Assn., 1974.

HALL, MARYANNE. *The Language Experience Approach for the Culturally Disadvantaged*. Newark Del.: International Reading Assn., 1972.

HARBER, JEAN R., and BEATTY, JANE N., comps. *Reading and the Black English Speaking Child: An Annotated Bibliography*. Newark, Del.: International Reading Assn., 1978.

HENDERSEN, ELLEN C. *Teaching Reading to Bilingual Children*. Jericho, N.Y.: Exposition Press, 1972.

HITTLEMAN, DANIEL R. *Developmental Reading: A Psycholinguistic Perspective*. Pp. 394–406. Chicago: Rand McNally College Publishing Co., 1978.

JASSOY, MARY E. "Migrant Children: "We *Can* Teach Them." In *Reading Interaction: The Teacher, the Pupil, the Materials*, edited by Brother Leonard Courtney. Newark, Del.: International Reading Assn., 1976.

JOHNSON, LAURA S. "Bilingual Bicultural Education: A Two-Way Street." In *Reading Interaction: The Teacher, the Pupil, the Materials*, edited by Brother Leonard Courtney. Newark, Del.: International Reading Assn., 1976.

LAFFEY, JAMES, and SHUY, ROGER, eds. *Language Differences: Do They Interfere?* Newark, Del.: International Reading Assn., 1973.

RAMIREZ, ARNULFO G.; ARCE-TORRES, EDGARDO; and POLITZER, ROBERT L. *Language Attitudes and the Achievement of Bilingual Pupils*. Research and Development Memorandum No. 146. Stanford, Calif.: Stanford University, Stanford Center for Research and Development in Teaching, 1976.

RANSOM, GRAYCE A. *Preparing to Teach Reading*. Pp. 439–63. Boston: Little, Brown, 1978.

RUDDELL, ROBERT B. *Resources in Reading-Language Instruction*. Englewood Cliffs, N.J.: Prentice-Hall, 1974.

SECTION D:
CLASSROOM
INSTRUCTION

SEITZ, VICTORIA. *Social Class and Ethnic Group Differences in Learning to Read.* Newark, Del.: International Reading Assn., 1977.

SIMONS, HERBERT D. "Black Dialect and Learning to Read." In *Literacy for Diverse Learners: Promoting Reading Growth at All Levels,* edited by Jerry L. Johns, Newark, Del.: International Reading Assn., 1974.

THONIS, ELEANOR W. *Literacy for America's Spanish Speaking Children.* Newark, Del.: International Reading Assn., 1976.

VICK, MARIAN L. "Relevant Content for the Black Elementary School Pupil." In *Literacy for Diverse Learners: Promoting Reading Growth at All Levels,* edited by Jerry L. Johns. Newark, Del.: International Reading Assn., 1974.

WELTY, STELLA. "Reading and Black English." In *Language, Reading, and the Communication Process,* edited by Carl Braun. Newark, Del.: International Reading Assn., 1971.

ZINTZ, MILES V. *The Reading Process: the Teacher and the Learner.* 2nd ed., pp. 397–457. Dubuque, Iowa: Wm. C. Brown Co., 1975.

Periodicals

ALLEN, VIRGINIA G. "The Non-English Speaking Child in Your Classroom." *Reading Teacher* 30, no. 5 (February 1977), pp. 504–8.

CAGNEY, MARGARET A. "Children's Ability to Understand Standard English and Black Dialect." *Reading Teacher* 30, no. 6 (March 1977), pp. 607–10.

DIXON, CAROL N. "Teaching Strategies for the Mexican American Child." *Reading Teacher* 30, no. 2 (November 1976), pp. 141–45.

"EDUCATION FOR THE SPANISH SPEAKING." *National Elementary Principal* 50, no. 2 (November 1970).

FEELEY, JOAN T. "Bilingual Instruction: Puerto Rico and the Mainland." *Reading Teacher* 30, no. 7 (April 1977), pp. 741–44.

FOERSTER, LEONA M. "Teaching Reading in Our Pluralistic Classrooms." *Reading Teacher* 30, no. 2 (November 1976), pp. 146–60.

GARCIA, RICARDO L. "Mexican American Bilingualism and English Language Development." *Journal of Reading* 17, no. 6 (March 1974), pp. 467–73.

GOODMAN, KENNETH S., with BUCK, CATHERINE. "Dialect Barriers to Reading Comprehension Revisited." *Reading Teacher* 27, no. 1 (October 1973), pp. 6–12.

HUTCHINSON, JUNE O'SHIELDS. "Reading Tests and Nonstandard Language." *Reading Teacher* 25, no. 5 (February 1972), pp. 430–37.

JOHNSON, KENNETH R. "Accountability and Educating Black Children in Reading and the Language Arts." *Language Arts* 54, no. 2 (February 1977), pp. 144–49.

JOHNSON, KENNETH R., and SIMONS, HERBERT D. "Black Children and Reading: What Teachers Need to Know." *Phi Delta Kappan* 53, no. 5 (January 1972), pp. 288–90.

JONES, VIRGINIA W. "Training Teachers of English for Alaska's Native Children." *Elementary English* 48, no. 2 (February 1971), pp. 198–202.

LATIMER, BETTYE I. "Telegraphing Messages to Children About Minorities." *Reading Teacher* 30, no. 2 (November 1976), pp. 151–56.

LÓPEZ, SARAH H. "Children's Use of Contextual Clues in Reading Spanish." *Reading Teacher* 30, no. 7 (April 1977), pp. 735–40.

NEY, JAMES W. "Bilingual Education in Sunday School Country." *Elementary English* 51, no. 2 (February 1974), pp. 209–14.

OVANDO, CARLOS J. "School Implications of the Peaceful Latino Invasion." *Phi Delta Kappan* 59, no. 4 (December 1977), pp. 230–34.

PHILION, WILLIAM L. E., and GALLOWAY, CHARLES G. "Indian Children and the Reading Program." *Journal of Reading* 12, no. 7 (April 1969), p. 553.

REED, LINDA. "ERIC/RCS: The Migrant Child in the Elementary Classroom." *Reading Teacher* 31, no. 6 (March 1978), pp. 730–33.

RUPLEY, WILLIAM H., and ROBECK, CAROL. "ERIC/RCS: Black Dialect and Reading Achievement." *Reading Teacher* 31, no. 5 (February 1978), pp. 598–601.

SMITH, NILA B. "Cultural Dialects: Current Problems and Solutions." *Reading Teacher* 29, no. 2 (November 1975), pp. 137–41.

Author Index

A

Aaron, Ira E., 65
Acinapuro, Philip J., 106, 120
Adams, Anne H., 120
Adams, Fay, 234, 380
Ahrendt, Kenneth M., 261
Alexander, J. Estill, 33
Allen, Claryce, 119
Allen, David P., 176
Allen, Roach Van, 20, 101, 119
Allen, Virginia G., 396–98, 404
Allington, Richard L., 176
Altick, Richard D., 235
Amidon, Edmund J., 33
Amster, Harriet, 201
Anastasiow, Nicholas, 65
Angelo, Evangeline B., 29
Arce-Torres, Edgardo, 403
Arthur, Sharon V., 362
Artley, A. Sterl, 140, 151–52, 176, 236, 373
Ashton-Warner, Sylvia, 32
Athey, Irene, 30
Atkinson, R. C., 120
Aukerman, Robert C., 91, 119, 362
Ausubel, Donald P., 33, 82

B

Bailey, Mildred H., 161
Barnhart, Clarence L., 175
Barr, A., 120

Barrett, Thomas C., 26, 52, 64, 91, 112, 119, 235, 302, 373
Barron, Roderick W., 176
Barth, Rodney J., 120
Beatty, Jane N., 391–92, 392–93, 403
Beck, Isabel L., 176
Becker, George J., 119
Beery, Althea, 64, 91, 112, 119, 235, 373
Benditt, Marcella, 97
Berger, Allen, 261
Berlyne, D. E., 7
Bernstein, Edgar, 86–87
Betts, Emmett A., 56
Bingham, Alma, 235
Biskin, Donald S., 236, 371
Blachowicz, Camille L. Z., 209–10
Blake, Howard E., 292–93
Blanton, William, 43
Blatt, Gloria T., 92
Bloom, Benjamin S., 31, 33, 68, 230
Blumer, Herbert, 33
Bond, Guy L., 68
Bonenfant, Richard G., 302
Borden, Juliet P., 92
Bormuth, John R., 116
Bortnick, Robert, 213
Botel, Morton, 56
Boyan, Catherine S., 236
Boyd, Rachel M., 65
Braun, Carl, 33, 48–50, 64, 119, 404
Brigham, Bruce W., 201
Browne, Margaret P. J., 29

Bruner, Jerome, 68
Bryan, George S., 247
Buck, Catherine, 404
Burke, Carolyn L., 60, 61
Burlando, Andrew A., 362
Burmeister, Lou E., 161
Buros, Oscar K., 42, 43, 44, 64
Burrows, Alvina T., 20
Busch, Jackie S., 120
Butler, Annie L., 92

C

Cagney, Margaret A., 404
Cameron, Jack R., 236
Campbell, J. D., 120
Carlson, Kenneth L., 302
Carroll, John B., 20, 176
Carton, Aaron S., 20
Carver, Ronald P., 261
Cazden, Courtney B., 20, 33
Chafe, Wallace L., 55–56
Chall, Jeanne S., 116
Chambers, J. Richard, 236
Chance, Larry L., 302
Chang, Lynette Y., 119
Charnock, James, 372–73
Cheek, Martha C., 57–58, 65
Cheyney, Arnold B., 302
Ching, Doris C., 395, 401, 403
Chomsky, Carol, 20, 21
Clary, Linda M., 236
Clements, Zacharie J., 200–201
Clymer, Theodore, 161
Collier, Calhoun C., 302
Colvin, Cynthia M., 112, 113

Conde, David, 403
Cook, Jimmie, 193–94, 201
Cooper, Charles R., 64
Courtney, Brother Leonard, 403
Cowe, Eileen, 21
Crabtree, Esther, 234, 380
Cramer, Ronald, 236, 362
Criscuolo, Nicholas P., 362
Cullinan, Bernice, 70
Cunningham, Dick, 302, 383
Cunningham, James W., 362
Cunningham, Patricia M., 11–12, 65, 362
Curry, Robert L., 378–79

D

Dale, Edgar, 79, 116, 190, 191–92, 194, 201
Dallman, Martha, 112, 119
Dauzat, Sam V., 64
Davis, A. L., 390
Davis, Anita P., 236
Davis, Joel J., 22
Dawson, Mildred A., 235
DeBoer, John J., 119
Deighton, Lee C., 201
Dennison, Paul E., 22
Devine, Thomas G., 22
Dieterich, Daniel, 120
Dixon, Carol N., 395, 404
Dohrman, Mary H., 284–85, 302–3
Downing, John, 22, 92
Duckworth, Eleanor, 9
Duker, Sam, 21
Dulin, Kenneth L., 302
Durkin, Dolores, 71, 73, 92, 112, 119, 176
Durrell, Donald, 236
Duscher, Raymond, 303
Dworkin, Nancy, 29
Dykstra, Robert, 33

E

Earle, Richard A., 64, 65, 302
Edmund, Rose M., 237
Ehri, Linnea C., 176
Eisiminger, Sterling, 94, 201
Elashoff, Janet D., 33
Elin, Rhoderick, 22
Eller, William, 235
Ellinger, Bernice D., 235
Emans, Robert, 161, 176

Ennis, Robert H., 220–21
Esler, William K., 303
Estes, Thomas H., 34

F

Fareed, Ahmed A., 215
Farr, Roger, 43, 65
Farrar, Nanette L., 362
Fay, Leo, 302
Feeley, Joan T., 404
Feldman, Jeffrey M., 176
Fennimore, Flora, 378
Figurel, J. Allen, 119, 229
Filler, Ronald C., 33
Fillion, Bryant, 10, 22
Fillmer, H. Thompson, 201, 383
Fillmore, Charles J., 300
Flanders, Ned A., 33
Fletcher, J. D., 120
Foerster, Leona M., 404
Foulke, Patricia N., 92
Friesen, Doris T., 92
Froese, Victor, 48, 64, 119
Fry, Edward, 116, 119
Fuller, Abraham, 96

G

Galloway, Charles G., 405
Gans, Roma, 100
Garcia, Ricardo L., 404
Gartler, Marion, 97
Garton, Sharon, 65
Gates, Arthur I., 27, 68, 98
Geis, Lynna, 378–79
Gerhard, Christian, 235
Gibson, Eleanor J., 21
Gluck, H. Robert, 261
Golinkoff, Roberta M., 240
Goodman, Kenneth S., 8, 21, 22, 34, 60, 65, 112, 176, 197–99, 201, 206, 235, 299, 404
Goodman, Libby, 70
Goodman, Yetta M., 60, 61, 214, 362
Gove, Mary K., 210–11
Grant, Barbara M., 21
Gray, William S., 225–26
Greene, Jennifer, 214
Groff, Patrick, 173, 261
Grommon, Alfred H., 43
Guice, Billy M., 57–58, 65
Guilford, John P., 370

Guszak, Frank J., 229
Guthrie, John T., 6, 176, 210, 227, 235

H

Hall, Maryanne, 92, 119, 403
Hammill, Donald, 70
Handley, Herbert H., 92
Hansell, T. Stevenson, 92
Harber, Jean R., 391–92, 392–93, 403
Harrell, Max M., 120
Harris, Albert J., 65
Harris, Beecher H., 362
Harris, Theodore L., 261
Harrison, Cathy B., 120
Harves, Gene R., 362
Haupt, Edward L., 55–56, 236
Hayakawa, S. I., 201
Heilman, Arthur W., 92, 119, 383
Heinrich, June S., 362
Hendersen, Ellen C., 403
Hennings, Dorothy D., 21
Henry, George H., 235
Henry, Nelson B., 34
Herber, Harold, 82, 228–29, 236, 302
Herold, Curtis P., 201
Higginbotham, Dorothy C., 22
Hillerich, Robert L., 65
Hittleman, Daniel R., 21, 61, 62, 63, 92, 403
Hjelm, Howard, 383
Hodges, Richard E., 21
Hogaboam, Thomas, 177
Holmes, Neal J., 376
Hoskisson, Kenneth, 92, 236, 371
Hough, John B., 33
Houts, Paul L., 43
Hunkins, Francis P., 229, 230–33
Hunt, Lyman C., Jr., 107–8, 119
Husek, T. R., 54
Hutchinson, June O'Shields, 404
Huttenlocher, Janellen, 22
Hynes, Dell, 33

J

Jacobson, Lenore, 29, 34
Jared, Lee Ann, 302

Jassoy, Mary E., 403
Jensen, Gale E., 33
Johansson, Bror A., 92
John, Vera P., 33
Johns, Jerry L., 65, 403, 404
Johnson, Dale D., 26, 51, 52, 65, 112, 113, 119, 120, 161, 176, 302
Johnson, Kenneth R., 404
Johnson, Laura S., 403
Johnson, Marjorie S., 65, 201
Johnstone, Julie P., 34
Jones, Margaret B., 236
Jones, Virginia W., 404
Jongsma, Eugene, 208

K

Kachuck, Beatrice L., 372
Karlin, Robert, 302, 375, 376
Katz, Leonard, 261
Kaufman, Bel, 34
Kennedy, Dolores, 236
Kidder, Carole L., 120
King, Ethel M., 92
King, Martha L., 235
Kirkland, Eleanor R., 22, 92
Kling, Martin, 261
Krause, Kenneth, 116–17
Kress, Roy A., 65

L

Ladevich, Laurel, 120
Laffey, James, 403
Lamb, Pose, 151, 177
Lamme, Linda L., 362
Lamoreaux, Lillian A., 100
Langendoes, D. Terence, 300
Lanier, Ruby J., 236
Larrick, Nancy, 362
Latmer, Bettye I., 405
Lawson, Anton E., 22
Lazar, May, 106
Lee, Doris, 235
Lee, Dorris M., 100
Lee, Harper, 69
Lees, Fred, 303
Levin, Harry, 21
Lindsay, E. J., 120
Lloyd, Dorothy M., 362
Lopardo, Genevieve, 213, 214
López, Sarah H., 400, 405
Lorenz, Estelle K., 201

Lundsteen, Sara W., 21, 236
Lynn, Bonnie, 383

M

MacDonald, James B., 34
MacGinitie, Walter, 65, 92
Maehr, Martin I., 34
Manis, Jerome G., 34
Marcel, Tony, 261
Marcus, Albert, 372
Mattleman, Marciene S., 292–93
McCabe, Patrick, 7–9
McCormick, Sandra, 363
McCracken, Robert A., 56
McCullough, Constance M., 140, 176, 234–35, 236
McDavid, Raven I., 390
McDonell, Gloria, 22
McKeown, Pamela, 362
Meltzer, Bernard M., 34
Mendelsohn, Leonard R., 261
Menyuk, Paula, 7–9, 21
Meredith, Robert, 21, 34, 176, 197–99, 206, 235, 299·
Merritt, King, Jr., 303
Merryman, Edward, 176
Miller, Wilma H., 367
Modlin, Marjorie, 236, 371
Moerk, Ernst L., 21
Monson, Dianne L., 20
Monteith, Mary K., 65
Mosedale, S., 261
Muller, Hans, 34
Musgrave, G. Ray, 119

N

Neilsen, Allan R., 33
Nelson, Joan B., 236
Neuwirth, Sharyn E., 236
Ney, James W., 405
Nielsen, Duane M., 383
Niles, Olive S., 21, 201
Nyquist, Ewald B., 362

O

O'Donnell, E. Michael, 92
Ollila, Lloyd O., 70, 92
Olson, David R., 22
Olson, Willard C., 106
O'Rourke, Joseph, 190, 191–92, 194, 201

Ovando, Carlos J., 405

P

Page, William D., 302, 363
Pauk, Walter, 261
Pearson, P. David, 120
Peebles, James, 261
Pehrsson, Robert, 213
Perfetti, Charles A., 177
Petty, Walter T., 201
Philion, William L. E., 405
Phillips, Nina, 402
Piaget, Jean, 7–9
Pienaar, Peter T., 120
Piercy, Malcolm, 7
Pikilski, Edna C., 236
Pipho, Chris, 65
Polcyn, Kenneth A., 111
Politzer, Robert L., 403
Popham, W. James, 54, 65
Powell, William R., 64, 91, 112, 119, 235, 373

Q

Quandt, Ivan, 34

R

Ramirez, Arnulfo G., 403
Rankin, Earl F., 65, 261
Ransom, Grayce A., 403
Rauch, Sidney J., 200–201
Raven, Ronald J., 223
Raymond, Dorothy, 92
Redmond, Lois A., 302
Reed, Linda, 396, 405
Reynolds, Charlotte, 84
Robeck, Carol, 392, 405
Robinson, Francis P., 373–74
Robinson, H. Alan, 26, 27, 41, 48, 59, 81, 84, 86, 92, 116–17, 137, 141, 142, 162, 186, 195, 197–99, 215–16, 221, 236, 260–61, 301, 302, 303, 374
Robinson, Helen M., 197–99
Robinson, Violet B., 70, 71
Rodgers, Denis, 300
Rogers, John R., 120
Rose, Arnold, 34
Rosecky, Marion, 120
Rosenthal, Robert, 29, 34
Rouch, Roger L., 119

Rubovits, Pamela C., 34
Ruddell, Robert B., 20, 21, 30, 34, 403
Rudman, Herbert C., 65
Rudman, Masha, 22
Rudorf, Hugh, 21
Rupley, William H., 22, 65, 303, 392, 405

S

Salzer, Richard T., 223
Sanacore, Joseph, 34
Sanders, Norris M., 230
Sawyer, Diane L., 383
Schell, Leo M., 235
Schoenfelder, Paula, 65
Schwartz, Robert M., 236
Seitz, Victoria, 404
Shablak, Scott L., 302, 383
Shapiro, Nathaniel, 215
Shepherd, David L., 8, 21
Shuy, Roger W., 34, 390, 403
Simons, Herbert D., 236, 404
Simula, Vernon L., 65
Sinatra, Richard C., 15–16
Singer, Harry, 20, 30, 34, 261
Skriba, Patricia, 65
Smith, E. Brooks, 21, 34, 176, 197–99, 206, 235, 299
Smith, Edwin H., 57–58, 65
Smith, Frank, 9–10, 21, 22, 34, 145, 176, 205, 235
Smith, Helen K., 107–8
Smith, James A., 21
Smith, Nila B., 22, 56, 60, 88–91, 141, 191, 199–200, 213, 243, 249, 255, 266, 282–83, 287–89, 301, 303, 405
Smith, Richard J., 51, 52, 65, 112, 113, 120, 161, 237, 302
Snow, Richard E., 33
Soar, Robert S., 34
Spache, Evelyn B., 92, 120, 161, 176, 230, 235, 259, 260, 302, 383
Spache, George D., 92, 116, 120, 161, 176, 230, 235, 302, 383
Spaulding, Robert L., 34
Stauffer, Russell G., 20, 48, 118, 120, 162, 176, 214, 236, 362, 370
Stephens, Kent G., 121
Stoll, Earline, 201
Strange, Michael, 176
Strickland, Dorothy S., 70
Sullivan, Joanna, 237
Swain, Merrill, 10, 22
Swalm, James, 261
Swiss, Thom, 120

T

Taba, Hilda, 237
Taylor, Wilson L., 59, 208
Thackray, D. V., 92
Thelen, Judith, 302
Thomas, Ellen L., 81, 86, 92, 137, 142, 162, 186, 195, 197–99, 236, 260–61, 301, 302, 374
Thompson, Richard A., 22
Thomson, Q. E., 17
Thonis, Eleanor W., 404
Thorndike, Edward L., 162, 175, 237
Tiegs, Ernest W., 234, 380
Tinker, Miles A., 176, 236
Tovey, Duane R., 22
Tuinman, J. Jaap, 43
Turner, Thomas N., 187, 188, 201, 237, 303

V

Vacca, Joanne L., 383
Vacca, Richard T., 92, 303, 383
Veatch, Jeanette, 106, 120
Venezky, Richard, 43
Vick, Marion L., 404
Vilscek, Elaine C., 119
Viorst, Judith, 209

W

Wallen, Carl J., 363
Waller, T. Gary, 21, 71
Watson, Dorothy J., 362
Weaver, Constance, 207
Weiner, Roberta, 363
Weinstein, Alfred B., 200–201
Welch, Carolyn, 56
Welty, Stella, 404
Wheat, Thomas E., 237
Wheeler, Alan, 120
Wheeler, Kirk, 120
Wheeler, Mary, 120
Wicklund, David A., 261
Wiederhold, J. Lee, 70
Woelfel, Sue, 235
Wolf, Judith G., 235
Wolf, Willavene, 235
Wollenberg, John P., 92
Wood, R. Kent, 111, 121

Y

Yonemura, Margaret, 388–89

Z

Zintz, Miles V., 49–50, 236, 404

Subject Index

A

Ability, definition of, 68
Advance organizers:
  definition of, 82
  examples of, 82–87
Affective factors, 26–31, 47
Affixes, 162–64, 169–70, 190
Agendas, 348–49, 367–68
Anaphora, 54–55, 59, 379–80, 383
Antonyms, 192
Application of reading, 225–26
Assessment of auditory and visual problems, 70
Assessment of reading abilities, 40–65
  attitude surveys, 51–52
  checklists, 48–50
  direct inquiry, 51
  informal inventories, 56–60
  informal tests, 53–56
  interviews, 52–53
  National Assessment of Educational Progress, 45–46
  observations, 47–48
  qualitative interpretation, 63
  Reading Miscue Inventory, 60–62
  self-evaluation, 63
  standardized tests, 40–45
Attention span, 31, 69
Attitude surveys, 51–52
Auditory factors:
  acuity, 70
  assessment of problems, 70
  discrimination, 70, 74

B

Basal readers:
  approach to instruction, 96–100
  defined, 10
  desirable uses, 99–101
  misuses, 98–99
Bibliographies:
  about approaches to instruction, 119–21
  of assessment sources, 64–65
  on comprehension, 235–37
  about content areas, 302–3
  about dialects and bilingualism, 403–5
  on dictionaries for grades four through eight, 284
  on encyclopedias for grades four and above, 287
  about intermediate levels and above, 383
  about primary levels, 362–63
  about psychological-sociological factors, 33–34
  on rates of reading and flexibility, 261
  on readiness, 91–93
  on sources of literature for children, 315–16
  on sources of literature in content areas, 311
  of test reviews, 43–44
  about thought and language, 21–23
  on vocabulary development, 201
  on word identification and approximation, 176–77
Bilingualism:
  definition of, 394
  learning patterns, culture, and, 395–98
  reading and, 398–402
Black English, 390–94
Book reports, 324–25, 333, 378

C

Card catalog, 290–91
Checklists, 48–50
Closure activities:
  cloze procedures, 58–60, 116, 118, 208, 214, 234
  instructional uses, 208–14, 382–83
  in intermediate grades and above, 211–13
  maze, 210
  Op-In, 213
  oral, 208
  primary, 209–11
  zip, 209–10
Cloze procedures, 58–60, 116, 118, 208, 214, 234
  (*see also* Closure activities)
Cognition:
  concrete operations, 8–9
  formal operations, 8–9

Cognition (*cont.*)
preoperational thought, 8
sensorimotor stage, 7–8
stages of, 7–9, 71
Compound words, 164–66,
190
Comprehension, 204–35
definition of, 205
foundations for, 74–75
growth areas in, 216–26
(*see also* Comprehension
growth areas)
measurement of, 44
principles for guiding, 207–
8
and purposes for reading, 6
strategies for developing,
205–16
Comprehension growth areas:
application, 225–26
critical reading, 220–25
interpretation, 218–20
literal, 216–18
Computers and reading, 112
Concept of reading, 41, 50
Concepts:
definition of, 180
development of, 180–86
Connectives, 300
Content areas:
geography, 268, 294–95
literature, 293, 296, 301
mathematics, 57–58, 266,
269, 271, 295, 297,
301
science, 57–58, 194, 265,
265–66, 268, 268–69,
271, 293–94, 296, 301,
311
social studies, 194, 266,
269, 271, 296–97, 301,
311
Context clues:
activities with, 142–44
and bilingualism, 399–401
in concept building, 184–85
dangers in overemphasizing,
142
types of, 140–42
Creative reading, 225–26
Criterion-referenced tests, 54
Critical reading, 220–25
Critical thinking, 194–96
(*see also* Critical reading)
Cultural factors:
background, 26–27, 387–90,
394–98, 402
materials, 113
patterns, 207

D

Diagnosis (*see* Assessment of
reading abilities)
Dialect, 28–29, 197, 390–94
Dictionaries:
for grades four through eight,
284
picture, 139–40, 148–49,
277
Dictionary skills, 173–75
Directed Reading Activity
(DRA), 354–56, 370,
372
Directed Reading-Thinking
Activity (DRTA), 356–
57, 370–71
Directions, following, 76, 291–
92, 347–48

E

Early readers, 71–73
Encyclopedias, 284–87
Evaluation of materials (*see*
Materials)
Evaluation procedures (*see*
Assessment of reading
abilities)
Experience charts and stories,
15, 102–5
Experiential background:
cultural, 26–27
defined, 68
individual, 27
linguistic, 27–29
as readiness factor, 78–80

F

Figurative language, 187–88
Flexibility of rates of reading
(*see* Rates of reading)
Fluency, 76–77, 242–45, 312

G

Games, discussion of, 145–47
Geography, 268, 294–95
Gilmore Oral Reading Test,
60–61, 63
Graphemes, 19, 29, 150

Gray Oral Reading Test, 60–
61, 63
Grouping:
history of, 342–43
individuals and, 315
interest, 109
skill, 109
small groups, 109, 344–45
static, 30
total class, 109, 343

I

Index, use of, 282–84
Individualized reading instruction:
commercial forms of, 110–11
evaluation of, 110
grouping in, 109
history of, 105–6
organizing for, 108–9
procedures in, 107–8
record-keeping in, 108
Informal assessment:
attitude surveys, 51–52
checklists, 48–50
closure procedures, 58–60
direct inquiry, 50
interests, 333
interviews, 52–53
observations, 47–48
qualitative interpretations of
tests, 63
reading inventories, 56–58
Reading Miscue Inventory,
60–62
reading tests, 53–56
self-evaluation, 63
writing questions for tests,
55–56
Informal reading inventories:
IRI, 56–57
Content-area inventory,
57–58
Informal tests:
criterion-referenced, 54
of skills, 54–55
writing questions for, 55–56
Intelligence (*see also* Cognition):
and environment, 389–90
and IQ tests, 43
Interests in reading:
ascertaining, 333
in intermediate grades and
above, 313
in primary grades, 312–13
stimulating, 308–22

Intermediate grades and above:
classroom organization, 367–68
closure activities, 211–13
concept development, 183–84
increasing rates of reading, 245–59
independent reading, 373–78
instructional plans, 370–73
language processing, 379–82
materials, 284–87, 368–70
readiness, 78–87
reading interests, 313
speaking, 13–14
study strategies, 267–68, 270, 272, 277–91
writing, 15
Interpretation, 218–20 (see also Comprehension and Comprehension growth areas)
Interviews, 52–53

J

Junior Great Books Program, 371–72

L

Language acquisition (see Oral language)
Language arts (see Language skills)
Language-experience approaches, 100–105
advantages and disadvantages of, 105
cloze procedure in, 214
experience charts in, 102–5
history of, 100–101
procedures in, 101–2
Language skills, 10–18
Learning centers, 349–50
Libraries:
classroom collection, 317–18, 326–27
public, 330–32
school, 327–29
Linguistic readers, definition of, 19
Linguistics defined, 18–19
Listening:
defined, 6

listening-reading transfer lessons, 11–12
relationship to reading, 11–12
Literal comprehension, 216–18 (see also Comprehension and Comprehension growth areas)
Literature:
appreciation of, 306–7, 310–12
interests and, 312–13
keeping records of, 323–24
patterns of writing in, 293, 296
personality development and, 306–8
reporting about, 324–25
and skill development, 312
stimulating interest in, 309–12, 313–22
vocabulary terms in, 301
Location of information:
alphabetizing, 276–77, 278–79
dictionary and glossary skills, 278–82
grades four and above, 277–91
index skills, 282–84
library skills, 289–91
parts of a book, 273–76, 278
primary grades, 273–77
readiness, 75–76
reading illustrations, 275–76, 287–89
reference materials, 277, 284–87
tables of content skills, 274–75

M

Materials:
basal, 10, 96–100, 368
curriculum, 369–70
evaluation of, 114–15, 117
language experience, 100–105
nature of, 31–32
readability of, 115–17
readiness for, 80–87
reading development, 368–69
reference, 139–40, 148–49, 277, 284–87
selection of, 29, 112–14
Mathematics, 57, 58, 266, 269, 271, 295, 297

Maze, 210
Memorization (see Recall)
Miscue analysis, 215 (see also Reading Miscue Inventory)
Morphemes, 19, 150

N

National Assessment of Educational Progress, 45–46
Nongraded primary, 346

O

Open school or classroom, 345–46
Op-In, 213
Oral language:
basing reading on, 20–29
development of, 6–9
interrelationships with reading, 9–14
relationship to writing, 9–10
relationship to written language, 28–29
understanding and respecting, 27–28
Oral reading, 13, 30, 353–54, 378–79
Organization:
for instruction in a classroom, 109, 342–45, 350–52
for instruction in a school, 345–46, 366–67
as a study strategy, 268–70
Orthography, definition of, 29

P

Parents:
and children's reading interests, 316–17
advising, 357–60
Phoneme-grapheme relationships defined, 150
Phonemes, 9, 28, 150
Phonics:
chart of consonants, 151
chart of vowels, 152
defined, 150, 162
generalizations, 161–62

Phonics (*cont.*)
 instructional procedures,
  153–58
 practice and maintenance
  activities, 158–61
 what to teach, 151–53
 when to teach, 150–51
Phonographological defined,
  134
Piaget's stages of cognitive development (*see* Cogni-
  tion)
Picture clues, 137–40, 183–84
Picture dictionaries, 139–40,
  148–49
Previewing, 81, 87–91, 248–50,
  255–57
Primary grades:
 advising parents, 357–60
 classroom organization, 343–
  45, 347–50
 closure activities, 209–11
 concept development, 180,
  182
 directed reading lessons,
  354–57
 fluency foundations, 242–45
 learning centers, 349–50
 nongraded plan, 346
 open school or classroom,
  345–46
 oral reading, 353–54
 planning, 350–52
 readiness for study strategies,
  267, 269–70, 272–73,
  273–77, 300–301
 reading interests, 312–13
 reading to children, 353
 reference materials, 277
 role of independent activities,
  347–49, 361–63
 speaking, 12–13
 writing, 15
Programs and approaches:
 basal reader, 96–100
 computer, 112
 individualized reading,
  105–10
 language experience, 100–
  105
 television, 111–12
Propaganda, 223–24
Psycholinguistics, 19
Psychological-sociological guidelines, 26–34
Purposes for reading, 31–32,
  227–28
 examples of, 227–28, 244,
  259–60
 readiness and, 82
 role of, 227

Q

Questions, 228–33
 analysis, 232
 application, 231–32
 comprehension, 231
 evaluation, 233
 interpretation, 219–20
 knowledge, 230–31
 literal, 217–18
 replacement for, 228–29,
  272
 synthesis, 232–33
 on tests, 55–56

R

Rates of reading, 240–61 (*see
  also* Scanning; Skim-
  ming)
 awareness of, 245–46
 flexibility of, 241–42, 254–
  61
 fluency foundations for,
  242–45
 instruments for pacing, 253
 previewing and, 248–50
 purpose and, 247–48
 thought units in, 246–47
 timing, 251–57
Readability, 115–17
Readiness:
 beyond prereading, 79–87
 definitions of, 68–69
 prereading, 69–78
 principles, 80–83
 procedures, 83–87, 87–91
Reading, definitions of, 6, 40
Reading interests (*see* Interests
  in reading)
Reading levels, defined, 41–42
Reading Miscue Inventory,
  60–62
Reading program, defined, 18,
  31
Reading programs (*see* Programs and approaches)
Reading skills:
 defined, 32
 sequence of, 31–32
Reading strategies defined, 32
Reading task defined, 227
Reading to children, 318, 353
Recall, 271–73
Reference materials:
 almanacs, 277
 atlases, 277

dictionaries, 139–40, 148-
  49, 277, 284
 encyclopedias, 277, 284–87
Retrospection, 214–16
Roots, 190

S

Scanning, 242, 245, 258–59,
  260
Science, 57–58, 194, 265, 265–
  66, 268, 268–69, 271,
  293–94, 296, 301, 311
Selection and evaluation:
 in developing interest in
  literature, 322
 of standardized tests, 40–41
 as study strategy, 265–68
Self-concepts, 30–31, 63, 70–
  71, 387–89
Self-evaluation, 63
Semantics defined, 9, 19, 28,
  135
Sexism, 113, 114–15, 195–96
Sight words, 144–50
Skill tests, 54–55
Skimming, 242, 258, 260–61
Social studies, 194, 266, 269,
  271, 296–97, 311
Sociolinguistics, definition of,
  19
Speaking:
 definition of, 6–7
 in intermediate grades and
  above, 13–14
 in kindergarten, 13
 in nursery school, 12
 in primary grades, 13
Spelling, 14
SQ3R, 373–74
Standard English defined, 28
Standardized tests:
 definitions related to, 40–41
 pros and cons of, 41–45
 selection and evaluation of,
  40–41
Strategies:
 for comprehending, 205–15
 defined, 32, 264
 study, 264–92
 survival, 292–93
 for unlocking words, 134–37
Structural analysis:
 affixes, 169–70
 common prefixes, 162
 common suffixes, 162, 164
 compound words, 164–66
 defined, 162

Structural analysis (cont.)
  inflectional endings, 167–69
  little words in big, 166–67
  meaning changes, 188–90
  syllabication, 170–72
Structural overview (*see* Advance organizers)
Study guides, 374–77
Study reading, 373–77
Study skills, 264 (*see also* Study strategies)
Study strategies, 264–93
  defined, 264
  following directions, 291–92
  foundations for, 75–76
  location of information, 273–91
  organization, 268–70
  recall, 271–73
  selection and evaluation, 265–68
  survival, 292–93
Survival strategies, 292–93
Syllabication, 170–72
Synonyms, 190–92
Syntax and syntactic, definitions of, 9, 19, 28, 135

T

Technology and reading, 350
Television and reading, 111–12
Tests (*see* Informal tests and Standardized tests)
Thought and language, 6–23 (*see also* Cognition)

Trade books defined, 10

U

Uninterrupted sustained silent reading, 353, 378

V

Viewing and listening, 12
Visual factors:
  assessment of problems, 70
  discrimination, 70, 73–74
  perception, 70
Vocabulary:
  activities for building, 196–97, 199–201
  concepts, 180–86
  connectives, 300
  content areas, 297–300, 301
  critical thinking, 194–96
  figurative language, 187–88
  foundations for, 73–75
  function words, 299–300
  guiding principles, 197–98
  multi-meaning words, 186–87, 298–99
  overlap words, 297–98
  personalized word collections, 196–97
  synonyms and antonyms, 190–92
  technical words, 297
  word origins, 192–94
  word structure, 188–90

W

Wide reading:
  for reading fluency, 244–45
  for vocabulary development, 197
Word identification and approximation:
  context clues, 140–44
  defined, 135
  dictionary usage, 173–75
  phonics, 150–62
  picture clues, 137–40
  sight words, 144–50
  strategies in, 134–37
  structural analysis, 162–73
Word origins, 192–94
Word structure (*see* Structural analysis)
Writing:
  intermediate grades and above, 15
  patterns of, 15–16, 293–97, 301
  prereading activities, 14–15
  primary grades, 15
Written language:
  defined, 19, 134
  relationship to oral language, 9–10